What is Neoclassical Economics?

Despite some diversification, modern economics still attracts a great deal of criticism. This is largely due to highly unrealistic assumptions underpinning economic theory, explanatory failure, poor policy framing and a dubious focus on prediction. Many argue that flaws continue to owe much of their shortcomings to neoclassical economics. As a result, what we mean by neoclassical economics remains a significant issue. This collection addresses the issue from a new perspective, taking as its point of departure Tony Lawson's essay 'What is this "school" called neoclassical economics?'.

Few terms are as controversial for pluralist and heterodox economists as neoclassical economics. This controversy has many aspects, because the term itself has different specifications and connotations. Within this multiplicity what we mean by neoclassical matters to pluralist and heterodox economists for two primary reasons. First, because it informs how we view and critique the mainstream; second, because the relationship between heterodox and mainstream economics influences how heterodox economists model, apply methods and construct theory. The chapters in this collection each have different things to say about these matters, with contributions ranging across the work of key thinkers, such as Thorstein Veblen and Kenneth Arrow, applied issues of non-linear modelling of dynamic systems and key events in the history of economics.

This book will be of use to those interested in methodology, political economy, heterodoxy and the history of economic thought.

Jamie Morgan is Reader at the School of Accounting, Finance and Economics, Leeds Beckett University, UK.

Economics as Social Theory
edited by Tony Lawson
University of Cambridge, Cambridge, UK

For a complete list of titles in this series, please visit www.routledge.com

Social theory is experiencing something of a revival within economics. Critical analyses of the particular nature of the subject matter of social studies and of the types of method, categories and modes of explanation that can legitimately be endorsed for the scientific study of social objects, are re-emerging. Economists are again addressing such issues as the relationship between agency and structure, between economy and the rest of society, and between the enquirer and the object of enquiry. There is a renewed interest in elaborating basic categories such as causation, competition, culture, discrimination, evolution, money, need, order, organisation, power probability, process, rationality, technology, time, truth, uncertainty, value, etc.

The objective for this series is to facilitate this revival further. In contemporary economics the label 'theory' has been appropriated by a group that confines itself to largely asocial, ahistorical, mathematical 'modelling'. Economics as Social Theory thus reclaims the 'theory' label, offering a platform for alternative rigorous, but broader and more critical conceptions of theorising.

Other titles in this series include:

1. **Economics and Language**
   Edited by Willie Henderson

2. **Rationality, Institutions and Economic Methodology**
   Edited by Uskali Mäki, Bo Gustafsson and Christian Knudsen

3. **New Directions in Economic Methodology**
   Edited by Roger Backhouse

4. **Who Pays for the Kids?**
   Nancy Folbre

5. **Rules and Choice in Economics**
   Viktor Vanberg

6. **Beyond Rhetoric and Realism in Economics**
   Thomas A. Boylan and Paschal F. O'Gorman

7. **Feminism, Objectivity and Economics**
   Julie A. Nelson

8. **Economic Evolution**
   Jack J. Vromen

9. **Economics and Reality**
   Tony Lawson

10. **The Market**
    John O' Neill

11. **Economics and Utopia**
    Geoff Hodgson

12. **Critical Realism in Economics**
    Edited by Steve Fleetwood

13. **The New Economic Criticism**
    Edited by Martha Woodmansee and Mark Osteen

14. **What do Economists Know?**
    Edited by Robert F. Garnett, Jr.

15. **Postmodernism, Economics and Knowledge**
    Edited by Stephen Cullenberg, Jack Amariglio and David F. Ruccio

16. **The Values of Economics**
    An Aristotelian perspective
    Irene van Staveren

17. **How Economics Forgot History**
    The problem of historical specificity in social science
    Geoffrey M. Hodgson

18. **Intersubjectivity in Economics**
    Agents and structures
    Edward Fullbrook

19. **The World of Consumption, 2nd edition**
    The material and cultural revisited
    Ben Fine

20. **Reorienting Economics**
    Tony Lawson

21. **Toward a Feminist Philosophy of Economics**
    Edited by Drucilla K. Barker and Edith Kuiper

22. **The Crisis in Economics**
    Edited by Edward Fullbrook

23. **The Philosophy of Keynes' Economics**
    Probability, uncertainty and convention
    Edited by Jochen Runde and Sohei Mizuhara

24. **Postcolonialism Meets Economics**
    Edited by Eiman O. Zein-Elabdin and S. Charusheela

25. **The Evolution of Institutional Economics**
    Agency, structure and Darwinism in American institutionalism
    Geoffrey M. Hodgson

26. **Transforming Economics**
    Perspectives on the critical realist project
    Edited by Paul Lewis

27. **New Departures in Marxian Theory**
    Edited by Stephen A. Resnick and Richard D. Wolff

28. **Markets, Deliberation and Environmental Value**
John O'Neill

29. **Speaking of Economics**
How to get in the conversation
Arjo Klamer

30. **From Political Economy to Economics**
Method, the social and the historical in the evolution of economic theory
Dimitris Milonakis and Ben Fine

31. **From Economics Imperialism to Freakonomics**
The shifting boundaries between economics and other social sciences
Dimitris Milonakis and Ben Fine

32. **Development and Globalization**
A Marxian class analysis
David Ruccio

33. **Introducing Money**
Mark Peacock

34. **The Cambridge Revival of Political Economy**
Nuno Ornelas Martins

35. **Understanding Development Economics**
Its challenge to development studies
Adam Fforde

36. **Economic Methodology**
An historical introduction
Harro Maas
Translated by Liz Waters

37. **Social Ontology and Modern Economics**
Stephen Pratten

38. **History of Financial Crises**
Dreams and follies of expectations
Cihan Bilginsoy

39. **Commerce and Community**
Ecologies of social cooperation
Robert F. Garnett, Jr., Paul Lewis and Lenore T. Ealy

40. **The Nature and State of Modern Economics**
Tony Lawson

41. **The Philosophy, Politics and Economics of Finance in the 21st century**
From hubris to disgrace
Edited by Patrick O'Sullivan, Nigel F. B. Allington and Mark Esposito

42. **The Philosophy of Debt**
Alexander X. Douglas

43. **What is Neoclassical Economics?**
Debating the origins, meaning and significance
Edited by Jamie Morgan

What is Neoclassical Economics?

Debating the origins, meaning and significance

Edited by Jamie Morgan

LONDON AND NEW YORK

First published 2016
by Routledge
2 Park Square, Milton Park, Abingdon, Oxon OX14 4RN

and by Routledge
711 Third Avenue, New York, NY 10017

Routledge is an imprint of the Taylor & Francis Group, an informa business

© 2016 selection and editorial material, Jamie Morgan; individual chapters, the contributors

The right of the editor to be identified as the author of the editorial material, and of the authors for their individual chapters, has been asserted in accordance with sections 77 and 78 of the Copyright, Designs and Patents Act 1988.

All rights reserved. No part of this book may be reprinted or reproduced or utilised in any form or by any electronic, mechanical, or other means, now known or hereafter invented, including photocopying and recording, or in any information storage or retrieval system, without permission in writing from the publishers.

Trademark notice: Product or corporate names may be trademarks or registered trademarks, and are used only for identification and explanation without intent to infringe.

British Library Cataloguing in Publication Data
A catalogue record for this book is available from the British Library

Library of Congress Cataloguing in Publication Data
What is neoclassical economics? : debating the origins, meaning and significance / edited by Jamie Morgan.
pages cm
Includes bibliographical references and index.
1. Neoclassical school of economics. 2. Economics—History. I. Morgan, Jamie, 1969- editor.
HB98.2.W496 2015
330.15'7—dc23
2015023160

ISBN: 978-1-138-96207-1 (hbk)
ISBN: 978-1-138-96209-5 (pbk)
ISBN: 978-1-315-65959-6 (ebk)

Typeset in Palatino
by Swales & Willis Ltd, Exeter, Devon, UK

Printed and bound in Great Britain by
TJ International Ltd, Padstow, Cornwall

Contents

List of figures	ix
List of contributors	x
Introduction: the meaning and significance of neoclassical economics JAMIE MORGAN	1
1 What is this 'school' called neoclassical economics? TONY LAWSON	30
2 From neoclassical theory to mainstream modelling: fifty years of moral hazard in perspective JOHN LATSIS AND CONSTANTINOS REPAPIS	81
3 Neoclassicism, critical realism and the Cambridge methodological tradition SHEILA DOW	102
4 Lawson, Veblen and Marshall: how to read modern neoclassicism ANNE MAYHEW	119
5 Lawson on Veblen on social ontology JOHN B. DAVIS	135
6 Why is this 'school' called neoclassical economics? Classicism and neoclassicism in historical context NUNO ORNELAS MARTINS	149

7 Ten propositions on 'neoclassical economics'   168
   JOHN KING

8 Neoclassical economics: an elephant is not a chimera
   but is a chimera real?   180
   BEN FINE

9 The state of nature and natural states: ideology and
   formalism in the critique of neoclassical economics   200
   BRIAN O' BOYLE AND TERRENCE MCDONOUGH

10 Heterodox economics, social ontology and the
   use of mathematics   221
   MARK SETTERFIELD

11 Is neoclassical economics mathematical? Is there a
   non-neoclassical mathematical economics?   238
   STEVE KEEN

12 Neoclassicism forever   255
   DON ROSS

13 Reflections upon neoclassical labour economics   273
   STEVE FLEETWOOD

   Index   311

Figures

11.1	A predator–prey model in the system dynamics program Minsky	242
11.2	Lorenz's model illustrating sensitive dependence on initial conditions	243
11.3	The dynamic path of the Lorenz model around its three unstable equilibria	244
13.1	A schematic overview of searching and matching	285
13.2	Equilibrium wages and market tightness (Pissarides, 2000 19)	287
13.3	Equilibrium vacancies and unemployment (Pissarides, 2000 20)	290

Contributors

John B. Davis is Professor of Economics, Marquette University, and Professor of Economics, University of Amsterdam. He is the author of *Keynes's Philosophical Development*, *The Theory of the Individual in Economics*, *Individuals and Identity in Economics* and co-author, with Marcel Boumans, of *Economic Methodology: Understanding Economics as a Science*. He is co-editor with Wade Hands of the *Journal of Economic Methodology*.

Sheila Dow is Emeritus Professor of Economics at the University of Stirling in Scotland and Adjunct Professor of Economics at the University of Victoria in Canada. Her main research interests lie in the history and methodology of economic thought and the theory of money, banking and monetary policy. Her most recent book is *Foundations for New Economic Thinking* (Palgrave Macmillan, 2012). She is co-editor of the WEA's online journal *Economic Thought: History, Philosophy and Methodology* and co-convenor of SCEME. Past roles include chair of the International Network for Economic Method and special advisor on monetary policy to the UK Treasury Select Committee.

Ben Fine is Professor of Economics at the School of Oriental and African Studies, University of London and Senior Research Fellow attached to the South African Research Chair in Social Change, University of Johannesburg. He currently sits on the Social Science Research Committee of the UK's Food Standards Agency for which he chaired the Working Group on Reform of Slaughterhouse Controls. He has received funding from the European Union Seventh Framework Programme (FP7/2007–2013) under Research, Technological Development and Demonstration Grant Agreement no. 266800, for research on Financialisation, Economy, Society and Sustainable Development (FESSUD). He is the author and contributing editor of many works including, with Dimitris Milonakis, *From Economics Imperialism to Freakonomics* (Routledge, 2009), which was awarded the 2009 Deutscher Prize, and *From Political Economy to Economics* (Routledge, 2009), which was awarded the 2009 Gunnar Myrdal Prize, and, with Kyung-Sup Chang and Linda Weiss, *Developmental Politics in Transition: The Neoliberal Era and Beyond* (Palgrave Macmillan, 2012).

Steve Fleetwood is Professor of Human Resource Management and Employment Relations at Bristol Business School at the University of the West of England, UK. He has two (linked) areas of interest. He writes about all aspects of work and employment, from how people find employment via labour markets, to what they do and how they are managed once they become employed. He also works in areas of philosophy and methodology of social science, especially critical realism, which he links to disciplines such as labour economics, political economy, organisation studies and human resource management. Steve gained a PhD in the Department of Economics at the University of Cambridge in 1994 and was previously employed by De Montfort University and Lancaster University – both in the UK. His recent work includes, co-edited with Zina de Abreu, *Women Past and Present: Biographic and Multidisciplinary Studies*, (Cambridge Scholars Publishing, 2014); and 'Do labour supply and demand curves exist?' (*Cambridge Journal of Economics*, 2014, 38(4): 1–27).

Steve Keen is Professor and Head of School of Economics, History and Politics at Kingston University, London. Professor Keen has produced more than 70 academic publications on a diverse range of topics including modelling financial instability, monetary macroeconomics, econophysics, chaos and complexity theory, Islamic finance, mathematical flaws in neoclassical microeconomics and logical flaws in Marxian economics. His most influential publications are *Debunking Economics* (Pluto Press, 2001) and 'Finance and economic breakdown: Modeling Minsky's "financial instability hypothesis"' (*Journal of Post Keynesian Economics*, 1995, 17(4): 607–635). His most recent publications explain why he and Wynne Godley and colleagues were the only ones to develop mathematical models that anticipated the global economic crisis of 2007–2008. Professor Keen was one of the handful of economists to realise that a serious economic crisis was imminent and to publicly warn of it, from as early as December 2005. This, and his pioneering work on complex systems modelling of debt-deflation, resulted in him winning the Revere Award from the *Real World Economics Review* for being the economist: 'who first and most clearly anticipated and gave public warning of the Global Financial Collapse and whose work is most likely to prevent another GFC in the future'. Keen's research speciality is monetary macroeconomic modelling. With the support of INET, he developed 'Minsky', an open source, cross-platform, visual monetary macroeconomic modelling program (see http://sourceforge.net/projects/minsky/). It was selected as project of the month in January 2014 from among Source Forge's 22,000 projects, and it is now available for use by other researchers. Professor Keen maintains an influential blog on economics. He also writes a column in *Forbes Magazine* – see http://www.forbes.com/sites/stevekeen/.

John King recently retired from teaching at La Trobe University, Australia, where he is now Emeritus Professor; he is also Honorary Professor at Federation University Australia. His continuing research interests are in the history of heterodox economic thought, in particular Marxian political economy and post Keynesian economics. Recent books include *The Microfoundations Delusion* (Elgar, 2012) and *David Ricardo* (Palgrave Macmillan, 2013). His *Advanced Introduction to Post Keynesian Economics* (Elgar, 2015).

John Latsis is Associate Professor in Social and Organisational Behaviour at Henley Business School. He previously held positions at Oxford, Nanterre and the European University Institute as well as a visiting scholarship at Harvard University. His research interests are in social theory and economic philosophy and cover questions about the nature of conventional behaviour and rule-following in social life, the influence of theory on economic action and the socio-economic dimensions of human need. His recent publications include articles in the *Cambridge Journal of Economics*, the *Journal of Institutional Economics* and the *British Journal of Sociology*. John is also an editor of *Economic Thought*, a journal published by the World Economics Association that focuses on the philosophy, methodology and history of economics.

Tony Lawson trained as a mathematician and was formerly a member of the Cambridge Growth Project under the leadership of Professor Sir Richard Stone. Lawson currently holds a professorial fellowship of the Independent Social Research Foundation. He is also Professor of Economics and Philosophy at the University of Cambridge and Professor of Economics at the National University of Ireland, Galway. Lawson sits on numerous editorial boards including the *Cambridge Journal of Economics* and *Feminist Economics* and is sole editor of the Routledge book series *Economics as Social Theory*. For over 20 years now Lawson has chaired the Cambridge Realist Workshop, and for more than 10 years he has chaired the Cambridge Social Ontology Group. He is also former Director of the Cambridge Centre for Gender Studies. Lawson has long been highly critical of the course of modern economics. Among his numerous publications are the books *Economics and Reality* (1997) and *Reorienting Economics* (2007). His various contributions are widely debated in scholarly journals and similar outlets including in Edward Fullbrook's (2009) *Ontology and Economics: Tony Lawson and his Critics*. His latest work is *The Nature and State of Modern Economics* (Routledge, 2015).

Nuno Ornelas Martins is lecturer in economics at the School of Economics and Management and CEGE at the Universidade Católica Portuguesa, a member of the Centro de Estudos de Gestão e Economia and a member of the Cambridge Social Ontology Group, UK. His research interests are social ontology, the Cambridge economic tradition, the capability approach to human development and the social surplus approach. He is the author of *The Cambridge Revival of Political Economy*, and in recent years has published articles in the *Cambridge Journal of Economics*, *Journal of Critical Realism*, *Journal of Post Keynesian Economics*, *Review of Political Economy*, *Journal of Economic Methodology*, *Review of Social Economy*, *American Journal of Economics and Sociology*, *Ecological Economics*, *Economic Thought*, *Evolutionary and Institutional Economics Review*, *New Political Economy*, *Journal for the Theory of Social Behaviour* and other journals.

Anne Mayhew is Professor Emerita at the University of Tennessee, and earned a PhD from the University of Texas (Austin) in 1966. Mayhew's scholarly work has focused on the contributions of Thorstein Veblen and other early twentieth-century American social scientists, with emphasis on the impact of technological and economic change on economic thought and public policy. She served as editor of *The Journal of Economic Issues* from 1991 to 2000. Her recent work includes *Narrating the Rise of Big Business in the USA: How Economists Explain Standard Oil and Wal-Mart* (Routledge, 2008); 'Copeland on money as electricity' in *Real World Economics Review* (2010); 'Money as electricity' in *Journal of Cultural Economy* (2011); and 'The backward art of thinking about consumer spending' in *Journal of Economic Issues* (2014).

Terrence McDonough is Professor of Economics at the National University of Ireland, Galway. His main interest is Marxian stage theories of capitalism and the periodisation of history. He has recently co-edited with Michael Reich and David Kotz *Contemporary Capitalism and Its Crises: Social Structure of Accumulation Theory for the 21st Century* (Cambridge University Press, 2010).

Jamie Morgan is former Coordinator of the Association for Heterodox Economics and co-edits *Real World Economics Review* with Edward Fullbrook. He is the author of *Private Equity Finance* (Palgrave Macmillan, 2009) and has published in *Cambridge Journal of Economics*, *Economy & Society*, *Journal of Institutional Economics*, *Sociology*, *Globalizations*, *Philosophy of the Social Sciences* and many other journals covering economics, sociology, philosophy and area studies. He is particularly interested in financialisation. After working for a number of years for Helsinki University he now works at Leeds Beckett University.

Brian O'Boyle is Economics Programme Director at St. Angela's College Sligo (a college of the National University of Ireland Galway). His principal research interest is in Marxist political economy, but he has also published in the area of Marxist philosophy of science. He recently received (with Terrence McDonough) an Outstanding Contribution Award at the Emerald Literary Awards for his Article 'Epistemological Problems and Ontological Solutions; A Critical Realist Retrospective on Althusser'. He has also published in *Capital and Class*, the *Cambridge Journal of Economics* and the *Journal for the Theory of Social Behaviour*. He recently co-authored (with Kieran Allen) *Austerity Ireland: The Failure of Irish Capitalism* (Pluto Press, 2013).

Constantinos Repapis is a Lecturer in Economics at the Institute of Management Studies, Goldsmiths, University of London. He is also a Fellow of the Political Economy Research Centre at Goldsmiths. After completing his PhD at the University of Cambridge, he lectured in economics at St. Peter's College, University of Oxford, and has held visiting positions in the University of Cyprus and St. Edmund's College, Cambridge. He research interests are in the history of economic thought and especially business cycle developments during the 1930s. Recently he has started working on the link between economic models and real world policy. His recent publications include articles in the *Cambridge Journal of Economics*, *Economic Thought* and *History of Political Economy*.

Don Ross is Professor of Economics and Dean of the Waikato Management School at the University of Waikato in Hamilton, New Zealand. He is also Professor of Economics at the University of Cape Town and Program Director for Methodology at the Center for Economic Analysis of Risk at Georgia State University. His areas of recent research include economic methodology, experimental economics of risk and time preferences in vulnerable populations, strategic foundations of human sociality and scientific metaphysics. He is the author or editor of 13 books and numerous journal articles, book chapters and policy reports.

Mark Setterfield is Professor of Economics in the Department of Economics at the New School for Social Research in New York. He is also a member of the Centre d'Économie de l'Université Paris N (CEPN) at l'Université Paris XIII (France), an associate member of the Cambridge Centre for Economic and Public Policy at Cambridge University (UK) and a senior research associate at the International Economic Policy Institute at Laurentian University (Canada). He is the author of *Rapid Growth and Relative Decline: Modelling Macroeconomic Dynamics with Hysteresis* (Palgrave Macmillan, 1997), editor (or co-editor) of seven volumes of essays, and has authored articles in numerous peer-reviewed journals including the *Cambridge Journal of Economics*, *Journal of Post Keynesian Economics*, *European Economic Review*, *Review of Political Economy*, *Journal of Economic Issues* and *The Manchester School*. He and co-author Gilberto Lima were winners of the 2010 Haralambos Simeonidis prize, awarded by the Brazilian Association of Graduate Programs in Economics for 'Pricing behaviour and the cost-push channel of monetary policy' *Review of Political Economy*, 2010, 22(1): 19–40.

Introduction

The meaning and significance of neoclassical economics

Jamie Morgan

Few terms are as controversial for pluralist and heterodox economists as neoclassical economics. This controversy has many aspects, because the term itself has different specifications and also connotations. Within this multiplicity, what we mean by neoclassical matters to pluralist and heterodox economists for two primary reasons (see Fullbrook, ed., 2003; Kitson, 2005; Garnett *et al.*, 2010). First, because what we mean affects how we view the mainstream, and so where pluralist and heterodox economists situate and pursue appropriate critique of, and constructive dialogue with, the mainstream. Second, because what we mean affects how we conceive heterodox economics in relation to mainstream economics, and this has significance for whether, and the way in which, heterodox economists model, apply methods and construct theory. The essays in this collection all have different things to say about these matters. Each is a response to Tony Lawson's recent essay 'What is this "school" called neoclassical economics?' (Chapter 1 of this collection). To make sense of Lawson's essay and also of the individual contributions, we first need to provide some context concerning the different ways in which the term neoclassical has had meaning.

A useful way to start here is to situate the term neoclassical to a familiar narrative. The narrative does not concern the substantive content of the term – we will get to that later – but is important because of the different ways one can develop the analysis of economics in relation to the term. In this narrative a self-identified neoclassical grouping (George Stigler, Paul Samuelson, Milton Friedman, etc.) came to dominate the discipline in the latter half of the twentieth century. In coming to dominate, the neoclassicals actively shaped the discipline in their own image (e.g. Mirowski and Plehwe, eds., 2009). This was particularly so in the USA and the UK, (see Lee, 2009; Lee *et al.*, 2013). In particular, the neoclassicals came to command the language of science and objectivity, effectively making these synonymous with their own work, irrespective of whether that work could then demonstrate that it was both scientific and objective in an appropriate sense. At the same time, the neoclassicals came to dominate the terrain of policy relevance.

As the neoclassicals became more dominant then they came to exercise greater control over departments, the curriculum, appointments, promotion, research agendas, journals and publications (creating self-reinforcing tendencies). Based on the positioning of the neoclassical, the very terms of debate then placed other approaches at a disadvantage, except in so far as any alternative accepted the terms of debate on neoclassical grounds. This effectively meant that 'legitimate' alternatives became points of departure *from* a neoclassical position, rather than more fundamental rejections of such a position. Neoclassicism thus came to influence its own terms of critique. As a corollary, because the neoclassicals commanded the language of science and objectivity, to reject neoclassicism entirely came to mean, in some unstated and pre-emptive fashion, to be anti-science, pejoratively subjective and policy irrelevant. This then also meant any attempt to position neoclassical theory and models through fundamental critique confronted a positional problem. Attempts to counter the neoclassical approach by claiming that it was unscientific, lacking in objectivity and dangerous or debilitating in policy terms were undermined. In making such claims one was saying more than that this theory or that postulate is incorrect or needs modification. As such one could easily fall outside what was legitimate across the developing range of mainstream economics.

The main consequence was then that neoclassical economics' domination extended from formal power, inhering in and exercised through the structures of the discipline, to the more informal way in which the discipline disciplined itself through the positioning of theory, method and critique. The combination served to narrow the field and marginalise critique. Concomitantly, economics became less pluralistic and less tolerant of difference. The very concept of difference narrowed.

I have used the term narrative here because the retrospective significance is of neoclassical as a story, but the use of the term narrative does not make it fictional or trivial, merely familiar and often repeated as a tale that has been told in pluralist and heterodox circles. For many pluralist and heterodox economists neoclassicism is a term with a cluster of negative connotations tied to cumulative histories: a scientism, an inability to recognise the failures and fallibility of one's own approach, a failure to see another's point of view, to appreciate the value of different perspectives, a concomitant disengagement from constructive dialogue, and so on.[1] Moreover, that cumulative history is lived experience and so the term neoclassical provokes a visceral response from many heterodox economists. For many heterodox economists neoclassical is not just another word, a neutral term deployed as a simple referent. It is too evocative for that. The term has history. However, once we recognise that it has a recent history then we can also recognise that there are different contexts one can apply to that recent history and these affect the way the neoclassical is given further significance.

Two ways to explore the neoclassical: diversity versus continuity in the mainstream

First, it is intrinsic to the previous narrative that the term neoclassical can be meaningfully applied to a specific grouping *within* the mainstream. Neoclassicals came to dominate the field, but not all mainstream economists self-identify as neoclassical and mainstream economists reflect on (or can be prompted to reflect on) the degree to which they are neoclassical. For example, in Colander and Klamer's (1987) well-known research on postgraduate teaching at US elite universities 'The Making of an Economist', postgraduate students were invited to rank the relevance of neoclassical economics (Colander and Klamer, 1987; Klamer and Colander, 1990). The conducted survey recognised that a neoclassical approach is one among several, though the inflection of the questions put to postgraduates also encompassed the notion that 'relevant' refers to *relevant as a theoretical view of the world*. Follow up research in 2005 revealed that elite university students continued to think neoclassicism was important (44% strongly agreed and 45% somewhat agreed, Colander, 2005a: 184). What is equally important here is that orientating on neoclassicals as a specific grouping *within* the mainstream lends itself to a focus on diversity *within* the mainstream.

The focus on diversity brings a particular context or emphasis to the neoclassical. Recall that in the narrative in the previous section one recognised feature of recent history has been the narrowing of the field and the command of that field, such that 'legitimate' alternatives became points of departure *from* a neoclassical position, rather than more fundamental rejections of such a position. However, the existence of constraint and the existence of domination do not necessarily prevent constructive or positive change. One is more likely to be orientated on this possibility of constructive change if one begins from a focus on the neoclassical as within the mainstream. Here the neoclassical becomes more of a fixed point and the use of the term can become contrastive – one designates this as neoclassical and that as something other, but both as mainstream.

Since it is differentiation from the neoclassical that becomes the focus, then this usage defines the neoclassical such that the mainstream exceeds the neoclassical. The emphasis can then be on dominance as a matter of degree and of possibly declining degree. One finds this, for example, in Colander *et al.*'s (2004) *Review of Political Economy* essay, which claims that the mainstream is undergoing a fundamental shift away from neoclassical economics (becoming more dynamic), a shift which, according to the authors, a simple neoclassical or orthodox-to-heterodox dichotomy cannot encapsulate (see also Colander, 2005b).

The point I want to make here is not concerned with whether in fact the claims made for diversity are well-justified. The point is simply that one important way in which the term neoclassical has been given significance has been as a referent for a relatively recent subset of the mainstream, albeit an extensive one, and with reference mainly to its recent or later twentieth-century history. This is an approach that leads to an emphasis on difference rather than commonality – and so is primed to seek and see both greater significance and greater potential in a changing mainstream into the twenty-first century. A typical focus becomes theory innovation, such as might be explored in behavioural economics, information-theoretic economics, etc. Here, the neoclassical is significant, but it is of declining significance *within* the mainstream.

There is, however, a second way in which the term neoclassical has been given significance. This second way uses neoclassical as broadly synonymous with the mainstream. It too recognises that a group of self-identified neoclassicals came to dominate the field in the second half of the twentieth century. However, the focus also places greater emphasis on further associated issues. In so far as this neoclassical group came to dominate in the later twentieth century, it was because the field was one conducive to such dominance. This focus places greater emphasis on a longer history, though the approach emphasising degree of difference is also not antithetical to history. The emphasis tends more to continuity than diversity. More accurately, the emphasis tends more to the *continuity that limits diversity*. This is a rather different approach to the narrative and the way 'legitimate' alternatives become points of departure *from* a neoclassical position.

In terms of history, the focus shifts to the emergence of the modern usage of the term neoclassical, any prior early usage of the term and also its prehistory. One finds this focus in the history of economic thought. For example, Aspromourgos (1986) explores the way in which neoclassical originally derived from Veblen's usage in a series of essays from 1900, but was also popularised as a self-identification and as a textbook designation based on a casual appropriation of the term by Samuelson from the third edition of *Economics* (Samuelson, 1955; see also Skousen, 1997) and also through commentary from Hicks (1939) and Stigler (1941).

However, history is not simply history. It is the operable dynamic in which knowledge is produced and reproduced. So, one can take a history of economic thought approach to the neoclassical, exploring the work of the thinkers on its own terms, but in a comparative sense. Author x developed theory y under the influence of thinker z, and one can do so with reference to contestation and development of meanings (Veblen meant x, and this emerged from y, but later self-identified neoclassicals meant z). But one can also go beyond this to consider the nature of continuity and so explore *the history* of the history of economic thought. The two main ways in which this has been executed have been through political economy and through the philosophy and methodology of economics. The two overlap in so far as both involve the identification of underlying characteristics of knowledge formation that are then transmitted as a matter of continuity.

The political economy critique takes as its point of inspiration Marx's critique of vulgar political economy. Classical political economy focused on the conditions of production and the creation and distribution of wealth in relation to social classes. Vulgar political economy ceased to focus on the problem of wealth creation as value inhering in labour and expressible in the relationships between social classes. The subsequent rise of marginalism and the work of Jevons, Walras, Menger, Marshall and others (albeit with different degrees of caveat and concern) then created the conditions in which modern economics could develop – a subjectivist focus on ahistorical individuals involved in universal behaviours amenable to simple mathematical expression. Here, the political economy critique goes beyond the observation that the internal dynamics of economics as a discipline narrowed the field in terms of concepts of science and objectivity (see Morgan and Rutherford, 1998). It places this in a broader context where knowledge is not just produced, favoured and reproduced internally, but also because it serves some purpose within a broader political economy (it is ideationally part of the reproductive processes of an economic system, even if its immediate advocates, producers and practitioners do not see it in quite these terms). Significantly, this approach emphasises that, although there may be a range of internal aspects identifiable as to what constitutes economics, they can be overwritten, modified and sometimes simply allowed to persist in deficient and contradictory forms, based on the overall reproduction of economics as knowledge *within and in relation to* an economic system as itself a place of power. Dimitris Milonakis and Ben Fine (2009) are perhaps the best-known proponents of this approach.

In the political economy critique the term neoclassical has a generalised meaning. In the contemporary period it is essentially synonymous with the mainstream, but this is because of the continuity within diversity of that mainstream based on its longer history, where there is a history of the history of economic thought. The claim is that the consequences of that history continue to be relevant today. Continuity limits diversity and so, from this point of view, it is reasonable to refer to the mainstream as neoclassical, irrespective of whether mainstream economists continue to *self-identify* as neoclassical and irrespective of some degree of innovation of theory within the mainstream. This is in so far as key characteristics continue to be produced and reproduced across the mainstream. So, there is here quite a different set of inferences drawn regarding the neoclassical than those drawn when one focuses on the neoclassical as a grouping *within* the mainstream and where the neoclassical is significant, but is of declining significance *within* the mainstream.

Arnsperger and Varoufakis (2003, 2006) provide one of the best-known political economy characterisations of neoclassical economics. They identify three components:

1 Methodological individualism: theory is constructed beginning from the individual and based on degrees of rationality. Any concept of structure used is weak, typically the sum of behaviours.
2 Methodological instrumentalism: behaviour is preference driven and means-end focused, eschewing more complex motivations and stances.
3 Theory is typically equilibrium directed: mathematical resolutions or demonstrations assume the existence of equilibrium, assume that a process exists by which it can be found and assume that no forces tend to permanently shift the system away from any and all equilibria; the mathematics can then be adjusted in order that this occurs.

What is immediately notable with regard to these components is that they are general and permissive. They enable actual theory to include a wide range of deviations from the most stringent expressions of rationality, optimisation and individuation of the agent. Moreover, Arnsperger and Varoufakis argue that it would be an error to focus on these more stringent expressions, since adherents to the three components too easily dismiss this, because these increasingly do not apply to their work and so they do not consider themselves (self-identify) as neoclassical in these terms. Rather, they refer to themselves in general as scientific economists and thereafter in terms of their theory focus (for example, behavioural). For Arnsperger and Varoufakis the power of the ideational aspects of neoclassicism are so embedded in the mainstream that adherents do not need to refer to themselves collectively in order to ensure that the components are reproduced. The critique is able to draw on work in sociology for evidence of this reproduction based on the, for a social science, unusual unity and concentration of power in economics as a discipline (for example, Fourcade *et al.*, 2015).

Clearly, the claims made differentiate this approach to the neoclassical from attempts to see greater significance in diversity, despite that both can call on survey research. For example, if we return to Colander's (2004) various collaborations, we find that the neoclassical is summarised as:

> In our view, neoclassical economics is an analysis that focuses on the optimizing behavior of fully rational and well-informed individuals in a static context and the equilibria that result from that optimization. It is particularly associated with the marginalist revolution and its aftermath. Leon Walras and Alfred Marshall can be viewed as its early and great developers, with John Hicks's *Value and Capital* (1939) and Paul Samuelson's *Foundations of Economic Analysis* (1947) as its culmination.
>
> (Colander *et al.*, 2004: 490–491)

Again this diversity position is not antithetical to history, but it is read to different purposes in the later twentieth century and into the twenty-first.

For Colander *et al.* (2004) it is in deviating from these stringent expressions that one becomes something other than neoclassical, and relatedly, the issue of self-identification (or recognition of the relevance) of these stringent expressions is also important. One finds this position also in Colander's *Journal of the History of Economic Thought* (Special Issue) essay in 2000[2]:

> Let me be clear about what I see as the largest problem with the use of the term. The problem is its use by some heterodox economists, by many non-specialists, and by historians of thought at unguarded moments, as a classifier for the approach that the majority of economists take today. We all, me included, fall into the habit of calling modern economics neoclassical when we want to contrast modern mainstream economics with heterodox economics. When we like the alternative, the neoclassical term is often used as a slur, with our readers or listeners knowing what we mean. Of course, historians of thought are far better at avoiding this 'slur' use than are others. The worst use, and the place one hears the term neoclassical most often, is in the discussions by lay people who object to some portion of modern economic thought. To them bad economics and neoclassical economics are synonymous terms.
>
> There is much not to like in current economics; but slurring it, by calling it neoclassical economics, does not add to students' understanding of the current failings of economics. *Economists today are not neoclassical according to any reasonable definition of the term. They are far more eclectic, and concerned with different issues than were the economists of the early 1900s, whom the term was originally designed to describe.* If we don't like modern economics, we should say so, but we should not take the easy road, implicitly condemning modern economics by the terminology we choose.
>
> (emphasis added, Colander, 2000: 129–130)

So, one thing we might note here is that, depending on the way the neoclassical is situated, it becomes significant in different ways, takes on different meanings and offers different emphases regarding the mainstream and its scope. The distinguishing feature of the different approaches is not the existence or absence of underlying or common characteristics by which the neoclassical is identified. The distinguishing feature is how they are situated and expressed (see Davis 2006, and to what purpose in terms of cycles of pluralism, Davis, 2008). Approaches that orientate on greater innovation within the mainstream tend to focus on more fixed characteristics of what the neoclassical is. They are fixed in recent history, though there may be a lineage attached to this, and as specifications of theory. They tend then to be identifiable in terms that deviate little from Hollis and Nell's (1975) classic early articulation of the grounds of neoclassical economics in the late twentieth century, *Rational Economic Man: A Philosophical Critique of Neoclassical Economics*. From these fixed beginnings diversity follows within the mainstream, but beyond the neoclassical. Approaches that orientate on greater conformity within the mainstream tend to focus more on flexible characteristics of what the neoclassical is. The very basis of the neoclassical can be more fluid and so any subsequent diversity is limited and becomes more a matter of continuity. So the mainstream (by any other name) remains essentially neoclassical. This brings us to the second form of the second way in which the neoclassical is given significance, the philosophy and methodology of economics. It is here that Lawson's work in general and recent essay on neoclassical economics (Chapter 1 of this collection) become points of reference.

The social ontology critique, mainstream or neoclassical?

Clearly, both the diversity and continuity approaches to the neoclassical involve issues of methodology and philosophy, though they are not reducible to methodology or philosophy only. Both may be interested in the degree to which theory changes, but both ultimately identify the nature of change as also a matter of identified common characteristics shared by theory. Methodology is, as such, a key area of focus for identification and critique of neoclassical economics and of the mainstream.

Social ontology is one of the most prominent contemporary approaches to methodology and philosophy of economics. Though ontology is a term used in a variety of ways in economics (see Mäki, 2001, 2002), social ontology is most closely associated with the Cambridge Social Ontology Group (CSOG) in general, and the work of Tony Lawson in particular (Pratten, ed., 2015). Although initiated earlier the approach came to prominence in the 1990s and did so in terms of an already existing set of foci and concerns in economics. As we noted in the narrative set out earlier, a defining aspect of mainstream economics has been the command of the language of science and objectivity. As a result, the existing discourse of philosophy and methodology in economics, with which social ontology then interacted, was focused on the nature of science and of objectivity. Its typical resources have included:

- issues in the philosophy of science based on contemporary concepts (positivism, empiricism, paradigms, research programmes, H-D models, I-P models, verification, falsifiability, confirmation, the appropriateness of natural science conceptualisations for a social science, the work of Blaug, Backhouse, Boland, Caldwell, Hands, Hausman, Weintraub, etc.);
- a focus on mainstream economists who have promulgated and justified problematic aspects of economic theorising (notably Becker,

Debreu, Friedman, Lucas, Samuelson, Stigler, and perhaps Arrow, Hahn, Robbins, and Solow);
- a focus on historical figures who have expressed reservations regarding key aspects of economic theory and economics as a discipline and/or have clearly expressed methodological tenets for economics based on what economics is, should be or could be in ways that have resonated with heterodox economists (Keynes, Kaldor, Kalecki, Marshall, Marx, Robinson, Sraffa, Veblen, etc. and the many subsequent works of Dobb, Harcourt, Hart, Pasinetti and so forth).

Social ontology has taken this existing discourse and has gradually changed its emphasis (see Dow, 1997 for an early take on the shift, or Dow, 2000). Adherents of CSOG have asked the deceptively simple question: To what degree is the arising economics orientated on realism? Realism is not the only form that explicit ontology could take, but it has been a significant one in economics thanks to the relative success of CSOG. Realists ask: What are the common characteristics of mainstream economics and what would reality need to be like in order for these characteristics to be adequate as an account of an economy? They claim that mainstream economists theorise and model in ways that assume and seek atomistic constant conjunctions or regularities in events. In so doing, mainstream economists adopt some combination of positivist and empiricist understandings of science, tied to a technical sense of objectivity rooted in quantitative methods. This philosophy of science is inappropriate for social reality since it requires reality to be one of closed systems. Persisting with closed-systems approaches means that mainstream theory will result in explanatory failure and this will become clearer at times when degrees of change in systems are more manifest (an apparent stability conflated with regularity breaks down).

Adherents to realist social ontology then claim that social reality, including an economy, is characterised by sets of structures of social relations and agents imbued with powers or capacities. The interaction of agents and structures produces events, which may be more or less stable based on the current dynamics of interaction. The resultant system(s) is/are one where the accumulation of activity can change the grounds on which the activity occurs, so any causation can also be shifting in its forms. Consequently, a system is recognisably complex, historical, contingent and in process (an open system). These characteristics *in general* are ones that many heterodox economists identify with. It is for this reason that realist social ontology has gained the prominence that it has. It resonates with aspects of Marxism, Post-Keynesianism, the new ecological economics and so forth. However, resonance is not the same as uncritical acceptance. Many heterodox economists may agree that open systems are important, but may dispute the sufficiency of ontology as a domain of argument, and the particulars of the arguments for the specifics of ontology, and how these affect theory, modelling and methods in economics. For example, despite that many heterodox economists support an open-systems approach, Lawson's (2006) essay, claiming that realist social ontology provides a unity-in-difference by which heterodox economics could be differentiated from the mainstream, and by which it can most appropriately and consistently develop, created some controversy.

For Lawson, social ontology is about bringing clarity to issues in economics that can be recognised and explored in many different domains. Social ontology serves an 'underlabouring' function (for example, Lawson, 1999: 14). The attempt by realist social ontology to clearly differentiate the mainstream from heterodoxy necessarily begs the question: How does one characterise and name the mainstream? It is, therefore, unsurprising that Lawson has eventually come round to considering the problem of what we mean by neoclassical economics. As we have shown, it is a term used in different ways for different purposes. It can be used as more of a fixed point within the mainstream or as synonymous with the mainstream. It can be explored in terms of theory and self-identification, or as an imposed categorisation. It can involve long and short histories of economics, the history of economic thought, the history of the history of economic thought and also methodological critique, drawing on many different resources.

For a philosopher, methodologist or social theorist 'underlabouring', the existence of multiplicity readily leads to the issue of clarification. Specifically, in the case of the usage of the term neoclassical it leads to the question, has multiplicity become an impediment to constructive argument regarding the mainstream and of heterodoxy in relation to the mainstream? As a corollary, can order be brought to the use of the term and does retention of the term serve any constructive purpose? These are the shaping concerns that seem to motivate Lawson's 'What is this "school" called neoclassical economics?' Though Lawson, does not say so in the essay, this way of thinking is integral to realist social ontology. It flows directly from one of its typical methods. 'Immanent critique' identifies tensions and inconsistencies in different approaches to a common problematic and then seeks to resolve them, typically by reformulating the conceptual framework of the problematic (for example, Bhaskar, 1989: 182; Lawson, 1997: 50–51).

Lawson's 'What is this "school" called neoclassical economics?'

So, the first chapter in this collection is Lawson's 'What is this "school" called neoclassical economics?', originally published in the *Cambridge Journal of Economics*. The essay takes as its point of departure that there are currently multiple uses of the term neoclassical and that this results, in general, in a looseness of usage that serves to direct attention away from the underlying problems that are common across mainstream economics. Multiplicity creates the potential for an adverse focus in various ways. It can lead to the inference that solving problems of neoclassical economics is sufficient to solve problems of the mainstream. However, this is so only in so far as fundamental problems of mainstream economics are solved and, for Lawson, these are problems common to the ontology. Specifically, the issue remains one of the ontology of closed systems rather than open systems. On this basis it makes sense to focus explicitly on the issue of ontology as a generalised problem of the mainstream, rather than to express this through designating the neoclassical, since this introduces a mediating term that invites confusion based on multiple uses.

Lawson thus recognises that it is possible to use the term as synonymous with the mainstream and as a subset of that mainstream, though his own position is closer to the methodological component in the political economy critique. However, he questions the strategic value in continuing to use the term, whether based on a methodological component or explored through history of economic thought, etc., because of its many uses. However, the argument is not then antithetical to history of economic thought, since he then argues that one can return to the original meaning of the neoclassical, as coined by Veblen (1900), in order to highlight the issue of ontology. The point then becomes to use the history of economic thought to draw a line under the usage of the neoclassical – to move beyond it (the term neoclassical rather than the issue of ontology). Moreover, it is intrinsic to Lawson's argument that it is worthwhile doing so, because recognising common issues of ontology is not the same as consistency in terms of expressing and applying ontology.

It is here that Lawson seeks to rehabilitate a reading of Veblen's original usage of neoclassical. In part 3 of his *Quarterly Journal of Economics* paper, Veblen (1900) distinguishes between two concepts of science: taxonomic science and evolutionary science. By taxonomic he means a focus on a normal situation, which is expressed and explored as a repetitive system, subject only to deviations and disturbing factors. By evolutionary science he means a focus on a system based on cumulative causation, such that change cannot be conceptualised as simply disturbing factors, which create deviations from a repetitive normal situation. The former broadly conforms to Lawson's closed system and the latter to his account of an open system. According to Lawson, Veblen introduces the term neoclassical as a designation for approaches which articulate, accept or advocate evolutionary science, but that simultaneously default to methods and applications that *do not* transcend the constraints of taxonomic science. So, neoclassical, in its original usage, refers to a mismatch or potential inconsistency in the work of economists. The mismatch is defined in terms of an inconsistency with regards to ontology.

Recall that the grounds of realist social ontology seem to provide a way to clearly differentiate the mainstream from heterodoxy based on an open- and closed-systems dichotomy. If the difference can be specified via ontology, then someone working from within realist social ontology will necessarily be sensitised to the issue of the significance of intermediate terms, such as the neoclassical within the mainstream, or as synonymous with, but in terms of which one must translate to, a mainstream. By rehabilitating Veblen's usage of neoclassical Lawson appears to be emphasising possible occlusion of (from within this logic of argument) the primary (though not sole) significance of social ontology in shaping economics. The return to Veblen's usage highlights potential problems from the point of view of social ontology. That is, because of the mismatch, there can be consequences that are as relevant for heterodox economists as they are for mainstream economists. *In practice* there may be no simple dichotomy between heterodoxy (historical-processual open systems) and the mainstream (atomistic constant conjunction closed systems), because there can be intermediate positions. Based on Lawson's reading of Veblen the neoclassical now becomes the third of three highly general, ontologically-orientated classifications of economics:

1   those who both (a) adopt an overly taxonomic approach to science, a group dominated in modern times by those who accept mathematical deductivism as an orientation to science for us all, and (b) effectively regard any stance that questions this approach, whatever the basis, as inevitably misguided [many within the mainstream];
2   those who are aware that social reality is of a causal-processual nature as elaborated above, who prioritise the goal of being realistic and who fashion methods in the light of this ontological understanding, and thereby recognise the limited scope for any taxonomic science, not least any that relies on methods of mathematical deductive modelling [many within heterodox economics];
3   those who are aware (at some level) that social reality is of a causal-processual nature as elaborated above, who prioritise the goal of being realistic, yet who fail themselves fully to recognise or to accept the limited scope for any overly taxonomic approach including, in particular, one that makes significant use of methods of mathematical deductive modelling [who may be self-identified heterodox economists].

(Lawson, Chapter 1: 63–64)

'What is this "school" called neoclassical economics?' thus provides a different inflection regarding Lawson's 2006 essay. In that essay the *potential* of heterodoxy is built from its common open-systems (historical-processual) ontology, which according to Lawson provides heterodoxy with its unity-in-difference. It is integral to 'What is this "school" called neoclassical economics?' that this potential can be undermined by a lack of attention to the significance of the consistency of social ontology for both theory and method.

Positions and provocations: the collected responses to 'What is this "school" called neoclassical economics?'

So 'What is this "school" called neoclassical economics?' recognises the multiplicity of uses of the term neoclassical, situates this to a problem of looseness and confusion, creating the potential for an adverse focus that may distract from underlying issues of common ontology, and then seeks to reintroduce a reading of Veblen's original usage in order to highlight the issue of ontology and the potential problems of ontology for both mainstream economics and heterodoxy. In so doing it takes a term with history and tries to reposition debate in order to reiterate the significance of social ontology. One can read this as a strategic provocation within the ongoing realist project in economics (see Morgan, 2015). The provocation is both emotional and cerebral. It is emotional, because the term is not neutral. It is *significantly* significant for many precisely because it has for so long embodied an 'us and them' quality, despite any ambiguity or multiplicity of use. Attempting to redefine the term, such that self-identified heterodox (for example, pluralist) economists become subject to the designation, neoclassical is clearly an act of provocation. This is by no means necessarily a negative, given what matters here is the nature of the response. This also leads to issues of substance.

Given the essay is an intervention in terms of recognised research interests and positions, it readily lends itself to responses from within, and shaped by, those recognised interests and positions. So, it seems to invite responses that consider the essay both from the point of view of, and also ranging across, continuity, conformity, history of economic thought, the political economy critique, and the methodology and philosophy of economics. This means that there are also multiple ways of reading Lawson's essay to some purpose, some more sympathetic, some less so. Reading Lawson on neoclassical economics is no less neutral than the term itself. Moreover, given the purpose of Lawson's essay is to reiterate the significance of social ontology through an exploration of what neoclassical means, then the essay readily lends itself to responses that also place that essay in a broader context – specifically different takes on the actual significance of realist social ontology. Here, there can be differences between the intent, and thus implication of, the author and the inferences drawn, and thus emphasis pursued by, interlocutors. In terms of positions and provocations the essay has proven amenable to responses that:

1 elaborate or build on the realist social ontology argument as is, tending to accept, confirm, illustrate or apply aspects of Lawson's argument regarding the neoclassical;
2 reconsider the derivation of meaning of the neoclassical in the light of Lawson's essay, considering the nature of multiplicity and ambiguity

of the term, and asking, to what degree is this multiplicity and received usage necessarily problematic;
3   extend the argument in terms of the adequacy or relevance of Veblen's definition, in and through the history of economic thought, the history of economics and issues of methodology;
4   extend the argument in terms of questioning the strategic value in rehabilitating Veblen's usage;
5   pursue a line of inference from Lawson's various statements, selected from across his published works, regarding the prevalence of deductive mathematical method in the mainstream as the dominant expression of closed systems, in order to question a strong association between deductive mathematical method only and the mainstream. That is, translate Lawson's position into one that focuses tightly on and rejects deductive mathematical method and then question whether this deductive mathematical method (rather than closed systems per se) is sufficient to define an economist as mainstream or neoclassical (in the non-Veblen sense);
6   qualify or bring into question the nature of the rehabilitated term in a contemporary context, based on the specifics of method. That is, explore the problem of a mismatch (on which the rehabilitated Veblen definition hinges) between closed systems, open systems and adequate economics. This takes two forms:

   a   the argument that there can be constructive uses of mathematics, that is, mathematics need not be based on closed systems, where formalism and constant conjunctions are problematic. There need be no mismatch between using mathematics and ontologically adequate economics. Economics can (and heterodox economics at its best does) theorise, model and apply dynamic systems, and these are equivalent to open systems;
   b   the argument that there can be constructive uses of a range of mathematically-statistically rooted methods, despite that they may be limited by closed-systems characteristics. Economics can apply and model using such methods in so far as this is done with appropriate understanding and contextualisation of their use.

The contributions to this collection range across all of these possibilities. The contributors include some of the best-known and respected names in methodology, political economy, heterodoxy and the history of economic thought.

Following Lawson's essay, in Chapter 2, John Latsis and Constantinos Repapis, both of whom are closely associated with CSOG, apply Lawson's triadic reformulation of basic categories of approaches to economics to the history of economic thought. Whilst one of Lawson's primary purposes in writing 'What is this "school" called neoclassical economics?' was to highlight that problems of multiple uses of the term might provide a reason to, having clarified its meaning, dispense with it, Latsis and Repapis argue that it may be worth preserving the term. Specifically, if the neoclassical refers to an ontological mismatch and the mainstream refers to a more consistent closed-systems approach to ontology, then one can trace the development from one to the other. For Latsis and Repapis:

> An unintended consequence of this clearly defined distinction between mainstream and neoclassical economics is that it provides us with a new tool to investigate important questions in the history of economic thought. For example: what is the historical relationship between mainstream and neoclassical economics? If the mainstream emerged from neoclassical contributions, how and when did this transition occur?

Latsis and Repapis explore the potential of this 'tool' in the case of Arrow's seminal 1963 paper on moral hazard. According to Latsis and Repapis, Arrow's paper is neoclassical, in so far as it recognises aspects of behaviour that cannot be reduced to atomistic relations expressible through mathematical formalism. However, the subsequent uptake and interpretation of moral hazard steadily focused on adverse selection in terms of rational action, translating the whole into a more consistent mainstream form. As such, this discourse illustrates a post-war transition from a neoclassical mismatch to mainstream model building, which shapes, sheds, distances and/or discards potential inconsistencies.

In Chapter 3 Sheila Dow argues that seeking to clarify general approaches to economics in terms of Lawson's triad operates on two levels. It provides a new general classification with a contemporary significance, but begs questions in terms of the nature and intent of the classification. She first places Lawson's essay in the context of his 2006 essay, which argued for realist social ontology as a point of unity for heterodox economics, and as a point of differentiation from mainstream economics, noting that whilst the new categorisation may seem clear in general it adds ambiguity in terms of detail. Specifically, and illustrated using Cambridge economists, there is significant scope to contest the degree to which any historical figure would fit solely into any of the three categories. However, for Dow, definitive historical categorisation of individuals may not be the context in which the essay is most appropriately judged. Rather it may work best as a rhetorical device creating a strategic provocation. That one can dispute which category an economist's work falls into might best be read as a challenge to actually justify in which category they do so. In this sense Lawson's paper might be considered important based on his motivating intent – seeking to encourage economists to consider the ontological basis of the economics that they do. As Dow states: 'disruption needs to be followed through with further development of what exactly in particular modelling exercises is incompatible with open-systems ontology, and whether the answer varies depending on the type of open-systems ontology under consideration'. So, unlike Latsis and Repapis, who focus on clarity in terms of the history of economic thought, Dow chooses to read Lawson's essay in terms of its productive ambiguity for methodological responses, subsequent to its significance for the history of economic thought.

In Chapter 4 Anne Mayhew also places Lawson's essay in terms of the history of economic thought. Specifically, she places the substantive definition of the neoclassical in the context of other relevant work by Veblen. The insight that a mismatch existed was for Veblen an observation of a state of affairs. He expected this state of affairs to change because the mismatch was (is) problematic and because institutional economics provided a way forward (fully evolutionary science). Lawson picks up this point and argues that the increasing mathematisation of economics based on arbitrary forms (whose methodological tenets required no substantive claim on reality) has extended the duration of the mismatch, whilst also augmenting mainstream economics. For Mayhew this may be the case, but is insufficient to account for the perpetuation of a mismatch and for the dominance of the mainstream along closed-systems lines. Here she makes the case that, as an institutional economist, Veblen also places the development of social science, including economics, within an institutional framework. Though people may show a collective tendency towards evolutionary science as a recognised superior account of the world, there may be little comfort in such a 'passionless' perspective. As such, both the public and policy makers may still tend to resist uncertainty, complexity and difficulty, preferring simple explanatory and policy narratives. This is an environment hostile to a fully realised evolutionary science, but conducive to both a mismatch and the mainstream. To fully appreciate the perpetuation of a mismatch and then also of the dominance of the contemporary mainstream, one must, therefore, place economic thought in terms of a socially situated history of economics. Mayhew illustrates her point using two crises of public policy in the USA: the anti-trust crisis and the Great Depression. For Mayhew, whilst Lawson's essay provides a significant service in terms of rehabilitating Veblen's use of the neoclassical and is 'highly convincing' as an account of closed systems and mathematics in economics, she is less convinced that: 'a revolution in mathematics is sufficient explanation of why economics remained "neoclassical"'. So, where Dow orientates on the sufficiency of Lawson's argument in terms of the need for constructive responses to its rhetorical intent as a means to provoke justifications of ontological consistency from economists, Mayhew orientates on sufficiency as a matter of the broader institutional framework of the history of economics as, implicitly, a matter of consistency for any fuller reading of Veblen.

In Chapter 5 John B. Davis also chooses to orientate on a more extensive engagement with Veblen. However, he does so on the grounds of methodology and philosophy of social science. His point of departure is that: 'Veblen is hardly only valuable to Lawson because his initial conception of the term and category is an obvious starting point'. One can also shift back and forth between Veblen and Lawson in order to disambiguate some of the key concepts of social ontology. Specifically, one can constructively clarify and extend some of the key concepts stated in the essay. Here Davis develops his own approach to reflexivity to explore the temporal significance of cumulative causation. It is the reflexivity of the human agent that links the future and the present, creating both non-identity between the past, present and future, but also continuity. Reflexivity is one way of accounting for why the social world is open and why it cannot be atomistic in the causal sense assumed by mainstream economics. Cumulative causation involves feedback and also process, but one must be careful to distinguish between change as always and everywhere occurring and change as a property of social reality. Given that change is a property only, then degrees of change and also limited or lack of change (stability) are also properties. Moreover, since process involves both agents and structures, one needs also to carefully conceptualise the context of interaction. For Davis a cumulative causation process is self-referential, acting upon itself, and thus potentially changing the components of its relevant parts. In so far as this is the case, both human action and social structures are emergent upon one another. At the same time not all aspects of social reality are necessarily internally related. According to Davis, these clarifications address possible problems with reading Lawson's essay in isolation. In particular, Lawson's emphasis that social reality is highly transient, always changing and internally related. Davis provides a different take than Lawson's own more extended work on these subject matters (Lawson, 1997, 2003, 2015b). However, he does so in order to place the essay in terms of two other points. Though Lawson does not reject *a priori* the use of mathematical modelling (rather he objects to the *a priori* default to its use), the emphasis on change seems to 'rule out *all* mathematical modelling' and serves to alienate some heterodox economists. So, much as Dow notes, the issue of a neoclassical mismatch needs some greater specification. Moreover, one can also consider a renewed mismatch to be important and productive in a transitional sense. It is precisely the lack of a mismatch that renders much of the mainstream currently moribund.

In Chapter 6 Nuno Martins, another member of CSOG, returns to the history of economic thought in order to consider the context in which Veblen coined the term neoclassical. Drawing on his recent text *The Cambridge Revival of Political Economy* (2013), Martins argues that classical political economy, properly interpreted, was actually a proto-evolutionary science in Veblen's sense. As such, the prefix neo is inappropriate to designate an evolutionary science-taxonomic science mismatch, since classical political economy was not taxonomic. Rather it was the subsequent vulgar political economists who might be categorised in this way.

One might, therefore, more appropriately term the work Veblen designates as neoclassical as (following Dobb and as Lawson also notes) counter-classical. Moreover, one might describe Marx as the last of the classical political economists and, if one were to use neo appropriately, to mean actually following from the classical in some recognisably continuous sense, one might describe Veblen as the first of the neoclassical economists. For Martins this creates some degree of reservation regarding Veblen's use of the term and Lawson's revival of it (in order then to perhaps argue for it to be discarded). Whilst Martins is supportive of the actual argument for ontology that Lawson sets out, he argues it might be strategically preferable to reclaim the term as a discursive move in a Gramscian war of position sense, in order to frame the classical theory of the surplus as an important contemporary, and consistent, expression of open-systems ontology.

In Chapter 7 John King also focuses on the issue of appropriate definition. Specifically, he considers ten propositions that address the looseness, diversity and adequacy of meaning of the neoclassical. For King Veblen's usage is figurative rather than precise and is intended to be disruptive. This, of course, is also Lawson's intention. However, by returning to Veblen's mismatch, Lawson is putting aside the more typical way in which it is used and so may be creating a problem of anticipated definition, since his new definition would not include many well-known mainstream economists who are typically referred to in this way. Though it remains the case that the term is used in a variety of ways within the history of economic thought and beyond, it is still possible to fix a generalised meaning for purpose, based for example on Colander's (2000) and Colander *et al.*'s (2004) approach. Moreover, if one does so, many economists would be situated somewhere along a spectrum in terms of the criteria and so there is no simple dual of mainstream-not mainstream or neo-not neo (accepting that the use of neo is idiosyncratic within economics, as Martins argues). For King, though Lawson's essay is valuable as a provocation and as a means to remind economists of the importance of methodology, the specific claim that mathematical deductivism is the root of an ontological mismatch may not be sufficient to establish that a given economic expression is problematic and thus neoclassical in Lawson's sense. Post-Keynesians, Marxists, etc. have all used formal mathematical expression, so there may be a need for more careful differentiation here. However, unlike Dow, King does not explicitly consider this as a burden of proof issue for those who use formalism, for example, who would describe themselves as heterodox or non-neoclassical (in the received sense based on, for example, Colander or Arnsperger and Varoufakis). Rather, King finds that being required by the terms of Lawson's essay to reconsider what the neoclassical may mean, ought to encourage more and not less work on the meaning of neoclassical economics within the history of economic thought, precisely because the term has turned out to be so problematic and varied in a way that has so far been little considered.

In Chapter 8 Ben Fine also considers the meaning frames of the neoclassical, the adequacy or relevance of Veblen's definition and the strategic value of rehabilitating that definition. He does so from within his well-established political economy critique of the mainstream and his ongoing critique of what he terms Critical Realism in Economics (CRE). Fine reads Lawson's argument as one that essentially claims that the looseness and or variety of accumulated usage and meanings of the neoclassical implies it has no real existence. What exists or endures is ontology and it is this that licenses Lawson's claim that one might dispense with the term neoclassical for the mainstream and rehabilitate Veblen's use (and perhaps dispense with it there also). For Fine, though Veblen's use may have some interest within the history of economic thought, the current contemporary use remains important. The neoclassical does exist and there is more involved here than common ontological characteristics. Whilst for Lawson economics places too little emphasis on ontology, and it is this that motivates his essay in the sense of the intention to provoke a focus on ontology, for Fine, Lawson's whole approach tends to overemphasise the significance of ontology in determining the form of mainstream economics and the importance of ontology in engaging in critique of that economics. Specifically, mainstream economics may have commonalities that both Lawson and the political economy critique share, but the commonalities they share are not sufficient to make the two approaches equivalent, since the political economy critique places a greater emphasis on the actual form of theory. According to Fine, there is more involved in mainstream economic theory than mathematical deductivism as a core characteristic and this characteristic is not always present. It is, therefore, potentially reductive to focus on ontology only and then on mathematical deductivism in particular. Moreover, even if the intent is not to be reductive in quite this way the unintended consequence can still be to marginalise the actual analysis, engagement and critique of the substantive forms of mainstream (neoclassical) theory, except in so far as one describes them as ontologically deficient. For Fine a set of flexible technical apparatus and technical architecture provide a fuller conceptualisation and explanation of the form, power, reproduction, expansion and continued dominance of mainstream (neoclassical) economics. So, whilst Fine continues to express considerable sympathy for Lawson's closed-systems critique of the mainstream, he continues also to affirm that the differences between a defining social ontology approach (rather than sometimes employing social ontology argument) and a political economy approach matters.

In Chapter 9 Brian O'Boyle and Terrence McDonough take up Fine's argument in order to provide a historical account of claimed differences between a social ontology and political economy approach. Whilst they accept Lawson's 'fundamental argument about the inappropriateness of closed models being used to investigate open systems', they are sceptical that one can redefine economics in terms of its methods via ontology.

For O'Boyle and McDonough this neglects the actual history of the history of economic thought and, in particular, the ideological formation of mainstream (as neoclassical) economics. They argue that the classical political economists sought to use Newton as an inspiration for a scientific-realist methodology (seeking real causes). However, the vulgar political economists and then the marginalists separated Newtonian mechanics from this Newtonian scientific-realist methodology and conjoined it instead with a Hobbesian approach, where theory is constructed from idealised axioms, which provide thin or superficial confirmation of some aspect of an economy, but are ultimately insulated from interrogation as real causes. Though theory became less scientific in a realist sense, it maintained the appearance of science based on both the expression of laws and the use of mathematics. Moreover, the theory form(s) served to justify, legitimate and/or defend a capitalist society. Vulgar political economy and then marginalism were initially a response to the ideational potential of classical political economy and of the work of Marx. So, for O'Boyle and McDonough the history of the history of economic thought both involves influences beyond the discipline and matters of methodology that are more than the realism and absence of realism expressed in theory. From this perspective they question the strategic value of referring to the mainstream primarily in terms of ontology and also rehabilitating Veblen's definition. It is worth noting here that they cover much of the same historical ground as Martins' essay in Chapter 6 (and his *The Cambridge Revival of Political Economy* (2013)), but read this to quite different effect. Specifically, they seek to differentiate political economy from social ontology on the grounds that historical continuity is expressed substantively (if flexibly) in the combination of methodological characteristics, theory, analytical techniques and a legitimating-reproductive role in actual economic relations and society. For O'Boyle and McDonough expressions of this combination can reasonably continue to be referred to as neoclassical.

In Chapter 10 Mark Setterfield responds directly to Lawson's underlying intent in writing his essay on neoclassicism. Lawson's intent was to provoke economists into considering the significance of ontology, based in particular on the problem of a potential mismatch between recognition of an open-systems reality and particular modes of expression and methods, which may follow closed-systems forms. According to Setterfield 'Lawson's is not an idle rhetorical strategy in a meaningless war of words and should not be treated as such. He raises issues of real substance that demand to be engaged'. For Setterfield 'mathematical modelling is not (or at least *need not be*) inconsistent with open-systems ontology'. One can adopt the open systems, *ceteris paribus* (OSCP) approach to modelling. OSCP models have a temporal frame of reference and may hold some transmutable aspects constant over a period, but the equation form allows any regularity to dissolve in the next period. As such, OSCP models do not rely on intrinsic or extrinsic closure or perpetual deterministic deep conditional parameters. Where conditional closures are introduced these take one of two forms. First, they can be introduced as analytical devices that hold constant some recognisably variable aspect of a system in order to demonstrate something about the operation of the system – they can serve a pedagogic function, and Keynes and Post-Keynesians have demonstrated the value of this many times. Second, they can be introduced as empirically grounded temporary sources of relative stability. Open systems tend to encourage the development of institutions and institutionalised behaviour that are intended to provide some degree of regularity as security in systems (reducing problems of uncertainty for economic agents). Structural modelling can seek to capture these and, again, Post-Keynesians have demonstrated this (an argument also recently pursued by Nell and Errouaki, 2013). In seeking to capture degrees of stability there is no presumption that an economic system is atomistic, merely that it may display properties that can appear atomistic in so far as they are more or less regular for some period. 'Sensitive', in the sense of carefully (realistically) conceived and empirically grounded, uses of mathematical modelling can then be compatible with the actual potentials of Lawson's own agent-structure open-systems approach. Here, Setterfield provides a response that addresses Dow's point that Lawson's essay requires heterodox economists to justify their use of methods that may be considered problematic. In so doing he also draws on Davis's point that Lawson's essay (rather than perhaps his work in general) seems to place a great deal of weight on change and transition rather than relative stability. Setterfield's point is not to contest the relevance of open systems, but rather to suggest stability within openness is also important, and the combination can be expressed mathematically, and can be done so quite differently by a heterodox economist than is typically the case for a mainstream economist. As such, a heterodox economist using mathematics need not (though in any given instance still could) be neoclassical in the Veblen sense.

In Chapter 11 Steve Keen, another prominent Post-Keynesian, also addresses the issue of a mismatch. Though Keen states he has 'great sympathy' for aspects of Lawson's general position, he too wishes to contest the inference that the use of mathematics is necessarily problematic for any economist who also acknowledges the adequacy of open systems. For Keen it does mathematics a disservice to associate its potential with mainstream economics. Mainstream economics is best defined today as neoclassical in Arnsperger and Varoufakis's sense of adhering to methodological individualism, methodological instrumentalism, contrived equilibria and Keen's own methodological barter (economic interaction is treated as though it involved the exchange of two commodities between two agents, and money's only role was to assist barter rather than to enable, construct, and sometimes confound, commerce in a system of finance). Keen also draws on the political economy critique to make the point that the use of mathematics in the mainstream is not just unreal in the ontological sense but also inauthentic, because many of the mathematical expressions lack genuine solutions. When problems arise they are not confronted in ways that change the conditions under which mathematics is used, rather problems are arbitrarily resolved, assumed away or simply ignored as inconvenient (for a classic exposition see Keen and Standish, 2006). As such, they are not mathematics but rather 'mythematics'. Closed-systems varieties of mathematics are used precisely in order to avoid confronting many of the problems that the four axioms create. Lawson's critique of atomism may then be relevant for linear systems, since these treat interactions between variables as additive (the contribution of one variable is not influenced by any other – a 'superposition'), but does not apply to nonlinear dynamic systems, since these are non-atomistic (a system variable can be significantly altered by the value of other system variables, and whilst a system may be determinant it is not deterministic or conducive to deduction or prediction of events, particularly over longer periods). For Keen it is ultimately inappropriate to identify the use of mathematical formalism per se by heterodox economists as conducive to a mismatch. Rather, one should focus on a more constructive frame of reference, which encourages economists to use better mathematics. For Keen, Lawson's triadic reformulation (paraphrased as the good, the bad and the ugly), though a deliberate provocation, may ultimately be unhelpful if one generalises to the extent that any and all uses of mathematics are both closed-systems-based and problematic.

In Chapter 12 Don Ross addresses a similar point to Keen, but does so from a different perspective. For Ross, Lawson orientates on a genuine problem of confusion and lack of clarity in how we conceptualise economics. However, according to Ross even an adequately pursued economics cannot escape the neoclassical tension and all economists must in the end be neoclassical to some degree. Ross's point of departure is that his own and Lawson's positions are divided by different varieties of realism. Ross draws on Peirce to develop a 'Rainforest Realism', which is irreducibly dynamic, but in which to be is to be a 'real pattern'. This realism attempts to identify causal relationships but considers the ordinary language approach to social ontology of Lawson to be inadequate to actually capture the complexity of the world as an empirical endeavour. An adequate *scientific* account of the world derives its concepts from complexity and also explores the patterns of that complexity. From this perspective Lawson's social ontology is (in a non-pejorative philosophical sense) 'folk ontology'. This position leads to a reversal of Lawson's argument regarding mathematics: 'The general structure of the world, which furnishes the modal background for all special structures, can only be represented mathematically' and 'Which patterns are real in the sense of being non-redundant cannot be inferred from human practice or language but can only be affirmed with more or less confidence on the basis of statistical modelling'. However, in so far as the two claims are accepted there is a real constraint on the capacity of science to investigate the world. The world is 'strange' beyond folk ontology and we currently lack the mathematical power to fully express this. Economists who do not deny the manifest complexity of the world are, therefore, restricted by the available mathematics and so must be neoclassical if they are to attempt to engage with the world effectively at all. Lawson's various critiques of econometrics, for example, may have some traction here in terms of substance, but not necessarily inference. One need not be pessimistic in this context because it is on the basis of accumulated expertise and experience that an economist can interpret their use and selection of models and applications and thus make causal sense of otherwise problematic issues, such as variation in the magnitude of coefficients or changes of sign for dependent variables between applications. Moreover, the computing power available to such an aware economist is continually increasing.

Clearly Ross's argument takes us far from Lawson's original position that there is a *problematic* mismatch between accepting open-systems ontology (evolutionary science) and the practices of some economists who accept the evolutionary science ontology – a default to closed systems (taxonomic science). For Ross the mismatch is a tension, but is unavoidable for good science because of the nature of the world. The tension is manageable and, in so far as it is unavoidable, it can be productive. Given the starting point is that science is mathematical and that the world can only be adequately conceptualised mathematically and can only be primarily interrogated mathematically (though the product of mathematics can then also be interpreted), Ross's position represents an extension that goes further than either Setterfield or Keen. They argue for compatibility based on some uses of mathematics, rather than primacy, where mathematics becomes *the* point of departure for an adequate (economic) science.

In the final chapter, Chapter 13, Steve Fleetwood, another well-known CSOG participant, brings us full circle. He starts from the position that Lawson's argument for social ontology is well-founded and that its extension in terms of a problematic mismatch, whose pivot is the use of mathematics, can be readily demonstrated using labour economics. For Fleetwood mainstream labour economics was formerly neoclassical in the received mainstream sense of embodying a strict series of conceptual commitments. Those commitments were: labour supply and demand as a point of reference, methodological individualism, rational maximisation and Pareto efficiency. However, mainstream labour economics has subsequently adopted a generalised searching and matching approach to labour markets. This has discarded labour demand and supply and Pareto efficiency and, in some of its guises, incorporates bounded rationality, information asymmetries, rule following and dynamism. As such, it makes claim to be more realistic. However, if one sets out the way in which conceptual innovations and concessions are introduced, they actually remain, in acknowledged ways, unrealistic (as simplifications, limitations, approximations, etc.). For example, in the formal expression of theory a decision rule is not the actual rule following behaviour of agents and does not take account of the variability of intent and outcome of activity that affects outcomes in real time. There remains, therefore, a mismatch between the claim of realisticness, some degree of awareness that systems are open, and the actual way in which theory is expressed. For Fleetwood the problem is an overwhelming commitment to express the theory in the given mathematical forms (in which the agent must also be to some tractable degree rational and where all decisions are consciously calculative). As such, in the case of labour economics at least, recent theory innovation has served to make economics neoclassical in Lawson's sense and this is most clearly exposed at a meta-theoretical (ontological) level.

Fleetwood's position orientates on a sense of the fluidity of commitments within the mainstream, similar to that identified by Arnsperger and Varoufakis, and considers these to be indicative of neoclassicism at the level of theory, therefore reading this rather differently than Keen. Moreover, he reads the relationship between mathematics and ontology that one might draw from Lawson rather differently than Setterfield or Ross. From Fleetwood's position, the concepts of 'folk ontology' are central to an adequate representation of agents in their activity and of the structures in terms of which they act (real rule following behaviour). It is by seeking to translate these into mathematical form that one violates the realisticness of concepts, becoming perhaps scientistic. Moreover, an open system is one where causation resides in powers and capacities of entities, which may be different than the specification of those powers or capacities in a mathematically stated dynamic system. So, the terms of use of key concepts are quite different here for Fleetwood. However, given that Lawson's triadic categorisation, and in particular the third neoclassical category, is about degrees of use and limits of application of theory and methods, one cannot read Fleetwood's position as a decisive refutation of any of the others in terms of the use of mathematics. One cannot definitively refute an argument for use based on an argument for consistency limitations only. The argument still begs demonstration regarding the degree to which a given form of theory and application provides genuine insight into economic phenomena as they occur. Clearly, many Post-Keynesians in particular think quite differently about this based on their actual uses of dynamic systems (see also Foster, 2005).

Conclusion: reversing the strategic provocation? Future issues for Lawson on the neoclassical and social ontology

If one reads across the contributions to this collection it is clear that Lawson's 'What is this "school" called neoclassical economics?' has done exactly what he intended. It has provoked a response requiring economists to consider what they mean by neoclassical, whether they continue to think the term has meaning and relevance and also, more fundamentally, in what sense it relates to the significance of social ontology. However, in so far as the term neoclassical has multiple meanings and the essay is being read from within the received research interests and positions of economists who have different starting points in terms of those multiple meanings, it is also equally clear that Lawson has not yet persuaded some of his interlocutors. To some degree this is less important than that the economists whose work is represented here took the time to carefully consider the argument. Difference and disagreement flow from different concerns and emphases, rather than from an intention to traduce. Vituperation and excoriation are absent. Collectively, these essays demonstrate that pluralism is alive and well in some areas of economics. More specifically, pluralism as a value orientation, where one is committed to constructively consider the value of an argument, even a highly critical argument, within and for economics (rather than one is prepared only to contest the technical aspects of a model form from a technical point of view), is alive and well.

Moreover, though one could read the essays as a confirmation of continued disagreement and difference, the collective outcome is by no means necessarily indicative of dissolution into greater confusion. It may well constitute a productive first set of reflections leading to hiatus. There is general agreement that issues of open and closed systems are significant and that better economics recognises that open-systems ontology is a more adequate account of social (economic) reality. Thereafter, differences and disagreements revolve around the particulars of closed and open systems and the sufficiency of social ontology. Lawson may well feel that some of the points considered are ones that work from CSOG and his own work beyond the neoclassical essay can provide responses to (see e.g. Lawson, 2015a, 2015b, 2016). For example, in terms of specifics he might make reference to the substance of the ontology for open systems based on causation inhering in powers or capacities of entities, expressible in terms of causal concomitance versus causal connection and in forms of demi-regularity, in order to further his case regarding the substantive basis of any stability in events and its breakdown. Relatedly he might refer to his Transformational Model of Social Activity and Population Variety Reproduction Selection model in order to contextualise his argument for transience in terms of change and continuity. He might also note that his scepticism regarding ideology is mainly framed in terms of its explicit influence as a reason for acting by mainstream economists (its role in their preference for methods), based on awareness, since he has also argued that politicised ideas and contexts are not irrelevant to economics and its reproduction.

However, it remains the case that despite these possible counters some political economists, Post-Keynesians and methodologists remain unconvinced. So, for example, Martins or Fleetwood may read social ontology as integral to political economy, but there is still a significant gap between say Fleetwood (2012) and Milonakis and Fine (2009, or Fine, 2013). Moreover, though Lawson might reasonably argue that he has answers of sorts or elaborations of kinds that respond to many of the points made in this collection, the question is still begged why he is read in the way he is, particularly by his more critical interlocutors. It struck me as editor of this collection that two important and related dividing lines, read in terms of transitions, seem to be discursively significant. First, the transition from social ontology as an *important domain of argument* and component in self-aware critique of and adequate construction of economics, to social ontology as a *primary explanatory component* accounting for the state of economics. More critical interlocutors tend to accept the former, but not the latter. Second, the transition from open systems as a recognisably more adequate account of social (economic) reality than closed systems, to the claim that mainstream economics is both overwhelmingly dominated by and adequately defined in terms of formalism and mathematical deductivism as expressions of closed systems; that any attempt to use these will likely *a posteriori* exhibit failure; that better ways to express an economic argument and pursue research (methods) exist; and so one should prefer other ways of doing economics. Again, more critical interlocutors tend to accept the former (reality is open), but reject the latter (mathematics has demonstrated itself to be and will continue to demonstrate that it is, incompatible with expressing in theory and exploring in practice an open-systems reality) *in so far* as this seems to be overly anti-mathematical in the social domain. For more critical interlocutors Lawson seems to push his argument too far and in doing so has failed to take them with him, despite general agreement regarding the former.

Lawson's neoclassical essay then becomes a further provocation in terms of which this debate is pursued. What does this suggest? Primarily that if Lawson wants to make his case he needs to continue to address core dividing lines. At the same time Dow's point that Lawson's neoclassical essay works best as a strategic provocation that creates a burden of proof, remains relevant. Specifically 'disruption needs to be followed through with further development of what exactly in particular modelling exercises is incompatible with open-systems ontology, and whether the answer varies depending on the type of open-systems ontology under consideration'. For hiatus to be followed by further constructive development would seem to require distributed responsibility. Some of the core questions that sceptics seem to require more persuasion in regard of include:

1   Is (a claim Lawson does not himself make) mathematical modelling of the sort utilized in modern economics necessarily closed-systems-based, even if open-systems directed?

2   Based on what meaning frames can a dynamic system and an open system be considered equivalent or different?
3   Is mathematical deductivism the only relevant form of closed systems in the context of modern economics?
4   Is an approach that incorporates some element of closed systems or a closed-systems method necessarily problematic to the point of failure, or merely (and unavoidably) conditionally difficult to develop and use?
5   What does it mean for social ontology to be both an account of economic reality and an explanatory component in the state of economics?
6   Is ideology relevant as a conditioning element of knowledge as a social product and, if not, what is the difference between ideology and influential ideas embedded in or significant for structures?

Answers to these and other questions necessarily have bearing on the reasons we gave at the beginning for why what we mean by the neoclassical matters. First, because what we mean affects how we view the mainstream and so where pluralist and heterodox economists situate and pursue appropriate critique of, and constructive dialogue with, the mainstream. Second, because what we mean affects how we conceive heterodox economics in relation to mainstream economics and this has significance for whether, and the way in which, heterodox economists model, apply methods and construct theory. I hope you find the following essays worthwhile and informative.

Notes

1   The point is the familiarity of this as a narrative for neoclassical economics, not whether one might dispute the degree of relevance for particular proponents. For example, Paul Samuelson was in many ways open-minded and highly engaged across many branches of theory and also the history of economic thought. As Kurz notes in Samuelson's obituary for *The European Journal of the History of Economic Thought* Samuelson was one of the most open-minded and curious economists of his acquaintance, and Kurz states he was 'one of the most knowledgeable, erudite and original scholars I have ever had the privilege to meet . . . Samuelson himself had at least two souls in his breast: he was a neoclassical economist and a Keynesian at the same time. He was rightly critical of attempts to reduce irreducibly heterogeneous things to some homogeneous substance, and he knew better than most economists about the variety, diversity and frequent incompatibility of economic ideas and points of view (Kurz, 2010: 519).
2   However, this essay also illustrates the problem of simple classifications of complex attempts to address difficult issues. The essay is also a history of economic thought and identifies a long timeline with some degree of significant change in the substance of neoclassical economics. Colander also states 'As I will discuss below, it is difficult to determine what that content is, and even if I wanted to kill the content, I have no role in determining content. The role of historians of thought is to record, not determine, content. What I am declaring dead is the term' (Colander, 2000: 127). This is curiously at odds with the substantive claim quoted in the 2005 essay, though it is consistent with the actual essay in which it appears.

References

Arnsperger, C. and Varoufakis, Y. (2003) Toward a theory of solidarity. *Erkenntnis* 59(2): 157–188.
Arnsperger, C. and Varoufakis, Y. (2006) What is neoclassical economics? *Post-Autistic Economics Review* 38, article 1.
Aspromourgos, T. (1986) On the origins of the term 'neoclassical'. *Cambridge Journal of Economics* 10(3): 265–270.
Bhaskar, R. (1989) *Reclaiming Reality*. London, UK: Verso.
Colander, D. (2000) The death of neoclassical economics. *Journal of the History of Economic Thought* 22(2): 127–143.
Colander, D. (2005a) The making of an economist redux. *Journal of Economic Perspectives* 19(1): 175–198.
Colander, D. (2005b) The future of economics: The appropriately educated in pursuit of the knowable. *Cambridge Journal of Economics* 29(6): 927–941.
Colander, D. and Klamer, A. (1987) The making of an economist. *Journal of Economic Perspectives* 1(2): 95–111.
Colander, D., Holt, R. and Rosser Jr, B. (2004) The changing face of mainstream economics. *Review of Political Economy* 16(4): 485–499.
Davis, J. (2006) The turn in economics: Neoclassical dominance to mainstream pluralism? *Journal of Institutional Economics* 2(1): 1–20.
Davis, J. (2008) The turn in recent economics and the return of orthodoxy. *Cambridge Journal of Economics* 32(3): 349–366.
Dow, S. (1997) Mainstream economic methodology. *Cambridge Journal of Economics* 21(1): 73–93.
Dow, S. (2000) Prospects for the progress of heterodox economics. *Journal of the History of Economic Thought* 22(2): 157–170.
Fine, B. (2013) Economics unfit for purpose. *Review of Social Economy* 71(3): 373–389.
Fleetwood, S. (2012) From political economy and economics and beyond. *Historical Materialism* 20(3): 61–80.
Foster, J. (2005) From simplistic to complex systems in economics. *Cambridge Journal of Economics* 29(6): 873–892.
Fourcade, M., Ollion, E. and Algan, Y. (2015) The superiority of economists. *Journal of Economic Perspectives* 29(1): 89–114.
Fullbrook, E. ed. (2003) *The Crisis in Economics*. London, UK: Routledge.
Garnett, R., Olsen, E. and Starr, M. (eds.) (2010) *Economic Pluralism*. London, UK: Routledge.
Hicks, J. (1939) *Value and Capital*. Oxford, UK: Clarendon Press.
Hollis, M. and Nell, E. (1975) *Rational Economic Man: A Philosophical Critique of Neoclassical Economics*. Cambridge, UK: Cambridge University Press.
Keen, S. and Standish, R. (2006) Profit maximisation, industry structure and competition: A critique of neoclassical theory. *Physica A* 370: 81–85.
Kitson, M. (2005) The economics of the future. *Cambridge Journal of Economics* 29(6): 827–835.
Klamer, A. and Colander, D. (1990) *The Making of an Economist*. Boulder, CO: Westview Press.
Kurz, H. (2010) Obituary: Aiming for a 'higher prize' Paul Anthony Samuelson (1915–2009). *The European Journal of the History of Economic Thought* 17(3): 513–520.

Lawson, T. (1997) *Reclaiming Reality*. London, UK: Routledge.
Lawson, T. (1999) Developments in economics as realist social theory, in Fleetwood, S. (ed.), *Critical Realism in Economics: Development and Debate*. London, UK: Routledge, pp. 3–20.
Lawson, T. (2003) *Reorienting Economics*. London, UK: Routledge.
Lawson, T. (2006) The nature of heterodox economics. *Cambridge Journal of Economics* 30(4): 483–505.
Lawson, T. (2015a) *Essays on the Nature and State of Modern Economics*. London, UK: Routledge.
Lawson, T. (2015b) Process order and stability in Veblen. *Cambridge Journal of Economics* 39(4): 993–1030.
Lawson, T. (2016) Comparing conceptions of social ontology: Emergent social entities and/or institutional facts? *Journal for the Theory of Social Behaviour* (forthcoming).
Lee, F. (2009) *A History of Heterodox Economics: Challenging the Mainstream in the Twentieth Century*. London, UK: Routledge.
Lee, F., Pham, X. and Gu, G. (2013) The UK research assessment exercise and the narrowing of UK economics. *Cambridge Journal of Economics* 37(4): 693–717.
Mäki, U. (ed.) (2001) *The Economic World View: Studies in the Ontology of Economics*. Cambridge, UK: Cambridge University Press.
Mäki, U. (ed.) (2002) *Fact and Fiction in Economics: Models Realism and Social Construction*. Cambridge, UK: Cambridge University Press.
Martins, N. (2013) *The Cambridge Revival of Political Economy*. London, UK: Routledge.
Milonakis, D. and Fine, B. (2009) *From Political Economy to Economics*. London, UK: Routledge.
Mirowski, P. and Plehwe, D. (eds.) (2009) *The Road from Mont Pelerin: The Making of the Neoliberal Thought Collective*. Cambridge, MA: Harvard University Press.
Morgan, J. (2015) What's in a name? Tony Lawson on neoclassical economics and heterodox economics. *Cambridge Journal of Economics* 39(3): 843–865.
Morgan, M. and Rutherford, M. (1998) American economics: The character of the transformation. *History of Political Economy* 30 (supplement): 1–26.
Nell, E. and Errouaki, K. (2013) *Rational Econometric Man: Transforming Structural Econometrics*. Cheltenham, UK: Edward Elgar.
Pratten, S. (ed.) (2015) *Social Ontology and Modern Economics*. London, UK: Routledge.
Samuelson, P. (1947) *Foundations of Economic Analysis*. Cambridge, MA: Harvard University Press.
Samuelson, P. (1955) *Economics*, 3rd ed. New York, NY: McGraw Hill.
Skousen, M. (1997) The perseverance of Paul Samuelson's economics. *Journal of Economic Perspectives* 11(2): 137–152.
Stigler, G. J. (1941) *Production and Distribution*. New York, NY: Macmillan.
Veblen, T. (1900) The preconceptions of economic science III. *Quarterly Journal of Economics* 14(2): 240–269.

1 What is this 'school' called neoclassical economics?

Tony Lawson

Introductory observations

More than a century ago, Thorstein Veblen introduced the term 'neoclassical' into economics *prima facie* to characterise a particular 'school'. The latter quotation marks were provided by Veblen himself, suggesting that there may be a sense, however, in which the object of focus was not really a school of thought at all. Even so, Veblen certainly had in mind the nature of the output of a set of contributors, as we shall see.

Currently, the term 'neoclassical' pervades the discourse of academic economics, being employed to denote a range of substantive theories and policy stances. It does not take too much research or reflection, however, to realise that not only is the Veblenian heritage typically not acknowledged (and conceivably not always appreciated) but the term is invariably employed rather loosely and somewhat inconsistently across different contributors.

For many the act of describing an economic contribution as neoclassical is considered a form of criticism, though usually when the term is so used it is without explanation or elaboration; it mostly signals dissent.[1] In similar fashion those who accept the term for their own output seem very often, and again mostly without definition or explanation, to suppose that any contribution they make is neoclassical in nature.

There are numerous more careful or systematic interpreters of the term, found typically (though not exclusively) amongst methodologists and/or historians of thought, who do seek to elaborate its meaning rather more cautiously. Here two strategies dominate.

First, there are those who suppose that intrinsic to the notion of neoclassical is a sense of both continuity and difference with something called classical economics. Certainly, if the category neoclassical economics is to be maintained it does seem *prima facie* reasonable to expect this to be the case. Yet those historians of thought and others who focus on this expectation[2] typically conclude that the criterion is not met and, most especially, that contributions classified as neoclassical fail to reveal meaningful *continuity* with any conception of classical economics.[3]

Second, there are those interpreters of the term who prioritise internal coherence (rather than continuity with some classical tradition) and instead seek to systematise any analytical features that are common to, or generative of, those contributions most widely accepted as somehow quintessentially neoclassical.

The conceptions developed by the latter set of interpreters do have significant features in common. Perhaps the most notable is the highly abstract nature of the characterisations advanced, very often taking the form of a set of 'axioms' or 'meta-axioms' or perhaps a 'meta-theory'. Additional commonalities are that the axioms identified tend to make reference to individuals as the units of analysis and indicate something of the states of knowledge and/or forms of typical behaviour of these individuals. In addition it is often the case that certain supposed (typically equilibrium) states of the economic system get a mention.

Thereafter, however, agreement is harder to find and significant variety creeps in. Sometimes individual knowledge is assumed to be in some sense 'perfect' or 'complete', sometimes systematically limited, and very often knowledge specifications do not figure explicitly at all. Behaviour is often treated as rational in some technical sense, though not always, and where it is, there is significant variety in the particular specifications. Further, there is wide disparity over whether equilibrium states are part of the essential framework of neoclassicism, and, where they are accepted as so, disagreement as to whether such states are held axiomatically always to prevail, or whether their possible existence is a matter of study, or something else; and so on. In short there is significant variety of interpretation of the term 'neoclassical economics' even across the more cautious interpreters.[4]

No less significant is the observation that the various substantive categories (rationality, equilibrium), which frequently occur across the conceptions of these more cautious interpreters, seem to be in declining use in modern economics discourse and despite the continuing prevalence of the category neoclassical economics. Others have noted the same developments. Thus David Colander *et al.* (2004), for example, insist that modern: 'economics is moving away from strict adherence to the holy trinity—rationality, selfishness, and equilibrium—to a more eclectic position of purposeful behaviour, enlightened self-interest and sustainability' (Colander *et al.*, 2004: 485); an assessment shared by John Davis (2005), amongst others.

If current use of the term 'neoclassical' has lost touch with its original meaning, does not live up to its billing of signalling continuity with a classical school and is not consistently or usefully interpreted even by those who seek internal coherence, it seems to be additionally the case that there is no real need for such a term anyway, at least not for capturing major developments and/or approaches within the modern economics academy.

The reason for so concluding is that the major research groupings or divisions of study of modern economics are more than adequately characterised without employing the term. Certainly the contemporary discipline is dominated by a mainstream tradition. But whilst the concrete substantive content, focus and policy orientations of the latter are highly heterogeneous and continually changing,[5] the project itself is adequately characterised in terms of its enduring reliance, indeed, unceasing insistence, upon methods of *mathematical modelling*. In effect it is a form of *mathematical deductivism* in the context of economics.[6] Deductivism is just the doctrine that all explanation be expressed in terms of 'laws' or 'uniformities' interpreted as (actual or 'hypothetical') correlations or event regularities (see later discussion and Lawson, 2003).

Moreover, if the contemporary mainstream project is appropriately characterised as one of mathematical modelling in economics, a form of mathematical deductivism, each of the various academic heterodox traditions that stand opposed to this hugely dominant mainstream project has its own self-identifying label, including post-Keynesianism, feminist economics, (old) institutionalism, Marxian economics, Austrian economics, social economics and numerous others. It is thus *prima facie* unclear that the designation 'neoclassical economics' is anywhere required.

Why it matters

But so what? Does any of this matter? After all, it might be argued, in all spheres of human activity many categories are seemingly used rather loosely and without agreement, but appear to do little harm; this, it might thereby be supposed, is the case with the use of the term 'neoclassical' in modern economics.

I suspect that in most contexts of human interaction more clarity is preferable to less. Of course, (lexical) ambiguity can sometimes be useful (for example, when an author does not want to reveal too much early on in a text) as can ambivalence (when a contributor is unable to weigh up the arguments and seeks to avoid making a commitment prematurely[7]); I doubt that either are ever entirely avoidable whatever a contributor's intentions. In addition the meanings of many (if not most) categories do evolve to an extent over time, and in any case may, in part at least, be determined (and so revealed only) in use. Certainly there is no desire here to reify or underplay nuance or performativity and so forth. However, in the current situation the manner in which, and wide disparity in the ways, the term 'neoclassical' is applied is not only productive of severe obfuscation, and seemingly increasingly so, it is also, or so I shall argue, positively debilitating of the discipline not least through hindering effective critique. Indeed, a major motivation of this article is precisely an assessment that the looseness with which this central term is interpreted (along with the toleration of this looseness) is a major factor inhibiting progress in economic understanding.

Not only is the economy in crisis but, as is now widely recognised, so is the discipline of economics itself. Yet the debate over the nature of the latter's problems, weaknesses and limitations has so far been mostly fairly superficial; indeed, it is apparent that within the academy there has been very little if any significant progress. A major reason for this, I will be arguing, is that loose and varying interpretations of neoclassical theorising, especially when standing in as forms of criticism and dismissal, actually serve to distract sustained reflective attention from the real, or more systematic, causes of the discipline's failings.

If I am correct in my assessment here that the term is not only without obvious use but also debilitating (the latter, as I say, being a contention defended later), a seemingly reasonable reaction is to suggest jettisoning the category 'neoclassical economics' altogether, as indeed has been the recourse of a few commentators (for varying reasons) previously.[8]

This, in effect, has tended to be my own previous orientation; I have rarely if ever employed the term in previous writings. But I have often been criticised for this, not least because a stance of non-recognition or non-engagement through avoidance is taken to be if not itself confusing then insufficiently critical (Fine, 2004; Bernard Guerrien, 2004), or even accommodating, of results maintained under the neoclassical head. Perhaps, too, the non-appearance (rather than an explication) of the term 'neoclassical' in analyses seeking to identify and illuminate the causes of problems of the discipline has in itself encouraged some to treat the latter analyses less seriously. Although I shall argue that theorising and policy stances labelled neoclassical are not the primary causes of the discipline's problems, I accept (below) they may often be manifestations of it; so that determining the relation of at least the seemingly most coherent account of neoclassical to the real causes of the discipline's problems, will hopefully provide practical insight. Moreover, I am aware that there is interest in, and I suspect there may be value to determining, how a conception of the contemporary mainstream economics as a form of mathematical deductivism, a conception I have long advanced, relates to at least the seemingly most sustainable conception of neoclassical economics. Furthermore, there is simply a repeatedly observed questioning of the nature of neoclassical thinking.

For various reasons, then, I take the opportunity here to elaborate that interpretation of the term that I believe to be the most sustainable. Let me stress at the outset that I do actually believe that a coherent construal is possible. I might also add that I am sympathetic to the idea that elaborating a coherent interpretation of such a pervasive term is an interesting intellectual project in itself. I also think it an intrinsically interesting exercise to systematically re-examine Veblen's purposes in formulating the term. But primarily, and more practically, the reason for seeking a coherent conception here is to facilitate clarity in the hope and expectation that, one way or another, this can contribute to advancing the discipline. If merely avoiding the use of the term is considered unhelpful and misleading for the reasons just given, then seeking as coherent an account as is feasible seems the obvious alternative recourse. Either way (if not through discarding the term altogether then through rendering it coherent), my aim is to help remove certain significant obstacles that obstruct the path of seriously addressing those factors that are the more fundamental causes of the modern discipline's increasingly widely recognised and indeed very widespread problems.

There is little point, of course, in my merely asserting a novel or alternative conception of neoclassical economics. Rather, any interpretation worth maintaining must fit at least the criteria implicit in criticising current uses above. The conception I advance does so. In particular, I argue for an interpretation that is (developmentally[9]): consistent with the historical origins of the meaning of the term given it by Veblen; is both continuous with, as well as different from, a meaningful conception of classical economics; is not only consistent with but in a sense encompasses seemingly all the explicit modern interpretations, not least those put forward by the more careful/cautious contributors and indeed, makes sense of and explains the latter; renders equally intelligible the contradictions of the wider, looser literature; possesses a clear referent, one that is currently without a category name; and is useful in at least (through all the foregoing) bringing clarity to academic discussion.

Obviously, I cannot, any more than anyone else, stipulate that a specific interpretation of the term be accepted, but I can hope to persuade that a particular version is more adequate than others, at least in terms of its ability to satisfy all of the various criteria of coherence already elaborated. Indeed, in terms of satisfying the noted criteria I suspect that the conception defended here may be as good as it gets. Whether this is ultimately good enough for the purposes laid out, and indeed whether the fact of a coherent interpretation of the term renders it worth persevering with, are matters that I also examine in due course.

In presenting and defending the interpretation I have in mind, Veblen's initial conception is an obvious starting point. Unfortunately, Veblen's conception needs a fair bit of elaboration to convey its essential meaning. This in part, I suspect, explains why it seems rarely to be seriously discussed or even acknowledged. I believe, though, that there are significant rewards to treating Veblen's analysis on these matters explicitly and systematically, to recovering his basic message. This I attempt to accomplish eventually below (where I find that in the few cases where Veblen is referenced on the matters before us, standard interpretations of his intentions are not quite right). Before I turn to such matters, however, I want first to expand a little on a central claim made in the introductory overview, concerning the real causes of the discipline's problems. The issues involved are likely not overly familiar to everyone; some of them require argumentation; many of them, as we eventually see, are highly relevant at some level for understanding Veblen's own conception of the neoclassical 'school'.

The real source of the discipline's problems

I have suggested that a widespread loose usage of the phrase 'neoclassical economics' or 'neoclassical theorising', especially in criticism, has tended to deflect from the real source of the discipline's problems, so I had better indicate here what the latter is and how the slack use of the category neoclassical economics hinders effective critique.

The source (as opposed to immediate manifestations) of the problems of the discipline of modern economics lies not at the level of substantive theorising at all but at the level of methodology and social ontology (the study, or a theory, of the nature of social reality). Modern economics, as has already been noted, is dominated by a mainstream tradition that insists on the repeated application of methods of mathematical modelling. The models actually employed, like all tools, are useful in some conditions and not in others As it happens the sorts of conditions under which the modelling methods economists have employed would be useful are found to be rather uncommon, and indeed unlikely, occurrences in the social realm. Alternatively put, the ontological presuppositions of the heavy emphasis on mathematical modelling do not match the nature of the 'stuff' of the social realm. The heavy use of these tools in conditions for which they are found to be inappropriate both explains the repeated explanatory failings of the discipline as well as why formulations are of a nature that are typically recognised by almost everyone as rather unrealistic. That, in summary, is the real cause of the discipline's problems.[10]

Let me briefly elaborate some of the detail of the argument. It can be noted first that mathematical methods and techniques of the sort employed by economists (use of functions, calculus and so forth) presuppose regularities at the level of events. Whether the latter are *a priori* hypothesised or *a posterior* 'detected', the successful application of economists' mathematical tools require event regularities or correlations. Systems in which such event regularities occur can be called *closed*. Deductivism, as already noted, is just the doctrine that all explanation be couched in terms of such (closed systems of) event regularities. Modern mainstream economics, if to repeat, is just a form of mathematical deductivism.

A social ontology or worldview that guarantees such event regularities is a world of isolated atoms. The term 'atom' here refers to anything that (if triggered) has the same independent effect whatever the context. Formulations couched in terms of atomistic factors allow the deduction and/or prediction of events. Or rather, they do so if nothing is allowed to interfere with the actions of the atoms. So to guarantee that at the theory level outcomes are truly predictable and/or deducible, the atoms must be assumed to act in isolation from any countervailing factors that could interfere with the outcomes.

This is the usual implicit ontology of mainstream mathematical modellers: a system of isolated atoms; indeed, a ubiquity of such systems. Very often specific substantive constructions employed take the form of conceptions of optimising (atomistic) individuals isolated in 'worlds' that each contains a unique optima, whereby the outcomes of agent interactions can be deduced. However, the latter type of set-up is not compulsory. Assumptions to the effect that individuals follow fixed rules are common, as are (or including) the algorithmic constructions of agent-based modelling and such like. But in almost all cases, the concrete theoretical specifications of economic mathematical modellers are implicitly in terms of – and so constrained to be formulations of – worlds of isolated atoms.

If there are exceptions to the latter sorts of formulations these arise in the few exercises where the emphasis on mathematical modelling is retained, but where the modellers seek to avoid the usual unrealistic (atomistic and isolationist) conceptions by downgrading the role of theorising almost entirely. In such cases attempts are usually made to avoid theorising in terms of causal factors altogether as the emphasis is placed more on data information than theorising, as or where faith is placed, as with some modern approaches to econometrics, in more or less simply uncovering event regularities.[11]

Once, however, we change tack and give primary attention not to mathematical modelling but to studying more directly the actual nature of social reality, a quite different and clearly more explanatorily powerful or superior conception emerges. According to this alternative social ontology, causality always matters and a more complex, processual account tends to dominate.

The conception of social ontology I have in mind is processual in that social reality, which itself is an emergent[12] phenomenon of human interaction, is recognised as being (not at all atomistic in the sense just noted but rather) highly transient, being reproduced and/or transformed through practice; social reality is in process, essentially a process of cumulative causation (see Lawson, 2012a). Furthermore, social reality is found to be composed of emergent phenomena that (far from being isolatable) are actually constituted in relation (that is, are internally related) to other things, and ultimately to everything else (for example, students and teachers, *qua* students and teachers, are constituted in relation to each other; so are employers and employees, landlords/ladies and tenants, creditors and debtors and so forth;[13] so, too, are money, markets, firms and so forth internally related under capitalism, and inherently transient). Constitutive social relations, in short, are a fundamental feature of social reality. So, social reality consists of emergent phenomena, constituting highly internally related causal processes.[14] For ease of exposition in what follows I often simply refer to this alternative worldview as a causal-processual or causal-historical ontology or some such.

Even this sketch, though unavoidably brief, is sufficient to indicate that from the perspective of the latter alternative ontology, the closed-system atomist and isolationist requirements of economic modelling are everywhere violated. In fact, the alternative ontology in question is more complex still, for the social world is additionally characterised by meaning, value and so on.

This latter conception, as I demonstrate elsewhere (see especially Lawson, 2003, chapter 2), is, if to repeat, significantly explanatorily superior as an account of the nature of social reality to the implicit worldview of systems of isolated atoms presupposed by the mainstream emphasis on certain techniques of mathematical modelling. It follows, accepting the alternative conception, that the failings of the discipline arise just because economists everywhere are seeking to provide analyses of a social system that is, amongst other things, open (in the sense of not consisting in event regularities), processual and highly internally related, in terms of formulations that require that the social realm be treated as if made of closed systems of isolated atoms So, in summary, the real source of the discipline's problems is the very emphasis on mathematical modelling that defines the mainstream, an emphasis that usually results in formulations implicitly constrained to be consistent with a deficient social ontology.

The mainstream/heterodox contrast and the category neoclassical economics

I noted in the introductory overview that if the mainstream project is usefully characterised as a form of mathematical deductivism, the heterodox traditions are already self-identifying without employment of the term 'neoclassical'. Matters would be analytically neat if the mainstream/heterodox differentiation coincided with the contrasting ontological conceptions already sketched and that it was recognised as doing so. Unfortunately, at least in terms of recognition, matters are not quite so straightforward. Let me elaborate a little, for the issues involved, we eventually see, also bear significantly on Veblen's conception of neoclassical economics.

Although the heterodox traditions of modern economics do, on grounds of pluralism at least, oppose the noted mainstream insistence on methods of mathematical modelling, this opposition to the mathematical emphasis is not always viewed as a sufficient basis, or even sometimes as any basis, for identifying heterodoxy *qua* heterodoxy, just because the ontological implications of this mathematical emphasis are not always recognised.

Rather, on the surface at least, the heterodox antagonism to mainstream contributions is typically manifested not in terms of ontology at all but as a reaction to the project's substantive theoretical and policy claims. These of course are easily seen to be unrealistic and lacking explanatory power. But then so are the substantive theories accompanying more or less all mathematical modelling endeavours of modern economics. Although various commentators often suggest otherwise, the academic discipline of economics has been characterised by explanatory failure along with clearly unrealistic formulations for rather a long time now.[15] In this context the term 'neoclassical' plays a role, in distracting from the nature of the limitations of modelling *per se*. With more or less all theories attached to models being necessarily unrealistic in significant ways (due to the isolationist atomistic underpinnings), it is all too easy for any contributor to dismiss any particular set of results or claims that clashes with his or her own beliefs as neoclassical (or perhaps as insufficiently neoclassical) and quickly run up alternative (equally unrealistic) formulations that generate preferred conclusions.

Such activity serves to convince hardly anyone to change their minds on anything, of course. Yet it pervades the modern discipline. In this way much if not most academic economic debate remains extraordinarily superficial, certainly insufficiently radical, not least at the level of policy analysis. The practices of labelling varying sets of theories 'neoclassical' helps sustain this superficiality precisely through encouraging the impression that the source of all problems lies at the level of substantive theories, with questionable claims and hypotheses reflecting no more than their formulator's erroneous beliefs about economic behaviour. In this way, any critical observer is encouraged in the view that there is no need to get beyond the level of substantive theorising and model building. In consequence, the more basic problems at the level of ontology remain insufficiently examined and indeed mostly neglected, so the emphasis on mathematical modelling remains largely unquestioned.[16]

Yet there is something of a paradox in all of this. Although debates and critiques within modern economics do in this way tend to remain overly superficial, on closer examination it is also apparent that the more sustainable causal ontology of openness, process, significant internal relationality and so on is nevertheless regularly, if often only implicitly, recognised, most especially by heterodox practitioners (see Lawson, 2006a). Or at least this alternative social ontology is often acknowledged in some manner within heterodox pronouncements and more general forms of reasoning. Indeed, specific heterodox traditions have tended to emphasise, or focus centrally and repeatedly on, different aspects of it; or rather, they have systematically focused on features that clearly presuppose it. Thus post-Keynesians effectively recognise the all-prevailing openness (or the rarity of closed systems) in their significant and enduring concern with uncertainty; feminist economists highlight relationality especially, not least in their concern with theorising issues of care, discrimination and oppression; institutionalists continually interest themselves in systematically studying both change and stability in social life, not least through their emphasis on technology and institutions; Marxian economists concentrate especially on elaborating the nature of the specific emergent internally related totality in motion that is capitalism; and so on (on all this see Lawson, 2003, chapter 7; 2006a).

In fact, a good deal of sustained heterodox research is couched in conceptual frameworks consistent with the sort of causal-processual ontological conception just described. All too often, however, this goes hand in hand with a lack of realisation that methods of mathematical modelling require formulations that are in severe tension with this ontology. This lack of realisation both underpins a misapprehension of the source of the unrealistic nature of many competing claims, as well as the recourse of many heterodox economists to using mathematical modelling methods in seeking to advance insights obtained by other means (see Lawson, 2009a, 2009b).

Reinforcing the confusion of this whole situation are frequently repeated accompanying assertions to the effect that a reliance on mathematical methods is somehow analytically neutral, that mathematics is no more than a language, or mathematical models are heuristic devices or some such – none of which withstand critical scrutiny (see Lawson, 2009c).

Of course, because heterodox economists typically prioritise the search for relevance rather than mathematical prowess *per se*, a result is that those heterodox economists who engage in mathematical modelling are, unlike their mainstream counterparts, usually very willing to acknowledge as legitimate (i.e. do not reject as unscientific or not 'proper' economics) the various insightful analyses by others that are not mathematical in any way. The defining feature of the mainstream is the *insistence* on methods of mathematical modelling.

In large part, however, heterodox economists who resort to forms of mathematical modelling fail to appreciate the tension between the ontological presuppositions of this activity and the sort of worldview they otherwise tend to acknowledge. Or where within heterodoxy, a continuing faith in, and/or resources allocated to, exercises in mathematical modelling are not accounted for by an inattention to ontological preconceptions of methods, the explanation is seemingly that the individuals in question entertain hopes of identifying certain contexts in which local closures (facilitating the appropriate use of mathematical methods) do, temporarily, obtain. Either way, the more fundamental problems of the discipline are usually sidestepped with the result that the inappropriate emphasis on mathematical modelling methods remains largely unchallenged.

So, to take stock, both the fundamental failings and the main divisions of modern economics can at some level be expressed in terms of ontological orientations. Or at least this is the real basis for the heterodox opposition to mainstream contributions. However, the picture is muddied by the fact that seemingly not all heterodox economists appreciate that methods of mathematical modelling carry ontological presuppositions, let alone presuppositions (closed systems of isolated atoms) that are inconsistent with world views broadly professed. A result is that the picture, if reasonably coherent at the level of ontological distinctions and grounding, is far less so in terms of actual practice. Whether or not the latter identified tension is a weakness of the conception maintained, it represents a theme to which I return in due course and suggest a critical re-evaluation.

A factor that contributes to the preservation of this confused situation is a constant if uncritical repetition of the refrain, at least within heterodoxy, that neoclassical (substantive) theorising is the cause of the problems, even though there is the noted lack of clarity over the meaning of such a term. This activity serves to focus attention on conflicts at the level of substantive theorising and policy formulation, and thereby away from the deeper fundamental tensions at the level of ontology that inhibit systematic progress on all sides of modern debate.

It is thus against the backdrop of this situation that I seek to elaborate a coherent conception of the term 'neoclassical economics', indicating how it relates to the various strands of the discipline. This latter task seems at least an appropriate and useful – and perhaps a necessary – undertaking if, as here, the goal is to help facilitate more effective critique within the current context, and thereby at least a possibility of progress in understanding.

I turn, then, to develop a conception of neoclassical economics that meets the criteria of coherence laid out in the introductory overview and can be viewed, in that sense at least, as more sustainable than the alternatives so far considered. To motivate the interpretation of neoclassical economics that I have in mind, I focus specifically on the analysis originally provided by Veblen. I do so not merely to emphasise historical lineage but also because Veblen's analysis and concerns prove extremely useful to achieving an interpretation that retains current relevance as well as overall coherence, as we will see.

Veblen's project

Those individuals or groups who formulate novel categories do so, of course, for purposes of drawing out similarities and differences that they regard as significant within a body of phenomena they are concerned to examine. A first objective here is to identify Veblen's larger purpose in coining the term 'neoclassical', to uncover the sorts of concerns that interested him and relative to which he felt it advantageous to draw certain distinctions.

This is a topic rarely addressed at any length. Those who acknowledge Veblen as the originator of the term mostly report that he introduces it to distinguish Marshall's marginalism, or at least to distinguish a marginalist tradition for which Marshall is a central or typical proponent. For these observers, the emphasis tends to be on Marshall's intention of continuing a form of economics that Veblen labels 'classical', justifying the formulation 'neoclassical'.[17] However, as already noted, these same observers mostly conclude that no significant commonality between the two projects actually exists.[18] Other contributors emphasise instead that the point of introducing the term 'neoclassical' is not merely to express commonality but also to differentiate, specifically to differentiate economists like Marshall from those whom Veblen labels 'Austrian'.[19]

There is some insight to all of this. However, a close examination of the original text, I shall argue, reveals that Veblen holds neither that Marshall typifies the neoclassical contribution nor that Marshall and/or those grouped with him are the only continuers of the classical tradition in question, nor even that it is Marshall's marginalism *per se* that determines his neoclassical credentials. I also argue that Veblen does after all establish a coherent and sustainable account of continuity between the contributions of those he labels 'neoclassical' and those he interprets as 'classical'; and that in so doing, Veblen is indeed also very concerned to establish distinctions between projects, albeit not especially with drawing a distinction between the line of thinking designated as neoclassical and Austrian contributions. In fact, to emphasise this latter distinction before others is to miss almost the entire point of Veblen's analysis.

Clearly I need to substantiate these introductory remarks as well as provide grounds for an alternative assessment. In seeking to do so I start by elaborating the nature of Veblen's broader project. That is, before turning to Veblen's actual introduction and use of the term 'neoclassical', I examine at some length the issues that motivate his analysis including the sorts of distinctions he seeks to draw.

Metaphysical preconceptions

In the 1900 paper in which the category neoclassical is first introduced, Veblen's ongoing relevant concerns are actually signalled by the paper's title: 'Preconceptions of economic science'. The sorts of preconceptions Veblen has in mind here are precisely those already discussed above, namely, the ontological presuppositions held by contributors to economic science. Veblen here (and in other papers written at the time, including his famous 'evolutionary essay' (1898) as well as two earlier papers also titled the 'Preconceptions of economic science' (1899a, 1899b)) uses the term 'metaphysics' rather than 'ontology', seeking to tease out the: 'underlying metaphysics of scientific research and purpose' (Veblen, 1900: 241); but his meaning of metaphysics is the same as that of ontology as used here. Throughout these papers Veblen's primary focus is not substantive theory but, as these titles suggest, the metaphysical preconceptions underpinning economic theorising.

Veblen's specific concern is to identify or distinguish competing 'grounds of finality' of economic contributions, meaning the conceptions of scientific formulations held as proper and providing the standard whereby analyses that conform might be regarded as potentially complete.

In the course of the three 'preconceptions' papers, Veblen at length traces out how: 'changes which have supervened in the preconceptions of the earlier economists constitute a somewhat orderly succession' (Veblen, 1900: 240), the most interesting feature of which has been a gradual change overtime in the received 'grounds of finality' presupposed in economics:

> The feature of chief interest in this development has been a gradual change in the received grounds of finality to which the successive generations of economists have brought their theoretical output, on which they have been content to rest their conclusions, and beyond which they have not been moved to push their analysis of events or their scrutiny of phenomena. There has been a fairly unbroken sequence of development in what may be called the canons of economic reality; or, to put it in other words, there has been a precession of the point of view from which facts have been handled and valued for the purpose of economic science.
>
> (Veblen, 1900: 240)

Motivating this analysis, however, is a concern to distinguish and contrast two specific and basic 'grounds of finality for science' especially. These relate to conceptions of science that Veblen usually terms 'taxonomic' and 'evolutionary' science, with the former taxonomic conception being: 'the economics handed down by the great writers of a past generation' (Veblen, 1899a: 121) and the latter evolutionary conception described as 'modern'.

Put simply, for Veblen a taxonomic science is a science of normalities or of the normal case. It presupposes normality in or underpinning and grounding the course of events.[20] This contrasts with, and indeed can be said to be the antithesis[21] of, a historical or evolutionary or 'matter of fact' orientation to science that presupposes nothing more than cumulative causal sequence. In the latter case any outcome or event is always caused by something that went before it, but is not in conformity with some pre-ordained pattern or regularity, nor in a manner serving some normative or laudable purpose and so forth.

Veblen notes in this regard that the evolutionary scientist: 'is unwilling to depart from the test of causal relation or quantitative sequence' (Veblen, 1898: 377), inquiring of everything only 'why?', and seeking an answer in terms of cause and effect. For the taxonomic economist, in contrast: 'this ground of cause and effect is not definitive' (Veblen, 1898: 378). Rather, the ultimate term in the systematisation of knowledge is something like a 'natural law', or an association of phenomena, an empirical generalisation, or possibly a correlation regarded as 'natural', or 'normal' or a 'consistent propensity' with any exceptions regarded as mere disturbing factors.

Veblen interprets all lines of economics up until the time he is writing, including those systematised as classical, as being essentially taxonomic in this sense. He has two related concerns in producing the set of three papers titled the 'Preconceptions of economic science' as well as his 'evolutionary essay'. The first is to trace how preconceptions of normality and regularity have changed and been rationalised in different periods, culminating with the classical economists of recent standing. The second and more important purpose is to examine how conceptions of normality in economics have fared in the face of the influence of the wider modern evolutionary sciences. In regard to the latter objective his concern is with understanding whether the taxonomic emphasis will continue to shape the methods of economic science.

> The question of interest is how this preconception of normality has fared at the hands of modern science, and how it has come to be superseded in the intellectual primacy by the latter day preconception of a non-spiritual sequence. This question is of interest because its answer may throw light on the question as to what chance there is for the indefinite persistence of this archaic habit of thought in the methods of economic science.
> (Veblen, 1898: 379)

In the endeavour of tracing out earlier preconceptions of normality and regularity, Veblen first notes how the: 'more archaic metaphysics of the science ... saw in the orderly correlation and sequence of events a constraining guidance of an extra-causal, teleological kind' (Veblen, 1900: 255). That is, the order that was experienced in social life was in effect interpreted as pre-ordained and external to the events unfolding. Starting from an analysis of this 'archaic metaphysics', Veblen at length traces out gradual changes in the underlying ontological preconceptions, running through those of the Physiocrats, Adam Smith, the utilitarian economists (especially Jeremy Bentham), and culminating in the more recent British contributors such as John Stuart Mill and especially John Elliott Cairnes.

A notable feature of the changing metaphysics throughout the period Veblen discusses is a continuous dissolution of 'animistic' preconceptions, a giving up of the idea that there is a spiritual force directing or guiding all developments including those classed as economics.

> The history of the science shows a long and devious course of disintegrating animism – from the days of the scholastic writers, who discussed usury from the point of view of its relation to the divine suzerainty, to the Physiocrats, who rested their case on an 'ordre naturel' and a 'loi naturelle' that decides what is substantially true and, in a general way, guides the course of events by the constraint

of logical congruence. There has been something of a change from Adam Smith, whose recourse in perplexity was to the guidance of 'an unseen hand', to Mill and Cairnes, who formulated the laws of 'natural' wages and 'normal' value.

(Veblen, 1898: 381)

As my intention here is to elaborate Veblen's notion of neoclassical economics and indicate its continuity with (as well as departure from) a classical economics, the segment of this history of metaphysics on which I mostly focus concerns precisely those developments in economics that Veblen systematises as classical.

It can be immediately noted that Veblen's use of this latter term is non-standard or anyway non-universal. As is well known, Karl Marx coined the term, or rather the category, 'classical political economy' in his *Contribution to the Critique of Political Economy* (Marx, 1977). Marx used it to denote that strand of economics, originating in France with Pierre le Pesant, sieur de Boisguilbert (1646–1714), running through William Petty (1772–1823) and reaching its high point with the contributions of Adam Smith and David Ricardo (1772–1823), where the focus is on the deeper structures of capitalism and in particular social relations, including relations of production. In coining the term, Marx sought to emphasise a contrast with the 'vulgar economy' that followed thereafter which puts aside any interest in real relations of production and focuses instead on superficial appearances.[22]

It is this latter set of contributions, Marx's vulgar economy, which Veblen essentially identifies as classical economics (as more or less did John Maynard Keynes and others later on). More specifically, for Veblen, the classical school consists of those British economists that came after, but were influenced by, Adam Smith, and culminated with those contributors that were to precede Marshall, most notably Mill and Cairnes.

Given that I explore Veblen's thinking and quote various passages by him, I take it as given in the discussion of the next two sub-sections that the referent of the term 'classical' conforms to Veblen's usage, although in due course I briefly return to the issue of these differing conceptions of classical and any bearing the fact of the difference has on a viable interpretation of the category neoclassical economics.

Veblen's classical economics

Thus interpreted, classical economics, to now use Veblen's rather than Marx's characterisations of the different strands of thought, is differentiated from its forerunners at a substantive level in that its focus is primarily no longer on production but on the: 'pecuniary side of life' constituting: 'a theory of a process of valuation' (Veblen, 1898: 424).

However, it is the metaphysical preconceptions of contributors to classical economics that most characterises the latter for Veblen, and he primarily focuses on them. These do develop somewhat over time, starting with 'remnants of natural rights and of the order of nature' but becoming:

> [i]nfused with that peculiarly mechanical natural theology that made its way into popular vogue on British ground during the eighteenth century and was reduced to a neutral tone by the British penchant for the commonplace – stronger at this time than at any earlier period.
> (Veblen, 1899b: 424)

Thus Veblen is explicit in regarding the significant difference between the early classical economics in the form of the utilitarianism and the contributions of Adam Smith, its forerunner, to lie neither in any attachment to a utilitarian viewpoint *per se* nor in any substantive conclusions or policies, but in metaphysical preconceptions (Veblen, 1899b: 411–412). For Smith the ultimate ground of economic reality is the design of God; the economic order is divinely instituted, and human beings are suitably deferential. For contributors to classical economics, the ultimate grounds are human nature and processes of valuation. For the utilitarian version of classical economics specifically, the ultimate ground lies in a simplistic hedonistic conception of the nature of human beings conceived essentially in terms of maximising pleasure and minimising pain.

> After Adam Smith's day, economics fell into profane hands ... the next generation do not approach their subject from the point of view of a divinely instituted order; nor do they discuss human interests with that gently optimistic spirit of submission that belongs to the economist who goes to his work with the fear of God before his eyes ... With Adam Smith the ultimate ground of economic reality is the design of God, the teleological order; and his utilitarian generalizations, as well as the hedonistic character of his economic man, are but methods of the working out of this natural order, not the substantial and self-legitimating ground ... Of the utilitarians proper the converse is true ... The substantial economic ground is pleasure and pain: the teleological order (even the design of God, where that is admitted) is the method of its working out.
> (Veblen, 1899b: 411–412)

In the course of the development of classical economics, as Veblen conceives it, the spiritual or: 'animistic preconception was not lost, but it lost tone' and: 'partly fell into abeyance'. It was mostly evident in: 'the unavowed readiness of the classical writers to accept as imminent and definitive any possible outcome which the writer's habit or temperament inclined him to accept as right and good'. Veblen thus writes of: 'the visible inclination of classical economists to a doctrine of the harmony of interests' and their readiness to: 'state their generalizations in terms of what ought to happen' (Veblen, 1899b: 424–425).

An operative term here is 'generalisations'. These are fundamental to the classical contributions as Veblen views them. However, uncovering these generalisations is not a straightforward matter. In discussing how they are derived, Veblen draws attention to a norm of procedure especially important to the later classical economics. Although the approach is heavily empirical, it involved not the direct observation of event regularities but their careful construction via interpreting the evidence at hand. Let me elaborate this assessment a bit.

In fact, Veblen is of the clear view that later 'avowedly classical economists', notably Cairnes and J. S. Mill, are essentially empiricists, who, in seeking their (empirical) correlations or laws, exclude all ideas of teleology or even causal continuity. Thus Veblen writes of: 'the abiding faith which these empiricists had in the sole efficacy of empirical generalization' (Veblen, 1900: 251) in which all notions of organic connection or causal continuity are to be avoided. Rather, they construe: 'causal sequence to mean a uniformity of co-existences and successions simply' (Veblen, 1900: 252).[23]

However, such empirical regularities, then as now, were nowhere in evidence. The novelty of the contributors of this period is to interpret regularities as the product of laborious interpretation.

> But, since a strict uniformity is nowhere to be observed at first hand in the phenomena with which the investigator is occupied, it has to be found by a laborious interpretation of the phenomena and a diligent abstraction and allowance for disturbing circumstances, whatever may be the meaning of a disturbing circumstance where causal continuity is denied.
>
> (Veblen, 1900: 252–253)

The perspective or set of preconceptions that ground this interpretive activity is summed up by the idea that all things ultimately tend towards (even if they are temporarily disturbed from) ends or patterns that the common sense of any era holds to be valuable or worthy. This, says Veblen, is the: 'standpoint of the classical economists in their higher or definitive syntheses and generalizations' (Veblen, 1898: 382). It is described as a standpoint of 'ceremonial adequacy', not least because the: 'ultimate laws and principles which they formulated were laws of the normal or the natural, according to preconception regarding the ends to which, in the nature of things, all things tend'; the latter in turn being ends that: 'the instructed common sense of the time accepts as the adequate or worthy end of human effort' (Veblen, 1898: 382).

Veblen's assessment of the later avowedly classical economists, then, is that their scientific preconceptions of normality took the form essentially of correlations or event regularities, albeit regularities about the normal or natural, understood as that which common sense determines as desirable. However, these had to be carefully read into actual economic outcomes. This is a method of analysis, peculiar to these classical economists that, according to Veblen, renders them a 'deductive school', and their science taxonomic.

> What is peculiar to the classical economists in this respect is their particular norm of procedure in the work of interpretation. And, by virtue of having achieved a standpoint of absolute economic normality, they became a 'deductive' school, so-called, in spite of the patent fact that they were pretty consistently employed with an inquiry into the causal sequence of economic phenomena. The generalization of observed facts becomes a normalization of them, a statement of the phenomena in terms of their coincidence with, or divergence from, that normal tendency that makes for the actualization of the absolute economic reality. This absolute or definitive ground of economic legitimacy lies beyond the causal sequence in which the observed phenomena are conceived to be interlinked. It is related to the concrete facts neither as cause nor as effect in any such way that the causal relation may be traced in a concrete instance. It has little causally to do either with the 'mental' or with the 'physical' data with which the classical economist is avowedly employed. Its relation to the process under discussion is that of an extraneous – that is to say, a ceremonial – legitimation. The body of knowledge gained by its help and under its guidance is, therefore, a taxonomic science.
> (Veblen, 1899b: 425)

The preconceptions of normality that underpin the analysis, to repeat, are that economic developments conform to correlations, albeit correlations that express features that common sense determines as desirable and can be apprehended only though significantly reinterpreting the evidence. As Veblen had earlier observed in his (1898) 'evolutionary essay':

> The ways and means and the mechanical structure of industry are formulated in a conventionalised nomenclature, and the observed motions of this mechanical apparatus are then reduced to a normalised scheme of relations ... With this normalised scheme as a guide, the permutations of a given segment of the apparatus are worked out according to the values assigned the several items and features comprised in the calculation; and a ceremonially consistent formula is constructed to cover that much of the industrial field. This is the deductive method. The formula is then tested by comparison with observed permutations, by the polariscopic use of the 'normal case'; and the results arrived at are thus authenticated by induction. Features of the process

that do not lend themselves to interpretation in the terms of the formula are abnormal cases and are due to disturbing causes. In all this the agencies or forces causally at work in the economic life process are neatly avoided. The outcome of the method, at its best, is a body of logically consistent propositions concerning the normal relations of things – a system of economic taxonomy.

(Veblen, 1898: 383–384)

Laws, then, are but laws of the normal case, sometimes interpreted as hypothetical or abstract, and this science, to repeat, is taxonomic.

The laws of the science – that which makes up the economist's theoretical knowledge – are laws of the normal case. The normal case does not occur in concrete fact. These laws are, therefore, in Cairnes's terminology, 'hypothetical' truths; and the science is a 'hypothetical' science. They apply to concrete facts only as the facts are interpreted and abstracted from, in the light of the underlying postulates. The science is, therefore, a theory of the normal case, a discussion of the concrete facts of life in respect of their degree of approximation to the normal case. That is to say, it is a taxonomic science (Veblen, 1900: 254–255).

Given this concern with the non-empirical normal or natural, it is unsurprising that a central category for describing economic states should be that of equilibrium. Thus Veblen in total traces the interpretations of normality from extra-causal teleological guidance of the ancients to the modern-day search for correlations and suchlike, as well as theories concerning conditions of economic equilibrium.

> The earlier, more archaic metaphysics of the science, which saw in the orderly correlation and sequence of events a constraining guidance of an extra-causal, teleological kind, in this way becomes a metaphysics of normality which asserts no extra-causal constraint over events, but contents itself with establishing correlations, equivalencies, homologies, and theories concerning the conditions of an economic equilibrium.
>
> (Veblen, 1900: 255)

Importantly for the issues before us, Veblen assesses that at the time he is writing, economics is experiencing change and moving in the direction of an evolutionary science. However, the degree of change achieved is regarded by Veblen as not yet sufficient for economic science to qualify as evolutionary, with hallmarks of taxonomic thinking remaining dominant.

> The process of change in the point of view, or in the terms of definitive formulation of knowledge, is a gradual one; and all the sciences have shared, though in an unequal degree, in the change that is going forward. Economics is not an exception to the rule, but it still shows

too many reminiscences of the 'natural' and the 'normal', of 'verities' and 'tendencies', of 'controlling principles' and 'disturbing causes' to be classed as an evolutionary science.

(Veblen, 1898: 381)

Veblen's conception of neoclassical economics

All that has been said on Veblen's concerns to this point, of course, has been motivated by a need to set the scene for a discussion of what Veblen might mean by the category 'neoclassical'. As we shall see, Veblen also refers to the same project intermittently as modernised or even quasi-classical economics.

Fundamental to Veblen's use of the term 'neoclassical' are precisely the metaphysical or ontological grounds of finality of science that form the focus of the three 'preconceptions' papers and, in particular, the contrasting preconceptions associated with taxonomic science on the one hand and with causal-historical or evolutionary science on the other. It is important to recall that Veblen believed himself to be writing at a time of transition in relation to the matters that concerned him (see Lawson, 2003, chapter 8). Although, as we have seen, Veblen motivates his preconceptions papers by enquiring into the possible persistence of the taxonomic approach, and certainly concludes that an adequate basis in evolutionary thinking has yet to be achieved, he elsewhere basically expresses the view that an evolutionary orientation to economics, and indeed to all social and political science, is ultimately unavoidable; specifically: 'The social and political sciences must follow the drift [towards becoming evolutionary sciences], for they are already caught in it'.[24]

In this assessment, Veblen has so far been proven to be quite wrong. When introducing the term 'neoclassical economics', Veblen is uncertain as to which of various projects that coexisted at that time will most endure, or, as he puts it, survive the processes of 'natural selection'. Nor is he clear as to which of the various contending contributors will be most involved in: 'continuing the main current of economic speculation and inquiry'. Nor even is he intending to give any relative evaluation of the specific claims of the two or three main 'schools' of theory; or at least, he intends not to do so beyond noting one obvious comparative 'finding'. However, it is in the context of noting this obvious finding that the term 'neoclassical' first appears. The relevant passage is as follows:

> With respect to writers of the present or the more recent past the work of natural selection, as between variants of scientific aim and animus and between more or less divergent points of view, has not yet taken effect; and it would be over-hazardous to attempt an anticipation of the results of the selection that lies in great part yet in the future. As regards the directions of theoretical work suggested by

50 Tony Lawson

> the names of Professor Marshall, Mr. Cannan, Professor Clark, Mr. Pierson, Austrian Professor Loria, Professor Schmoller, the group – no off-hand decision is admissible as between these candidates for the honor, or, better, for the work, of continuing the main current of economic speculation and inquiry. No attempt will here be made even to pass a verdict on the relative claims of the recognized two or three main 'schools' of theory, beyond the somewhat obvious finding that, for the purpose in hand, the so-called Austrian school is scarcely distinguishable from the neoclassical, unless it be in the different distribution of emphasis.
>
> (Veblen, 1900: 260–261)

So Veblen does indeed introduce the term 'neoclassical' in a passage that indicates a 'school' that it is not the same as the Austrian. He does so, however, only to point out that for 'the purpose in hand' the neoclassical and Austrian school are actually 'scarcely distinguishable'.

What is this 'purpose in hand'? It is, as it has been throughout the three preconceptions essays, to determine the accepted 'grounds of finality' or the ontological preconceptions of science, of groups of economists. In particular, Veblen is concerned to examine if and how the taxonomic orientation is giving way to evolutionary thinking or science. In the passage that immediately continues that just noted, he substitutes 'modernised' for 'neo' in qualifying classical, indicating that he regards the terms as equivalent, and makes it very clear that with regard to this 'purpose in hand' the interesting and significant contrast (to neoclassical economics) is provided *not* by the Austrians but by the 'historical and Marxist schools'.

> The divergence between the modernized classical views, on the one hand, and the historical and Marxist schools, on the other hand, is wider – so much so, indeed, as to bar out a consideration of the postulates of the latter under the same head of inquiry with the former. The inquiry, therefore, confines itself to the one line standing most obviously in unbroken continuity with that body of classical economics whose life history has been traced in outline above. And, even for this phase of modernized classical economics, it seems necessary to limit discussion, for the present, to a single strain, selected as standing peculiarly close to the classical source, at the same time that it shows unmistakable adaptation to the later habits of thought and methods of knowledge.
>
> (Veblen, 1900: 261)

Whatever else neoclassical economics is, then, it is clearly not on a par with the historical or Marxist schools. But if neoclassical economics and the 'modernised classical school' are the same project, it is equally apparent (from the final sentence of the last noted passage) that Veblen is intending to limit discussion not to neoclassical thinking as a whole, but to a single 'strain' of it. It is in consideration of this single strain or subset of neoclassical thinking, we will see, that Marshall enters the picture.

What is the nature of this 'strain'? According to Veblen, although the producers of neo or modernised classical economics stand 'peculiarly close to the classical source' they are differentiated from their classical predecessors in being aware of and positively orientated to evolutionary thinking. The strain or subgroup on which Veblen focuses includes those who best exemplify this positive orientation. This is his meaning in observing of this 'strain' that: 'it shows unmistakable adaptation to the later habits of thought and methods of knowledge'.

Marshall and Keynes

In identifying this specific strain (which shows unmistakable adaptation to the historical or evolutionary approach) Veblen proceeds merely by illustrating it with reference to two of its developers. One is the philosopher of science, John Neville Keynes (the father of John Maynard Keynes), the other is the economist (and Keynes family friend), Alfred Marshall.

> For this later development in the classical line of political economy, Mr. Keynes's book may fairly be taken as the maturest exposition of the aims and ideals of the science; while Professor Marshall excellently exemplifies the best work that is being done under the guidance of the classical antecedents.
> (Veblen, 1900: 261–262)

So Marshall's contributions do not so much *typify* neoclassical economics as represent a specific strand of it that represents the best work done within that line of thinking, in effect moving it further away from its taxonomic classical heritage. The contributions of both Keynes and Marshall are presumably singled out because, under the principle of charity, if a line of thinking is to be criticised for its fundamental nature, and this indeed is Veblen's intention, it is always better to illustrate with the best of work in that line.

Veblen certainly discusses these noted contributors at some length. But his main point throughout is that no matter how ready they are to acknowledge causal processes, and in particular causal histories of structures like institutions in line with causal-processual ontology underpinning historical and evolutionary science, even Keynes and Marshall are unable in practice to break with the taxonomic ideal of science, particularly at the level of method, and this prevents the achievement of a meaningful account of the genesis and developmental continuity of such phenomena.

Veblen is clearly positively disposed towards aspects of the stances adopted by both Keynes and Marshall. He acknowledges of Keynes, for example, that not only does he interpret the aims of modern economic science as having less of the 'hypothetical' character assigned it by Cairnes (that is, as dealing less closely with the ascertainment of the normal case) but he also takes: 'fuller account of the genesis and developmental continuity of all features of modern economic life' giving: 'more and closer attention to institutions and their history'. Nevertheless a break with taxonomy is not achieved in practice. Rather: 'There is a curious reminiscence of the perfect taxonomic day in Mr. Keynes's characterization of political economy as a "positive science," the sole province of which is to establish economic uniformities' (Veblen, 1900: 264). Moreover, observes Veblen: 'in this resort to the associationist expedient of defining a natural law as a "uniformity", Mr. Keynes is also borne out by Professor Marshall' (Veblen, 1900: 265).

So the taxonomic approach that typifies the classical school survives even in the writings of Keynes and Marshall, albeit the case that notions of normality no longer express economic developments considered desirable, but rather those situations, now considered to exist at the level of the actual course of events, which conform to empirical regularities or economic uniformities. This, of course, is all quite inconsistent with Veblen's conception of evolutionary thinking.

Indeed, although (or perhaps because) Marshall is apparently more adapted to modern science than most economists, he is interpreted by Veblen as being especially inconsistent on these matters. For, despite observing that Marshall occupies himself with investigating the nature of institutions and is positively disposed to incorporating insights of evolutionary thinking, Veblen also observes that throughout this work the: 'taxonomic bearing is, after all, the dominant feature' (Veblen, 1900: 263).

This is not to say that Marshall is not considered to make a substantial contribution. Indeed, Veblen even suggests that despite: 'survivals of the taxonomic terminology, or even of the taxonomic canons of procedure' the latter: 'do not hinder the economists of the modern school from doing effective work of a character that must be rated as genetic rather than taxonomic' (Veblen, 1900: 265).[25] The problem, though, according to Veblen, is that the evolutionary thinking is in the end rather superficial; in particular there is little attempt to fashion relevant methods of analysis. The special 'strain' of neoclassical thinking represented by Keynes and Marshall is singled out precisely to illustrate that even this most adapted and aware strain (which: 'exemplifies the best work that is being done under the guidance of the classical antecedents') fails to get beyond taxonomic science at the level of method.

In short, a feature of contributions of both Keynes and Marshall that is significant with regard to the sorts of issues that interest Veblen is a tension bordering upon inconsistency. It is a tension between method and ontology/metaphysics (or more accurately between the ontological presuppositions of taxonomic method and a causal-processual social ontology). Certainly Veblen finds in these contributors a greater awareness (than is revealed by the earlier classical economists) of issues that are central to the historical evolutionary approach of the sort he favoured, but taxonomy in terms of method remains dominant.

It is precisely this tension, which is first illustrated using the contributions of Keynes and Marshall that I take to be the essence of neoclassical economics, according to Veblen. In other words, the defining feature of all neoclassical economics is basically an inconsistent blend of the old and the new; it is in effect an awareness of the newer metaphysics of processual cumulative or unfolding causation, combined with a failure to break away from methods of the older taxonomic view of science that are in tension with this modern ontology.

Neoclassical economists are classical in their acceptance of a taxonomic orientation to science that does not rely on the design of God, albeit a taxonomic stance now primarily revealed at the level of method. But at that level of explicit ontological or metaphysical preconception, neoclassical economists reveal unmistakable adaptation to the viewpoints of the evolutionary sciences, warranting the qualifier 'neo'.

Neoclassical economics more generally

Within neoclassicism it is the strain or subset of neoclassical thinking represented by Marshall and Keynes that in Veblen's assessment is the more adapted to evolutionary thinking. As such, Marshall and Keynes are viewed as the more scientifically advanced contributors to, rather than as typifying, neoclassical economics, though even these do not escape the classical taxonomic heritage. Equally, however, Veblen is clear that an air of evolutionism does characterise all neoclassical output, allowing it in fact to be associated at least superficially with work of the early generation of Darwinians. Hence the tension or inconsistency revealed to be present in Keynes and Marshall does characterise all of neoclassical argumentation. Specifically neoclassical economists have done little to develop or to apply methods of analysis that are appropriate to evolutionary preconceptions.

> All this gives an air of evolutionism to the work. Indeed, the work of the neo-classical economics might be compared, probably without offending any of its adepts, with that of the early generation of Darwinians, though such a comparison might somewhat shrewdly have to avoid any but superficial features. Economists of the present day are commonly evolutionists, in a general way. They commonly accept, as other men do, the general results of the evolutionary speculation in those directions in which the evolutionary method has made its way. But the habit of handling by evolutionist methods the facts with which their own science is concerned has made its way among the economists to but a very uncertain degree. The prime postulate of evolutionary

> science, the preconception constantly underlying the inquiry, is the notion of a cumulative causal sequence; and writers on economics are in the habit of recognizing that the phenomena with which they are occupied are subject to such a law of development. Expressions of assent to this proposition abound. But the economists have not worked out or hit upon a method by which the inquiry in economics may consistently be conducted under the guidance of this postulate.
> (Veblen, 1900: 265–266)

At best neoclassical economists have limited their analyses to aspects of the social world that appear least unpromising for handing with taxonomic methods. This, on occasion at least, is how Veblen describes Marshall specifically, that is, as merely limiting the scope of economics to the few situations where the conditions of such a taxonomic approach may conceivably prevail. In particular, where some innovation has occurred the taxonomic approach of this sort, with its 'statements of uniformities', may be able to say something of the conditions of survival of the innovation, though even here Veblen remains sceptical.

> Taking Professor Marshall as exponent, it appears that, while the formulations of economic theory are not conceived to be arrived at by way of an inquiry into the developmental variation of economic institutions and the like, the theorems arrived at are held, and no doubt legitimately, to apply to the past, and with due reserve also to the future, phases of the development. But these theorems apply to the various phases of the development not as accounting for the developmental sequence, but as limiting the range of variation. They say little, if anything, as to the order of succession, as to the derivation and the outcome of any given phase, or as to the causal relation of one phase of any given economic convention or scheme of relations to any other. They indicate the conditions of survival to which any innovation is subject, supposing the innovation to have taken place, not the conditions of variational growth. The economic laws, the 'statements of uniformity', are therefore, when construed in an evolutionary bearing, theorems concerning the superior or the inferior limit of persistent innovations, as the case may be. It is only in this negative, selective bearing that the current economic laws are held to be laws of developmental continuity; and it should be added that they have hitherto found but relatively scant application at the hands of the economists, even for this purpose.
> (Veblen, 1898: 266)[26]

Finally, it is not merely Keynes and Marshall who abandon the idea that correlations carry some kind of normative appeal; it is a feature of neoclassical economics more generally. Economics remains taxonomic for neoclassical economists essentially because of the presumed form of its results, as presupposed by its methods of correlation analysis. Only now the correlations or uniformities that are produced or sought after are interpreted (if ultimately somewhat mysteriously) as laws of everyday conduct.

> In consonance with this quasi-evolutionary tone of the neo-classical political economy, or as an expression of it, comes the further clarified sense that nowadays attaches to the terms 'normal' and economic 'laws'. The laws have gained in colorlessness, until it can no longer be said that the concept of normality implies approval of the phenomena to which it is applied. They are in an increasing degree laws of conduct, though they still continue to formulate conduct in hedonistic terms; that is to say, conduct is construed in terms of its sensuous effect, not in terms of its teleological content. The light of the science is a drier light than it was, but it continues to be shed upon the accessories of human action rather than upon the process itself. The categories employed for the purpose of knowing this economic conduct with which the scientists occupy themselves are not the categories under which the men at whose hands the action takes place themselves apprehend their own action at the instant of acting. Therefore, economic conduct still continues to be somewhat mysterious to the economists; and they are forced to content themselves with adumbrations whenever the discussion touches this central, substantial fact.
> (Veblen, 1900: 267–268)

In summary, I am suggesting that Veblen introduces the term 'neoclassical' to distinguish a line of thinking that is ultimately characterised by possessing a degree of ontological awareness whilst persevering with a methodology inconsistent with this awareness; it is a line of thinking identified precisely by this ontological/methodological tension or inconsistency. Its practitioners recognise that social reality is a historical process of cumulative causation, but nevertheless continue to rely upon methods that require of reality that it conforms to given correlations, that render the science as still taxonomic.

As I noted earlier, deductivism is the term used to designate any explanatory reliance on methods that presuppose event correlations. Veblen's neoclassical economists, then, can be characterised as acknowledging the social world everywhere as historical, as processual, but nevertheless simultaneously treating it using taxonomic and specifically deductivist methods that presuppose that social reality is anything but.

It warrants emphasis that, so interpreted, Veblen's neoclassical economics is neither identical to nor subsumes marginalist economics under its head. Of course all versions of marginalist economics are taxonomic. But not all contributors to marginal economics, at least 100 years ago, adopt or reveal adherence to the sort of causal-processual ontology that

Veblen attributes to the neoclassicals. Veblen's main focus in discussing theorising under the marginalist head is John Bates Clark. But Clark's position is interpreted as basically classical, or at least a near derivative that is *not* distinguished by some revealed support for a causal-processual metaphysics.[27]

In short, neoclassical economists approach the analysis of social reality armed with inappropriate tools, with the result that they fail to illuminate, or at best they limit the scope of economics to those few cases, if any, where localised stabilities or uniformities may occur. Whatever else it may be, neoclassical economics, according to Veblen, is a line of thinking that falls short of determining methods that are appropriate to addressing the causal-processual nature of social reality that its practitioners nevertheless, at some level, widely recognise.

Although recognition of a causal-processual ontology is regarded by Veblen as an advance of neoclassical over classical thinking, the persistence with taxonomy (in the form of deductivism) is the dominating feature that determines the form of the research findings. That is why it makes sense for Veblen to have characterised the project or strand of thinking in question not, say, as post- or counter-classical, but as modernised or neoclassical, signalling that it constitutes a continuation of the same basic taxonomic project, at least at the level of method, even if its 'adepts' at some level hold to a worldview ultimately inconsistent with such a taxonomic orientation.

Parenthetically, the interpretation of the term 'neoclassical' that I am advancing here may remain coherent even if or where, instead of Veblen's interpretation of classical economics, Marx's alternative and original interpretation of classical is preferred.[28] For on both interpretations, the term 'neoclassical' expresses a tension between method and ontology, and in both cases neoclassical is seen to be both a continuation of, as well as a departure from, classical thinking. The difference is that on Veblen's interpretation it is the adherence to taxonomic method that expresses the continuity of the later neoclassical economists with classical thinking, whereas on Marx's interpretation it is the recognition of a causal-processual ontology that plays this role. Alternatively put, for Veblen the causal-processual ontological commitments account for the prefix 'neo' in neoclassical, whilst from the point of view of Marx's interpretation the overly taxonomic (deductivist) orientation to method might be said to legitimise its use. Either way, as I say, the label 'neoclassical economics' seems not entirely inappropriate.[29]

The rise of mathematical modelling in economics

In viewing neoclassical economics as founded on inconsistency, Veblen expected it ultimately to prove unsustainable. Indeed, as already noted, he thought that the social and political sciences were already caught up in processes leading to the inexorable rise of evolutionary science, or anyway of science grounded in an ontology of causal processes (Veblen, 1898: 396–397; Lawson, 2003, chapter 8), a development that would have entailed the relative demise of all overly taxonomic (including deductivist) approaches. What Veblen could not foresee is that taxonomy in the form of deductivism specifically was later to acquire a new lease of life by way of unprecedented developments in the field of mathematics.

Ever since the Enlightenment various economists had been seeking to mathematise the study of the economy. In this, at least prior to the early years of the twentieth century, economists keen to mathematise their discipline felt constrained in numerous ways, and not least by pressures by (non-social) natural scientists and influential peers to conform to the 'standards' and procedures of (non-social) natural science, and thereby abandon any idea of constructing an autonomous tradition of mathematical economics. Especially influential, in due course, was the classical reductionist programme, the idea that all mathematical disciplines should be reduced to or based on the model of physics, in particular on the strictly deterministic approach of mechanics, with its emphasis on methods of infinitesimal calculus. Moreover, the intellectual context throughout was one in which, amongst these scientists and mathematicians in particular, there was an enduring belief that mathematical methods were unlikely to be of relevance to the analysis of society (on all this, see Lawson, 2003, chapter 10).

However, in the early part of the twentieth century changes occurred in the interpretation of the very nature of mathematics, changes that caused the classical reductionist programme itself to fall into disarray. With the development of relativity theory and especially quantum theory, the image of nature as continuous came to be re-examined in particular, and the role of infinitesimal calculus, which had previously been regarded as having almost ubiquitous relevance within physics, came to be re-examined even within that domain.

The outcome, in effect, was a switch away from the long-standing emphasis on mathematics as an attempt to apply the physics model, and specifically the mechanics metaphor, to an emphasis on mathematics for its own sake.

Mathematics, especially through the work of David Hilbert, became increasingly viewed as a discipline properly concerned with providing a pool of frameworks for *possible* realities. No longer was mathematics seen as the language of (non-social) nature, abstracted from the study of the latter. Rather, it was conceived as a practice concerned with formulating systems comprising sets of axioms and their deductive consequences, with these systems in effect taking on a life of their own. The task of finding applications was henceforth regarded as being of secondary importance at best, and not of immediate concern.

This emergence of the axiomatic method removed at a stroke various hitherto insurmountable constraints facing those who would mathematise the discipline of economics. Researchers involved with mathematical projects in economics could, for the time being at least, postpone the day of interpreting their preferred axioms and assumptions. There was no longer any need to seek the blessing of mathematicians and physicists or of other economists who might insist that the relevance of metaphors and analogies be established at the outset. In particular it was no longer regarded as necessary, or even relevant, to economic model construction to consider the nature of social reality, at least for the time being. Nor, it seemed, was it possible for anyone to insist with any legitimacy that the formulations of economists conform to any specific model already found to be successful elsewhere (such as the mechanics model in physics). Indeed, the very idea of fixed metaphors or even interpretations, came to be rejected by some economic 'modellers' (albeit never in any really plausible manner).[30]

The result was that, in due course, deductivism in economics, through morphing into mathematical deductivism on the back of developments within the discipline of mathematics, came to acquire a new lease of life, with practitioners (once more) potentially oblivious to any inconsistency between the ontological presuppositions of adopting a mathematical modelling emphasis and the nature of social reality. The consequent rise of mathematical deductivism has culminated in the situation we find today.

Implications for the contemporary situation

It will no doubt be apparent by now where I am headed with all this. I am suggesting that central to Veblen's characterisation of neoclassical economics is a particular tension or inconsistency – specifically, a tension of ontological perspective and method (or the latter's ontological presuppositions) that, as I noted at the outset, is a prevalent feature of much economics produced today. Certainly the interpretation of the term in this manner is useful in that it picks out the practices of a prominent group of modern economics. Moreover, it picks out a group and a set of practices that are so far unidentified by any label and yet arguably warrant being so identified to draw attention to the inconsistencies of the positions taken.

Somewhat ironically, then, albeit particularly advantageously, if the suggested interpretation of the term 'neoclassical' is accepted, usage of the category would serve to draw attention to precisely that inconsistency (of preconceptions of certain modelling practices with otherwise revealed ontological commitments), which the manner of its current usage helps obfuscate. The effect, in short, would be to reverse the term's current role in the discipline; its usage would contribute to identifying, revealing and/or signalling the tension in question, rather than, as at present, serving to mask or otherwise divert attention from it.

I do not suggest that the content of the taxonomic endeavour of Veblen's time matches the content of modern taxonomic endeavour or even that the latter is at all uniform or consistent. Nor do I pretend that Veblen possessed anything like the developed account of the causal-processual social ontology outlined earlier and defended elsewhere. He only rarely mentions social relations for example; nor does he advance a systematic theory of an emergent social reality. He does, though, recognise that social reality is not well characterised by conceptions of normality at the level of or underpinning actual events and indeed observes that actual social events advance typically in causal sequence only. Nor, as already noted, do I suggest that Veblen anticipated that taxonomic science would persist in economics in the form of mathematical deductivism. But the tension he identifies remains evident and still warrants attention. As such, it is not unreasonable to hold that there is usefulness, in addition to any historical legitimacy, to employing the term 'neoclassical economics' to express this particular tension.

There are clearly many currently who both adhere to taxonomic and specifically deductivist methods and yet at some level also acknowledge the open causal-processual nature of social reality. The central difference between the current situation and that which Veblen addresses is that deductivism today, the production of formulations couched in terms of event-level uniformities, is, to repeat once more, more pervasively bound up with the drive to mathematise the discipline; it takes the form of methods of mathematical modelling.

The coherence of the conception of neoclassical

So is it really the case that I am suggesting that all mathematical modellers in modern economics, who at some level appear to subscribe to the causal-processual worldview, including those who self-identify as heterodox, are appropriately characterised as (modern-day) neoclassical economists? I re-emphasise that the group under focus here is not the set of mathematical deductivist modellers *per se*, but that subset of the latter who at some level simultaneously accept a historical or causal-processual ontology.

I certainly think this is the most coherent rendering of the category of neoclassical economics in that it constitutes a strategy and, seemingly the only one, which allows the term to be interpreted in a manner that meets all the criteria earlier set out. Let me briefly elaborate how it does so.

The interpretation provided is clearly developmentally consistent with historical lineage, as we have seen; indeed, I suggest that it is effectively Veblen's conception. Moreover, it expresses a strand of thinking that is both continuous with and a departure from a position that has been prominently characterised as classical. It also possesses a meaningful referent or object of analysis, namely, that group of economists who at some level accept the causal-processual ontology yet for some reason feel unable, unwilling or unmoved to abandon deductivism. It is *prima facie* useful just in that it picks out and identifies a group of economists who are prominent and significant in their impact on the contemporary discipline and economy, but who currently have no alternative identifying label. Finally, the interpretation I am proposing not only generalises all the loose attributions of neoclassical, as well as the alternative contending systematic conceptions, revealing them to be in effect special cases of deductivism, of the taxonomic approach to economics, but can make sense of the form of the latter more cautious systematisations as well. Let me now elaborate the latter claim a little.

From the perspective of the conception set out, the explanation of the nature and variety, as well as the limitations, of the accounts of the term advanced by the more cautious/careful interpreters is that the latter have resulted from attempts to uncover the most general, core or generative features of contributions widely regarded as neoclassical, whilst their formulators were mistakenly working under the apprehension that these features must be stated in substantive economic terms.

I suggest that the core feature of neoclassical economics is adherence not to any particular substantive features but to deductivism itself in a situation where the general open-processual nature of social reality is widely recognised at some level. Certainly Veblen's central focus and concern in using the term is preconceptions (of economics) rather than conceptions (of economics). Thus from the perspective of this understanding the presumption that the core features must lie at the level of substantive economic specification, even if it takes a highly abstract form, is, as I say, mistaken. The result is that these more cautious interpreters of neoclassical economics have come as close to the interpretation I propose as seems feasible, whilst sticking to the self-imposed constraint of interpreting neoclassical economics only in substantive economic terms.

I re-emphasise that deductivism entails reliance on correlations. The desire to theorise in a manner that produces results taking the form of correlations or event regularities in turn encourages the treatment of economics in terms of systems of isolated atoms. At the same time, the traditional view of the object of economics is in terms of consumption (demand) and production (supply). Thus I am suggesting that the varying conceptions of neoclassical economics outlined earlier are explained as attempts to steer as close as possible to the above features, namely, correlations involving closed systems of isolated atoms, whilst maintaining a concern with consumption and production; in other words, whilst acting under the erroneous constraint of characterising neoclassical economics in terms of substantive economic categories.

The point here, of course, is that although the deductivist orientation encourages substantive formulations that are implicitly in terms of isolated atoms, there is no unique way of generating them. This explains the sorts of conceptions held, and/or conclusions reached, both by those who have sought to establish commonalities between Veblen's classical and neoclassical economics and by those who have sought to draw out general or generative features of prominent (if often recent) accounts widely regarded as neoclassical.

Thus, turning first to those in the former group, we can see that they have failed to find continuity in Veblen's conceptions of classical and neoclassical just because continuity has been sought at the level of the 'substantive content' (Aspromourgos, 1986: 269) of theories (whether in economics or psychology) or of 'economic ideas' (Fayazmanesh, 1998: 90), but not at the level of accepted preconceptions of science. In this Veblen's focus on the continuing taxonomic emphasis with its implicit ontological presuppositions is overlooked. Yet it is precisely an adherence to the latter by Marshall and others that constitutes the features that render the latter contributors continuous with the classical tradition.

If we turn to the second group, namely, those that have sought to categorise neoclassical economics through seeking generalities across prominent contributions, we can just as equally make sense of, and indeed explain, the sorts of results produced here. Commonalities arise because these interpreters, in seeking generality across numerous contributions, have formulated their conceptions in highly abstract terms whereby, given the ontological constraints of the reliance on methods of mathematical modelling on the contributors on which they focus, these abstract accounts have tended to take the form of varying versions of isolated human individuals as atoms, with specifications concerning knowledge and behaviour serving precisely to constrain conceptions of human beings so as to render them atomistic. Yet significant variation is nevertheless equally found across the versions of neoclassical economics so determined just because there is no unique way to generate substantive formulations consistent with the taxonomic and specifically deductivist orientation, that is which presuppose closed systems of isolated atoms.

The atomistic condition for a closure requires only that the (atomistic) factors in question have the same separate and independent effect whatever the context. Rendering formulations of human individuals so that they are atomistic in this sense is the purpose of and mostly achieved via the rationality assumption/axiom, of course. But there are various versions even of the latter. In some cases the specification of this (rationality) constraint is absurdly unrealistic (as when individuals are assumed to be continuous calculative optimisers); in other cases it is overly simplistic (as when individuals are assumed to be merely fixed-rule followers). The feature in all this that warrants emphasis (and tends to be overlooked) is that the primary purpose of any rationality axiom is just to fix individual behaviour in some way to render it atomistic and so tractable. The precise (set of) assumption(s) whereby this is done is secondary to this requirement.

This is why some of the more careful interpreters of neoclassical economics have recognised that all that is needed in this regard is 'an acceptance of some rationality axiom' (see, for example, Hahn, 1984, 1985). Alternative interpretations of neoclassical economics that have individuals continually following maximising behaviour in the name of rationality no doubt capture a good deal of the actual literature, but stipulations do not need to be this specific. We can now also see why others have been (even) more cautiously abstract, for only fixity of response to stimuli is actually required in the process of satisfying conditions of closure (i.e. in which event regularities can be derived). Of course, there are numerous different specifications that will achieve this.

We can further explain the widely varying assessments of and uncertainty concerning the need to include some notion of equilibrium theorising in the characterisation of neoclassical economics. For although theorising in terms of this category is usually of a sort that can be regarded as taxonomic in Veblen's sense, and is a practice pursued by Marshall and since figured widely in the economics literature, a concern with equilibrium theorising is not in and of itself an integral part of any modern mathematical deductivist framework. Rather, in the context of modern economics especially, equilibrium is basically a solution concept, given a system of equations. Where such a system is generated under deductivist thinking, a question that can in some contexts be meaningfully addressed is whether the resulting set of equations is mutually consistent. Is there a vector of values consistent with them all? The solution concept, especially where prices are involved, is often called an equilibrium state. When economists enquire whether an equilibrium state exists, they are merely inquiring as to whether a set of equations has a solution (see Lawson, 2005, 2006b). In this manner we can understand why, at least from a mathematical point of view, such a concern may be of interest, and thereby we can explain the (former) high frequency of appearance of the category equilibrium in the economics literature. However, the set of steps involved in examining whether there exists a solution to a set of equations is not *per se* a requirement of adhering to deductivism and is notably absent from many contributions widely perceived as neoclassical. So we can easily understand why some of the more cautious interpreters never mention equilibrium in their definition of neoclassical economics (for example, Weintraub, 2002), whilst others accept no more than a qualified 'commitment to study equilibrium states' (for example, Hahn, 1984, 1985).

From the perspective set out, all other looser interpretations of neoclassical economics can equally be rendered intelligible, including those that seek to tie the category to laissez-faire ideology, or to competing claims about the functioning of markets, or use it to promote notions of efficiency and so on. In contemporary economics, all designations are applied to substantive claims and policy proposals formulated in accordance with the constraints of taxonomic, essentially mathematical modelling exercises, so that where commitment to a social system as being causal-processual in nature is at some level implied, all are appropriately characterised as neoclassical according to the conception I am advancing.

Perhaps the interpreter of neoclassical economics that comes closest to the conception defended here is Fine (2006). Consistent with deductivism being the problem, Fine does not interpret neoclassical in terms of the particular specifications of human beings or states of the economy or whatever that have been adopted to guarantee that event regularities can be derived; rather, he interprets neoclassical economics in terms of the regularities themselves, or at least in terms of functions expressing them. Thus for Fine the defining feature is the 'technical apparatus or architecture' the 'most fundamental' of which is 'the use of utility and production functions'. From this perspective, Fine is able to recognise that additional common objects of focus like equilibrium states are encouraged but not necessary.

> Enduring commitment to this technical apparatus explains the persistence but not the necessity of equilibrium, efficiency, laissez-faire ideology, the optimising individual and so on. To a large extent, even those approaches on the edge within the mainstream take this technical apparatus at least as point of departure, adding other forms of behaviour or modifying technical assumptions or, because institutions, history, path dependence, aggregation now matter, glorifying previous inconveniences as the way forward to add wrinkle or complexity.
>
> (Fine, 2006: 3)

Where Fine's analysis proves deficient is that his emphasis on utility and production functions forces him to interpret other manifestations of deductivism as merely 'wrinkles or complexity'. In truth modern mathematical economists have gone way beyond resting their attention on demand and supply conditions in the economy as a whole. Yet still the deductivism remains, generating, as always, unrealistic formulations. These are readily dismissed by heterodox critics, very often as being neoclassical. Now, at least where recognition of causal-processual ontology is at some level revealed, this designation can be rendered coherent.

Taking stock and reassessment

In short, I am suggesting that there are three basic divisions of modern economics that can be discerned in the actual practices of modern economists. These are:

1   those who both (a) adopt an overly taxonomic approach to science, a group dominated in modern times by those that accept mathematical deductivism as an orientation to science for us all, and (b) effectively

regard any stance that questions this approach, whatever the basis, as inevitably misguided;
2   those who are aware that social reality is of a causal-processual nature as elaborated above, who prioritise the goal of being realistic and who fashion methods in the light of this ontological understanding and thereby recognise the limited scope for any taxonomic science, not least any that relies on methods of mathematical deductive modelling; and
3   those who are aware (at some level) that social reality is of a causal-processual nature as elaborated above, who prioritise the goal of being realistic, and yet who fail themselves fully to recognise or to accept the limited scope for any overly taxonomic approach including, in particular, one that makes significant use of methods of mathematical deductive modelling.[31]

If members of group 1 not only include but (with the pervasive modern dogmatic insistence on methods of mathematical modelling) more or less reduce to the contemporary mainstream; and those in group 2 constitute the coherent core of modern heterodoxy; it is members of group 3, again mostly made up by those that utilise mathematical methods, that most qualify as modern neoclassical economists. Groups 1 and 3 are both overly taxonomic in Veblen's sense, whilst only members of group 2 are coherently engaged in Veblen's idea of historical or often broadly evolutionary or modern science.

What to do with the category of neoclassical economics?

To return to a question already posed but not really answered, am I seriously suggesting that we employ the term 'neoclassical' to refer to the third of the identified groups of economists, which will clearly include many who self-identify as heterodox? I repeat that I am certainly suggesting that to use the term 'neoclassical' in this fashion is the most appropriate and coherent use of the category for the reasons already given; although a better categorisation might be non-dogmatic taxonomists or non-dogmatic deductivists, in contrast with the dogmatic (mathematical) taxonomists/ deductivists that are the mainstream.

If used in this way, then as noted, the term would serve no longer to mask but to bring repeatedly to the fore a basic tension that lies at the core of the discipline's problems. It is a tension that a consideration of Veblen's analysis reveals has long been in play. Using the term in this manner may encourage thereby a somewhat more critical orientation or greater reflexivity on the part of those unreasonably enamoured of any overly taxonomic emphasis at the substantive level, including especially any form of deductivism. So there are certainly grounds for doing so.

All things considered, however, in the end I do not really think it reasonable to distinguish or identify any group on the grounds of a shared fundamental inconsistency. My aim here, in reporting my findings, is, in the end partly rhetorical, namely, to point out that if coherence in use is required, then according to the seemingly most sustainable conception, many of those who use the term 'neoclassical' as an ill-defined term of abuse can be viewed ultimately as engaged in unwitting self-critique. But I am hoping, more fundamentally, that it is enough in this manner to communicate (in a yet further way) that in modern economics there prevails largely unrecognised a basic tension between ontology and method, one that hinders serious attempts to overcoming the real problems of the discipline.

My suggestion, then, is that rather than distinguish/identify a group on the grounds of a fundamental inconsistency in (ontological) theory and (methodological) practice, the term 'neoclassical economics' should be dropped from the literature, as a few others have already suggested. In other words, I return to my previously held position, albeit now re-evaluated in the light of possessing a seemingly (and perhaps the only) coherent notion of the category of neoclassical economics. All the various questions or lines of reasoning that served to motivate the quest for a coherent interpretation are effectively answered or otherwise already addressed. But once addressed there seems to me to be emergent further grounds, now, to abandon the term. Given that the term as interpreted here signals intrinsic inconsistency, or at best severe tension, it is more reasonable, and significantly less uncharitable, to focus on displaying the latter as a seemingly genuine if long-lasting error than to apply a label with negative connotations to those who implicitly make it, as if implying that they consciously choose to be permanently in error. I doubt that many knowingly wish to build a school on the foundation of an inconsistency.

In this I also suspect that I am continuing in the spirit of Veblen. When Veblen uses the term, as we have seen, it was not intended to denote a school of thought at all; he merely wished to focus, in one specific paper, on one line of thinking (which he expected to be highly transient) that had come out of classical reasoning (as he interpreted it), was open to ongoing (broadly evolutionary) scientific developments of his day but which had not yet adjusted scientific method accordingly. The prefix 'neo' is employed by Veblen just as a serviceable adjective for this discussion and was interchanged with qualifiers like 'modernised', 'quasi' and perhaps others.

Certainly I am not aware that Veblen uses the term 'neoclassical' outside the preconceptions paper in which it is introduced, and I suspect that he would be astounded at the widespread use of the term throughout the discipline today. Veblen's point when coining the term was simply to bring to prominence the limitations for economics of persevering with the taxonomic ideal in science and in particular with adopting a taxonomic science in the form of seeking uniformities at the level of events. That there are problems with adopting any overly taxonomic approach was a central message found in various of his numerous methodological essays, not least in the preconceptions paper in which the term 'neoclassical' is coined; whatever the fate of the category neoclassical, it is a message that is certainly no less relevant today.

Conclusion

Throughout his methodological writings, Veblen is acutely aware that all scientific undertakings carry within them metaphysical preconceptions regarding the 'grounds of finality' to which results must conform to be regarded as potentially satisfactory. Two basic approaches are distinguished: the (overly) taxonomic and the (broadly) evolutionary. The difference between them is: 'a difference of spiritual attitude or point of view ... it is a difference in the basis of valuation of the facts for the scientific purpose, or in the interest from which the facts are appreciated' (Veblen, 1898: 377). The only preconception of the modern, broadly evolutionary historical scientist is that events unfold in causal sequence. Thus the 'modern scientist is unwilling to depart from the test of causal relation or quantitative sequence', and in responses to all questions of economics the modern scientist 'insists on an answer in terms of cause and effect'. In contrast the taxonomic scientist insists on (or holds preconceptions of science requiring) something more, whether that something extra takes the form of outcomes regarded as natural or normal or laudable, tendencies to these outcomes, ameliorative trends, or simply correlations at the level of events. Mathematical deductivism is just the very dominant contemporary form.

I have suggested, drawing on Veblen, that the most coherent interpretation of neoclassical economics is of an inconsistent stance of: (1) recognising the historical processual ontology of unfolding causal sequence at the level of events; whilst (2) simultaneously seeking to combine this recognition with a taxonomic orientation in the form of deductivism at the level of method that is inappropriate to it. That is, I suggest that interpreted most coherently, the category designates a deep tension, the very one that the currently loose usage of the term serves to mask.

Even if the foregoing does identify a coherent interpretation of neoclassical economics, I suggest further that it is likely better, on balance, to abandon the category. Though others have reached a similar conclusion, they are often quick to stress that in dropping the term they do not wish to imply criticism of any content the term may be used to express.[32] In contrast, I suggest that the reason to discard the term (or otherwise to employ a coherent interpretation) is precisely to facilitate more appropriate and telling criticism than hitherto, in evidence of the content of modern economics, including any expressed through the term itself. This indeed is the point of this exercise of attempted clarification.

The contemporary discipline of economics, most now agree, has lost its way. It is easy enough to demonstrate that this is due largely to the widespread contemporary persistence with methods of mathematical modelling (whether through mainstream insistence or through heterodox confusion/optimism) in conditions where this persistence is unwarranted. The ultimate solution and, as Veblen clearly saw, basis for any relevant economics, lies first in uncovering the nature of social reality and second, and certainly no less important, in taking seriously any ontological or metaphysical insights so uncovered in fashioning the methods of economic science. It is to understand the nature of society and then to ensure that research methods are appropriate to that nature. It is to render actual a situation that Veblen long ago thought inevitable. More concretely, it is to replace the current, yet long outlived fixation on seeking or constructing accounts of event correlations with a serious concern to develop an ontologically grounded causal-explanatory social science.

Notes

1 Not infrequently those who use the label to designate others are in turn often so labelled themselves by their opponents. Thus Paul Krugman (2009) refers to 'monetarist' and 'freshwater economist' opponents as neoclassical, whilst he in turn is criticised by Steve Keen (2012) as being neoclassical; and so on.
2 Almost universally amongst those who seek to uncover a significant element of continuity between neoclassical and classical economics, neoclassical economics is interpreted as a set of 'marginalist' theories and classical economics is used to designate whatever came before it. Unfortunately, however, the term 'marginalism' is itself variably interpreted. Some commentators use the category for Alfred Marshall's contributions; others for the contributions of William Stanley Jevons, Carl Menger and Léon Walras; and still others for marginalism in general, including the writings of John Hicks and Paul Samuelson, and especially the latter's (Hicks-inspired) supposed 'grand neoclassical synthesis'. For a brief but systematic coverage of the various interpretations of marginalist economics, see especially Antonietta Campus (1987). For a discussion of marginalism in relation to interpretations of neoclassical specifically, see Tony Aspromourgos (1986).
3 Certainly this is the view of most scrutinisers of claims to continuity. Thus Maurice Dobb (1973: 248), for example, examines Joan Robinson's description of marginalist theories of distribution as neoclassical and finds it so unlike (his conception of) classical economics that he suggests that *counter-classical* would be a better designation. In similar fashion Joseph Schumpeter (1954) examines the: 'habit, which has developed especially in the United States, of describing the "marginalist" theories as neo-classic', but concludes (focusing on the 'pure-theory' aspect in particular) that: 'there is no more sense in calling the Jevons-Menger-Walras theory neoclassic than there would be calling the Einstein theory neo-Newtonian' (Schumpeter, 1954: 919). Milan Zafirovski defends at length the thesis:

[t]hat this neoclassical nomenclature for marginalism was problematic to the extent that marginalism, especially its early version in Walras, Menger, and especially Jevons, was a non- and even counter- or 'anti-classical' rather than 'newly' classical, as the term neoclassical would suggest.

(Zafirovski, 1999: 46)

Also, Aspromourgos (1986) finds that it was: 'only with Hicks and Stigler, in the 1930s and 1940s, [sic] that the term was extended to embrace marginalism in general' finding, however, that: 'Neither of them offered any substantial notion of continuity between classics and marginalists' (Aspromourgos, 1986: 266). This literature is usefully summarised by Aspromourgos (1986), who himself does notably turn to Veblen to locate the origin of the term 'neoclassical', suggesting that for Veblen, the: 'central figure in this neoclassical school is Marshall' (Aspromourgos, 1986: 266). Searching for continuity of neoclassical with the classical school at the level of substantive content, however, Aspromourgos concludes that Veblen fails to provide it in the essay in which the term 'neoclassical' is coined; instead: 'Only in a later essay does Veblen suggest some substantive content for the continuity he perceived' (Aspromourgos, 1986: 266); even this Aspromourgos seems to find unsatisfactory (see especially, Aspromourgos, 1986: 269). Finally, I note too that Sasan Fayazmanesh (1998) focuses almost exclusively on Veblen and examines three possible interpretations of what continuity may have meant for him, but concludes that: 'none [. . .] presents a clear and viable argument in support of the continuity of economic ideas' (Fayazmanesh, 1998: 90).

4   Consider first the view of Frank Hahn, someone who identifies with the label 'neoclassical'. Although not always consistent (compare Hahn, 1982: 354, with specifications found in Hahn, 1984, 1985), Hahn (1984, 1985) identifies the following restricted set of features of the 'neoclassical' economic theory project as essential: (1) an individualistic perspective, a requirement that explanations be couched solely in terms of individuals; (2) an acceptance of some rationality axiom; and (3) a commitment to the study of equilibrium states. Here the category equilibrium is explicitly referenced, though noticeably there is no presumption that an equilibrium state 'holds' or 'exists' in any sense. Rather, for Hahn, the task of determining whether an equilibrium state exists in some model is precisely the sort of activity intended by a commitment to the study of such states. Turning to a view from the history of economic thought, Roy Weintraub (2002) rather suggestively concludes that: 'we are all neoclassical now'. The reason for this assessment, it seems, is that supposedly all academic economists teach neoclassical economics to students; for this is the substantive content of modern economic textbooks that all economic teachers use. This content, we are informed, is, or conforms to, a meta-theory, meaning: 'a set of implicit rules or understandings for constructing satisfactory economic theories', and any substantive theory consistent with this meta-theory qualifies as neoclassical. The particular set of understandings or 'fundamental assumptions' that render a theory neoclassical are: '1. People have rational preferences among outcomes. 2. Individuals maximize utility and firms maximize profits. 3. People act independently on the basis of full and relevant information. Theories based on, or guided by, these assumptions are neoclassical theories' (Weintraub, 2002). Notably, and in contrast to Hahn, Weintraub nowhere in his

definition makes reference to the study of equilibrium states. A second difference is the insistence by Weintraub that individuals possess: 'full and relevant information'. Turning next to a view from economic methodology, Christian Arnsperger and Yanis Varoufakis (2006) take the view that the essence of neoclassical economics reduces to three meta-axioms:

> It is hard to imagine how any standardly trained economist could deny that her theoretical practices digress from the three methodological moves mentioned above: *Methodological individualism, methodological instrumentalism and methodological equilibration*. For simplicity we shall henceforth refer to them as *the neoclassical meta-axioms*.
>
> (Arnsperger and Varoufakis, 2006)

Notice that the third meta-axiom is simply 'the axiomatic imposition of equilibrium'. In their analyses, Arnsperger and Varoufakis, in agreement with those already noted, conclude that any axioms about individual behaviour are unable to guarantee equilibrium states, but, believing such states to be essential to neoclassical theorising, make the fact of equilibrium states an axiomatic assumption. No claim about individual possessing full information is seemingly included. Turning finally to some views from the heterodox traditions, Geoffrey Hodgson, who has contributed much to institutionalist economics, offers the following interpretation drawing on the observations of Gary Becker:

> Let us attempt to identify the key characteristics of neoclassical economics; the type of economics that has dominated the twentieth century. One of its exponents, Gary Becker (1976: 5) identified its essence when he described: 'the combined assumptions of maximizing behavior, market equilibrium, and stable preferences, used relentlessly and unflinchingly'. Accordingly, neoclassical economics may be conveniently defined as an approach which: (1) assumes rational, maximizing behaviour by agents with given and stable preference functions, (2) focuses on attained, or movements towards, equilibrium states, and (3) is marked by an absence of chronic information problems.
>
> (Hodgson, 1999: 29)

In contrast, the Marxian economist, Ben Fine, insists that neoclassical economics is not couched in terms of rationality or equilibrium specifications or indeed any specifications regarding features of 'agents' or states of the economy. Rather it is essentially:

> [t]he technical apparatus or architecture established by the mainstream from the marginalist revolution onwards. Most fundamental is the use of utility and production functions, with accompanying assumptions to allow the theory to proceed regardless of any other considerations – methodology, realism, other theory, empirical evidence *and* mathematics – to the contrary.
>
> (Fine, 2006: 2)

Clearly, each of these conceptions, though sharing some features with a selection of others, is unique in various ways. There is no consensus on interpretation, neither *prima facie* is there any obvious basis for choosing between them; in particular there is not an interpretation provided that seems to generalise or generate the others. Of course all I offer here is an indicative selection of assessments for the purpose of illustration.

5 On all this see especially Lawson (2012b). Others have emphasised the same features. For example, Colander *et al.* (2004) emphasise the 'changing face of mainstream economics' and criticise heterodox economists for failing to notice such ongoing developments. Specifically, these authors criticise heterodox contributors for adopting an overly: 'static view of the profession' (Colander *et al.*, 2004: 486); for simplistically referring to the current mainstream as neoclassical; and for missing the: 'diversity that exists within the profession, and the many new ideas that are being tried out' (Colander *et al.*, 2004: 487). In fact, Colander *et al.* (2004) insist that: 'Mainstream economics is a complex system of evolving ideas' (Colander *et al.*, 2004: 489) and refer to the: 'multiple dimensionalities that we see in the mainstream profession' (Colander *et al.*, 2004: 489). They acknowledge though that the mainstream is tied to its mathematical modelling methodology.

6 Interestingly, none of those who seek seriously and systematically to characterise neoclassical economics appear to do so according to the use of mathematical modelling *per se* (see note 5, for example); of course it was long after Veblen was writing that such modelling practices became dominant in economics.

7 Or a contributor may have something to hide.

8 See, for example, Aspromourgos (1986: 296), Colander (2000: 127) or Fayazmanesh (1998: 75) or Hicks (1983: xiii–xiv).

9 As already noted, few categories remain entirely fixed in their meaning over time. However, there is a sense in which those that prove helpful evolve systematically in the light of new understandings, changing conditions and evolving related needs. This is a case of (the broader notion of) developmental consistency (see Lawson 1997, 2003 for a discussion of this notion).

10 On all this, see especially Lawson (1997, 2003, 2012b).

11 For a good discussion of this sort of (de-privileging of theory) approach to econometrics, see Katerina Juselius (2010).

12 'Emergence' is a term that expresses the appearance of novelty or something previously absent or unprecedented. Emergent causal properties are often the primary focus of the philosophy-leaning literature that employs the category, though where they exist they must be the properties of something, an emergent entity or some such. An emergent entity, where addressed, is usually found, or anyway held, to be composed out of elements deemed to be situated at a different (lower) level of reality to itself, but which have (perhaps through being modified) become organised as components of the emergent (higher level) entity or causal totality. 'Emergence', then, as widely interpreted is ultimately a compositional term and involves components being organised rather than aggregated. Elsewhere I argue that social phenomena, though emergent from and always dependent on non-social natural phenomena are causally and ontologically irreducible to the latter (see especially Lawson, 2013b, but also 1997, 2012a, 2013a).

13 All such constitutive relations are relations of power couched in terms of differing rights and obligations (see Lawson, 2012a, 2013a).

14 For a comprehensive account, again see for example Lawson (2003, chapter 2; 2012a, 2013a). For discussions of the causal and ontological irreducibility of emergent social processes see especially Lawson (2012a, 2013a, 2013b).
15 The discipline has been in such a state for more than half a century indeed (see, e.g. Lawson, 2003, chapter 1).
16 Thus we find the same old mistakes being repeated even in projects like the setting up of the Institute for New Economic Thinking (INET), an organisation whose stated intention is precisely to transform the discipline of economics in the light of its failings to provide much understanding of the ongoing crisis. Although George Soros, the founder of the institute, does reveal an awareness that the reliance on mathematics may at least be something to question (see, e.g. Soros, 2009; Lawson, 2013c), for most of his close associates the idea that there might be something problematic about the emphasis on forms of mathematical technique does not appear even to cross their minds. This is easily seen, for example, from a quick scan of the numerous presentations made at the inaugural (2010) conference, held at King's College, Cambridge (all the numerous contributions are posted on the INET website or can be found on YouTube. See, for example, http://ineteconomics.org/initiatives/conferences/kings-college or http://www.youtube.com/ watch?v=SdZgD1DCNq4). Almost all presentations focus on modelling methods and details. The one issue that is rarely even hinted at is that we might also question the very emphasis on mathematical modelling itself; the discussion throughout is only and continually about how economists should go about finding 'better' mathematical models (for a discussion of the 2010 INET presentations, see Lawson, 2012b).
17 For example, Aspromourgos takes the view that:

> The term was coined by Veblen in 1900, and subsequently employed by others, in order to characterise the Marshallian version of marginalism. This is a 'satisfying' result to the extent that Marshall, more than any of the other marginalist founders, sought to present his theory as having a substantial continuity with classical economics.
> (Aspromourgos, 1986: 266)

After a few paragraphs Aspromourgos adds:

> After Veblen, a number of other early instances of the term [neoclassical] amount to a broad acceptance of Veblen's view and therefore need not detain us in detail. They all place Marshall at the centre of a neoclassical economics and there is ample evidence that they derived from Veblen.
> (Aspromourgos, 1986: 266–267)

Aspromourgos mentions in particular that on this matter: 'Hamilton (1923), Homan (1928: 262, 387, 401) and Mitchell (1967, vol. ii: 208, 215, 217–218, 220) evidently followed Veblen's lead' (Aspromourgos, 1986: 267). Fayazmanesh (1998) advances a different interpretation to that of Aspromourgos but is still of the view that: 'The term "neoclassical" was coined by Veblen apparently based on the assumption that the marginal school is a continuation of the "classical school"' (Fayazmanesh, 1998: 92).
18 One of the more positive assessors is Aspromourgos, who allows a part of what he takes to be Veblen's basis of commonality to be correct 'to an extent':

'Veblen conceived Marshallian economics to be "neoclassical" because it had in common with the classics a utilitarian approach and employed a hedonistic psychology. To an extent this argument was correct, at least with regard to the utilitarianism' (Aspromourgos, 1986: 269).

19 Although frequently heard, I am not sure this is a view often sustained by serious historians of thought. Nevertheless it is regularly found in 'popular' or easy access sources. For example, at the time of writing an initial draft of this article (July 2012) the Wikipedia entry on 'Neoclassical Economics' informs us that: 'The term was originally introduced by Thorstein Veblen in 1900, in his article "Preconceptions of Economic Science", to distinguish marginalists in the tradition of Alfred Marshall from those in the Austrian School'. See http://en.wikipedia.org/wiki/Neoclassical_economics. Moreover, if this sentence found in Wikipedia is in turn entered in quotation marks into Google, we find it repeated identically in several thousand additional sources.

20 Of course, Veblen is quite aware that all sciences deal to some degree in taxonomy meaning classification, his own contributions included. He is critical, though, of taxonomy for the sake of taxonomy:

> There is no intention here to decry taxonomy, of course. Definition and classification are as much needed in economics as they are in those other sciences which have already left the exclusively taxonomic standpoint behind. The point of criticism, on this head, is that this class of economic theory differs from the modern sciences in being substantially nothing but definition and classification. Taxonomy for taxonomy's sake, definition and classification for the sake of definition and classification, meets no need of modern science. Work of this class has no value and no claims to consideration except so far as it is of use to the science in its endeavor to know and explain the processes of life.
>
> (Veblen, 1908a: 112–113)

In a later passage where he discusses hedonistic science, it is clear that by a 'system of taxonomic science' specifically, he means:

> [a] science of normalities. Its office is the definition and classification of 'normal' phenomena, or, perhaps better, phenomena as they occur in the normal case. And in this normal case, when and so far as the laws of nature work out their ends unvitiated, nature does all things well. This is also according to the ancient and authentic canons of taxonomic science.
>
> (Veblen, 1908a: 122)

21 Veblen notes of himself that: 'In speaking of this matter-of-fact character of the modern sciences it has been broadly characterized as "evolutionary"; and the evolutionary method and the evolutionary ideals have been placed in antithesis to the taxonomic methods and ideals of pre-evolutionary days' (Veblen, 1899a: 123).

22 Or as Marx (1974) writes:

> Once for all I may here state, that by Classical Political Economy, I understand that economy which, since the time of W. Petty, has investigated the real relations of production in bourgeois society in contradistinction to vulgar economy, which deals with appearances only, ruminates without

ceasing on the materials long since provided by scientific economy, and there seeks plausible explanations of the most obtrusive phenomena, for bourgeois daily use, but for the rest, confines itself to systematizing in a pedantic way, and proclaiming for everlasting truths, the trite ideas held by the self-complacent bourgeoisie with regard to their own world, to them the best of all possible worlds.

(Marx, 1974, chapter 1, note 33)

23 According to Veblen:

Nothing of the nature of a personal element was to be admitted into these fundamental empirical generalizations; and nothing, therefore, of the nature of a discretionary or teleological movement was to be comprised in the generalizations to be accepted as 'natural laws'. Natural laws must in no degree be imbued with personality, must say nothing of an ulterior end; but for all that they remained 'laws' of the sequences subsumed under them. So far is the reduction to colorless terms carried by Mill, for instance, that he formulates the natural laws as empirically ascertained sequences simply, even excluding or avoiding all imputation of causal continuity, as that term is commonly understood by the unsophisticated. In Mill's ideal no more of organic connection or continuity between the members of a sequence is implied in subsuming them under a law of causal relationship than is given by the ampersand. He is busied with dynamic sequences, but he persistently confines himself to static terms. Under the guidance of the associational psychology, therefore, the extreme of discontinuity in the deliverances of inductive research is aimed at by those economists – Mill and Cairnes being taken as typical – whose names have been associated with deductive methods in modern science. With a fine sense of truth they saw that the notion of causal continuity, as a premise of scientific generalization, is an essentially metaphysical postulate; and they avoided its treacherous ground by denying it, and construing causal sequence to mean a uniformity of co-existences and successions simply.

(Veblen, 1900: 252)

24 In fact Veblen concludes his evolutionary essay as follows:

The later method of apprehending and assimilating facts and handling them for the purposes of knowledge may be better or worse, more or less worthy or adequate, than the earlier; it may be of greater or less ceremonial or aesthetic effect; we may be moved to regret the incursion of underbred habits of thought into the scholar's domain. But all that is beside the present point. Under the stress of modern technological exigencies, men's everyday habits of thought are falling into the lines that in the sciences constitute the evolutionary method; and knowledge which proceeds on a higher, more archaic plane is becoming alien and meaningless to them. The social and political sciences must follow the drift, for they are already caught in it.

(Veblen, 1898: 396–397)

25 More expansively, Veblen writes:

But this and other survivals of the taxonomic terminology, or even of the taxonomic canons of procedure, do not hinder the economists of the modern school from doing effective work of a character that must be rated as genetic rather than taxonomic. [. . .] Professor Marshall shows an aspiration to treat economic life as a development; and, at least superficially, much of his work bears the appearance of being a discussion of this kind. In this endeavor his work is typical of what is aimed at by many of the later economists. The aim shows itself with a persistent recurrence in his Principles. His chosen maxim is, "Natura non facit saltum," [nature takes no leaps] – a maxim that might well serve to designate the prevailing attitude of modern economists towards questions of economic development as well as towards questions of classification or of economic policy. His insistence on the continuity of development and of the economic structure of communities is a characteristic of the best work along the later line of classical political economy.

(Veblen, 1900: 265)

26 Without mentioning, and perhaps unaware of, Veblen's earlier critique, Stephen Pratten (1998) provides a thesis on Marshall that is highly consistent with Veblen's assessment. Veblen, as noted, takes the view that by adhering to taxonomic methods Marshall is forced to concentrate at best on areas or topics, if any, where taxonomic analysis seems less unreasonable. Pratten argues this same thesis at length and in detail. Most fundamentally, Pratten notes that on publishing his *Principles* in 1890, Marshall anticipates that a second volume will follow, an anticipation still in place a decade later when Marshall is explicitly conceiving of this project as involving a 'biological perspective' (in place of the mechanical stance of the earlier analysis). The second volume never appeared, of course, and the reasons for this have been much debated in the history of economic thought. Pratten's contribution is to explain this puzzle in terms of the inconsistency between Marshall's ontology and method. Specifically, noting how Marshall's project of achieving a 'biological perspective' entailed taking seriously the sort of causal-processual ontology discussed here, Pratten demonstrates that the feature that was: 'preventing Marshall from realizing his planned program of research lay in his conception of the nature of science – a conception that was simply inadequate to his chosen project' (Pratten, 1998: 122). Thus Pratten traces how Marshall's commitment to a taxonomic (constant conjunction or correlation seeking) conception of science: 'feeds into characteristic trajectories in certain parts of his substantive analyses' (where the method seems least unpromising) but 'systematically diverts [Marshall] from more fruitful paths'. The result is that those: 'aspects of Marshall's work that are not propelled by this standard perspective are not systematically developed' (Pratten, 1998: 123). Pratten concludes:

Marshall's continuing commitment to the standard constant conjunction view [of the form of scientific results] represents one obvious constraint blocking his analysis of economic change, organic development, and so forth. More specifically, I have argued that Marshall's project of promoting, within a proposed second volume of the *Principles*, an economics more sensitive to the nature of its subject matter is frustrated by his inability to shrug off this inherited conception of science.

(Pratten, 1998: 158–159)

27 Thus, in a paper titled 'The limitations of marginal utility', notably published in 1909, some nine years after the final preconceptions paper, Veblen notes of this version of marginalism in particular:

> The limitations of the marginal-utility economics are sharp and characteristic. It is from first to last a doctrine of value, and in point of form and method it is a theory of valuation. The whole system, therefore, lies within the theoretical field of distribution ... Within this limited range marginal utility theory is of a wholly statical character. It offers no theory of a movement of any kind, being occupied with the adjustment of values to a given situation. Of this, again, no more convincing illustration need be had than is afforded by the work of Mr. Clark, which is not excelled in point of earnestness, perseverance, or insight. For all their use of the term 'dynamic', neither Mr. Clark nor any of his associates in this line of research have yet contributed anything at all appreciable to a theory of genesis, growth, sequence, change, process, or the like, in economic life ... They have had something to say as to the bearing which given economic changes, accepted as premises, may have on economic valuation, and so on distribution; but as to the causes of change or the unfolding sequence of the phenomena of economic life they have had nothing to say hitherto; nor can they, since their theory is not drawn in causal terms but in terms of teleology.
>
> In all this the marginal utility school is substantially at one with the classical economics of the nineteenth century, the difference between the two being that the former is confined within narrower limits and sticks more consistently to its teleological premises. Both are teleological, and neither can consistently admit arguments from cause to effect in the formulation of their main articles of theory ...
>
> The infirmity of this theoretical scheme lies in its postulates which confine the inquiry to generalizations of the teleological or 'deductive' order. These postulates together with the point of view and logical method that follow from them, the marginal utility school shares with other economists of the classical line – for this school is but a branch or derivative of the English classical economists of the nineteenth century. The substantial difference between this school and the generality of classical economists lies mainly in the fact that in the marginal utility economics the common postulates are more consistently adhered to at the same time that they are more neatly defined and their limitations are more adequately realized.
>
> (Veblen, 1909: 620–622)

In the final paragraph, Veblen clearly does allow of the marginal utility school that it may be derivative (rather than a branch) of the English classical economists of the nineteenth century. But as I say, if there is a difference it is not that marginalists are thought to reveal acceptance of a causal processual ontology. Rather it reflects the marginalists' greater consistency in treatment of common postulates.

28 I am grateful to Nuno Martins for drawing this to my attention.

29 Of course the ontological orientation (found to be inconsistent with deductivism) that Veblen finds some awareness of in his neoclassical economists is that which grounds evolutionary economics and so is regarded by Veblen as non-taxonomic. This contrasts with the ontological orientation (inconsistent with deductivism) that is found in the classical (political) economy of the likes of Adam Smith, which is still regarded as overly taxonomic not only by Veblen but also in effect by Marx himself in his critique of classical political economy (Marx repeatedly rejects attempts to naturalise the political economy of capitalism or to represent generalities of capitalism by appeal to universalities of natural law. Marx's own understanding of capitalism, as I interpret it, is, at least in large part, an inherently historical system-in-process that is anarchic, crisis prone, and subject to a non-predetermined trajectory of development, and so is essentially non-[certainly non-overly] teleological in Veblen's sense – though it must be noted that Veblen mostly seems to interpret it as effectively otherwise, or anyway as non- or insufficiently Darwinian; see especially Veblen, 1906). But Marx identifies 'classical political economy' as a contrast to 'vulgar economy' to stress the former's concern with underlying causal structures and especially social relations in opposition to the *superficiality* (not taxonomic emphasis *per se*) of vulgar economy's preoccupation with mere appearances and correlations. Whether we adopt the perspective of Veblen or Marx it remains the case that the ontological/methodological tension found in writers such as Marshall is such that one or other side of this latter tension/opposition can coherently be regarded as classical from each perspective, *according to that perspective's own terms and interpretations*, with the totality reasonably employing the adjunct 'neo'. Of course, where numerous later interpreters of Marx proceed by understanding Marx not as merely critically transforming but also developing, and so himself as working *within*, the classical political economy tradition (see, e.g. Kurz, 2010; Martins, 2012, 2013), then any overly teleological elements in earlier contributors such as Adam Smith might in consequence (arguably) be interpreted as contingent, non-necessary features of that classical political economy *tradition* anyway.

30 It is worth noting that Veblen was never oblivious to how a desire on the part of some to employ mathematical methods tended to preserve the taxonomic (specifically deductivist) emphasis. Indeed (writing eight years after the preconceptions papers but prior to the developments within the field of mathematics), Veblen observes that the main argument against the causalist ontology of evolutionary thinking (and so its implications for method) is that causal forces cannot be directly observed (they are merely 'metaphysical' postulates) and so should be discounted. He is aware that such a stance is apparent even amongst some 'modern scientists'. But Veblen observes that it is especially evident amongst those disposed to employing mathematical functions. Thus although he regards as established the characterisation of reality as a process of consecutive causal change, he acknowledges that it: 'is by no means unusual for modern scientists to deny the truth of this characterization, so far as regards this alleged recourse to the concept of causation' [and] 'even deny the substantial continuity of the sequence of changes that excite their scientific attention' (Veblen, 1908b: 33). Notably:

This attitude seems particularly to commend itself to those who by preference attend to the mathematical formulations of theory and who are chiefly occupied with proving up and working out details of the system of theory which have previously been left unsettled or uncovered. The concept of causation is recognized to be a metaphysical postulate, a matter of imputation, not of observation; whereas it is claimed that scientific inquiry neither does nor can legitimately, nor, indeed, currently, make use of a postulate more metaphysical than the concept of an idle concomitance of variation, such as is adequately expressed in terms of mathematical function.

(Veblen, 1908b: 33)

Veblen actually sets about demonstrating that such arguments are untenable, that we all implicitly or explicitly must invoke notions of causal powers and continuity (again, see Lawson, 2003, chapter 8).
31 Edward Fullbrook (2009: 6–7) lists some possible strategies for those who recognise the relevance of the ontology in question but are resistant to adapting methods appropriately.
32 Colander (2000), for example, takes steps to: 'declare the term neoclassical economics dead', but immediately adds: 'Let me be clear about what I am sentencing to death – it is not the content of neoclassical economics' (Colander, 2000: 127).

References

Arnsperger, C. and Varoufakis, Y (2006) What is neoclassical economics? *Post-Autistic Economics Review* 38: 1–8.
Aspromourgos, T. (1986) On the origins of the term 'neoclassical'. *Cambridge Journal of Economics* 10(3): 265–270.
Becker, G. S. (1976) *The Economic Approach to Human Behavior*. Chicago, IL: University of Chicago Press.
Campus, A. (1987) Marginalist economics, in Eatwell, J., Milgate, M. and Newman, P. (eds) *The New Palgrave: A Dictionary of Economics*. London, UK: Macmillan.
Colander, D. (2000) The death of neoclassical economics. *Journal of the History of Economic Thought* 22(2): 127–143.
Colander, D., Holt, R. P. and Rosser, J. B. (2004) The changing face of mainstream economics. *Review of Political Economy* 16(4): 485–500.
Davis, J. B. (2005) Heterodox economics, the fragmentation of the mainstream and embedded individual analysis, in Garnett, R. and Harvey, J. (eds) *The Future of Heterodox Economics. Essays in Honour of Paul Dale Bush*. Ann Arbor, MI: University of Michigan Press, pp. 53–72.
Dobb, M. (1973) *Theories of Value and Distribution since Adam Smith*. Cambridge, UK: Cambridge University Press.
Fayazmanesh, S. (1998) On Veblen's coining of the term 'neoclassical', in Fayazmanesh, S. and Tool, M. R. (eds) *Institutionalist Method and Value*, vol. 1. London, UK: Edward Elgar.
Fine, B. (2004) Addressing the critical and the real in critical realism, in Lewis, P. (ed.) *Transforming Economics: Perspectives on the Critical Realist Project*. London, UK: Routledge, pp. 202–226.

Fine, B. (2006) *Critical Realism and Heterodoxy*. Mimeo, SOAS. Available at: http://eprints.soas.ac.uk/7024/1/lawsonono.doc (accessed 27 July 2015).

Fullbrook, E. (2009) Introduction to ontology and economics: Tony Lawson and his critics, in Fullbrook, E. (ed.) *Ontology and Economics: Tony Lawson and His Critics*. London, UK: Routledge, pp. 1–12.

Guerrien, B. (2004) Irrelevance and ideology. *Post-Autistic Economics Review* 29, article 3.

Hahn, F. H. (1982) The neo-Ricardians. *Cambridge Journal of Economics* 6(4): 353–374.

Hahn, F. H. (1984) *Equilibrium and Macroeconomics*. Oxford, UK: Basil Blackwell.

Hahn, F. H. (1985) *In Praise of Economic Theory*. Jevons Memorial Fund Lecture, delivered at University College, London, UK. Available at: http://www.worldcat.org/title/in-praise-of-economic-theory-the-jevons-memorial-fund-lecture-delivered-at-university-college-london-23-november-1984/oclc/470708868 (accessed 2 August 2015).

Hamilton, W. H. (1923) Vestigial economics. *New Republic*, 4 April.

Hicks, J. R. (1983) *Classics and Moderns* (Collected Essays on Economic Theory, vol. 3). Oxford, UK: Basil Blackwell.

Hodgson, G. M. (1999) False antagonisms and doomed reconciliations, in *Evolution and Institutions: On Evolutionary Economics and the Evolution of Economics*. Cheltenham, UK: Edward Elgar: 23–45.

Homan, P. T. (1928) *Contemporary Economic Thought*. New York, NY: Harper and Brothers.

Juselius, K. (2010) Time to reject the privileging of economic theory over empirical evidence? A reply to Lawson. *Cambridge Journal of Economics* 35(2): 423–436.

Keen, S. (2012) *Instability in Financial Markets: Sources and Remedies*. Paper presented at Berlin meetings of the Institute for New Economic Thinking (INET). Available at: http://ineteconomics.org/sites/inet.civicactions.net/files/keen-steve-berlin-paper.pdf (accessed 1 July 2012).

Krugman, P. (2009) How did economists get it so wrong? *New York Times Magazine*, 2 September. Available at: http://www.nytimes.com/2009/09/06/magazine/06Economic-t.html?pagewanted=all (accessed 1 July 2012).

Kurz, H. D. (2010) Technical progress, capital accumulation and income distribution in classical economics: Adam Smith, David Ricardo and Karl Marx. *European Journal of the History of Economic Thought* 17(5): 1183–1222.

Lawson, T. (1997) *Economics and Reality*. London, UK: Routledge.

Lawson, T. (2003) *Reorienting Economics*. London, UK: Routledge.

Lawson, T. (2005) The (confused) state of equilibrium analysis in modern economics: An (ontological) explanation. *Journal for Post Keynesian Economics* 27(3): 423–444.

Lawson, T. (2006a) The nature of heterodox economics. *Cambridge Journal of Economics* 30(2): 483–507.

Lawson, T. (2006b) Tensions in modern economics. The case of equilibrium analysis, in Mosini, V. (ed.) *Equilibrium in Economics: Scope and Limits*. London, UK: Routledge, pp. 133–149.

Lawson, T. (2009a) The current economic crisis: Its nature and the course of academic economics. *Cambridge Journal of Economics* 33(4): 759–788.

Lawson, T. (2009b) Contemporary economics and the crisis. *Real-World Economics Review* 50: 122–131.

Lawson, T. (2009c) On the nature and roles of formalism in economics: Reply to Hodgson, in Fullbrook, E. (ed.) *Ontology and Economics: Tony Lawson and His Critics*. London, UK: Routledge, pp. 189–231.

Lawson, T. (2012a) Ontology and the study of social reality: Emergence, organisation, community, power, social relations, corporations, artefacts and money. *Cambridge Journal of Economics* 36(2): 345–385.

Lawson, T. (2012b) Mathematical modelling and ideology in the economics academy: Competing explanations of the failings of the modern discipline? *Economic Thought: History, Philosophy and Methodology* 1(1): 3–22.

Lawson, T. (2013a) Emergence and social causation, in Greco, J. and Groff, R. (eds) *Powers and Capacities in Philosophy*. London, UK: Routledge, pp. 285–307.

Lawson, T. (2013b) Emergence, morphogenesis, causal reduction and downward causation, in Archer, M. (ed.) *Social Morphogenesis*. New York, NY: Springer, pp. 61–84.

Lawson, T. (2013c) Soros's theory of reflexivity: A critical comment. Mimeo. Cambridge, *Revue de Philosophie Economique* 14(1): 29–48.

Marshall, A. (1890) *Principles of Economics*. Available at: http://www.econlib.org/library/Marshall/marPCover.html (accessed 27 July 2015).

Martins, N. (2012) Sen, Sraffa and the revival of classical political economy. *Journal of Economic Methodology* 19(2): 143–157.

Martins, N. (2013) Classical surplus theory and heterodox economics. *American Journal of Economics and Sociology* 72(5): 1205–1231.

Marx, K. (1974) *Capital: A Critical Analysis of Capitalist Production*, vol. 1, Engels, F. (ed.). London, UK: Lawrence and Wishart.

Marx, K. (1977) *A Contribution to the Critique of Political Economy*. Moscow, Russia: Progress Publishers.

Mitchell, W. C. (1967) *Types and Economic Theory*, 2 vols, Dorfman, J. (ed.). New York, NY: Kelley.

Pratten, S. (1998) Marshall on tendencies, equilibrium, and the statical method. *History of Political Economy* 30(1): 122–163.

Schumpeter, J. A. (1954) *History of Economic Analysis*. Schumpeter, E. B. (ed.). London, UK: George Allen and Unwin.

Soros, G. (2009) *The Crash of 2009 and What it Means: The New Paradigm for Financial Markets*. New York Public Affairs.

Veblen, T. (1898) Why is economics not an evolutionary science? *Quarterly Journal of Economics* 12(4): 373–397.

Veblen, T. (1899a) The preconceptions of economic science I. *Quarterly Journal of Economics* 13(2): 121–150.

Veblen, T. (1899b) The preconceptions of economic science II. *Quarterly Journal of Economics* 13(4): 396–426.

Veblen, T. (1900) The preconceptions of economic science III. *Quarterly Journal of Economics* 14(2): 240–269.

Veblen, T. (1906) The socialist economics of Karl Marx and his followers. *Quarterly Journal of Economics* 20(4): 575–595.

Veblen, T. (1908a) Fisher's capital and income. *Political Science Quarterly* 23(1): 112–128.

Veblen, T. (1908b) The evolution of the scientific point of view. *University of California Chronicle* 10(4); reprinted in Veblen, T. (1990) *The Place of Science in Modern Civilization*. New Brunswick, NJ: Transaction Publishers (page references to the latter).

Veblen, T. (1909) The limitations of marginal utility. *Journal of Political Economy* 17(9): 620–636.
Weintraub, E. R. (2002) Neoclassical economics, in *Concise Encyclopaedia of Economics*. Library of Economics and Liberty, Liberty Fund. Available at: http://www.econlib.org/library/Enc1/NeoclassicalEconomics.html (accessed 27 July 2015).
Zafirovski, M. (1999) How 'neo-classical' is neoclassical economics? With special reference to value theory. *History of Economics Review* winter: 1–15.

2 From neoclassical theory to mainstream modelling

Fifty years of moral hazard in perspective

John Latsis and Constantinos Repapis

Introduction

Tony Lawson asks why and under what circumstances we should use the term 'neoclassical' to refer to a specific school of economics. His answer is both nuanced and strategic. It is nuanced in the sense that, though Lawson believes that a conception of neoclassicism can be salvaged, that conception differs significantly from accounts defended by neoclassical economists themselves and by prominent historians of economic thought. It is strategic in the sense that, following a careful reconstruction of how Veblen's original conception of neoclassicism might be extended to strands of modern economics, Lawson eventually suggests that the term should be abandoned.

We begin with what we see as a major, but under-emphasised, contribution of Lawson's paper: rendering the distinction between *neoclassical* and *mainstream* economics more precise. As Lawson points out, the frequent elision of the older conception of neoclassicism and the modern mainstream by historians, philosophers and practising economists has been intellectually stultifying, supressing debate and neutralising effective critique. First, we briefly present Lawson's analysis and contextualise it. We then go on to show that Lawson's apparent rejection of the neoclassical label may not be desirable in the context of research in the history of economic thought. While we agree that a reformulated conception of neoclassical economics may be of limited use for understanding the state of modern economics, it can nevertheless serve as a powerful analytical tool when analysing historical debates. It provides us with a way to address an important historiographical problem in the evolution of twentieth-century economic thought. This is to chart the transformation of economics from the pre-WWII neoclassical theory to modern mainstream modelling. While this is a complex and multi-layered problem, we use Lawson's distinction to investigate a particular transformation that relates to healthcare economics: the introduction and subsequent use of the concept of 'moral hazard' by economists.

As recent policy debates have shown, models of moral hazard are now at the core of the discipline of economics to such an extent that they have been utilised as analytical and policy tools in a wide variety of contexts (Latsis and Repapis, 2014). We trace the humble origins of moral hazard as a peripheral element of Kenneth Arrow's *The American Economic Review* article 'Uncertainty and the welfare economics of medical care' (Arrow, 1963). This seminal article is widely regarded as a key contribution to neoclassical economics, because it effectively launched health economics as a field and is also considered to be one of the pioneering contributions to the literature on informational asymmetries. Our discussion of Arrow (1963) reveals the tension between ontology and method that is characteristic of Lawson's use of the term 'neoclassical'. More importantly, however, by fitting Arrow's contribution into Lawson's mould, we gain a new perspective on and a better understanding of the debates surrounding the paper, its initial reception and its subsequent use.

We then highlight tensions that arose almost immediately between Arrow, the architect of what quickly came to be seen as a new framework for analysing healthcare, and those who wished to appropriate his insights to develop various subfields within economics. Differences in political ideology and theoretical assumptions are apparent in several cases, but the most pervasive and the least noticed tension can be identified at a deeper level. While Arrow struggled with the mismatch between ontology and method that is typical of neoclassical theorising, most critics were blind to these concerns. Our analysis suggests that Arrow is a neoclassical in Lawson's sense; however, many of his interlocutors – both followers and critics – are not. Framing the debate in terms of the tension between ontology and methodology that is characteristic of Lawson's version of neoclassicism provides a new perspective on the remarkable intellectual trajectory of one of Arrow's key contributions to economic theory.

Ontology and method in the neoclassical school

Lawson starts with two puzzles that arise from the current use of the term 'neoclassical' in economics: first, that it is used in a vague and undisciplined way by both critics and supporters; and second, that this usage undermines clear discussion and effective critique. These two observations point to the same problem, which is that because it is difficult to define neoclassicism in a non-controversial and widely accepted manner, it is unclear which authors or contributions can be called neoclassical in a meaningful way. The critique of neoclassical economics can thus be said to miss its target, because the definitions used by critics are at odds with each other, or with the definition used by defenders or the self-perception of the economists the term intends to describe. In addition, continuing debates about the 'true nature' of neoclassicism can deflect attention away from the failings of modern economics, adding further confusion to the use of the term 'neoclassical'. Lawson's article seeks to address the interpretative puzzle by showing that a coherent conception of neoclassicism can be reconstructed based on Veblen's (1900) early definition of the term. He does not claim to be able to resolve the second puzzle, arguing that the terminology of neoclassicism should be abandoned (at least insofar as it relates to current debates).

Lawson's definition of neoclassical economics draws heavily on Veblen, who was responsible for coining the term at the turn of the twentieth century. As Lawson (Chapter 1: 40–41) explains, Veblen's neologism was carefully chosen to reflect both the influence of the modern 'evolutionary' approach (neo) and continuity with the older 'taxonomic' approach (classical). He also recognised the tension that this juxtaposition of old and new had on the key neoclassical contributions of the late nineteenth century by Alfred Marshall and John Neville Keynes.

> I am suggesting that Veblen introduces the term 'neoclassical' to distinguish a line of thinking that is ultimately characterised by possessing a degree of ontological awareness whilst persevering with a methodology that is inconsistent with this awareness; it is a line of thinking identified precisely by this ontological/methodological tension or inconsistency. Its practitioners recognise that social reality is a historical process of cumulative causation, but nevertheless continue to rely upon methods that require of reality that it conforms to given correlations, that render the science as still taxonomic.
> (Lawson, Chapter 1: 55)

Lawson updates this definition by translating it into the language of social ontology. Veblen's emphasis on taxonomy is identified with what Lawson calls deductivism, and thus with the methods of mathematical modelling. Veblen's conception of an 'evolutionary approach' is seen as equivalent to Lawson's preferred ontology, which sees the social realm as a causal-processual open system. Thus, according to Lawson, neoclassical economists are:

> [t]hose who are aware (at some level) that social reality is of a causal-processual nature ... who prioritise the goal of being realistic, and yet who fail themselves fully to recognise or to accept the limited scope for any overly taxonomic approach including, in particular, one that makes significant use of methods of mathematical deductive modelling.
> (Lawson, Chapter 1: 63–64)

Lawson's paper is concerned with the current state of economic theorising and brings forth two rather controversial consequences of this revised understanding of neoclassical economics:

1   That the term 'neoclassical' picks out a group of economists who do not share a common core or set of assumptions in terms of substantive

theorising, but rather are joined by their failure to recognise a fundamental inconsistency between ontology and method in their work.
2 That many mathematically orientated, but self-defined heterodox economists could now be identified with this revised neoclassical category.

While this analysis raises a host of questions for the types of modern economic analysis, an important consequence is to use Lawson's argument to clearly delineate the previously sketchy boundaries between neoclassical and mainstream economics. The defining feature of mainstream economic analysis is that it does not suffer from the 'neoclassical tension' attributed to neoclassical theorising because, to paraphrase Lawson, mainstream economists are those who are: (a) wedded to mathematical deductivism as the all-consuming scientific method; and (b) regard all analysis that deviates from this stance as lacking knowledge-building content (Lawson, Chapter 1: 64).

Our focus in the remainder of this chapter engages directly with this distinction. Despite its controversial nature, we accept the fundamental plausibility of Lawson's redefinition of neoclassical economics as both coherent and consistent with the historical origins of the term. However, we believe that the redefinition of neoclassicism has consequences that go beyond the contemporary debate about the state of modern economics and, indeed, beyond the current opposition between heterodox and mainstream economists. An unintended consequence of this clearly defined distinction between mainstream and neoclassical economics is that it provides us with a new tool to investigate important questions in the history of economic thought. For example: What is the historical relationship between mainstream and neoclassical economics? If the mainstream emerged from neoclassical contributions, how and when did this transition occur?

In order to shed some light on these important questions, we have adapted an illustrative case study focusing on the genesis of the concept of moral hazard in the economics literature. Our argument is that the introduction of moral hazard in Arrow's (1963) seminal paper on healthcare bears all the hallmarks of Lawson's neoclassicism. These are: inconsistency between ontology and method; tension between a commitment to understand the phenomena and a commitment to modelling them in a particular way; and a desire to understand the specificity of the system under investigation (healthcare), while respecting the formal constraints of the 'economic approach' to analysing social problems. This internal struggle was ignored by subsequent economists who saw the article simply as a progenitor of mainstream economic analysis, thus misunderstanding its neoclassical stance. However, in order to see how this break occurred we first revisit Arrow's (1963) seminal paper and give a reading of the article from this viewpoint.

A reading of Arrow (1963)

Arrow opens his article with: 'This paper is an exploratory and tentative study of the specific differentia of medical care as the object of normative economics' (Arrow, 1963: 941). This sentence encapsulates what Arrow attempts to do: to describe the provision of medical care in the USA during the early 1960s and discuss why this provision seems to be so far removed from the competitive market model. He explains the analytical findings of the competitive model, the two welfare theorems, and finishes by noting: 'if ... the actual market differs significantly from the competitive model ... the separation of allocative and distributional procedures becomes, in most cases, impossible' (Arrow, 1963: 943). In this passage the tension characteristic of neoclassical contributions first appears: Arrow explicitly considers the distance between model and reality. If reality cannot be described in an accurate fashion by the paradigm, then it follows that questions about distribution and efficiency (what the mainstream would call positive and normative analysis), that formally arise in this literature, cannot be transferred to the real world.

The question of how to compare real life – the set of practical problems raised by the functioning of the healthcare[1] system – with the competitive model presents a methodological problem for Arrow. He points out that the methodological controversy has raged for more than a century, but acknowledges Friedman's (1953) well-known instrumentalist argument as an influential contribution that claims to resolve the controversy by focusing solely on a model's ability to predict (Arrow, 1963: 944). However, without giving a decisive argument against Friedman, Arrow rejects the approach of focusing on price and quantity predictions as the only relevant data that can be used to test the competitive model. Instead, he investigates: 'the institutional organisation and observable mores of the medical profession' (Arrow, 1963: 944). Here again we see clear evidence of the neoclassical tension: Arrow seeks to compare the model with a realistic account incorporating the socio-economic context rather than relying on a simplistic quantitative approach.

More specifically, he examines whether the preconditions for a competitive market system in medical care are actually met. These preconditions are: (1) *existence* of competitive equilibrium; (2) *marketability* of all goods and services; and (3) *nonincreasing returns* (Arrow, 1963: 944). Marketability is identified as the main problem and is seen as a broader issue than the one analysed within the traditional externalities literature. Again, Arrow gives a very open and informal definition, writing: 'it will be sufficient to identify nonmarketability with the observed absence of markets' (Arrow, 1963 945). He focuses on two issues that create nonmarketability: risk and uncertainty. With risk he notes that while, due to illness and risk pooling, a well-developed market should exist, it does not actually exist in practice (Arrow, 1963: 945). As for uncertainty, he writes that with: 'uncertainty, information or knowledge becomes a commodity' (Arrow, 1963: 946). In this context, it can be argued that Arrow sees information problems as related to environmental factors rather than only behavioural responses to stimuli. It follows that uncertainty is a natural hindrance to a well-functioning market. But when markets fail to operate, nonmarket institutions occasionally fill the existing gap and in healthcare the government and other charitable institutions play this role. With this observation Arrow ends his extensive introduction and forges ahead with a survey of the healthcare market, focusing on the elements that distinguish it from the competitive model.

Arrow's survey focuses both on the supply and demand characteristics of the healthcare market. A recurrent theme in this section is the issue of trust and the existence of institutions and behaviour that lie outside the competitive model. Arrow describes the behaviour of physicians in detail, noting that there are very strong social and moral norms governing their behaviour. In order to illustrate this he explains that: '[a physician's] behaviour is supposed to be governed by a concern for a customer's welfare which would not be expected of a salesman' (Arrow, 1963: 949). Divergence from the competitive model is not only restricted to the action of physicians. Arrow also speaks of the prevalence of non-profit hospitals and even non-profit educational establishments training students to become doctors at subsidised cost. While profit seems to play a reduced role in the provision of healthcare, trust appears central. Patients trust doctors, non-profit hospitals and educational establishments that give accreditation. The patient-doctor relationship is extensively explored and trust is important there in order to deal with the complex nature of medical care and the uncertainty of disease. Arrow notes a special aspect of this relationship, the 'informational inequality' between doctors and patients, something both parties are aware of. Finally, he notes that there is some friction between competitive business practices and trust. Physicians are expected to: provide advice that is: 'completely divorced from self-interest'; treatment that responds to 'objective needs' and not financial considerations; and certificates that confirm the existence of illnesses truthfully and not to please customers (see Arrow, 1963: 950). Thus, the physician is trusted not to abuse their special position by engaging in competitive practices that are both commonplace and arguably necessary in other markets.

Having provided this elaborate and realistic description of the healthcare market, Arrow proceeds to compare it with two versions of the competitive model, first under certainty, and then under uncertainty. When he considers the comparison with the competitive model under certainty,[2] he finds that there are four major departures: nonmarketability, increasing returns, entry requirements for physicians and price discrimination. The analysis generally follows well-established economic arguments that would have been familiar to the academic reader of the period. For example, he discusses problems of externalities, or how licensing laws restrict entry or how price discrimination may be used to maximise profits for a collective monopoly. The neoclassical tension is once again clear in this discussion as he disagrees with the standard interpretation of price discrimination as simply maximising profits for the medical profession and argues that the incidence of charity by the medical profession shows: 'the relevance and importance of social and ethical factors' (Arrow, 1963: 957).

However, it is in the comparison of the medical market with the competitive model under uncertainty that Arrow breaks new ground. He starts his analysis by characterising optimal or ideal insurance, noting that when you have risk-averse individuals, an actuarially fair or almost fair insurance scheme is welfare improving due to risk pooling. Drawing on standard methodological tools, he provides formal proofs (in an appendix) for this analytical result, which show that: 'the nonexistence of suitable insurance policies... implies a loss of welfare' (Arrow, 1963: 959). But this analytical finding presents two puzzles: first, why should this be the case? And second, what is the scope for government action? Arrow writes: 'It follows that the government should undertake insurance in those cases where this market, for whatever reason, has failed to emerge. Nevertheless, there are a number of significant practical limitations on the use of insurance' (Arrow, 1963: 961). The discussion that follows is tentative and is obviously intended to be exploratory. In it Arrow faces the consequences of the juxtaposition of his formal methodology and the reality of the American healthcare system. He attempts to blend abstract economic analysis of the theoretical problems associated with insurance in a market economy with empirical descriptions of actual gaps in insurance coverage.

It is in this discussion that Arrow introduces the problem of moral hazard. He writes: 'one of the limits which has been much stressed in insurance literature is the effect of insurance on incentives. What is desired in the case of insurance is that the event against which insurance is taken be out of the control of the individual' (Arrow, 1963: 961). Later on he notes: 'It is frequently observed that widespread medical insurance increases the demand from medical care' (Arrow, 1963: 961). Nevertheless, in these crucial pages moral hazard is not given a more exact definition, and, interestingly, the incentives problem noted *en passant* and quoted above is not formally explored. This is in contrast to the way Arrow discussed the ideal insurance case, where the analytical results were clearly presented in the text and formal proofs provided in the appendix. Instead, in the case of moral hazard, Arrow gives a general discussion noting that there are behavioural responses, which may be relevant to his analysis. Rather than providing a formal framework to analyse these responses, he provides an illustrative example: if you insure your house against fire, then there is the issue of carelessness and even arson, and similar problems may also arise in medical insurance. He then notes that: 'to some extent the professional relationship between physician and patient limits the normal hazard in various forms of medical insurance' (Arrow, 1963: 961), though this is far from a perfect check. Interestingly he argues that where there is scrutiny and control of payments by third parties (other than the doctor and patient) then this may be effective in reducing moral hazard. Furthermore, this may explain why, in some areas of healthcare, insurance policies are more widespread than others, as some activities like surgery are under third-party supervision whereas others, like GP visits, are not.

In the last section of the paper Arrow is preoccupied with the problem of what happens when, due to the practical limitations discussed above, appropriate insurance markets do not, or have not, developed. He writes: 'in the absence of ideal insurance, there arise institutions which offer some sort of substitute guarantees' (Arrow, 1963: 965). This is because with uncertainty:

> [the patient] would want some guarantee that the physician is using his knowledge to the best advantage. This leads to the setting up of a relationship of trust and confidence, one which the physician has a social obligation to live up to.
>
> (Arrow, 1963: 965)

This relationship of trust, which he observed when he was doing a survey of the medical care market in the previous section, is not incidental to the workings of that market, but instead serves an economic purpose – it fills a gap created by the problem of uncertainty. This nonmarket mechanism has its own rules that may actually further remove it from the competitive model. Arrow observes that: 'one consequence of such trust relations is that the physician cannot or at least cannot appear to act, as if he is maximizing his income at every moment in time' (Arrow, 1963: 965). And again that: 'the very word, "profit" is a signal that denies the trust relations' (Arrow, 1963: 965). Therefore trust is constitutive of the workings of the healthcare market and it manifests itself across the key relationships that form the basis of the healthcare system: between patient and physician, in the certification and licencing of physicians by academic and other regulatory institutions, or even in the non-profit organisations that own and run hospitals.

In the conclusion Arrow clearly states that his analysis of the healthcare market has two significant implications for economic theory. First, the observation that: 'the failure of the market to insure against uncertainties has created many social institutions in which the usual assumptions of the market are to some extent contradicted' (Arrow, 1963: 967). There are a host of interpersonal relations that have economic importance and these nonmarket relations create: 'guarantees of behaviour which would otherwise be afflicted with excessive uncertainty' (Arrow, 1963: 967).

Second, this means that the competitive model has natural limits in its descriptive powers. It is an important part of the economic canon, but it cannot be the full picture, for there are other institutions in existence organised across fundamentally different lines. Taken in conjunction with the preceding discussion of healthcare, the conclusion of Arrow's paper stands out as a remarkably clear exemplar of what Lawson has called neoclassicism. There is an explicit avowal of the descriptive inadequacy of the standard economic paradigm and of the existence of institutions that have developed and function in ways that are incompatible with it. This is a powerful indicator of the tension that persists between Arrow's concern to describe and understand socio-economic reality and the ontology imposed by standard techniques. There is also an equally explicit avowal of the limitations of the methodology of the competitive model as a tool. This is evident in his decision not to invoke a standard account in terms of event regularities in the analysis of moral hazard (as contrasted with the formal treatment of insurance in the appendix). The last line of the article provides an elegant summary of the neoclassical tension at work: 'The logic and limitations of ideal competitive behaviour under uncertainty force us to recognize the incomplete description of reality supplied by the impersonal price system' (Arrow, 1963: 967).

Early reception: the first seven years

Arrow's article received attention from the moment it was published. In fact, even when the article was still in proofs Arrow presented it in the 'secret' seminar in Cambridge, as he was visiting Cambridge for the academic year of 1963–4,[3] which means that the article was rapidly becoming well-known on both sides of the Atlantic. In the first 7 years since its publication Arrow was cited 18 times in economics journals. These included one citation each in the following journals: *The Review of Economics and Statistics* (Feldstein, 1970); *The Quarterly Journal of Economics* (Akerlof, 1970); *American Journal of Agricultural Economics* (Ball and Wilson, 1968); *Journal of Law and Economics* (Lees, 1962); *The Journal of Business* (Pashigian et al., 1966); *The Journal of Risk and Insurance* (Pauly, 1970); and *The Journal of Human Resources* (Baird, 1970). There were three citations in *Economica* (Foldes, 1967; Williamson et al., 1967; Lindsay, 1969). There were also eight in *The American Economic Review* (Arrow, 1965b, 1968; Boland, 1965; Lees and Rice, 1965; Diamond, 1967; Pauly, 1968; Crew, 1969; Newhouse, 1970). Of these eight, two were by Arrow in reply to published comments on his original paper. These early published comments and Arrow's replies constitute two distinct theoretical debates that set the scene for the subsequent interpretation and use of the article. There are substantial differences in what these two debates focused on, but also on how they relate to the transformation of economics and in particular the emergence of modern mainstream economic theorising.

The first citation of Arrow (1963) is by the British economist, D. S. Lees (1962), in an article that analyses the UK National Health Service (NHS) from a libertarian perspective. Lees argues that the basic problem of the NHS is not the nationalisation of the healthcare industry, but the abolition of prices for the services provided. This outcome makes healthcare a service outside what the market economy provides. The article continues by composing a list of arguments in favour of abolishing prices in medical care and then rebutting each in turn. One of the reasons tendered is that: 'medical care is "different" from other things that are normally bought and sold in markets' (Lees, 1962: 114). It is in relation to this objection that Lees references Arrow (1963) and writes that he finds the arguments in Arrow unconvincing. He concludes by saying that even if the government objective is to enforce equality of consumption of medical care, it does not follow that: 'a non-market situation, one in which there are no prices is inescapably necessary to achieve this purpose' (Lees, 1962: 116). He goes on to argue that this outcome can also be achieved through the market and indeed this would be more compatible with how a free society works.

A second paper by Lees and Rice (1965) is the first of the two comments published in *The American Economic Review* in response to Arrow's original paper.[4] They start by quoting the following passage from Arrow: 'for present purposes, it will be sufficient to identify nonmarketability [of risk-bearing] with the observed absence of markets . . . It follows that the government should undertake insurance in those cases where this market, for whatever reason, has failed to emerge' (Arrow, 1963: 945, 961, quoted in Lees and Rice, 1965: 141). They make the following two counterpoints to Arrow's claim: (1) due to the buyer's and seller's costs, the absence of insurance policies for certain risks may be the optimal market response, not an inability of the market to develop; and (2) that it takes time for new types of insurance markets to emerge, but they do so eventually. The first point is formally explored and shows that there may be optimal reasons for markets not emerging for some types of insurance. This argument is qualitatively different to the second one. There the authors argue that markets develop over time, as new needs create conditions for the emergence of products. They then suggest that since markets fill that gap in the long run, and since markets are assumed to be a desirable form of social organisation, then: 'whatever role government is to play in this transition, it would at least seem inappropriate to create permanent institutions to deal with what is essentially a temporary problem' (Lees and Rice, 1965: 153).

Lees's libertarian position is implicit in both papers. He sees a fundamental antagonism between two types of social organisation – the market and the state – in which healthcare is a key battleground. His repeated critique of Arrow, despite its occasionally formalistic presentation, is firmly motivated by this normative perspective, as he identifies Arrow as a defender of intervention in healthcare markets and hence, by proxy, a proponent of a state-sponsored healthcare system. Arrow's response to Lees effectively recognises the normative flavour of the debate, though he seeks to separate analytical claims from 'normative implications'. In the case of the former, he argues that not all institutional structures 'out there' can be analysed through the lens of market competition, citing a real world example to illustrate his point:

> [t]he Blue Cross-Blue Shield network is by no stretch of the imagination an example of a competitive market in health insurance. On the other hand, it would clearly be incorrect to regard it as a profit-maximizing monopoly. What has happened is a voluntary association has essentially played the role of a surrogate government
> (Arrow, 1965b: 156)

What remains from this exchange is a genuine disagreement about the ability of the market system to deliver appropriate services in the healthcare sector. The debate of Lees and Rice vs. Arrow is ideologically charged, but it appears that the interlocutors understand that their disagreement is on personal values and competing systems of social organisation.

The second debate on Arrow's paper was with Mark Pauly, following a comment published in *The American Economic Review* in 1968. Pauly starts by reviewing the exchange between Arrow, Lees and Rice, stating that there are actually better reasons than transaction costs for why: 'some insurances are not offered commercially' (Pauly, 1968: 532). Pauly then turns to his main theme, the exploration of the problem of moral hazard, since: 'in the controversy that followed [the exchange between Lees, Rice and Arrow] moral hazard seems to have been completely overlooked as an explanation of why certain types of expenses are not insured commercially' (Pauly, 1968: 535, footnote 3). Furthermore, he argues that in the 1963 article: 'Arrow appears to consider moral hazard as an imperfection, a defect of physical control' or a 'practical limitation' on the use of insurance, which does not: 'alter the case for [the] creation of a much wider class of insurance policies than now exist' (Pauly, 1968: 535, footnote 3). Instead, Pauly presents moral hazard in a completely different light. He starts by offering a formal definition, which is that by lowering the marginal cost of care to the individual, you will increase usage of medical care. This behavioural response is not a characteristic of the personality of the individual, an aspect taken into account in the insurance literature,[5] but is a rational reaction. He insists that: 'the response of seeking more medical care with insurance than in its absence is a result not of moral perfidy, but of rational economic behaviour' (Pauly, 1968: 535). This choice of words can appear odd. What exactly does Pauly mean? Arrow, when quoting this line by Pauly in his rejoinder, adds: 'Mr. Pauly's wording suggests that "rational economic behaviour" and "moral perfidy" are mutually exclusive categories. No doubt Judas Iscariot turned a tidy profit from one of his transactions, but the usual judgement of his behaviour is not necessarily wrong' (Arrow, 1968: 538).

This a core disagreement between the two theorists that deserves further analysis. By analogy, Pauly's argument may be recast in the following way: the fall of a large asteroid on planet earth that extinguishes all life is not the outcome of divine will, but simply the outcome of the laws of physics. By implication, any discussion of ethics in the situation of healthcare, is as irrelevant and 'unscientific' as a discussion of theology in physics. A key disagreement, then, is whether human behaviour is completely determined by the axioms of rational choice in the same way that the law of gravity completely describes planetary movements. Here Pauly adopts the mainstream stance since he accepts the axiomatic straightjacket imposed by his formalisation of moral hazard. Arrow, on the other hand, is motivated by an attempt to understand the problems that might actually arise in healthcare insurance markets, rather than those imposed by the structure of the model.

By accepting the logic behind this analogy we can analyse the rest of Pauly's argument in relation to moral hazard. If individuals are atomised and rational in the technical economic sense and isolated from any cultural, ethical or social factors, then healthcare insurance faces the following problem. If the government decides to insure everyone against medical expenses, then the outcome is: 'to reduce the price charged to the individual at the point of service from the market price to zero' (Pauly, 1968: 532). There is a subtle, but very important, difference between Lees and Rice's argument that prices are abolished and Pauly's argument that prices are reduced to zero. According to Pauly, the government, by covering healthcare costs, sets a specific price for the good in what effectively remains a market system. This world, populated by isolated atoms whose behaviour is mechanically determined by implicit or explicit price signals, responds to institutional change only through the effect it has on the money denominated price of the good in question; the relevant event regularity in Lawson's terms.[6]

With a price of zero, the reader is lead to believe that demand will increase. The reason for this is because healthcare is treated like any other consumer good, with a possible range of demand elasticities. Pauly notes that if demand for healthcare goods is perfectly inelastic then moral hazard is not a problem, as demand would not increase with decreasing prices. It is interesting to observe here that Pauly is resting on very strong assumptions inherited from the competitive model: every economist knows that if the price of apples decreases, people will buy more apples. But how does this translate in the real world market for medical care? In what way can consumers take advantage of the zero price? Will they undergo surgery when it is not medically necessary? Will they stay in hospital longer than required? Will they consume more pills or use more medical devices than they need? Or might they abuse their local GP privileges and clog waiting rooms? Pauly uses the visits to a physician's office as an example of a situation when an: 'increase in use in response to a zero price would be relatively great' (Pauly, 1968: 535). But he makes a broader point, and this is that when you have inelastic demand and uncertainty, (as is the case with surgery) then insurance is provided through the market already, as moral hazard would not be a problem.[7]

The outcome of this formalisation of the moral hazard is that when insurance should be provided it is already provided by the market. If it is not provided by the market, it can only be because the individual who purchases it has a tendency to overuse the services provided. Because the provider expects this rational reaction he charges more for the insurance than what is actuarially fair. But at these prices the individual finds it optimal not to buy insurance, as it is too expensive for the cover he needs. If the government provides this insurance and taxes the individual, the problem of overuse is still there and the government substitutes one problem for another. Individuals will complain about high taxes to finance the system of provision and the solution will not be politically sustainable. After all, if they were willing to pay the cost of provision given the expectation of overuse, the market would have provided the service without government intervention. Therefore, according to Pauly's analysis, government action is redundant and harmful in all situations.

This argument achieves an elegant transformation of the problem of market failure. It starts as in Arrow (1963) by presenting an ideal market in which appropriate insurance would exist if it was not for the adverse, but rational behavioural response. This response gives rise to the actual market situation in which optimality means that: 'some uncertain medical care expenses will not and should not be insured' (Pauly, 1968: 537). It then measures any government intervention, either outright central provision or policies in the form of coinsurance and deductibles against the outcomes that the existing market can deliver, finding that no intervention, in this situation, can offer any improvement. By improvement what is meant here is very specific: moving closer to the idealised market represented by the competitive model in which the appropriate prices for the efficient provision of insurance exist.

In his rejoinder Arrow starts by briefly stating the analytical finding that Pauly presents and agreeing with him that in such a situation optimality will not be achieved: 'either by the competitive system or by an attempt by the government to simulate a perfectly competitive system' (Arrow, 1968: 537). But then he questions Pauly's 'exclusive emphasis' on market incentives. He notes that insurance with rationing would solve the problem and lists the following different ways rationing can take place:

> (1) there might be a detailed examination by the insurance company of individual cost items allowing those that are regarded 'normal' and disallowing others, where normality means roughly what would have been bought in the absence of insurance; (2) they may rely on the

> professional ethics of physicians not to prescribe a frivolously expensive cost of treatment, at least where the gain is primarily in comfort and luxury rather than in health improvements proper; (3) they may even, and this is not as absurd as Mr. Pauly seems to think, rely on the willingness of the individual to behave in accordance with some commonly accepted norms.
>
> (Arrow, 1968: 538)

This list is an explicit avowal of the neoclassical tension apparent in Arrow's original paper. While the first of the three reasons can be analysed within Pauly's narrow incentive framework, the following two cannot. Broader ethical and institutional factors that are drawn from observation and experience of the functioning of real healthcare services in society are the source of Arrow's critique. For Arrow shows the limits of this framework of analysis, as he writes:

> [t]he lesson of Mr. Pauly's paper is that the price system is intrinsically limited in scope by our inability to make factual distinctions needed for optimal pricing under uncertainty. Nonmarket controls, whether internalized as moral principles or externally imposed are to some extent essential for efficiency.
>
> (Arrow, 1968: 538)

Unlike the previous debate, the Arrow vs. Pauly controversy cannot be analysed simply as an ideological disagreement, although they do occupy different sides of the ideological spectrum. A deeper philosophical divide separates the two authors, despite their reliance on a common technical toolbox to articulate their arguments. Pauly follows what was to become the standard mainstream approach by decontextualising the analytical framework and producing a model of moral hazard that is specifically defined, formally precise and highly portable between different real world applications. Arrow, on the other hand, refuses to ignore the complexity and openness of a real healthcare system when addressing problems of allocation and the real distribution. As a result the technical apparatus of modern economics can only take him so far and he recognises its weaknesses and limits when he faces them.

This exchange is also an early indication of the changes that would eventually lead to the dominance of a modern mainstream in which the scientific status of economics is judged purely on methodological grounds. This is evident in the disagreement between Arrow and Pauly on the relevance of ethics in the analysis of human conduct. In the coda of his response, Arrow writes:

> [o]ne of the characteristics of a successful economic system is that the relations of trust and confidence between principal and agent are

sufficiently strong so that the agent will not cheat even though it may be 'rational economic behaviour' to do so. The lack of such confidence has certainly been adduced by many writers as one cause of economic backwardness.

(Arrow, 1968: 538)

Marshall – the archetypal neoclassical in both Veblen's and Lawson's terms – wrote the following in the first chapter of his *Principles on Economics* on the advances of modern society:

> [m]odern methods of trade imply habits of trustfulness on the one side and a power or resisting temptation and dishonesty on the other, which do not exist among a backward people ... Adulteration and fraud in trade were rampant in the middle ages to an extent that is very astonishing, when we consider the difficulties of wrong-doing without detection at that time.
>
> (Marshall, 1890: 18)

Arrow and Marshall clearly share an ontological perspective that links economic behaviour to broader social processes and aims to extend beyond the limits imposed by their reliance on deductive techniques.

Pauly, in contradistinction, was looking ahead to how economic theory was to develop in subsequent decades. He returned to healthcare markets in 1970 in an article that further developed the concept of moral hazard by analysing 'different varieties' of this problem in healthcare and other types of insurance (Pauly, 1970). In this paper he finds that a price of zero creates all kinds of distortions in a market system, but notes that interventions that appropriately alter incentives may have a positive effect in the market. More importantly, 1970 is a watershed date for economic theory, because it marks the publication of Akerlof's celebrated 'market for lemons' article (Akerlof, 1970). Akerlof not only cites Arrow (1963) but starts his article by noting that: 'this paper presents a struggling attempt to give structure to the statement: "Business in underdeveloped countries is difficult"; in particular, a structure is given for determining the economic costs of dishonesty' (Akerlof, 1970: 488). While this seems to be an allusion to the literature that Arrow was also pointing at in his response to Pauly, it becomes quickly apparent that the terms of the discussion have changed. The basic problem is one of information between different market participants and Akerlof rigorously shows that asymmetries of information create all types of problems for efficient market interaction. Even dishonesty is treated in informational terms; if purchasers know who the dishonest sellers are, there would be no inefficiencies in the market. In fact, Akerlof returns to the problem of public healthcare, and adds the following observation to the Arrow vs. Pauly discussion:

He [Arrow] emphasizes 'moral hazard' rather than 'adverse selection'. In the strict sense 'moral hazard' is equally disadvantageous for both governmental and private programs; in its broader sense which includes 'adverse selection', 'moral hazard' gives a decided advantage to government insurance programs.

(Akerlof, 1970: 493)

Akerlof is ideologically on the same side as Arrow, favouring government insurance programs. However, he uses Pauly's mainstream framework to make his argument and leaves behind him the neoclassical tension we located in Arrow (1963). The idealised market system in which informational problems do not exist is the measuring rod not only for any existing market but also for any government intervention. What Pauly identified as a behavioural response – a 'rational reaction' by agents – thus received its final transformation and subsequent standardisation into an informational problem. This pushed any discussion of social norms and their ethical underpinnings into the background, as economics established itself on new ground, which encompassed the whole ideological spectrum by distancing it from real world problems.

Becoming a classic: the next 40 years

Arrow's paper on medical care is one of the most heavily cited papers ever published by *The American Economic Review*. As an indication of its success, it has 1,528 articles citing it in the web of science core collection and more than 6,000 in Google scholar (search on 6 February 2015). It was also chosen as one of the 20 most important articles published in *The American Economic Review* in its first 100 years. Furthermore, it has not only became a key text in economic theory, but it is also widely cited by academics and policymakers in a number of other fields, including law, sociology, political science, health policy and insurance. In fact, as Mark Peterson shows, while in the first decade of its publication it held greater significance for economists, by the 1990s it had become a focus of attention for non-economists as well (Peterson, 2001: 825).

The neoclassical tension apparent throughout the paper explains both its early success within economics and its enduring influence in the other social sciences and policy circles. It is beyond the scope of this section to describe the whole interdisciplinary literature that follows Arrow's (1963) article. Surveys on the impact of Arrow's article in a variety of fields can be found in Vol. 25, No. 5, of the *Journal of Health Politics, Policy and Law* published in October 2001. There an array of articles by leading scholars in their fields is joined with a forward by Mark Pauly and a postscript by Arrow, giving a more complete view of the impact Arrow's article had across disciplines including economics in its first 40 years since publication. However, for our purposes, it is sufficient to point out that, while social scientists who were unhampered by the ontological limitations of the economic method took a variety of different messages from Arrow's article, the economic use of his arguments has been much more limited.

Arrow is generally seen as providing a pioneering and influential analysis of healthcare, but among economists he is generally cited as the source of the modern conceptualisation of a type of market failure. In this context, his introduction of the idea of moral hazard has been extremely influential and it is as a forerunner of the moral hazard and asymmetric information literature that the article is principally remembered in mainstream economics today.[8] In other words, it is principally Pauly's interpretation of Arrow's paper that has dominated economics. The neoclassical tension that Arrow clearly struggled with when beginning the economic analysis of healthcare, has been set aside. Instead Arrow's paper is now seen as a necessary but incremental stage in the 'progressive' mainstream project of transforming health economics into a formal subfield populated by microeconomic models of asymmetric information. The committee that chose the top 20 articles ever published in *The American Economic Review* makes this last point explicitly:

> This paper provided a framework for thinking about the economics of the market for medical care using the language and tools of modern microeconomics. It argued that the aforementioned market is beset by market failures because consumers are exposed to risks that are not fully insurable (in large part due to problems of moral hazard), and because they lack the information and expertise required to assess risks and treatments. It hypothesized that various salient features of the institutions governing the provision of medical care are best understood as social adaptations aimed at redressing the resulting inefficiencies. It also noted that in some cases those institutional adaptations undermine competition and perversely contribute to inefficiency. Though written well prior to the emergence of the formal literature on asymmetric information, the paper anticipated many of the central issues that continue to occupy health economists today.
> (Arrow *et al.*, 2011: 2)

A more eclectic and partial way to see how the paper entered the canon of mainstream economics is to observe that it has been cited in three Nobel laureate lectures: those of Kenneth Arrow, James Mirlees and Joseph Stiglitz. This, in itself, is remarkable enough, as none of these Nobel Prizes were particularly related to developments in the healthcare market. However, in all three cases it is the wider ramifications of the abstract findings of the paper that make it key in the literature that these lectures survey. First, Kenneth Arrow himself mentioned the paper in his 1972 lecture, when discussing general equilibrium and uncertainty, noting that 'moral hazard' is a problem when you have unobservable behaviour and insurance.

He then writes: 'I would hold that the allocational difficulties arising from the inequality in information are of importance in such diverse fields as medical care and racial discrimination' (Arrow, 1974: 269) before referring to the (1963) article. Then, James Mirlees in 1996 devotes a section of his lecture on moral hazard, and after defining the concept notes: 'Medical care has been regarded as a prime example in the economics literature, perhaps surprisingly' (Mirrlees, 1997: 1323) before referring both to Arrow (1963) and Pauly (1968). Finally, Joseph Stiglitz devotes a section of his lecture on 'Sharecropping and the general theory of incentives', arguing that with imperfect information, people's incentives became a problem. Therefore: 'the adverse effect of insurance on incentives to avoid the insured-against contingency is referred to as moral hazard' (Stiglitz, 2002: 465). In a footnote he notes that the concept comes from insurance literature and adds: 'Not taking appropriate care [when having insurance] was thought to be "immoral"; hence the name' (Stiglitz, 2002: 465, footnote 10) before referring to Arrow's work (Arrow, 1963; 1965a) as an important precursor for the literature on moral hazard that followed.

This short history illuminates how mainstream economics integrated Arrow's work with developments in economic theory over the next 50 years. Pauly in his forward of a special issue of the *Journal of Health Politics, Policy and Law*, celebrating in 2001 almost 40 years of Arrow's article, eloquently writes:

> The introduction to health economics of the topic of moral hazard ignited a firestorm of interest in the impact of insurance on the process of care, with both theoretical and empirical dimensions. The major empirical topic was the measurement of the extent of moral hazard, and the major theoretical question was how that magnitude would affect the ideal design of an insurance policy that relied on patient cost-sharing to limit medical spending.
>
> (Pauly, 2001: 830)

This research agenda persists to this day as economists continue to explore the empirical and theoretical complications of the problem of incentives in markets with different varieties of imperfect information (see, e.g. Einav *et al.*, 2013).

Conclusion

We began our argument by noting that Tony Lawson's reinterpretation of neoclassicism provides much needed clarity to the discussion about what neoclassical economics is and how and when we should use the term. This clarity comes at a price insofar as the critique of modern economic theorising is concerned, because it would essentially define neoclassicism through its deficiencies and hence it could be seen as an attempt to pathologise neoclassical economists. As Lawson notes, it would also necessarily lead to the reclassification of many heterodox economists as 'neoclassical'. In the preceding chapter, we have set aside these concerns without wishing to deny their importance. This is because we intended to explore an under-researched corollary of Lawson's argument. When applied to the question of the transformation of economic thought in the twentieth century, Lawson's revised conception of neoclassicism has important uses and yields novel insights. Our example, drawing on the history of healthcare economics, seeks to illustrate this. First, we have demonstrated that interpreting Arrow's 1963 paper as suffering from 'neoclassical tension' is crucial to understanding the debates that emerged after it was published, but also important in placing this contribution in the canon of neoclassical theory that preceded it. Second, we have shown that by mapping the key differences between mainstream economics and neoclassicism we can similarly illuminate our understanding of the appropriation, formalisation and development of Arrow's ideas by subsequent theorists. Thus we demonstrate that this distinction can be used to analyse an important chapter in the history of economic analysis, the post-war transition from neoclassical theory to mainstream model building.

Notes

1 For consistency with the rest of the chapter we use throughout this section the term healthcare instead of medical care. It is important here to note that Arrow explicitly avoided the term healthcare in his original contribution, noting that his article is about the conditions of providing medical coverage to individuals. In his opening paragraph he stresses that there are many factors that influence health and medical coverage is only one of them, but that that is what he intends to investigate (Arrow, 1963: 941). This may be seen as another example of the neoclassical tension in Arrow's article. Nevertheless, economists today use healthcare to denote this field of economic analysis and for consistency we also follow this use.
2 He defines conditions of certainty as: 'consumers are presumed to be able to distinguish qualities of the commodities they buy' (Arrow, 1963: 956).
3 This is noted by G. C. Harcourt who attended the seminar. Private correspondence with the authors.
4 There is also a contribution by Vincent Boland (1965), challenging some of the technical outcomes of the (Lees and Rice, 1965) comment, but his contribution is peripheral to our analysis here, other than an indication of how widely Arrow's original paper and subsequent comments were read by the academic community.
5 Pauly mentions reactions like 'hypochondria' and 'outright fraud' as issues that concern insurance writers (see Pauly, 1968: 535).
6 Importantly, shame or other emotions are not taken into account, although even someone who is committed to developing and using this type of mechanistic framework of analysis may argue that this influences the implicit price of 'freely' provided healthcare, so that prices do not have to go exactly to zero.

7 In this example Pauly is actually echoing what Arrow originally wrote in his 1963 article (see Arrow, 1963: 962), where surgery is viewed as less subject to moral hazard than GP prescriptions are. However, this occurs for different reasons. Arrow stresses third-party supervision during surgery, whereas Pauly stresses the elasticity of demand for the particular good.
8 But not exclusively. For example, Newhouse's (1970) frequently cited article deals with a theory of non-profit institutions, by presenting an economic model of a hospital and this follows one of the insights found in Arrow (1963). But on the whole, it is safe to say that these other strands of research are nowhere near in volume and influence in comparison to the moral hazard literature.

References

Akerlof, G. A. (1970) The market for 'lemons': Quality uncertainty and the market mechanism. *The Quarterly Journal of Economics* 84(3): 488–500.

Arrow, K. J. (1963) Uncertainty and the welfare economics of medical care. *The American Economic Review* 53(5): 941–973.

Arrow, K. J. (1965a) *Aspects of the Theory of Risk-Bearing (Yrjo Jahnsson Lectures)*. Helsinki, Finland: Yrjo Jahnssonin Saatio.

Arrow, K. J. (1965b) Uncertainty and the welfare economics of medical care: Reply (The implications of transaction costs and adjustment lags). *The American Economic Review* 55(1/2): 154–158.

Arrow, K. J. (1968) The economics of moral hazard: Further comment. *The American Economic Review* 58(3): 537–539.

Arrow, K. J. (1974) General economic equilibrium: Purpose, analytic techniques, collective choice. *The American Economic Review* 64(3): 253–272.

Arrow, K. J., Bernheim, B. D., Feldstein, M. S., Macfadden, D. L., Poterba, J. M. and Solow, R. M. (2011) 100 years of 'The American Economic Review': The top 20 articles. *The American Economic Review* 101(1): 1–8.

Baird, C. W. (1970) A proposal for financing the purchase of health services. *The Journal of Resources* 5(1): 89–105.

Ball, D. S. and Wilson, J. W. (1968) Community health facilities and services: The manpower dimensions. *American Journal of Agricultural Economics* 50(5): 1208–1222.

Boland, V. F. (1965) Uncertainty and the welfare economics of medical care: Comment. *The American Economic Review* 55(5): 1172–1173.

Crew, M. (1969) Coinsurance and the welfare economics of medical care. *The American Economic Review* 59(5): 906–908.

Diamond, P. A. (1967) The role of a stock market in a general equilibrium model with technological uncertainty. *The American Economic Review* 57(4): 759–776.

Einav, L., Finkelstein, A., Ryan S. P., Schrimpf, P. and Cullen, M. R. (2013) Selection on moral hazard in health insurance. *The American Economic Review* 103(1): 178–219.

Feldstein, M. S. (1970) The rising price of physician's services. *The Review of Economics and Statistics* 52(2): 121–133.

Foldes, L. (1967) Income redistribution in money and in kind. *Economica* 34(133): 30–41.

Friedman, M. (1953) The methodology of positive economics, in *Essays in Positive Economics*. Chicago, IL: Chicago University Press, pp. 3–43.

Latsis, J. and Repapis, C. (2014) A model intervenes: The many faces of moral hazard. *Cambridge Journal of Economics* 38(4): 743–760.

Lawson, T. (2013) What is this 'school' called neoclassical economics? *Cambridge Journal of Economics* 37(5): 947–983. Also published in this book as Chapter 1, and page numbers cited refer to those in this book.

Lees, D. S. (1962) The logic of the British National Health Service. *Journal of Law and Economics* 5: 111–118.

Lees, D. S. and Rice, R. G. (1965) Uncertainty and the welfare economics of medical care: Comment. *The American Economic Review* 55(1/2): 140–154.

Lindsay, C. M. (1969) Medical care and the economics of sharing. *Economica* 36(144): 351–362.

Marshall, A. (1890) *Principles of Economics*. London, UK: Macmillan.

Mirrlees, J. A. (1997) Information and incentives: The economics of carrots and sticks. *The Economic Journal* 107(444): 1311–1329.

Newhouse, J. P. (1970) Toward a theory of nonprofit institutions: An economic model of a hospital. *The American Economic Review* 60(1): 64–74.

Pashigian, B. P., Schkade, L. L., Menefee, G. H. (1966) The selection of an optimal deductible for a given insurance policy. *The Journal of Business* 39(1): 35–44.

Pauly, M. V. (1968) The economics of moral hazard: Comment. *The American Economic Review* 58(3): 531–537.

Pauly, M. V. (1970) The welfare economics of community rating. *The Journal of Risk and Insurance* 37(3): 407–418.

Pauly, M. V. (2001) Forward. *Journal of Health Politics, Policy and Law* 26(5): 829–834.

Peterson, M. A. (2001) Kenneth Arrow and the changing economics of health care. *Journal of Health Politics, Policy and Law* 26(5): 823–828.

Stiglitz, J. E. (2002) Information and the change in the paradigm in economics. *The American Economic Review* 92(3): 460–501.

Veblen, T. (1900) The preconceptions of economic science III. *Quarterly Journal of Economics* 14(2): 240–269.

Williamson, O. E., Olson, D. G. and Ralston, A. (1967) Externalities, insurance, and disability analysis. *Economica* 34(135): 235–253.

3 Neoclassicism, critical realism and the Cambridge methodological tradition[1]

Sheila Dow

Introduction

Tony Lawson (Chapter 1) has made a significant contribution by putting the category 'neoclassical' under the spotlight and by considering its relevance both for orthodox economics and for heterodox economics. The term has for a long time been applied generally to mainstream economics, but lately has not seemed a good fit, or is being used in very different ways, leading to its falling into relative disuse. Lawson's (Chapter 1) paper invites us to contemplate a specific use of the term (inspired by Veblen) and to consider how that meaning relates both to the mainstream and to heterodox economics. He concludes that the most useful configuration is three categories: orthodox economics, heterodox economics and neoclassical economics, which is in a state of tension between the first two. Lawson's focus continues to be to address the problems with mainstream economics: 'the real source of the discipline's problems is the very emphasis on mathematical modelling that defines the mainstream, an emphasis that usually results in formulations implicitly constrained to be consistent with a deficient social ontology' (Lawson, Chapter 1: 37). The particular motivation for attempting to clarify further categorisations is that: 'the slack use of the category "neoclassical" economics hinders effective critique' (Lawson, Chapter 1: 35).

The classification draws on Lawson's distinction between closed and open systems applied to the subject matter and to its analysis: the underlying ontology and the methodology employed, respectively. Lawson's (1997) particular definition of a closed social system is that it is characterised by empirical regularities with respect to events.[2] These regularities are the manifestations of uniformities, which can be identified by deductive, axiomatic logic expressed in formal mathematical modelling. An open social system, on the other hand, is complex and evolving in a way that does not yield either axioms or laws, which can be taken as universally true. Rather it consists of multiple causal tendencies, which do not normally generate event regularities and whose character and interrelationships differ in time and space in a non-deterministic manner. Formal deductive mathematics is therefore an unsuitable methodology for analysing open systems, although some formal mathematical argument may contribute alongside other methods.

Lawson's (Chapter 1) categorisation of economics is defined in terms of these distinctions: orthodox economics professes a closed-system methodology, implying a closed-system ontology, while heterodox economics professes an open-system ontology and therefore an open-system methodology. Neoclassical economics involves the contradiction of an open-system ontology alongside a closed-system methodology. He argues:

> The most coherent interpretation of neoclassical economics is of an inconsistent stance of: (1) recognising the historical processual ontology of unfolding causal sequence at the level of events; whilst (2) simultaneously seeking to combine this recognition with a taxonomic orientation in the form of deductivism at the level of method that is inappropriate to it. That is, I suggest that interpreted most coherently, the category designates a deep tension, the very one that the currently loose usage of the term serves to mask.
> (Lawson, Chapter 1: 66)

If only this contradiction could be addressed, it is implied, economics could settle properly into a duality of orthodoxy/heterodoxy reflecting closed/open-system ontologies respectively. Of course, the critical realist argument includes a justification of the belief that social ontology must conform to an open system; the purpose of Lawson (1997) was therefore to point to the contradiction between the only justifiable (open-system) social ontology and the closed-system methodology of orthodox economics. Addressing this contradiction would require all of economics to employ an open-system methodology based on an open-system ontology.

The new focus on a contradiction between an open-system ontology and a closed-system methodology has particular relevance for new developments in mainstream economics, which fall into Lawson's neoclassical category, making it clear in what sense they differ from heterodox economics. Behavioural economics is a case in point, where efforts are made to build on the understanding of real behavioural processes, and yet the compulsion is to tailor this understanding to modifications to the traditional axiomatic structure (Dow, 2013). Lawson (2009) has already pointed to the ontology-methodology inconsistency in well-meaning efforts to put forward alternative explanations of the crisis by developing alternative models (Lawson, 2009). But compared with the contribution of Lawson's definition of neoclassical economics for our understanding of mainstream economics, the much more important and controversial argument in my view is that a significant portion of heterodox economics should be classified as neoclassical. In posing this challenge, Lawson (Chapter 1: 65) aims to address the 'debilitating' stand-off between orthodox and heterodox modellers who share an open-system ontology, and to do this by arguing for attention to methodological issues.

Lawson had earlier effectively equated heterodoxy with critical realism, defining it as follows: 'it is an appraisal that mathematical methods are mostly inappropriate to social analysis that ultimately underpins the heterodox opposition. In short, I am contending that the essence of the heterodox opposition is ontological in nature' (Lawson, 2006: 493). But he proceeded to note that this social ontology is often implicit. In this more recent article Lawson (Chapter 1) argues that the cost of not making heterodox ontology explicit has been that the implications for methodology in many cases have not been taken on board:

> In fact, a good deal of sustained heterodox research is couched in conceptual frameworks consistent with the sort of causal-processual ontological conception just described. All too often, however, this goes hand in hand with a lack of realisation that methods of mathematical modelling require formulations that are in severe tension with this ontology.
> (Lawson, Chapter 1: 39)

A particular constituency of heterodox economics to whom this argument is relevant is those who see philosophical and methodological argument as a distraction; of these, many may not in fact use orthodox methodology, but the challenge to them too is to be methodologically aware, and to articulate and defend one's philosophical and methodological position. The argument which has long been addressed to mainstream economists by Lawson (among others) on the importance of philosophical and methodological awareness, is here being addressed also to heterodox economists.

The specific argument that many heterodox economists are 'neoclassical' is challenging, and is more difficult for the reader to address, because of the absence of concrete examples. We will address it here first in general terms, by focusing on the whole business of classification. We will explore the issues raised by classification being used as an epistemological tool, and its further roles with respect to ontology and as a rhetorical tool. These issues are particularly important for critical realism because of its stance on boundaries, and even more important given Lawson's adoption of Veblen's term for mainstream methodology: 'taxonomic'. In order to address these issues, we then consider Lawson's argument against the backdrop of the Cambridge tradition as a way of trying to make the issues more concrete.

The nature and role of classifications of economics

Lawson's three-way classification of economics is novel, compared to the conventional two-way classification between mainstream/orthodox economics and heterodox economics. It encourages reflection on the nature of all such classifications. In particular, there seems to be a tension between the urge to classify (most clearly in the critical realist version of the distinction between closed-system and open-system approaches), implying boundaries, and the critical realist form of open-system thinking, which aims to avoid thinking in terms of boundaries. There is a substantive question as to whether the boundaries Lawson sets up by his categorisation are illuminating or whether they gloss over the possibility of other categorisations (such as theoretical content; see Fine, Chapter 8, this volume). But we focus here on the prior question as to the function and implications of classification itself, which applies also to the previous two-way classification (see further, Mearman, 2012).

The urge to classify is the key defining characteristic of what Foucault (1991 [1966], 1992 [1969]) called the classical episteme, or the age of representation. Classification arose from a separation (atomisation) of elements of what had previously, in the age of resemblance, been understood as parts of an organic whole (Vigo de Lima, 2010). While in the age of resemblance knowledge was drawn from history and the emphasis was on connections, in the age of representation knowledge was regarded as universal and the emphasis was on distinctions; the resulting taxonomies were based on resemblance within categories, but distinctions between them. Tellingly, Foucault identified Hume and Smith as being on the cusp of the transition from the age of resemblance to the modern episteme, the age of representation, i.e. as retaining aspects of the older episteme (see further, Dow, 2009). Thus for Smith (1980 [1795]) new theories arise from seeing new patterns among observed phenomena, i.e. the making of new connections in the imagination (Loasby, 2003). But, rather than theoretical patterns being taxonomic, their value was primarily psychological and their form could be expected to change according to context: knowledge was provisional, in that further new patterns might emerge as history unfolded. But as the age of representation proceeded and classical economics developed, the tendency to seek universal theories became more marked and Hume and Smith's approach was largely misunderstood from that new perspective.[3]

Some classification is inevitable – it is inherent in language itself. But Foucault referred to different conceptions of classification, which can help us understand Veblen's depiction of the mainstream/classical approach as 'taxonomic' as corresponding to Foucault's 'classical' representation by means of classification. The categories of the age of resemblance were more fluid, evolving over time, and the distinctions were more porous and vague, corresponding to the 'modern' approach to classification discussed by Mearman (2012). It also corresponds to Keynes's epistemology, where vagueness was a virtue of the human logic he developed to address an open system (Coates, 1996; Davis, 1999). Lawson (Chapter 1: 32) does note that there can sometimes be virtue in 'loose' use of terminology ('(lexical) ambiguity'). Nevertheless the purpose of the article is to offer a clear, consistent category of neoclassical economics for general application:

> Few categories remain entirely fixed in their meaning over time. However, there is a sense in which those that prove helpful evolve systematically in the light of new understandings, changing conditions and evolving related needs. This is a case of (the broader notion of) developmental consistency.
>
> (Lawson, Chapter 1: 33)

Thus Lawson draws on Veblen for a category for modern application. He aims for precision in his definition of neoclassical economics on the grounds that a loose use of the term has inhibited understanding. This precision of categorisation is a characteristic of the dualistic thinking typical of mainstream economics (Dow, 1990); Lawson seeks to introduce a tripartite division to replace the orthodox-heterodox dual, but the critique of dualism can apply equally to three: 'all-encompassing, mutually-exclusive categories with fixed meanings' rather than two. In developing and refining the concept of duals, Mearman (2005) criticises the critical realist form of the closed-system/open-system dual on grounds which cut across Lawson's (Chapter 1) argument. Thus Davis (2009) argues against the use of fixed categories for economics, while Mearman (2011) argues against the 'rhetoric of distinction'. The closed-system/open-system distinction need not in fact be dualistic. Chick and Dow (2012 [2005]) consider closed and open systems in non-dualistic terms by setting out the conditions, which all have to be met by a closed system, while there is a range of possibilities for systems to be open because any one condition (or combination of conditions) has not been met. Mearman's analysis (building on Mearman, 2005) suggests that a useful approach would be to classify along a spectrum between poles.[4]

As an open-system thinker, we would expect Lawson to employ categories in the sense of the age of resemblance, i.e. categories which are vague, evolving and whose boundaries may shift over time. Certainly there has been evolution and the identification of new boundaries in the form of his exploration of Veblen's understanding of neoclassicism as an additional category. But the classification of these boundaries is anything but vague – it is crystal clear in the distinction between a closed-system ontology and an open-system ontology. Further it is a new classification which, rather than being mutable, can be applied across the history of heterodox economics as well as orthodox economics. It is a continuing refrain from orthodox economists in response to heterodox critiques that the mainstream has evolved in ways that are not being accounted for. Yet Lawson has always argued persuasively that his critique continues to hold. Has he in fact developed a taxonomy of economics?

The key distinction for Lawson is between theorising which is consistent with open-system social reality, and orthodox theorising, which is only consistent with a closed-system reality (which Lawson, as a heterodox economist, argues is a fiction). The open-system/closed-system classification is treated as an absolute, i.e. taxonomic; only once the distinction (with its methodological implications) is recognised, as Lawson advocates, will economics conform to a heterodox-orthodox duality. The distinction is maintained by Lawson (2004) in response to the argument that differences between heterodox schools of thought derive from (open-system) ontological differences within a non-dualistic structure (Dow, 2004). Nevertheless, while Lawson aims for philosophical precision with respect to the definition of heterodox economics as a whole, he employs non-taxonomic categorisation in his treatment of schools of thought within heterodox economics, defining them in a loose, open-ended way in terms of 'ontological commitment'.

Where the ontological difference between orthodoxy and heterodoxy bites is at the methodological level. The methodological implication of a closed-system approach is the reliance, indeed insistence, on deductive mathematical formulation of theory amenable (even if only in principle) to empirical testing. The ontological implication is that the economy is characterised by event regularities, which are the manifestation of universal laws. The focus of Lawson (Chapter 1) is the argument that some heterodox economists adopt this methodological stance in spite of espousing an open-system ontology. Lawson has been careful to argue (as did Keynes) that a pluralistic, open-system methodology can include mathematics. It is the *insistence* that arguments be expressed mathematically, and that this mathematics has a deductivist structure (built on supposedly universally true axioms), which is problematic because such formulations cannot correspond to an open-system reality. This is the key inconsistency – between theorising and reality – which critical realism addresses.

But mathematics can be used for partial analysis; a mathematical model is a closed system in the sense that only certain variables are considered and their interrelationships assumed to take a particular form. But the boundaries of the closed system can be mutable, in application to different contexts, and vague, allowing a range of meanings (as in 'the' rate of interest, for example). Accordingly, the assumptions are likely to differ from one partial analysis to another, standing in the way of a deductive, axiomatic structure. Keynes advocated mathematics only for expressing partial logical arguments contributing to a wider analysis, but not for quantification, and certainly not for quantitative prediction.

But, if we are talking about *insistence* on deductivist mathematics and the *extent* to which an argument is mathematical and deductivist, we are getting away from absolute distinctions and into matters of degree. There seems to be a parallel between an extension of Lawson's discussion on ontology and Keynes on probability; in the latter case, the earlier understanding of Keynesian uncertainty in dualistic terms relative to certainty has given way to a more complex understanding of shifting degrees of uncertainty between the poles of certainty and complete ignorance.[5] Is it still satisfactory to understand closed-system theorising and methodology in dualistic terms, or is it time to move on? Again it could be argued that it is an empirical question how far mainstream economists and heterodox economists insist on deductivist mathematical formulations of theory. But, again for Lawson, it would be a matter of definition: where this insistence is associated with a closed-system ontology we have orthodox economics; where it is associated with an open-system ontology we have neoclassical economics.

How far mathematical formulations account for the full argument could also be seen as an empirical question. But to consider how far this could be a matter of definition raises issues with respect to the structure of argument, for which we turn now to questions of rhetoric.

Classification and rhetoric

The rhetoric literature has provided empirical evidence on the form and content of argument in relation to professed methodology (Klamer, 1983; McCloskey, 1985 were the pioneering texts in modern times). In particular, McCloskey drew the distinction between the (closed-system) official discourse of mainstream economics and the (open-system) unofficial discourse. The evident need for this unofficial discourse demonstrates the inconclusive nature of closed-system argumentation, consistent with an open-system ontology (and evident similarly in the failure of the Bourbaki project to build a complete, closed mathematical system). Even in articles apparently relying on formal, deductivist reasoning, other forms of reasoning are shown to be used as rhetorical devices, designed to persuade as to the meaning and credentials of the formal argument. It may be that awareness of the range of methods actually employed informally by mainstream economists has allowed them to brush off accusations of closed-system thinking. Lawson (Chapter 1) has now addressed the incidence of a tension between a professed open-system ontology and closed-system methodology among heterodox economists as well as orthodox economists. But the rhetoric literature has already pointed to a tension among mainstream economists between a professed closed-system methodology and an open-system methodology in practice. This is a tension within methodology, which differs from the tension Lawson identifies with neoclassical economics, and follows from the need to theorise, communicate and persuade.

While the official discourse of orthodox economics purports to rely solely on formal modelling, it is clear in the official discourse of heterodox economics that formal modelling is only one among many methods employed in a pluralist methodology. The distinction between official and unofficial discourse in orthodox economics is not apparent in heterodox economics, since any formal mathematical reasoning tends to be only a contributor to argument. The other factor relates to the sociology of the discipline, which enforces closed-system methodology in the official discourse of economics as a whole. This sociology is critical for the type of knowledge generated, determining the methodology employed by publications in 'leading' journals and in funded research and thereby hiring practices and education. Thus the official mainstream discourse is propagated, and provides the context for heterodox economists and their methodology.

Rhetorical considerations are important for any discussion of classification and particularly any discussion of the meaning of neoclassicism and the term's fall from favour. Identifying mainstream economics as 'neoclassical' rather than 'economics' had implied a critical stance. I was told some time ago by a leading mainstream economist that he stopped reading anything once the term 'neoclassical' turned up, because he assumed it would be critical. Now it is a matter for debate whether heterodox economists should use the term 'mainstream' or 'orthodox' because of the different rhetorical force of each term.

Lawson's own work can be analysed from a rhetoric perspective. There is no question that Lawson has been tremendously persuasive among heterodox economists, convincing a high proportion about the importance of social ontology and its implications for methodology. It is inherent in Lawson's philosophical position that theorising cannot yield law-like truths, but rather expresses powers operative in generative mechanisms, such that persuasion is an integral element in successful argument. As Keynes (1973 [1934]: 470, emphasis in original) put it:

> In economics you cannot *convict* your opponent of error, you can only *convince* him of it. And, even if you are right, you cannot convince him, if there is a defect in your powers of persuasion and exposition or if his head is already so filled with contrary notions that he cannot catch the clues to your thought that you are trying to throw at him.

It has been argued above that Lawson builds up a clear-cut distinction between closed and open-system approaches, which seems somewhat inconsistent with his own non-taxonomic thinking. But we have to consider how far this distinction is being employed for rhetorical force and accounts for critical realism's success. There has over the last few decades been a steady building up of awareness among heterodox economists that their methodological approach is different from orthodoxy and that there are good reasons to justify that difference. Critical realism has provided a substantial philosophical foundation for this difference. How far has it been persuasive by posing a duality between orthodoxy and heterodoxy, supporting heterodoxy's growing sense of identity?

Some time ago, Lawson (2002) explicitly addressed the fact that his philosophy is expressed in a rationalistic manner, which seems at odds with critical realist philosophy:

> It must also be acknowledged that (essentially ontological) arguments of the sort sketched here and elaborated elsewhere (e.g. Lawson, 1997) are somewhat rationalistic, and that this especially always carries dangers. Although such arguments as I defend currently seem (to me) to be as sustainable as others with which they compete, they are of course fallible and partial, and may yet turn out to be quite dramatically wrong, at least in certain significant respects. It may be found that, on occasion, aspects of the social world after all approximate a closure, for example. Or new mathematical methods may yet be devised which are found to be (more) appropriate to open systems. Who knows?
>
> (Lawson, 2002: 80–81)

The rhetorical aspect within the current social structure of the discipline is then made explicit:

> The reason (rationalistic) ontological analysis remains so important at this juncture is just that such an evolutionary scientific process is currently blocked. Or rather the environment of selection is so determined that, for the time being, any flourishing (that is, widespread) practice must be of a mathematical form. Real progress, that is, in social understanding, is, in other words, undermined by the pervasive insistence in faculties of economics that the only (or almost only) permitted form of activity involves the wielding of mathematical models. It is this dogma, this constraint on evolutionary progress in knowledge, that makes the input from (somewhat rationalistic) ontology at this point so important.
>
> (Lawson, 2002: 81)

Lawson (Chapter 1: 65) makes explicit the rhetorical case for focusing on neoclassical economics as a vehicle for drawing attention to inconsistencies between ontology and methodology:

> My aim here, in reporting my findings, is, in the end partly rhetorical, namely, to point out that if coherence in use is required, then according to the seemingly most sustainable conception, many of those who use the term 'neoclassical' as an ill-defined term of abuse can be viewed ultimately as engaged in unwitting self-critique. But I am hoping, more fundamentally, that it is enough in this manner to communicate (in a yet further way) that in modern economics there prevails largely unrecognised a basic tension between ontology and method,

one that hinders serious attempts to overcoming the real problems of the discipline.

In using the term 'tension' (interchangeably with 'inconsistency'), Lawson may be intending to signal the meaning of consistency which accords with open-system thinking. While 'inconsistency' has a clear (classical logic) meaning within a closed system of thought, it is harder to identify within an open system of thought (Dow, 1990, 2014). When does difference, e.g. as between different strands of partial analysis, reveal a regrettable logical inconsistency, and when does it simply reflect the nature of a pluralist methodology? Even within orthodox economics, Weintraub (2002) argues that applied mathematics (characteristic of much of mainstream economics) inevitably involves inconsistencies, which pure mathematics (the method of pure mainstream theory) can avoid.

For Lawson the critical inconsistency is between methodology and reality. But this may not be so straightforward either. We therefore need to explore further what we need to look for when seeking out inconsistencies within otherwise apparently heterodox economics. Do the heterodox economists Lawson has in mind *insist* on deductive mathematical reasoning for their official and unofficial discourse, and is it regarded as sufficient for economic argument? As a limited empirical exercise, we turn now to the Cambridge tradition in economics for evidence on economic methodology and its philosophical underpinnings.

Classicism and neoclassicism at Cambridge

The difficulty in applying the classification suggested by Lawson to any economist or group of economists is evident as soon as we attempt to put it into practice. The examples in the history of thought literature are legion of disagreements as to how to interpret and categorise the methodological approach of leading figures. The history of economics at Cambridge is an interesting case in point, not least because of Martins' (2013) exercise in pulling out features in the history of economic thought at Cambridge, which allow him to identify a Cambridge tradition stemming from Ricardo, through Marx, and built up by Marshall, Keynes, Sraffa, Sen, and (at the philosophical level) by Lawson's critical realism. The argument is that there has been a consistency of approach, applied at different levels (see further, Dow forthcoming). Yet Lawson, following Veblen, identifies the classical approach, on which the mainstream has built, with Ricardo. Martins (chapter 6, this volume) challenges this treatment of Ricardo and classical economics. The categorisation of Marshall is equally contentious; while Martins, following Harcourt (2012 [2003]: 201), sees Marshall as the initiator of the Cambridge tradition, which includes critical realism, Lawson follows Veblen in categorising him as neoclassical.

For Lawson, the litmus test is whether or not an economist insists on formal deductivist mathematics and regards such argument as sufficiently demonstrative: the characteristics of a closed-system methodology. The view of formal mathematical argument being necessary and sufficient follows from deductivism. But it is so in the sense that it is regarded as a superior 'language' by which to express deductive logic. We know from the history of mathematics and from the economic rhetoric literature that mathematical argument is not in fact sufficient; it is necessarily accompanied by other forms of argument. This renders formalist deductivism incoherent as a positive methodology. Where the insistence on formal mathematical treatment has greatest impact is rather, as Lawson points out, in its negative form: the view that non-mathematical argument does not meet methodological requirements for good theory.

There has been a common thread within Cambridge of objections to this view, beginning with Malthus's critique of Ricardo's methodology on ontological grounds (Cremaschi and Dascal, 1996), such that Malthus would seem to fit into the heterodox category better than Ricardo. Marshall explicitly demoted the mathematical method by confining mathematical derivations to footnotes. He wrote to his protégé, J. N. Keynes, as follows: 'I take an extreme position as to the *method & scope* of economics. In my new book I say of *methods* simply that economics has to use every method known to science' (emphasis in original, as quoted by Groenewegen, 1995: 415). Yet J. N. Keynes himself arguably actively (even if inadvertently) promoted deductivism in the Millian tradition (Deane, 1983, 2008). Veblen identified Marshall and J. N. Keynes as the best (in the sense of least contradictory) examples of neoclassical economists by his definition, both displaying open-system ontological positions, while using the deductive mathematical method. But this is inconsistent with what Marshall himself said about his methodology. He certainly facilitated others in building up a deductive mathematical structure, but he himself did not insist on it. This unresolved contradiction in Marshall has long been understood to explain his inability to produce the second volume of the (1890) *Principles of Economics*. Indeed Lawson's hesitation to apply his own criterion strictly is evident in the following passage:

> In short, a feature of contributions of both Keynes and Marshall that is significant with regard to the sorts of issues that interest Veblen is a *tension bordering upon inconsistency*. It is a tension between method and ontology/metaphysics (or more accurately between the ontological presuppositions of taxonomic method and a causal-processual social ontology).
>
> (Lawson, Chapter 1: 52, emphasis added)

In contrast to his father and to Marshall, J. M. Keynes, consistently and repeatedly discussed the problems with insistence on deductivist mathematical formulation, on ontological grounds, in a manner consistent with the methodology he himself employed. Keynes therefore fits clearly into the heterodox category and indeed his philosophy has provided inspiration for critical realism. Yet he used mathematical expression at times, as an exercise in logic, rather than with a view to quantification. The aim was not to establish laws (confirmed by repeated instances) since the organic nature of the socio-economic system could not yield them. Similarly, he did not rule out quantitative analysis as such but rather, in his debates with Tinbergen, explored the conditions, which would need to be met in order for econometric analysis to be warranted (O'Donnell, 1997).

But how are we to classify those who came after Keynes? Arguably the 'circus' around Keynes found it difficult to break away from Pigovian deductivism (Ambrosi, 2003). For example, even by the time of the capital controversies, Joan Robinson appeared to accept the mainstream positivist methodology in that she aimed her critique at the realism of assumptions and the internal consistency of its logic. The controversy came to be epitomised for many by the 'reswitching' problem, which demonstrated by means of deductivist mathematical reasoning that capital and its return need not be inversely related (Harcourt, 1972). Similarly Sraffa expressed his critique of mainstream economics in terms of a formal mathematical system, albeit one which differed from mainstream marginalist analysis and which aimed to avoid fictional assumptions (Velupillai, 2008). Since both Robinson and Sraffa professed an open-system ontology, are they therefore neoclassical by Lawson's definition? On the other hand, while Hahn clearly employed a formal deductivist mathematical methodology, he could also be said to have had an open-system ontology in (at times) arguing that formal general equilibrium had no real-world counterpart; the mathematics was to be a matter of logic rather than quantification (see e.g. Hahn, 1985). His mathematics was quintessentially deductivist, but was he too neoclassical?[6]

It is clearly important to explore what we mean by 'deductive mathematics'; Martins (2013) in particular makes much of the significance of different types of mathematics, beginning with Newton. For Newton it was important that mathematical argument correspond to real experience, building on common sense understandings, so he relied on classical geometry as separate from arithmetic. Rather than separating induction and deduction, however, he combined the two in a process of abduction whereby hypotheses were derived from the operation of the mind on observation and then exposed to further observation. The result was provisional principles rather than universal laws. In contrast, Descartes applied deductive logic to fictional concepts (such as irrational numbers, infinity and points), to be tested against the enumeration of instances. While Newton relied on classical geometry as separate from arithmetic, Descartes combined the two in analytical geometry (Martins, 2013: chapter 5).

While for Newton geometrical argument related directly to real experience, the calculus did not necessarily have any real counterpart.

Keynes was to develop further the use of mathematics within a system of abductive logic, eschewing concepts without real-world correspondence, while the mainstream employed logical positivism with its clear separation between mathematical deduction, from unverified premises about rational optimising behaviour, and empirical testing. Keynes's deductions were applied rather to assumptions which were simplifications (based on 'stylised facts') rather than fictions (e.g. the falling marginal propensity to consume). As such the conclusions reached were provisional, depending on the persistence of the simplified relation, and conditional on other aspects of the system. The key was that an abductive approach is not capable of yielding a complete deductive system, so inevitably mathematical argument is bound to be only one of many methods to be used. Any formal model, even one which deduces a partial argument rather than a general argument on the basis of assumptions, is temporarily closed. But the point of abductive reasoning is that this closure is temporary, yielding only provisional conclusions, which may change as the assumptions may be replaced. It made no sense in abductive logic to insist on mathematical expression in general, or to regard it as sufficient for argument. This stance has been continued at Cambridge, notably by Harcourt (2001 [1996]), with his 'horses for courses' approach and by Lawson with his critical realism.

But we have seen that what has been identified as a(n implicitly heterodox) Cambridge tradition, seems to have involved significant components of what Lawson defines as neoclassical economics. Any such discussion of a body of research, which has evolved over time, subject to a range of influences, is bound to be controversial such that there is scope for much disagreement as to what exactly is neoclassical in the Cambridge tradition. In a way that is the point. The triad has rhetorical force and poses good questions, but in such a categorical philosophical way that it is difficult to operationalise.

Conclusion

By opening up debate on the category of neoclassical economics, a coherent framing has been offered for discussing such subjects as the Cambridge tradition in economics, even though any conclusions on specific economists can only arise out of debate and possibly not even then. More widely, by drawing attention to ontological issues, Lawson invites further debate as to their implications, the nature of closed and open systems, and so on. I have engaged in similar exercises, with the same aim of promoting methodological awareness. In this commentary my aim has been to make a further contribution to the debate by approaching this new classification with a different framing – responding in kind to an exercise in open-system analysis.

This different framing has aimed at specific application of Lawson's new categorisation, resulting in a range of questions. In seeking to apply Lawson's classification to modern heterodox economics more widely, is it modelling that is an indicator of neoclassicism by Lawson's definition, or only deductivist modelling based on fictional assumptions and/or deductivist modelling as sufficient for argument? How far is the injunction against deductivist modelling open to misinterpretation as an injunction against all modelling? Mearman (2005) argues that the critical realist presentation of orthodoxy-heterodoxy as mutually exclusive has discouraged heterodox economists from employing mathematical modelling when it would, in fact, have been a useful contributor to theorising. By the same token, how far can the mainstream reject critical realist arguments more readily when these arguments are (mis?)interpreted as an anti-mathematics position?

Good rhetoric is persuasive; it appeals to many aspects of epistemology, including reason and evidence. Just as rational economic man is a fiction, so mainstream economists build knowledge on more than narrow rational argument, inevitably opening up possibilities for contradiction, which, in an open system of thought, need not necessarily be of concern (only a matter for argument and debate). The important contradiction for a policy-related subject to avoid is that with reality. But that too is a matter for argument if (as I would argue) there are different understandings of open-system reality. Where Lawson (2002) himself has admitted he needs to be careful is the scope for contradiction in using rationalist argument to counter rationalism. But, as Morgan (2015: 864) suggests, the rhetorical purpose here may well be more disruption than persuasion: 'every now and then, it is better to be the Sex Pistols than The Carpenters'. The way in which neoclassical heterodox economists take the argument will be different from mainstream reactions. But disruption needs to be followed through with further development of what exactly in particular modelling exercises is incompatible with open-system ontology, and whether the answer varies depending on the type of open-system ontology under consideration.

Having launched this salvo at economics normally regarded to be heterodox, Lawson proceeds to suggest that the term 'neoclassical' no longer be used, not least because a philosophical inconsistency is a poor basis for a school of thought. In the end, the message is the one consistently pushed by Lawson: that all economists should reflect on their ontology and consider how far it is consistent with their epistemology and methodology. The aim is to root out the type of problematic inconsistencies which are apparent in orthodox economics, but which Lawson implies are evident also in heterodox economics. In other words, this time the message is being addressed explicitly to heterodox economists as well as orthodox economists. The onus is on all economists to be able to justify their methodology; rather than accepting automatically the current orthodox presumption in favour of formal mathematical modelling, economists should be able to justify their use (and choice) of mathematics on a case-by-case basis. If heterodoxy is distinguished by its open-system ontology and therefore its open-system epistemology and methodology, it is important for heterodox economists to be aware of this and able to justify their practice accordingly.

Notes

1 This chapter has benefited from comments and suggestions from John Davis, Andrew Mearman and Jamie Morgan.
2 Chick and Dow (2012 [2005]) offer a more general definition.
3 Indeed this misunderstanding persisted in the early accounts of critical realism, such that the resemblances between critical realism and Hume were not recognised (Dow, 2002).
4 Given the different ways in which open systems do not satisfy the conditions for a closed system, classification may involve a range of dimensions.
5 Again, the range may span different dimensions, i.e. not necessarily be linear.
6 Could it even be that Becker was heterodox? Heckman (2015) argues that Becker used the abductive, rather than deductive, method and, in effect, that he employed an open-system ontology.

References

Ambrosi, G. M. (2003) *Keynes, Pigou and the Cambridge Keynesians*. London, UK: Macmillan.
Chick, V. and Dow, S. ([2005] 2012) The meaning of open systems. *Journal of Economic Methodology* 12(3): 363–381. Reprinted in Dow S. (ed.) *Foundations for New Economic Thinking: A Collection of Essays*. London, UK: Palgrave Macmillan, pp. 178–196.
Coates, J. (1996) *The Claims of Common Sense*. Cambridge, UK: Cambridge University Press.
Cremaschi, S. and Dascal, M. (1996) Malthus and Ricardo on economic methodology. *History of Political Economy* 28(3): 475–511.
Davis, J. B. (1999) Common sense: A middle way between formalism and post-structuralism? *Cambridge Journal of Economics* 23(6): 503–513.
Davis, J. B. (2009) The nature of heterodox economics, in Fullbrook E. (ed.) *Ontology and Economics: Tony Lawson and his Critics*. London, UK: Routledge, pp. 83–92.
Deane, P. (1983) The scope and method of economic science. *Economic Journal* 93 (March): 1–12.
Deane, P. (2008) Keynes, John Neville (1852–1949), in Durlauf, S. N. and Blume, L. E. (eds) *The New Palgrave Dictionary of Economics*, vol. 4. London, UK: Palgrave Macmillan, pp. 725–726.
Dow, S. (1990) Beyond dualism. *Cambridge Journal of Economics* 14(2): 143–158. Reprinted in *Foundations for New Economic Thinking*. London, UK: Palgrave Macmillan, 2012, pp. 52–71.
Dow, S. (2002) Historical reference: Hume and critical realism. *Cambridge Journal of Economics* 26(6): 683–697.

Dow, S. (2004) Reorienting economics: Some epistemological issues. *Journal of Economic Methodology* 11(3): 307–312.
Dow, S. (2009) Hume and the Scottish enlightenment: two cultures. *Revista de Economia* 35(3): 7–20.
Dow, S. (2013) Mark Blaug on formalism and reality: The case of behavioural economics. *Erasmus Journal for Philosophy and Economics* 6(3): 26–43.
Dow, S. (2014) *Consistency in Pluralism and Microfoundations*. PKSG Working Paper 1408. Available at: http://www.postkeynesian.net/downloads/wpaper/PKWP1408.pdf.
Dow, S. (forthcoming) Cambridge's contribution to methodology in economics, in Cord, R. (ed.) *The Palgrave Companion to Cambridge Economics*. London, UK: Palgrave Macmillan.
Fine, B. (chapter 8, this volume) Neoclassical economics: An elephant is not a chimera but is a chimera real? In Morgan, J. (ed.) *What Is This 'School' Called Neoclassical Economics? Debating the Issues*. London, UK: Routledge.
Foucault, M. (1991 [1966]) *The Order of Things*. London, UK: Routledge.
Foucault, M. (1992 [1969]) *The Archaeology of Knowledge*. London, UK: Routledge.
Groenewegen, P. (1995) *A Soaring Eagle: Alfred Marshall 1842–1924*. Cheltenham, UK: Edward Elgar.
Hahn, F. H. (1985) *In Praise of Economic Theory*. Jevons Memorial Fund Lecture, delivered at University College, London, UK. Available at: http://www.worldcat.org/title/in-praise-of-economic-theory-the-jevons-memorial-fund-lecture-delivered-at-university-college-london-23-november-1984/oclc/470708868 (accessed 2 August 2015).
Harcourt, G. C. (1972) *Some Cambridge Controversies in the Theory of Capital*. Cambridge, UK: Cambridge University Press.
Harcourt, G. C. (2001 [1995]) How I do economics, in Medema, S. G. and Samuels, W. J. (eds) *How Do Economists Do Economics*. Cheltenham, UK: Edward Elgar, pp. 93–102. Reprinted in *50 Years a Keynesian and Other Essays*. London, UK: Palgrave Macmillan, pp. 323–333.
Harcourt, G. C. (2012 [2003]) The Cambridge economic tradition, in King, J. E. (ed.) *The Elgar Companion to Post Keynesian Economics*. Cheltenham, UK: Edward Elgar, pp. 44–51. Reprinted in *The Making of a Post-Keynesian Economist*. London, UK: Palgrave Macmillan, pp. 201–210.
Heckman, J. J. (2015) Gary Becker: Model Economic Scientist. IZA Discussion Paper 8827. Available at: http://ftp.iza.org/dp8827.pdf (accessed 17 August 2015).
Keynes, J. M. (1973 [1934]) *Towards the General Theory, The Collected Writings*. Part I: Preparation Volume XIII. London, UK: Macmillan, for the Royal Economic Society, pp. 337–653.
Klamer, A. (1983) *Conversations with Economists*. Totowa, NJ: Rowman and Allanhold; also published as *The New Classical Macroeconomics*. Brighton, UK: Wheatsheaf, 1984.
Lawson, T. (1997) *Economics and Reality*. London, UK: Routledge.
Lawson, T. (2002) Mathematical formalism in economics: What really is the problem? In Arestis, P., Desai, M. and Dow, S. (eds) *Methodology, Microeconomics and Keynes*. London, UK: Routledge, pp. 73–83.
Lawson, T. (2004) Reorienting economics: On heterodox economics, themata and the use of mathematics in economics. *Journal of Economic Methodology* 11(3): 229–240.

Lawson, T. (2006) The nature of heterodox economics. *Cambridge Journal of Economics* 30(4): 483–505.
Lawson, T. (2009) The current economic crisis: Its nature and the course of academic economics. *Cambridge Journal of Economics* 33(4): 759–777.
Lawson, T. (2013) What is this 'school' called neoclassical economics? *Cambridge Journal of Economics* 37(5): 947–983. Also published in this book as Chapter 1, and page numbers cited refer to those in this book.
Loasby, B. J. (2003) Closed models and open systems. *Journal of Economic Methodology* 10(3): 285–306.
Martins, N. (2013) *The Cambridge Revival of Political Economy*. London, UK: Routledge.
Martins, N. (Chapter 6, this volume) Why is this 'school' called neoclassical economics? Classicism and neoclassicism in historical context, in Morgan, J. (ed.) *What Is Neoclassical Economics? Debating the origins, meaning and significance*. London, UK: Routledge.
Marshall, A. (1890) *Principles of Economics*. Available at: http://www.econlib.org/library/Marshall/marPCover.html (accessed 27 July 2015).
McCloskey, D. N. (1985) *The Rhetoric of Economics*. Brighton, UK: Wheatsheaf.
Mearman, A. (2005) Sheila Dow's concept of dualism: Clarification, criticism and development. *Cambridge Journal of Economics* 29(4): 619–634.
Mearman, A. (2011) Pluralism, heterodoxy and the rhetoric of distinction. *Review of Radical Political Economics* 43(4): 552–561.
Mearman, A. (2012) 'Heterodox economics' and the problems of classification. *Journal of Economic Methodology* 19(4): 407–424.
Morgan, J. (2015) What's in a name? Tony Lawson on neoclassical economics and heterodox economics. *Cambridge Journal of Economics* 39(3): 843–865.
O'Donnell, R. (1997) Keynes and formalism, in Harcourt, G. C. and Riach, P. A. (eds) *A 'Second Edition' of the General Theory*. London, UK: Routledge, pp. 131–165.
Smith, A. (1980 [1795]) The history of astronomy, in Wightman, W. L. D. (ed.) *Essays on Philosophical Subjects*. Oxford, UK: Oxford University Press.
Velupillai, K. V. (2008) Sraffa's mathematical economics: A constructive interpretation. *Journal of Economic Methodology* 15(4): 325–342.
Vigo de Lima, I. (2010) *Foucault's Archaeology of Political Economy*. London, UK: Palgrave Macmillan.
Weintraub, E. R. (2002) *How Economics became a Mathematical Science*. Durham, NC: Duke University Press.

4 Lawson, Veblen and Marshall
How to read modern neoclassicism

Anne Mayhew

Introduction

In "What is this 'school' called neoclassical economics?" Tony Lawson makes two major contributions. He identifies and clarifies how and why Thorstein Veblen differentiated between his own approach and that of both classical and, as he christened them, neoclassical economists. Lawson also makes clear Veblen's argument that neoclassicism was the result of an incomplete movement away from classical ontology. In the late nineteenth century, newly emerging neoclassical economists, along with many scientists in other disciplines, came to appreciate the causal-processual nature of reality but, in the case of the neoclassicals, this was coupled with a continuing commitment to a taxonomic method. This commitment results in an inconsistency between the concept of reality and tools used to analyze it. Veblen saw the inconsistency as most likely a phase to be passed through on the way to a more thoroughly evolutionary approach. Lawson, writing a century later, describes many economists as having become stuck in the neoclassicism that has become a long-lasting condition rather than a passing phase.

I find Lawson's argument highly convincing. However, what he does not do is convince me that a revolution in mathematics is a sufficient explanation of why economics remained "neoclassical" in spite of tendencies to break away from the limits imposed by devotion to deduction as method.

My comments on Lawson's success and partial failure will come in two parts. I begin by using Veblen's general theory of the development of modern science to elaborate Lawson's summary of the move toward a new ontology in late nineteenth- and early twentieth-century economics. In setting forth that general theory, Veblen also suggested that there might be limits to humankind's willingness to accept scientific explanations. That suggestion will be the basis for my argument in the subsequent section of the paper that Lawson is wrong in identifying the availability of reconceived mathematics as the major reason why economics got stuck in a neoclassical mold. There is more, I shall argue, to the continued acceptance of method that is inconsistent with evolutionary ontology than the availability of a new approach to mathematics. If I am correct in this argument, this also means that devotion to mathematics is *a*, but not *the* defining characteristic of modern-day neoclassicism.

Lawson on Veblen and Veblen on economics

Lawson's careful examination of why Veblen chose to describe some of the best (in his view) economic analyses at the beginning of the twentieth century as "neoclassical" begins with explication of what "classical" economic analysis meant for Veblen. In doing this, Lawson relies upon the three "preconceptions" articles in which Veblen first introduced the term "neoclassical" (Veblen, 1900). For my purposes, I want to put Veblen's (1900) argument, and Lawson's treatment of that argument, into the broader context that Veblen developed in an article published in 1906: "The Place of Science in Modern Society," where he presented a general theory of the development of science. (For a more thorough treatment of the 1906 article, see Mayhew, 2007). In that general theory Veblen attributes the increased use of: "impersonal, dispassionate insight into the material facts with which mankind has to deal" to an innate human characteristic: idle curiosity. He wrote:

> This idle curiosity formulates its response to stimulus, not in terms of an expedient line of conduct, nor even necessarily in a chain of motor activity, but in terms of the sequence of activities going on in the observed phenomena.
>
> (Veblen, 1906: 7)

In informal language, we might say that Veblen rested the development of science and technology on "just messing around" in the process of teleologically-driven everyday practice. As humans act in purposeful and habitual fashion to achieve ends, they are also, said Veblen, prone to idle and non-purposeful activity. As they so engage, they do things differently; habit and purpose are, at least briefly and quite incidentally, not in control of human action and thought. Through this idle process, knowledge of how to manipulate the world around us grows, and, very gradually, new explanations are required.

Idle curiosity, thought Veblen, was a lasting human trait that had led to a gradual accretion of knowledge about causal sequences in nature, which, in turn, led to changes in interpretation of nature with resulting changes in metaphysical (or, in Lawson's terms, ontological) preconceptions. The "interpretation" of the facts under the guidance of this idle curiosity may take the form of anthropomorphic or animistic explanations of the "conduct" of the objects observed (Veblen, 1990: 7).

In the course of the nineteenth century, interpretations became more causal and processual, a consequence that fed back upon itself through technological development, which then led to the acceleration of both scientific knowledge and of the technological change that occurred in the middle of the nineteenth century.[1] As evolutionary interpretations spread, the study of economies was not left unaffected. The change, as Lawson emphasizes in his summary of Veblen, was gradual and involved a: "dissolution of 'animistic' preconceptions," as the nature of humankind and nature replaced an active spiritual force in explanations of how events occurred (Lawson, Chapter 1: 42).

In many ways Veblen's (1906) paper is, as I have already said, a more general statement of the argument that he offered in the "preconceptions" papers. What is important, however, for my purposes, is the conclusion that Veblen reached in 1906. After describing the gradual move from animism to the idea of natural laws to the causal-processual, or evolutionary, explanations that are modern science, Veblen raised doubts about whether or not this movement could be sustained. His question and conclusion are so important for my argument that I am going to quote him at some length:

> While the scientist's spirit and his achievements stir an unqualified admiration in modern men, and while his discoveries carry conviction as nothing else does, it does not follow that the manner of man which this quest of knowledge produces or requires comes near answering to the current ideal of manhood, or that his conclusions are felt to be as good and beautiful as they are true. The ideal man, and the ideal of human life, even in the apprehension of those who most rejoice in the advances of science, is neither the finikin skeptic in the laboratory nor the animated slide-rule. The quest of science is relatively new ... The [human] race reached the human plane with little of this searching knowledge of facts, and throughout the greater part of its life-history on the human plane it has been accustomed to make its higher generalisations and to formulate its larger principles of life in other terms than those of passionless matter-of-fact. This manner of knowledge has occupied an increasing share of men's attention in the past, since it bears in a decisive way upon the minor affairs of workday life; but it has never until now been put in the first place, as the dominant note of human culture. The normal man, such as his inheritance has made him, has therefore good cause to be restive under its dominion.
> (Veblen, 1906: 30–31)

Veblen was writing not about economics, but about science and society more generally. As Lawson emphasizes, Veblen thought that economists had made only partial progress toward the "passionless matter-of-fact" understanding of economies, but he was, in 1900 at least, optimistic that further progress might be made The relevance of his warning in 1906 about science in general to what actually happened in the discipline of economics requires further exploration and it is to that task that I now turn.

Why did so many economists get stuck?

Lawson argues (Chapter 1: 63–64) that those who should rightly be called "neoclassical," in a Veblenian sense, are those (Lawson's group 3, Chapter 1: 63) who:

> [a]re aware (at some level) that social reality is of a causal-processual nature as elaborated above, who prioritise the goal of being realistic, and yet who fail themselves fully to recognise or to accept the limited scope for any overly-taxonomic approach including, in particular, one that makes significant use of methods of mathematical deductive modelling.

A characteristic of this work is that it often begins with a causal-processual description of social reality and then proceeds to deduction. The work done by economists of this group gives an appearance of being based on sound observation of reality. At times the slide (or leap) from the causal-processual perspective to pure deductivism is obscured by the language of mathematics although often not entirely. In all cases, the power of mathematical reasoning is either implicitly or explicitly offered as justification for departure from observed reality.

A review of the journals in which most economists publish reveals that, as Lawson says, neoclassical economists live in a world of two parts: a world of socioeconomic evolution and a world in which truth is derived by deduction about an unchanging world. The process whereby observation led to changes in explanation and in ontology, a process occurring in other areas of inquiry as Veblen wrote, was at some point interrupted in the discipline of economics. The question is why? Lawson's explanation is that mathematics changed. He writes:

> Mathematics, especially through the work of David Hilbert, became increasingly viewed as a discipline properly concerned with providing a pool of frameworks for *possible realities*. No longer was mathematics seen as the language of (non-social) nature, abstracted from the study of the latter. Rather, it was conceived as a practice concerned with formulating systems comprising sets of axioms and their deductive consequences, with these systems in effect taking on a life of their own.
>
> (Lawson, Chapter 1: 57)

Lawson also notes that Veblen, writing in 1908, commented on the proclivity of economists who favored mathematic tools to reject: "the causalist ontology of evolutionary thinking" (Chapter 1, note 30: 76). However, says Lawson, it was a change in mathematics itself that allowed this proclivity to become dominant among economists. Although Lawson wrote in 2003 of an: "enormous, almost uncritical, awe of mathematics in modern Western culture" (Lawson, 2003: 245), in "What is this 'school' called neoclassical," he certainly seems to be saying that had mathematics not changed drastically, then even this powerful cultural pattern would not have been sufficient to get economists stuck in the neoclassical transition.

My contention is that the changes in mathematics were permissive rather than causal. Briefly put, my argument is that Veblen's normal man, who is neither: "finikin skeptic nor animated slide-rule" has been reluctant or unwilling to accept the uncertainty that evolutionary thinking requires in areas of vital public interest. Or, perhaps better put, "normal people" who are also citizens and voters have been unwilling to accept uncertainty where certainty is offered as an alternative, and where automaticity can be substituted for human application of policy. Those who have wanted to offer certainty in service to their policy patrons and in the interests of their own standing in their academic discipline, found reconceived mathematics a most useful tool to convey that certainty while also giving an appearance of scientific neutrality. Within the discipline there were powerful incentives to retain the "principles," mastery of which set economists apart from their fellow social scientists. But without external pressures this might not have been sufficient. Three well-documented aspects of the story of how the discipline of economics turned into mathematical discourse can be offered in support of my argument.

Consider first the intradisciplinary pressures. Although the subfield of mathematical economics can reasonably be said to have started early in the second half of the nineteenth century with the work of Stanley Jevons and others, it was not until the decade of 1925–1935 that there was a pronounced increase in the use of mathematical discourse in the leading Anglo-American and French journals (Mirowski, 1991: 150). Mirowski writes of a "watershed" during that decade that occurred with a: "change in the neoclassical research program" (a program that he, like Lawson, equates with mathematical discourse). This watershed was: "multi-faced, including not only more self-consciousness in the formalization of discrete models" but also, among other issues: "a cautious accommodation with stochastic mathematics" (Mirowski, 1991: 151).

The uneasy and cautious accommodation, as well as the awkwardness of combining the classical ontology with processual method, is illustrated by the fierce debates that took place over how to use measured quantities and prices of a commodity purchased (the case in point was sugar) to estimate the relationship between price and quantity. How, in other words, were the demand schedules that played such a central part in the principles of economics that Alfred Marshall had enunciated, to be measured in an age of increased emphasis upon measurement. What statisticians measured were quantities sold at a range of prices. These observed quantities and prices could be conceived of as intersections of theoretical supply and demand curves. But the goal, inherited from the structure of prior analysis, was to derive points along an unmeasurable demand schedule.

It is possible to imagine that economics might have developed along the lines laid out in the work of Henry Schultz and others who were concerned with estimating elasticity of demand in the real world of American agricultural markets. (See Morgan, 1990, chapter 5 for discussion of Schultz's 1928 work in the context of the debates about the use of statistical data in the 1920s and 1930s.) The view that won out, however, was that expressed by Ragnar Frisch and Frederick Waugh in the first issue of *Econometrica*. This view is succinctly expressed in a passage quoted by Morgan:

> An empirically determined relation is "true" if it approximates fairly well a certain well-defined *theoretical* relationship, assumed to represent the nature of the phenomenon studied. There does not seem to be any other way of giving a meaning to the expression "a true relationship." For clearness of statement we must therefore first define the nature of the *a priori* relationship that is taken as the ideal.
> (Frisch and Waugh, 1933: 38, as quoted by Morgan, 1990: 150)

What this meant in practice was that data should be pre-adjusted to eliminate time trends and other variables that could be considered as disturbances to the *true* relationship. As Morgan goes on to say: "An empirical relationship could then be considered 'true' if it approximated the postulated theoretical relationship" (Morgan, 1990: 150). In the practice of econometrics, the principles that Marshall enunciated in the early 1890s, principles derived by synthesizing the wisdom of the classical era, were preserved as the basic and not to be doubted structure of "true" economic analysis. Quantitative tools were to be used in aid of "proving" a series of postulated theoretical relationships and those relationships were to be those derived from the much earlier classical economics. Through the 1930s there had been a lively possibility that quantitative tools would be used in aid of what Wesley Mitchell, in his Presidential address to the American Economic Association in 1924, forecast to be a reformulation of economic theory that would more closely mirror the real world that could increasingly be described in statistical terms (Mitchell, 1925). The pressure to hew to true economic analysis was crucial in preventing this reformulation.

Pressures from outside the discipline for policies that would serve the public good in politically acceptable ways reinforced the intradisciplinary incentives for conformity to accepted principles. Two episodes in the development of economic theorizing in the course of the watershed decade of the 1930s show how pressing public issues, along with powerful interests associated with those issues, combined to give major advantage to economists who offered certainty based on timeless principles and what they could claim was scientific neutrality. Classical ontology, the source of the theoretical relationships deemed to be "true" provided the certainty, and mathematical discourse gave a patina of science.

Episode 1: what should economists say about trusts and what should be done about them?

In the first part of the twentieth century, particularly in the U.S., the issue of what to do about "trusts" gained urgency. Furthermore, even in England, where the issue did not have the public prominence that it did in the U.S., the issue of how to define competition and monopoly, two key terms in the classical taxonomy, was important. Marshall originally wrote *Principles of Economics* in 1890 and subsequently modified it through successive editions. In the Preface to the eighth edition of his *Principles of Economics*, written in 1920, Marshall said that when: "any branch of industry offers an open field for new firms which rise to the first rank, and perhaps after a time delay, the normal cost of production in it can be estimated with reference to 'a representative firm'" (Marshall, 1920: xiii). Study of such firms, Marshall continued: "belongs properly to a volume on Foundations" and, he continued: "So also does a study of the principles on which a firmly established monopoly, in the hands of a Government department or a large railway, regulates its prices." What did not fit into his book of *Principles* were the newly emerging trusts and combinations. Said Marshall:

> But normal action falls into the background, when Trusts are striving for the mastery of a large market, when communities of interest are being made and unmade; and, above all, when the policy of any particular establishment is likely to be governed, not with a single eye to its own business success, but in subordination to some large stock-exchange manoeuvre, or some campaign for the control of markets. Such matters cannot be fitly discussed in a volume on Foundations: they belong to a volume dealing with some part of the Superstructure.
> (Marshall, 1920: xiv)

What Marshall did was to relegate discussion of "giant businesses" to his *Industry and Trade* (published in 1919) where he described the growth of pools, trusts, and giant businesses in America. He wrote:

> [i]n the last few decades America has developed the scientific application of economic doctrines to many practical problems, with great energy and thoroughness. More perhaps than any other country, she has learnt that *general propositions in regard to either competition or monopoly are full of snares*; and that some of the most injurious uses of monopoly, being themselves extreme forms of competition, are not to be restrained by the advocacy of free competition.
> (Marshall, 1919: 512)

Remember that Marshall was one of the economists who Veblen thought most likely to escape the classical ontology and Marshall's words vividly describe some of the difficulty in doing so. He wanted to retain the words competition and monopoly but could not, being the honest observer that he was and, writing in the second decade of the twentieth century, give precise meaning to these terms. (See Hart, 2003 for a good discussion of Marshall's dilemma.) However, it was on the western side of the Atlantic that confusion about how to define the core concepts of "competition" and "monopoly" took on greatest urgency. Public anger over the formation of the Standard Oil Trust in 1879 and the trusts and combinations in a number of other industries that followed rapidly thereafter, led many states and, in 1890, the U.S. Congress, to pass "antitrust" legislation. In the words of the Sherman Act: "every contract, combination in the form of trust or otherwise, or conspiracy, in restraint of trade or commerce" became illegal.

Many economists today do not know that their predecessors were not only *not* involved in drafting this legislation but, when they said anything about it, most often opposed it. The reasons for opposition and then an about face and embrace of the Sherman Act in the 1930s clearly illustrate the dilemma that the rise of the trusts created for economists. The classical understanding of the core concepts, competition and monopoly, could no longer be used to describe the rapidly changing reality of the American economy. Competition was widely described, by economists and the public alike, as "ruinous" and, as Marshall and many other economists recognized, the trusts were neither "natural" monopolies nor the result of government charters (Morgan, 1993; Mayhew, 1998, 2007).

While World War I raised a host of new economic issues, the question of what to think and do about big businesses continued to be a major focus of attention in the U.S. Passage of the Clayton and Federal Trade Commission Acts in 1914 encoded the conclusion that had been reached by John Bates Clark and John Maurice Clark (1971), a father and son duo who tried to bridge the divide between classical and evolutionary thinking, that the new giants could be controlled by *potential* competition, which could be ensured by the courts. To do this the judicial system would need to enforce the legal requirement of a "fair field," but did not necessarily need to dissolve the new combinations. (For more on the concept of a "fair field," see Mayhew, 2007: 69–71). Rather than finding all restraint of trade illegal as the wording of the Sherman Act would seem to have required, the Supreme Court in 1911, and with subsequent affirmation, held that reason should be used to determine the context and consequences of restraint of trade. But this solution did not provide automatic solutions; it required regulation and an active judiciary and there could be no clear and scientifically "best" outcome. What the Clarks and others thought would be the best that could be achieved would be a "fair playing field" for all firms. The power of firms, not only over price but also over the playing field, would have to be regulated in the public interest. The behavior of firms, their response to rivals and to consumers of their output, could be judged reasonable and fair or not, but regulators would always be required to say which.

In the course of the 1930s two things happened that gave life to a new classically based taxonomy of industrial structure; one that could, it came to be alleged, eliminate the need for constant judicial oversight of the entire field of firm action that the Clarks envisioned as the span of required regulation. In the political arena of the 1930s, there was a turn away from acceptance of the inevitability of industrial behemoths and of the need for active regulation in the public interest. The advisors to Franklin Delano Roosevelt, who advocated active planning of the economy, were replaced by those who thought that vigorous enforcement of increasingly narrowly construed antitrust laws would be sufficient to create an economy that would operate as if it were competitive (Barber, 1996). At the same time, developments within the discipline of economics changed the policy conversation in a way that fit and fed the New Deal administrators' desire to downplay the issue of corporate power and for automaticity (or, in other words, neutrality) in policy making. Following on from the work of Edward Chamberlain (1933) and Joan Robinson (1933), Edward S. Mason published a schema in 1939 in which industrial structure and the related conduct and performance of firms were laid out along a spectrum from highly competitive to monopolistic, where competition and monopoly retained the meanings that they had had in Marshall's *Principles*. In other words, the classical taxonomy was revived. Robinson, Chamberlain, and finally Mason had solved the problem that Marshall could not. They made it possible to talk about "trusts" in a book on economic principles, for now these trusts were placed along a spectrum.

What was very important was that the spectrum was one in which place was determined by control over prices and output. Other aspects of corporate power, such as Marshall had mentioned when he wrote of corporate goals such as: "subordination to some large stock-exchange manoeuvre, or some campaign for the control of markets", were pushed firmly to the background of industrial policy. Of particular importance in economists' acceptance of this new neoclassical taxonomy of firms was the new University of Chicago approach to corporate power. The administration of antitrust policy passed, after World War II, into the hands of bright young economists who had, in their own words, experienced a "religious conversion" at the University of Chicago (Kitch, 1983). This was a conversion in which difficulties that large, complex firms had presented for adoption of Marshall's *Principles*, and the Smithian propositions upon which they were based, were swept away. According to Milton Friedman, one aspect of the conversion was belief that vigorous application of the antitrust laws could result in something like the theoretical state of perfect competition (Kitch, 1983: 178).

128 *Anne Mayhew*

What is of particular importance here is that a major stumbling block to mathematical discourse had been removed. In place of the "snares" that Marshall had found in trying to use the concepts of competition and monopoly to talk about an economy populated with a variety of multi-plant, multi-product combinations, economists had now created an ordered universe of categorized types. Rather than accepting that there were very large firms that exercised enormous power over resource development and allocation, and over widely geographically dispersed areas, "firms" became the firms of Marshall's *Principles*. Control over price became the only aspect of firm power that was considered of relevance both in most antitrust practice and in core economic theory. The theory of the firm and of prices was made safe for mathematical discourse, though it must be noted that mathematical discourse followed rather than led. I will return to this point later.

Episode 2: what should economists say about the Great Depression and what should be done about it?

A second great crisis of public policy in the third through fifth decades of the twentieth century was, of course, the crisis of dealing with the disastrous decline in industrial output, agricultural prices, trade, and employment that we now identify as the Great Depression. The story of how analysis of this crisis was tamed so as to be consistent with a mathematical approach is much better known to most economists than the story of taming the trusts, so I will treat it briefly. It was John Maynard Keynes who, perhaps appropriately given Veblen's identification of his father, John Neville Keynes, and of family friend and mentor, Alfred Marshall, as transitional figures, made what came to be regarded by most economists as the most dramatic break with classical thinking about the overall performance of economies (or what we would today call macroeconomics). The extent of Keynes' break with an established classical tradition and the extent of his departure from the approach taken by Marshall in *Principles of Economics* can and has been extensively debated. But, it is without doubt that Keynes insisted that the future was likely to be different from the present and that it was an unknowable future. The subversive (for classical ontology) nature of Keynes' analysis may be summarized in two brief quotes from the 1937 article in which he responded to criticisms of his (1936) book *The General Theory of Employment, Interest and Money*. He noted that Ricardo, Marshall, and:

> [r]ecent writers ... were still dealing with a system in which the amount of the factors employed was given and the other relevant facts were known more or less for certain. This does not mean that they were dealing with a system in which change was ruled out, or even one in which disappointment of expectation was ruled out.

But at any given time facts and expectations were assumed to be given in a definite and calculable form... Actually, however, we have, as a rule, only the vaguest idea of any but the most direct consequences of our acts.

(Keynes, 1937: 212–213)

Also, a few paragraphs later: "I accuse the classical economic theory of being itself one of these pretty, polite techniques which tries to deal with the present by abstracting from the fact that we know very little about the future" (Keynes, 1937: 215).

How Keynes' theory, which was about uncertainty, was tamed by J. R. Hicks and his IS-LM approach, by Paul Samuelson and his neoclassical synthesis, by "hydraulic Keynesianism" and, more recently turned into New Keynesian analysis, is a story that does not require repetition. What is important here is that analysis that dealt with the real and evolving economy has been transformed into analysis that ignores the causal-processual nature of social reality. Furthermore, once again, a crisis in public policy was converted into events to be handled by automatic responses (such as fiscal "fine tuning" or some form of monetary policy) generated through mathematical formulae.

Certainty, automaticity, and the persistence of the neoclassical trap

The evolution of economic analysis in the twentieth century was as contingent and non-teleological as the economy that was the purported focus of that analysis. When Veblen wrote his "preconceptions" papers it seemed possible and even probable that the processual nature of economic activity would cause economists to abandon the taxonomic analyses that required assumption of a fixed set of variables and relationships. Veblen found reason to think that economics might become an evolutionary science in the work of such prominent scholars as Alfred Marshall and John Neville Keynes. Lawson's important contribution is to explain how a revolution in mathematics allowed economists to avoid this evolutionary path. The availability of mathematical tools that did not require a commitment to a specific model of reality allowed economists to adopt a mathematical discourse that obscured the non-evolutionary, taxonomic nature of their analysis, even when they claimed to be analyzing the processual nature of economies. The neoclassical trap that Veblen thought might be transitory become persistent.

My argument in this paper is that a more complete, but in no way contradictory, explanation of the persistence of the neoclassical trap is gained by adding the human desire for certainty noted by Veblen in 1906 to the appeal of apparently scientific mathematical methods as explanation for what happened to economics. The way in which intradisciplinary allegiance to "principles," faith in superiority of mathematical discourse, and a strong desire for certainty combined to produce the economic analysis of twenty-first-century mainstream texts and journal articles becomes complex and interactive.

Intradisciplinary pressures led early econometricians to find ways of reconciling the wealth of statistical data being collected by governmental and quasi-governmental agencies (the National Bureau of Economic Research in the U.S., for example) with the "true relationships" that were laid down for economists by Alfred Marshall in the 1890s and again by Paul Samuelson in the 1950s. Had the "principles" that Marshall laid out been modified in light of the kind of analysis of demand schedules offered by Henry Schultz and others in the 1920s and 1930s, then the "principles" that are still used to "think like an economist" might have become less restrictive of the kind of analyses held in esteem. Instead, both because of and as a consequence of the trimming and pruning of evidence so that it would fit inherited "true relationships," the use of mathematical discourse was made more elegantly abstract. Today, the passage from learning economic principles and in doing so learning to think like an economist moves quickly into mathematical discourse, so that young scholars never realize what must be left out for the sake of that abstract discourse.

Aiding and abetting this slide into mathematics as economics is a deeply embedded perception that mathematics is the language of science and science requires mathematics. This certainly gave an advantage to those who led the charge to mathematize economics in the 1920s and 1930s. What I suggest, however, is that what tipped the scale away from the kind of evolutionary analysis that seemed to be emerging in early twentieth-century economics, was the human desire for certainty that was noted by Veblen in 1906 and, particularly, the desire for certainty as it is manifested among policy makers who seek automaticity rather than an appearance of discretionary (and therefore potentially blameworthy) policy formation. Two examples—the development of U.S. antitrust policy and the wide adoption of a kind of "hydraulic Keynesianism"—are offered as examples of how evolutionary processes were trimmed and pruned to make discretionary policies seem appropriate solutions for major public problems.

Acceptance of more or less automatic policies and the certainty of outcome that has been claimed for them required two things. The first is that a lot of earlier institutional analysis had to be trimmed away. Alfred Marshall, along with many others, knew that the power of the "trusts" was of concern not simply because of their control over output and prices but also because in the real world of these trusts: "communities of interest are being made and unmade" and stock-exchange maneuvers or campaigns for control of markets were likely to guide firm behavior. To move from this recognition to the simplified world of firms that could be arrayed along a spectrum of greater or lesser degrees of control over price and output, required significant removal of institutional detail, removal that Marshall himself could not achieve in order to bring the behavior of the emerging trusts into his compilation of principles. The later analysis of Robinson, Chamberlain, and Mason was undoubtedly successful, because it offered policy makers a way to simplify and make more or less automatic their exercise of power in the contested arena of government and business relationships. It was also analysis that appealed to economists, because it aided mathematical discourse and gave disciplinary status to those who pursued it.

A similar process played out in the 1930s and 1940s as economists on both sides of the Atlantic advised governments about finance of war, but also about prevention of the macroeconomic disasters of the 1930s. Once again, promise of more certain solutions achieved with a minimum of possibly fallible human decision-making held enormous appeal. Also, at the same time, apparent and elegant mathematical proofs of this possibility could be published to disciplinary acclaim.

It may be easier to see how this unholy marriage of disciplinary loyalty (or perhaps of disciplinary separation from allegedly sloppier social sciences), admiration for mathematics, and a desire to satisfy a deeply embedded human need for certainty and automaticity came about than it is to explain its persistence in the face of repeated practical failures. Since 2007–2008, much has been written, and not just in heterodox and normally critical outlets, about the failure of economists to predict accurately or to offer effective solutions to current problems. Yet there is little evidence of wholesale questioning or rejection of the marriage of taxonomic method, mathematical discourse, and a search for certainty. Why not? Why does the neoclassical trap persist in the face of apparent failure of neoclassical economics to live up to its claim of scientific reliability?

My suggestion is that the interaction of the forces that have made the neoclassical trap a persistent one has led to a further trap. When critics of neoclassicism note the failures of the approach as either explanatory science or a sufficient basis for good policy formation, the response is most often that the critics should provide a better alternative. What this most often means is that critics should provide other models that can be stated using the prevailing tools of mathematical discourse and that they can provide models with a high degree of certainty. These attributes of modern neoclassicism are taken by most to be required characteristics of good economic practice. Tony Lawson's analysis of the role of mathematical discourse in establishment economics, in combination with Veblen's (1906) warning about the human desire for certainty, can explain how this acceptance has come to coexist with a general recognition among neoclassical economists that social reality is processual.

Tony Lawson's careful explication of Veblen's concept of "neoclassical economics" makes it possible to read the work of most economists writing today as a mixture of a classical ontology based upon understanding the world in terms of fixed categories, in combination with recognition that the data presented are derived from a world in which categories and interrelationships are constantly shifting. The legerdemain that permits this combination of a taxonomic approach with a reality that contravenes the very existence of the categories required of a taxonomy, is the legerdemain of modern mathematics. Mathematical reasoning from a set of axioms, along with the cultural power of mathematics and its apparent scientific neutrality, has allowed a neoclassical accommodation of inconsistent ontology and method. A human desire makes this accommodation particularly attractive to those who seek through public policy to reduce the uncertainty that we humans fear, an uncertainty that is a necessary trait of a processual world. Alfred Marshall realized that he could not state the reality of modern economies in terms of the principles that he sought. Veblen did not try and thought that an evolutionary science of economics would be possible if economists would abandon the effort. He did, however, think that mankind might not be able to live without the fixity that an unchanging taxonomy provided. Unfortunately, he may have been right about that.[2]

However, to look on the bright side, Lawson has made a giant contribution in providing a close reading of Veblen to give precision to the term neoclassical. His analysis helps us understand the role that mathematics plays in providing camouflage for the unreality of the classical taxonomy and in giving an appearance of scientific authority to neoclassical analysis. It is nice to think that economists and users of economic analyses might heed Lawson's argument and recognize the importance of continuing the move to the processual-causal analysis that Marshall ventured part way on and that John Maynard Keynes took. Were this to happen, the pessimistic Veblen of 1906 would be proved wrong. To repeat: economic analysis is evolutionary and contingent so perhaps this might happen. Tony Lawson has moved us along that possible path.

Notes

1 In *The Gifts of Athena* (Mokyr, 2002) economic historian, Joel Mokyr, provides detailed accounts of technological change to illustrate how a new feedback mechanism between science and technology developed in the nineteenth century in Western Europe. His explanation focuses on a shift from pre-Industrial Revolution changes in technology that had: "narrow epistemic bases and thus rarely if ever led to continued and sustained improvements" (Mokyr, 2002: 19). During the nineteenth century organized scientific investigation, based on causal-processual ontology, was undertaken in support of enhanced production. Mokyr's account offers strong support for Veblen's interpretation of changes in nineteenth-century thought. (For more on this see Mayhew, 2007: 8–10.)
2 In email conversation Jamie Morgan makes the important point that a criticism of Thomas Piketty's (2014) book *Capital in the Twenty-First Century* is that his "laws" of capitalism require neoclassical and highly determined relationships along with

a taxonomy that is inherited and not reflective of twenty-first-century realities. As Morgan puts it: "several critics on the Left have noted that his work would look quite different if stated as highly contingent and variable." I agree and suspect that the commercial success of Piketty's (2014) book depends in large measure on his willingness to sacrifice reality of analysis to the appeal that "laws" have for a humankind that wants to think that what happens is not up to us, but to some natural (if not quite divine) plan. For more on this see Varoufakis, 2014.

References

Barber, W. J. (1996) *Designs within Disorder: Franklin D. Roosevelt, the Economists, and the Shaping of American Economic Policy, 1933–1945*. Cambridge, UK: Cambridge University Press.

Chamberlain, E. H. (1933) *The Theory of Monopolistic Competition*. Cambridge, MA: Harvard University Press.

Clark, J. B. and Clark, J. M. (1971) *The Control of Trusts*. New York, NY: Macmillan.

Hart, N. (2003) Marshall's dilemma: Equilibrium versus evolution. *Journal of Economic Issues* 37(4): 1139–1160.

Keynes, J. M. (1936) *The General Theory of Employment, Interest and Money*. New York, NY: Harcourt, Brace and Company.

Keynes, J. M. (1937) The general theory of employment. *The Quarterly Journal of Economics*, 51(2): 209–223.

Kitch, E. W. (1983) The fire of truth: A remembrance of law and economics at Chicago, 1932–1970. *Journal of Law and Economics* 21(1): 163–234.

Lawson, T. (2003) *Reorienting Economics*. London: Routledge.

Lawson, T. (2013) What is this "school" called neoclassical economics? *Cambridge Journal of Economics* 37(5): 947–983. Also published in this book as Chapter 1, and page numbers cited refer to those in this book.

Marshall, A. (1919) *Industry and Trade*. London, UK: Macmillan.

Marshall, A. (2013 [1920]) *Principles of Economics*. 8th edition. Basingstoke, Hampshire: Palgrave Macmillan.

Mason, E. (1939) Price and production policies of large-scale enterprise. *American Economic Review* 29(1): 61–74.

Mayhew, A. (1998) How American economists came to love the Sherman Antitrust Act, in Morgan, M. S and Rutherford, M. (eds) *From Interwar Pluralism to Postwar Neoclassicism*. Durham, NC and London, UK: Duke University Press, pp. 179–201.

Mayhew, A. (2007) The place of science in society: Progress, pragmatism, pluralism, in Knoedler, J., Prasch, R. E. and Champlin, D. P. (eds) *Thorstein Veblen and the Revival of Free Market Capitalism*. Cheltenham, UK and Northampton, MA: Edward Elgar, pp. 1–16.

Mirowski, P. (1991) The when, the how and the why of mathematical expression in the history of economic analysis. *Journal of Economic Perspectives* 5(1): 145–157.

Mitchell, W. C. (1925) Quantitative analysis in economic theory. *American Economic Review* 15(1): 1–12.

Mokyr, J. (2002) *The Gifts of Athena: Historical Origins of the Knowledge Economy*. Princeton, NJ and Oxford, UK: Princeton University Press.

Morgan, M. (1990) *The History of Econometric Ideas*. Cambridge, UK: Cambridge University Press.

Morgan, M. (1993) Competing notions of "competition" in late nineteenth-century American economics. *History of Political Economy* 25(4): 563–604.

Piketty, T. (2014) *Capital in the Twenty-First Century*. Cambridge, MA and London, UK: The Belknap Press of Harvard University Press.

Robinson, J. (1933) *The Economics of Imperfect Competition*. London, UK: Macmillan.

Schultz, H. (1928) *Statistical Laws of Demand and Supply with Special Application to Sugar*. Chicago, IL: University of Chicago Press.

Varoufakis, Y. (2014) Egalitarianism's latest foe: a critical review of Thomas Piketty's *Capital in the Twenty-First Century*. *Real–World Economics Review* 69. Reprinted in Fullbrook, E. and Morgan, J. (2014) (eds) *Piketty's Capital in the Twenty-First Century*. London, UK: WEA/College Publications, pp. 35–62.

Veblen, T. B. (1900) The preconceptions of economic science III. *Quarterly Journal of Economics* 14(2): 240–269.

Veblen, T. B. (1906) The place of science in modern civilization. *The American Journal of Sociology* 11(5): 585–609.

Veblen, T. B. (1990) The evolution of the scientific point of view. *The Place of Science in Modern Civilization*. New Brunswick, NJ and London, UK: Transaction Publishers.

5 Lawson on Veblen on social ontology

John B. Davis

Tony Lawson's "What is this 'school' called neoclassical economics?" draws on Thorstein Veblen's original use of "neoclassical economics" to critically interpret contemporary employment of the term, and argue for jettisoning the category of neoclassical economics altogether on the grounds that its use obfuscates effective critique of mainstream economics (Lawson, Chapter 1; also cf. Lawson, 2003: 184–217). The looseness with which he believes the term and category have been generally applied has, in his view, allowed a whole range of disparate arguments about neoclassicism to compete for attention, resulting in a failure on the part of many commentators to see what is fundamentally problematic about mainstream economics. However, Veblen is hardly only valuable to Lawson, because his initial conception of the term and category is an obvious starting point. His primary value resides in his evolutionary approach to science and associated critique of what he regarded as a primitive metaphysics of science particularly in the economics of his own time. Lawson regards this critique as close to his own critique of mainstream economics and sees a discussion of Veblen's view of neoclassicism as an opportunity to refocus contemporary discussion about the nature of neoclassicism on its untenable metaphysical preconceptions. His arguments are specifically directed at self-identified heterodox economists who, in his view, too often fail to see that the real source of economics' current problems lies not at the level of its substantive theorizing—that is, the content of economic doctrines—but at the level of methodology and social ontology—the study of the nature of social reality. Veblen used the term "metaphysics," but the term "ontology" has essentially the same meaning. In Lawson's language, then, the problem that Veblen identified remains the chief problem of mainstream economics today, namely, that it operates with a deficient social ontology. I am broadly sympathetic to this argument and think that recourse to Veblen's evolutionary thinking is a helpful way to examine what is deficient in mainstream economics' social ontology. In this chapter I will attempt to contribute to their approach by further discussing some of the more important themes they emphasize.

Lawson on Veblen

Lawson's own social ontology critique of the mainstream is well known, but comparing Veblen's critique may cast additional light on it and perhaps further develop it as well. Let us begin with Lawson's recent statement of the argument. First, then, he argues that the near-universal practice in economics of approaching every question as an exercise in mathematical modeling reflects the mistaken presupposition that what gets modeled adequately captures the nature of the social realm. Specifically, such modeling assumes that the social world can be represented in terms of collections of event regularities, which are stable and predictable—"closed systems" as he labels them. Lawson denies, however, that the social realm can be represented in this way, and his reason for this points to his main ontological critique of mainstream. Second, then, he argues that, in order to apply their mathematical techniques, and thereby reason in closed-system terms, the mainstream sees the social world in terms of event regularities, because in its associated worldview the "stuff" that the world is made up of are isolated atoms. Atoms are not labeled as such for reasons of size, as the word suggests, but rather on account of their nature as isolated, unchanging entities. What specifically defines these entities' isolation and unchanging nature, then, is that they always have the same independent and invariable causal effects in their interaction with other atoms, whatever the context. It is this conception that thus underlies the mainstream supposing there exist stable and predictable event regularities in the world, which in turn underlies its commitment to mathematical modeling, which together give an ontological view that constitutes the real source of mainstream economics' failure as a discipline for Lawson.

This critique then tells us where to look if we are to develop a social ontology for economics adequate to its subject matter and why Veblen plays a key role for Lawson. An ontologically "open" world, Lawson argues, cannot be represented as a collection of event regularities, because the world cannot be made up of atoms exercising independent and invariable causal effects on one another. We can see why, when we consider Veblen's evolutionary historical approach and alternative causal theory based on his idea of a cumulative causal sequence, an understanding Veblen emphasized is absent from neoclassical economics.

> The prime postulate of evolutionary science, the preconception constantly underlying the inquiry, is the notion of a cumulative causal sequence... Expressions of assent to this proposition abound. But the economists have not worked out or hit upon a method by which the inquiry in economics may consistently be conducted under the guidance of this postulate.
>
> (Veblen, 1900: 266)

A cumulative causal sequence, or cumulative causation, is the idea that through positive feedback processes the operation of causality in the world continually feeds back upon and transforms the conditions on which causality operates, so that cause-effect relations must continually evolve and can never be constant, even if they appear to us to be nominally the same over time. Thus, since the things or entities occupying the world are subject to causal processes, it follows that just as cause-effect relations are continually being transformed, so these things or entities occupying the world must also be in continual transformation. The idea that atoms are the "stuff" of the world is clearly inconsistent with this, and thus Lawson sees Veblen's conception as a fundamental contribution to anti-atomist reasoning about the social realm. Indeed, for him, Veblen's conception of an evolutionary historical world requires that the social world be seen as "open."

For both Lawson and Veblen, then, the social world is evolutionary and historical, because it is continually being transformed. Further, an evolutionary historical approach to science rules out what Veblen termed a taxonomic approach to science, which is grounded in the assumption that the social realm is stable and unchanging and which presupposes that the world is governed by regularities subject to classification in terms of "normal" or "natural" phenomena. A taxonomic approach is what Lawson sees as being involved in many current, even critical accounts of neoclassicism. Thus the problem he believes these accounts suffer from is that, by referring to a neoclassical approach, they implicitly make the debate a matter of which "normal" phenomena economics ought to investigate, whereas what debate should rather focus upon is how we understand a social reality in which the phenomena do not have this character at all. Better, then, to simply abandon the term "neoclassical" and work from the beginning with the idea that social phenomena unfold in an evolutionary way.

A further look at Veblen's cumulative causation idea

I agree, then, that Veblen's cumulative causation idea is an important contribution to philosophy of science, and that we need to understand and develop this core idea in order to explain how cause-effect relationships constantly evolve and explain the nature of the social realm. The basic idea cumulative causation employs is the non-identity of cause-effect sequences over time. In addition, Veblen allows for something in the way of similarity of cause-effect sequences over time, since as an evolutionary view cause-effect sequences at later times derive somehow from cause-effect sequences at earlier times. This means that the cumulative causation idea combines the concepts of non-identity and continuity, though while it is straightforward to state the first concept, the boundaries on the latter concept are difficult to explain in an evolutionary way. Let me attempt to illustrate this by giving a reflexivity interpretation of the cumulative causation idea, since reflexivity can be shown to be essential to at least the non-identity side of the idea.

Reflexivity is a property of human action in the social realm whereby there is a causal feedback loop between how the views people have of the future and the habits they sustain feedback on and influence what they do in the present, and how what they do in the present feeds forward on and influences their views and habits in the future. Thus in a reflexive social world, the influence of human action on cause-effect sequences means they can never be the same over time—the non-identity side of the idea—and the simple view of causality some have, where no feedback loops exist and the present strictly determines the future, as in the mainstream's invariable effects, atomist ontology, must be rejected. Essentially, on a cumulative causation understanding, the so-called atoms are constantly evolving through the feedback loop process in virtue of agents continually acting on the conditions of action through time. Indeed, they cannot be atoms in the sense of unchanging entities. So reflexivity effectively explains the non-identity side of the cumulative causation idea. Yet Veblen's idea also allows for some notion of continuity in cause-effect sequences in the social realm. Let us then use this same feedback loop analysis to move from the non-identity side of the idea to this more difficult one, by distinguishing two polar views of how continuity might be understood and then using that distinction to lay out an intermediate ground to explain cumulative causation.

At one extreme, the continuity in both entities and cause-effect sequences might be thought so minimal as to be basically non-existent. I characterize this case as a Heraclitian world, after the pre-Socratic Greek philosopher, Heraclitus of Ephesus. Heraclitus believed that change characterized everything (*Panta rhei* in Ancient Greek, meaning "everything flows") and is famous for expressing this in terms of the notion that one can never step into the same river twice. Yet Heraclitus was also a proponent of a "unity of opposites" idea, which is manifest in the river image as well. That is, to be able to say one cannot step into the same river twice—his idea of all-encompassing change—one needs to presuppose the same river, albeit having the property of moving—the opposite of the idea of all-encompassing change. We can interpret this combination as a comment on the viability of this polar extreme as a reading of Veblen's continuity idea. In effect, if taken to this extreme, namely, as there being no continuity in the world whatsoever because all is change, the continuity concept becomes paradoxical and incoherent.

At the other extreme, a continuity in entities and cause-effect relations might be taken to the point of excluding change altogether. If we stay with the pre-Socratic world, the historic opponent of Heraclitus was Parmenides of Elea, who essentially argued that the concept of truth requires we say that nothing changes and change is only an appearance. On this view, truth implies that what is, simply is, and can never be but what it is. More fully, Parmenides' metaphysical-logical argument (using a kind of *reductio* indirect reasoning) was that what is must always have been the case, because if what is had never existed, it would have to have been in a state of becoming and the concept of becoming is incoherent, because it requires that something come out of nothing. But surely this view too is paradoxical and, accordingly, neither should this polar extreme reading be seen as a viable way of interpreting Veblen's continuity concept.

How, then, can we use the reflexivity formulation of cumulative causation to interpret continuity in a way that gives us a characterization of the concept intermediate to these extremes? An advantage of a reflexivity formulation is that it is true to Veblen's emphasis on historical time. The feedback loop analysis, then, cannot be described without placing agents in time, or in effect seeing them straddling time in that their actions always link the future and the present. What this implies, then, is that when agents change what they are doing in the present in light of their view of the future, they change what they are doing according to their understanding of how existing cause-effect sequences can be exploited to achieve their future goals, so that it is human action, understood reflexively, which creates continuity between non-identical cause-effect sequences across time. This role human action plays gives us an interpretation of continuity for the cumulative causation idea in which change presupposes a stability about cause-effect in the present, and this stability simultaneously lays the basis for change in cause-effect sequences in the future. On this intermediate ground reading, therefore, neither polar extreme reading provides a tenable account of Veblen's cumulative causation idea, neither Heraclitus' all-is-change nor Parmenides' there-is-no-change. I suggest, then, that we employ this intermediate interpretation both as an explanatory tool for investigating the ontology of the social realm and also to avoid polar extreme views of cause-effect sequences that might make the cumulative causation idea vulnerable to easy critique, undermining its plausibility.

Returning to Lawson's critique of the mainstream ontological preconceptions, we find three positions he emphasizes that a cumulative causation view implies about the nature of social reality: (1) it is processual and highly transient; (2) its phenomena are characterized by emergence and the appearance of novelty; and (3) its phenomena are constituted in relation to one another, or the entities of the social world are internally related (Lawson, Chapter 1: 36). These ideas are all important for developing an alternative social ontology for economics and in need of further discussion if we are to take Lawson's advice to stop talking about neoclassicism and focus on social ontology. I take them in order.

Social reality as processual and highly transient

Saying that social reality is processual and highly transient can be taken in two ways, which may seem indistinguishable but are different. One can say it is the nature of social reality that it is processual and highly transient in itself, or one can say it is a property of social reality that it is processual and highly transient. The former view is a Heraclitian one and is inherently paradoxical. How can one refer to anything that constantly changes? There is no "thing" one can refer to if that "thing" is always different. The latter view that it is rather a property of social reality that it is processual and highly transient is what Heraclitus' own unity of opposites idea can achieve if we charitably read him as positing the river to be able to say you cannot step into it twice. Then one refers to the river as a single "thing" to be able to ascribe to it the property of always moving. As a pre-Aristotelian, Heraclitus lacked the substance-property distinction and thus employed the more awkward "unity of opposites" idea. However, Lawson inherits millennia of philosophical thinking and can thus be fairly ascribed the view that a key property of social reality is that it is processual and highly transient, rather than the view that social reality is in itself processual, as he seems to say in his paper.

If this seems an unnecessary semantic point, note that it implies, oddly perhaps given his emphasis on social reality being highly transient, that we can say what the *un*changing nature of social reality is or what social reality always and necessarily is. Specifically, what social reality for Lawson is, and always is, is a system of change, or in the terms he specifically employs to say this that include reference to human action, social reality is and always is an agency/structure interaction in which agency and structure are each continually undergoing change and the relationship between agency and structure is also always undergoing change (e.g., Lawson, 2003: 49ff). As I interpret how he has generally explained this idea across his writings, agency, a principle of human action, conditions social structures, which, as constituted out of social relationships, condition human action. My interpretation may not do justice to how Lawson understands this idea, but I believe it is sufficient to make my main point here, namely, that Lawson's idea that: "social reality is processual" is not the untenable, Heraclitian all-is-change polar extreme sort of view, despite his apparent statements to this effect, but rather the perhaps not best expression of his view that the given, unchanging nature of social reality itself is as an agency-structure interaction.

What follows from this is that, while indeed it is a property of social reality that it is processual and highly transient, since this is what seeing the agency/structure pair as interaction requires, it is also—to put this in quite the opposite way—a property of social reality that it is recurringly stable and temporarily unchanging. That is, when we adopt an agency/structure interaction view, social reality has both the property of change and also the property of stability. While this may seem to simply introduce another paradox, it need not be taken this way. Indeed, Veblen's cumulative causation thinking works along just these lines without being paradoxical, since as an evolutionary view cause-effect sequences at later times derive from cause-effect sequences existing at earlier times. Earlier sequences are then in effect temporarily stable and at least for a time relatively unchanging since they provide the basis for change, and yet since later sequences are different, cumulative causation exhibits transience in cause-effect sequences as well. Put in terms of Lawson's agency/structure interaction view, human action presupposes social structures, so social structures must be stable enough to provide a basis for human action. Yet human action also transforms social structures, demonstrating their changing character. In other words, as in Veblen's cumulative causation evolutionary historical view, so in Lawson's agency/structure model there is not only change but importantly also stability within a process of change. Thus, we can confidently say that neither Veblen nor Lawson are Heraclitians!

Thus it is not accurate to simply say that social reality is processual and highly transient, as this is an incomplete characterization of the properties of social reality. I make this argument because it seems that the emphasis in "What is this 'school' called neoclassical economics?" is too strong on the side of social reality seen as changing, and too weak on the side of social reality seen as in some manner unchanging. This is not just a philosophical point, because Lawson uses this emphasis to essentially rule out *all* mathematical modeling and include any event regularities in the domain of social ontology. For many heterodox economists, who are otherwise quite sympathetic to much of his argument, and who in many instances also hold an evolutionary understanding of social reality, this move ultimately renders Lawson's critique of the mainstream ineffective. Some critics charge his argument rules out all quantitative reasoning in economics. No doubt this is too strong, and Lawson denies he does. It is the modeling and exclusive recourse to event regularities that is the problem. But where is the line between use of quantitative reasoning and mathematical modeling? I make no attempt to revisit this debate and only note that it is clearly hard to discuss substantive theorizing in economics (the doctrines we discuss) if social reality is seen purely as processual and highly transient. What would one refer to if what one refers to is not what it is because it has already changed? This would then leave critical theory isolated within the space of methodology.

So it is tempting to conclude that the emphasis in this current reading of Veblen represents a step back from his agency/structure interaction analysis, and is not helpful to the interpretation of Veblen either. However, I withhold this judgment, because Lawson has things to say about emergence and internal relations in the social world that gives us both a different view of his argument and more weight to his agency/structure interaction thinking.

Emergence and the appearance of novelty

The concept of emergence is fundamental to an alternative social ontology, since it requires rejection of the mainstream economics idea that social reality is constituted out of atoms that always have the same independent and invariable causal effects in their interaction with other atoms, whatever the context. If the stuff of social reality always works in the same invariable way, there can be nothing new or novel in the world, and science then becomes a taxonomic exercise in the classification of "normal" or "natural" phenomena. Emergence is also intrinsic to the idea that a fundamental property of social reality is change, since the concept is defined by the idea that what emerges is not reducible to that from which it emerges. That is, emergent or novel phenomena are "emergent upon" phenomena to which they are related, but which cannot fully explain them. Further, the concept of emergence is fundamental to the agency/structure model since agency and structure constitute two different dimensions of social reality that condition one another, so that each must be emergent upon the other.

In "What is this 'school' called neoclassical economics?" then, Lawson says that social reality is: "an emergent phenomenon of human interaction" (Lawson, Chapter 1: 36). It seems it should be that social reality is an emergent phenomenon of agency/structure interaction, though it may have been intended that "human interaction" means "agency/structure interaction." Thus, if we describe the agency/structure interaction in a reflexive way in terms of feedback loops, we would say that people act with an expectation of the future together with an understanding of the nature of their actions and their possible consequences as conditioned by social structures, and that the effects of their actions in the present then condition the evolution of social structures. Thus, both human action and social structures are emergent upon one another. Similarly, when we think of change in Veblen's cumulative causation terms, an historical evolution of cause-effect sequences exhibits emergence in that cause-effect sequences at later times are emergent upon cause-effect sequences of earlier times in the sense that the former are related to, but not fully explainable in terms of, the latter.

Emergence is thus fundamental to agency/structure reasoning and cumulative causation, but how can the idea actually be explained, given critiques of the idea dating back as far as Parmenides, which argue that emergence essentially means that something comes out of nothing. Lawson's strategy, then, is to explain emergence in terms of different levels of social reality and how entities combine across them.

> An emergent entity ... is usually found, or anyway held, to be composed out of elements deemed to be situated at a different (lower) level of reality to itself, but which have (perhaps through being modified) become organised as components of the emergent (higher level) entity or causal totality. 'Emergence', then, as widely interpreted is ultimately a compositional term and involves components being *organised rather than aggregated*.
> (Lawson, Chapter 1, note 12: 70, emphasis added; also cf. 2003: 43–44, and Lawson 2013a)

Clearly there is a metaphorical quality to this reference to higher and lower levels, since the evolution of social reality for Veblen or Lawson does not really occur in any sort of Euclidian spatial framework, and I accordingly recommend that this language be set aside or used with proper caveats. More work is done in explaining the concept, however, in the comparison between the different ways in which components of entities get combined, with the difference being between when they are organized and result in emergent entities versus when they are aggregated without resulting in emergent entities. However, the difference between these cases is not immediately clear, because an aggregation of a set of components is also an organization of them. So clearly Lawson has a particular kind of organization in mind. What is it?

As a first pass, we can use the idea of organic connection to say that emergent entities are somehow "more than the sum" of their components, thus not reducible to them, thus emergent upon them. To make this conception persuasive, we would need to be able to distinguish it from non-emergent entities whose components are merely aggregated and are not "more than the sum" of their components. Yet the "more than the sum" idea is vulnerable to the eyes of the beholder problem. An aggregation of a set of components is not organic for Lawson, but another person might see this producing a novel entity if the aggregation was new to them and served some distinct purpose. Then a non-organized entity would also be an emergent one, and the idea of being organized loses its leverage. Putting aside the eye of the beholder problem, even aggregated entities, taking the meaning of aggregation to be that they are additively assembled, can be irreducible to their components, as in the famous sand pile example (Bak *et al.*, 1987). As grains of sand are added to a pile of sand, at some transition point the pile collapses, so it follows that the pile has a property over and above its character as an aggregation of sand grain components. Thus, it is not clear what distinguishes organization and aggregation. One might then just abandon the distinction and say that all combinations of components produce novel, emergent entities. But this strategy faces the problem of telling us why combination generates something novel and emergent. Might not the *disorganization* of an entity produce something novel and emergent? Then we run the risk of being pushed to the conclusion that everything is emergent, and the term collapses simply on the results of change.

I suggest, then, we rather adopt a Veblenian reflexivity defense of emergence in virtue of how a reflexivity analysis works through the property of self-referentiality. Thus, when we explain cumulative causation we say that the operation of causality in the world continually feeds back upon and transforms the very conditions on which causality operates, and that cause-effect relations continually evolve and are never constant because of this. A cumulative causation process is self-referential, then, in the sense that it references and operates upon itself and, in virtue of this, continually changes its own components, thereby securing novelty through time. In contrast, with aggregation the aggregated entity does not act on the character of its components. In the sand pile example, the sand grains are not changed in themselves by their aggregation, including if the pile collapses or otherwise changes its character. In effect, they are like Lawson's atoms, invariable and constant in their effects in combination with one another. Thus, however they are piled, there is nothing ontologically novel and emergent in this as compared to what occurs in a self-referential process in which entities that combine components always change their components. To defend emergence, then, I believe we need to understand process reflexively in this way, whether in connection with a Veblenian evolutionary model or in connection with the agency/structure interaction model. As noted above, what a reflexivity analysis does is make time intrinsic to explaining the phenomena of the social realm; that is, make our explanation truly historical. Time is absent from the organization-aggregation argument for emergence, so that argument seems vulnerable to being simply a taxonomic strategy without genuine causal dimensions. With this in mind, let us turn to the last topic, the internal relatedness of social reality.

The internal relatedness of social reality

Lawson emphasizes that the internal relatedness of social reality grounds the place of emergence in an alternative social ontology.

> Furthermore, social reality is found to be composed of emergent phenomena that (far from being isolatable) are actually constituted in relation (that is, are internally related) to other things, and ultimately to everything else (for example, students and teachers, *qua* students and teachers, are constituted in relation to each other; so are employers and employees ... and so forth) ... Constitutive social relations, in short, are a fundamental feature of social reality.
> (Lawson, Chapter 1: 36)

Emergent phenomena, then, are emergent upon social relatedness, as in the student-teacher example. Students and teachers are what they are only in relation to one another. If they are what they are in some way apart from their relation to one another, they would be externally rather than internally related. Were they externally related, they would be like atoms, acting as their natures determined irrespective of the context of interaction. So internal relatedness is comprehensive, as it were, of the things related. This means that since the things related internally are still distinguishable—students and teachers are still different from one another—there is something over and above them being the different types of entities they are that explains their difference. What is over and above them, then, is emergent upon their difference. Emergence, then, is an intrinsic characteristic of the internal relatedness of the world.

This argument works best, one can see, with pair-wise relations, because it is plausible that the things paired, say students and teachers, lack meaning apart from their relation to one another. What is a teacher but a teacher of students? The argument is less clear when non-pair-wise relations come into play. What is the relation of student to employer? By the standard of internally related student-teacher pair, it seems student and employer are externally related. Arguments to the effect that student and employer are ultimately internally related through some chain of pair-wise relations are strained and on the surface implausible, if only because the standard of internal relatedness is the close connection of cases such as student and teacher. The back-up argument would be to say something like, everything under capitalism is internally related, using the "under capitalism" expression as a systemic internal relation device. Yet this argument is sufficiently tendenticus as to be little more than a way of assuming the conclusion, where those who are candidates to accept it simply share a broad-based desire to see capitalism as being at the root of everything.

It seems more reasonable to conclude, then, that not all things are internally related (as no doubt Lawson also believes). At least the burden of argument should rest on those who suppose they are. Another possible problem with internal relatedness, I think, can be set aside. If the meanings and nature of student and teacher are not fully, but only partially, exhausted by their relation to one another (a kind of hybrid relationship), their degree of internal relatedness could still be argued to support emergent phenomena. So we would still be entitled to say that in a world in which internal relatedness is in some degree constitutive of social reality, we have elements of a way of understanding emergence. I say "elements" for two reasons.

First, because though we can see the outline of the argument that the comprehensiveness of an internal relation generates phenomena over and above what we know about what it relates to, the claim that these phenomena are novel and emergent remains to be demonstrated persuasively. Above, I have already argued that the "more than the sum" organicism idea is not likely to do the job. But there is another perhaps more serious problem in explaining emergence in terms of internal relations: if what constitutes the phenomena to be judged to be emergent is the highly related nature of the entities related, why should the constituted phenomena even be regarded as emergent and novel? Why are not any "new" phenomena already comprehended under the relatedness of the entities? In effect, why should there be anything new under a sun that shines so brightly? Granted, this is a skeptical argument, and skeptical arguments should be sometimes dismissed out of hand. But I pose this argument nonetheless, because the connection between internal relatedness and emergence has not been set out beyond the language of things being constituted together.

Second, then, I say there are "elements" of an argument here for emergence, because the case has been made entirely on the structural side of the agency/structure analysis in terms of relations as if agency and human action plays no role and can be ignored. In defense of Lawson, he does emphasize human practice when he argues for a processual conception, so we should assume that he is thinking in terms of agency/structure interaction as in his earlier writings. In my view, however, the self-referentiality argument I gave in the last section about how to justify emergence through a reflexivity interpretation of Veblen and the agency/structure view, still holds. The self-referentiality it depends upon only explains emergence by supposing agents operate on what in effect are the conditions of their own agency, namely, social structures. Just as for Veblen, causality is cumulative, because the operation of causality in the world transforms the conditions of causality, so in agency/structure interaction emergent phenomena exist because agents' actions continually transform the social structures that condition action.

The risk of minimizing action and agency is that one's vision of social reality can then veer toward becoming an entirely relational one, as in the position advanced by F. H. Bradley (1893), a neo-Hegelian proponent of view that "all relations are internal." A particular problem with this approach is that once one sees everything as internally related, one is likely to adopt the viewpoint of the whole and be left pitching one's arguments in terms of systems and social totalities. Then again, everything (and nothing) ends up being novel and emergent. In contrast, the advantage of the agency/structure interaction approach is it includes a principle not reducible to relations, that is, the principle of action. By nature, action changes the world and so generates emergent phenomena. The world may well still be highly internally related as Lawson claims. Yet, that agency influences structure can also be disruptive of systems of internal relations, as when employees reject or resist hierarchical power arrangements in their relations with employers. I conclude, therefore, that the idea that social reality is highly internally related is important to an alternative social ontology, but that this idea needs to be used in a measured way that recognizes not only the importance of human action but also the diversity of relational forms.

What is this "school" called neoclassical economics?

Lawson concludes his paper by saying that in modern economics there is a: "basic tension between ontology and method ... that hinders serious attempts to overcoming the real problems of the discipline" (Lawson, Chapter 1: 65). If the mainstream method is that of mathematical modeling and event regularities, and its implicit ontology is that of atoms constantly exercising invariable effects, then this thesis seems confusing since mainstream method and ontology rather appear to mutually support one another, as I interpreted Lawson's argument at the outset. If there were evidence of any commitment to an evolutionary ontology in the mainstream, it would indeed make sense to say there exists a tension between method and ontology. But I see very few mainstream economists entertaining any sort of evolutionary historical thinking, and most are fully committed to mathematical modeling. I agree, following Veblen, that this makes mainstream economics what he calls a taxonomic science dedicated to identifying "natural" and "normal" relationships. Thus the rise of behavioral economics can simply be interpreted as the investigation of previously unexplored "natural" and "normal" relationships. I also agree that the method and ontology of the mainstream has hindered the development of the discipline. But what rather seems to hinder the development of the discipline is the *lack of tension* between method and ontology in mainstream economics.

Veblen coined the term "neoclassical" to classify all forms of economics that failed to adopt an evolutionary historical approach and settled for being a taxonomic one. Since this seems to continue to characterize the mainstream today, the implication seems to be that we should retain his usage instead of jettisoning the term. I am sympathetic to Lawson's desire to shift discussion from what neoclassicism is, substantively to the project of developing an alternative evolutionary social ontology, though this does not mean substantive critique should be overlooked. But it may better serve that goal to emphasize what the social ontology of the mainstream is, flagging it as neoclassical and emphasizing the interlocking nature of its ontology and method. Bringing Veblen's approach into the foreground seems to be an appropriate way to make a sharp distinction between the evolutionary and neoclassical method-ontology approaches.

This then raises an interesting issue for heterodox economics: Lawson's ultimate target in his paper. His concern seems to be that many heterodox economists ostensibly reason in a non-evolutionary way or taxonomically, simply posing their preferred "natural" and "normal" relationships (e.g., provisioning) as alternative to mainstream ones (e.g., efficiency). But in fairness, I believe many heterodox economists, who are not explicit about evolutionary processes, would be seen to be committed to evolutionary ontologies when pressed. So, in contrast to neoclassical method and ontology that line up, heterodox economists are indeed at risk of involving themselves in the "tension between ontology and method," which Lawson attributes to the mainstream. I would only suggest that the tension he sees in heterodoxy is not as basic as the one he attributes to the mainstream. One of the defining characteristics of heterodox economics (cf. Davis, 2008: 360), I suggest, is to reason relationally in agency/structure terms. Surely this presupposes an evolutionary view of the world?

Acknowledgement

I am grateful to Steve Fleetwood, Anne Mayhew, Robert McMaster, and Jamie Morgan for very helpful comments on a previous version of this chapter.

References

Bak, P., Tang, C. and Wiesenfeld, K. (1987) Self-organized criticality: An explanation of 1/f noise. *Physical Review Letters* 59(4): 381–384.
Bradley, F. H. (1893) *Appearance and Reality*. Oxford: Clarendon Press.
Davis, J. (2008) The turn in recent economics and return of orthodoxy. *Cambridge Journal of Economics* 32(3): 349–366.
Lawson, T. (2003) *Reorienting Economics*. London, UK: Routledge.
Lawson, T. (2013a) Emergence, morphogenesis, causal reduction and downward causation, in Archer, M. (ed.) *Social Morphogenesis*. New York, NY: Springer, pp. 61–84.
Lawson, T. (2013b) What is this 'school' called neoclassical economics? *Cambridge Journal of Economics* 37(5): 947–983. Also published in this book as Chapter 1, and page numbers cited refer to those in this book.
Veblen, T. (1900) The preconceptions of economic science III. *Quarterly Journal of Economics* 14(2): 240–269.

6 Why is this 'school' called neoclassical economics?

Classicism and neoclassicism in historical context

Nuno Ornelas Martins

Introduction

Tony Lawson (Chapter 1) recently provided a stimulating and provocative account of neoclassical economics. According to Lawson (Chapter 1), neoclassical economics is characterised by a methodological inconsistency. Drawing upon Thorstein Veblen's (1900) usage of the term neoclassical, Lawson (Chapter 1) argues that neoclassical economists adopt: 'a taxonomic orientation in the form of deductivism at the level of method', which is inconsistent with the 'historical processual ontology of unfolding causal sequence at the level of events' (Lawson, Chapter 1: 66). That is, neoclassical economists are a group of economists who employ deductivist methods, which presuppose closed systems (that is, systems in which regularities of the form 'if event X then event Y' are ubiquitous) while simultaneously acknowledging that the social realm is a dynamic and evolving open system.

Lawson (1997, 2003a) characterises mainstream economics as an uncritical commitment to the use of mathematico-deductivist methods, which presuppose closed systems and are therefore inappropriate for the analysis of open systems such as the social realm. Many authors have criticised Lawson for failing to note that many mainstream economists acknowledge that the social realm is an open system – see Fleetwood (1999), Lewis (2004), Graça Moura and Martins (2008) and Fullbrook (2009) for some of those critiques and for some responses to those critiques. We can now see that those economists, who are committed to mathematico-deductivist methods, but believe that the social realm is an open system, are simply what Lawson (Chapter 1) calls neoclassical economists. Thus Lawson (Chapter 1) notes that: 'the group under focus here is not the set of mathematical deductivist modellers *per se*, but that subset of the latter who at some level simultaneously accept a historical or causal-processual ontology' (Lawson, Chapter 1: 59).

Lawson's conclusion is that the term neoclassical economics ultimately denotes a methodological inconsistency. I will argue that this happens primarily because neoclassical economics suggests a false idea of continuity with classical political economy, a continuity which, in truth, does not exist. In fact, the conception of 'classical economics' that Veblen adopts does not characterise adequately the classical project. Classical political economy was, in fact, when properly understood, an approach which shared many commonalities with Veblen's own approach.

As I shall argue, there is nothing in Veblen's approach that makes it incompatible with classical political economy, as defined by Karl Marx. Quite the contrary, classical political economy is an approach centred on the production and distribution of the surplus which is continued by Marx and Veblen, who pointed out how a given social class appropriates part of the surplus produced by another class. The surplus approach stands in stark contrast to the scarcity approach that was developed after the marginal revolution, which focuses on scarcity rather than on the surplus. I will argue that the term neoclassical, if used to denote any tradition at all, should be used to denote a tradition that somehow continues the classical surplus approach. Furthermore, if the continuous use of the term neoclassical to denote the project usually associated with it throughout the twentieth century makes the proposed usage problematic, then the term should be dropped in order to avoid confusion, as Lawson (Chapter 1) suggests.

Neoclassical economics and closed systems

When employing the term neoclassical economics, Veblen (1900) intends to identify a tension between what he calls the 'teleological' premises and 'taxonomic' method of classical economics on the one hand, and the new developments brought by authors who draw upon classical economics in order to study evolutionary processes on the other.

The classical method, according to Veblen, consists in finding uniformities, which assume the form of a 'natural law', while presupposing a teleological conception according to which the economy tends to a normal position. According to the classical method so defined, economic science consists in a taxonomic exercise, that is, in the identification of natural laws, which characterise the normal position, in order to then inspect whether existing reality fits or not into those natural laws, or normal position of the economy.

Veblen (1898) advances instead an evolutionary approach, where social reality is seen as a process of change, which cannot be aptly characterised in terms of natural laws. However, Veblen (1900) also notes that some authors who adopt the classical method seem to presuppose an evolutionary, rather than a teleological, conception of reality. As Lawson (Chapter 1: 51) explains, Veblen (1900: 261–262) identifies the work of Alfred Marshall as the 'best work', which engages in the study of evolutionary processes drawing upon the classical approach, and sees the contribution of John Neville Keynes as the 'maturest exposition' of the methodology which underpins the perspective adopted by Marshall.

For Veblen (1900) neoclassical economists adopt a method (the classical method), which is inconsistent with the processual nature of reality which they seem to accept. Drawing upon Veblen's original usage of the term neoclassical, Lawson (Chapter 1) argues that the term can be best used to characterise economists who adopt a classical taxonomic approach, of finding natural laws from which specific events can be deduced while nevertheless possessing a 'new' vision of reality according to which: 'social reality is a historical process of cumulative causation' (Lawson, Chapter 1: 51).

Hence, the prefix 'neo' denotes a new vision of reality, informed by an evolutionary perspective, while the term classical refers to the influence that the old taxonomic approach still has on economists like Marshall and Keynes. Marshall, like Veblen, was influenced by the evolutionary perspective of Herbert Spencer and Charles Darwin, which brought the 'new' elements that Marshall included in his neoclassical approach, leading to a tension between a 'new' evolutionary perspective and a 'classical' taxonomic approach.

As Lawson (Chapter 1: 56) also notes, Veblen (1909: 620–622) sees the marginalist approach of authors like John Bates Clark as: 'a branch or derivative of the English classical economists of the nineteenth century', with the difference being that the marginalists adhere more consistently to the postulates of the classical method. That is, the marginalists adopt more consistently a taxonomic approach while presupposing a teleological conception of reality. Marshall's approach is neoclassical in the sense that it moves beyond other marginalist authors who did not go beyond the classical teleological conception.

There is, however, an important methodological difference that emerges with the marginal revolution, namely the adoption of differential calculus. Differential calculus had already been applied within economics in the first half of the nineteenth century by authors like Johann Heinrich Von Thünen and Augustin Cournot. In his *Principles of Economics*, Marshall (1890) refers to Cournot's principle of continuity and Von Thünen's principle of substitution as key elements of his approach. At the end of the preface of the first edition of his *Principles*, Marshall (1890) notes that under the guidance of Cournot (and also Von Thünen, to a lesser extent), he learned to focus not so much on aggregate quantities, as the classical authors did (and his student John Maynard Keynes would also do) but rather on increments of quantities and on the stable equilibrium between marginal increments of demand and of the cost of production.

In his *Industry and Trade*, Marshall (1919) notes that the method of focusing on marginal increments, which Cournot and Von Thünen used, is an application of Newton's and Leibniz's differential calculus. Newton and Leibniz studied cases of infinitesimal changes and reached the conclusion that we can focus on the direct effect of an increment while neglecting the indirect effects, which occur due to the impact of a given increment on another increment. Marshall argued that we can thus focus on the direct effect of a change in 'X' on 'Y', while neglecting the indirect effect, such as the effect of 'X' on another variable 'Z', which in turn has an influence on 'Y'.

Since the increments Newton and Leibniz were considering were infinitesimally small, the impact of an infinitesimally small increment (of 'X' on 'Z') on another infinitesimally small increment (of 'Z' on 'Y') was, as Marshall says, a second order of smalls, and thus a very small thing of a very small thing, which can be neglected. Following the method of Newton and Leibniz, Marshall argued that if the period of time is small enough so that the changes are small, we can focus on the direct effect of 'X' on 'Y' while assuming everything else (the indirect effects which take place through other variables 'Z') to remain constant, for a time, in a pound called *ceteris paribus* – see Martins (2013: chapter 1) for a discussion.

As Marshall explains, his method of focusing on direct effects while assuming that everything else remains constant presupposes that we can focus on constant conjunctions of the form 'if X then Y', while neglecting other conditions 'Z'. Lawson (1997) designates systems in which constant conjunctions of this kind are ubiquitous as closed systems. Lawson (1997) further explains that mainstream economics can be best understood as a commitment to mathematical deductivist methods, which presuppose closed systems, that is, presuppose constant conjunctions of the form 'if X then Y'.

Differential calculus, which leads us to focus on the effect of a given marginal change 'X' on another variable 'Y' became widespread in mainstream economics, in fields such as microeconomics (where it is used in utility maximisation, profit maximisation and cost minimisation), econometrics (where it is used in estimation techniques such as the least squares method, the method of maximum likelihood and the generalised method of moments) and macroeconomics (where optimisation techniques are often used, not least when searching for microeconomic microfoundations based on utility maximisation). Other mathematical tools developed within mainstream economics, such as fixed point theorems (widely used in game theory and general equilibrium theory), presuppose closed systems too – see Lawson (2003a: chapter 10) or Martins (2013: chapter 5) for a discussion.

Drawing upon Veblen's (1900) original definition of neoclassical economics, Lawson (Chapter 1) suggests that neoclassical economics can be best characterised as an inconsistency between a taxonomic approach, which includes the use of mathematico-deductivist methods that presuppose closed systems on the one hand, and a processual conception of reality that presupposes open systems on the other hand. The recognition that the world is an open system follows from Marshall's endorsement of an evolutionary perspective. The emphasis on closed systems, in turn, follows from Marshall's method of focusing on the direct effects of 'X' on 'Y', which allowed Marshall to focus on the partial (or particular) equilibrium of a given market, while neglecting other effects, which were assumed to be infinitesimally small, for a certain amount of time at least. In particular, Marshall was able to define supply and demand curves, which are assumed to be independent of one another, as long as everything else remains constant, for a time, in a pound called *ceteris paribus*.

Classical political economy and vulgar economy

Piero Sraffa (1925, 1926) showed the inconsistencies of Marshall's partial equilibrium analysis. In economics we are typically not concerned with infinitesimal increments. Thus, the marginalist method of focusing on marginal changes of a given factor, while assuming everything else is constant, is misguided. In particular, Sraffa showed that it is not reasonable to assume that supply and demand curves are independent, although his critique can be applied to marginal analysis in general – see Martins (2013) for a discussion with reference to Sraffa's unpublished manuscripts.

Sraffa (1960) defines 'classical political economy' according to Marx's original definition, which is very different from the definition of classical political economy adopted afterwards by Marshall, Veblen and Keynes. Marx (and Sraffa) used the term classical political economy in order to designate the approach of authors like William Petty, Richard Cantillon, François Quesnay, Adam Smith and David Ricardo, an approach which runs from the late seventeenth century to the early nineteenth century. Marx distinguishes this group of classical economists from the group he called 'vulgar' economists, which includes such economists as Thomas Robert Malthus, John Stuart Mill, William Nassau Senior, John Elliot Cairnes and most of the nineteenth-century economists often designated as 'Ricardian' economists (who, according to Marx, were not really following Ricardo's classical approach, but rather 'vulgarising' it).

Marx argues that the classical economists were concerned with the underlying causes of value, which are found in the objective process of production. The classical authors focused on objective entities when measuring cost, such as labour time, or the quantity of land which is necessary to sustain a labourer who engages in a certain quantity of working time. The 'vulgar' economists from Malthus to Cairnes, in contrast, can be identified as those who, instead of looking at the underlying causes of value, focused on superficial phenomena, like supply and demand, and adopted a subjective conception of cost, which makes it difficult to compare costs that cannot be objectively measured.

The emphasis on subjective aspects is connected to the use of supply and demand as the ultimate determinants of value. In order to achieve a conception where supply and demand are ultimate and independent forces, the vulgar economists conceptualised supply and demand as forces driven by subjective desires, which are exogenously given. For the classical authors, in contrast, effective demand was not an independent or exogenous force, since it was defined with reference to the natural price, which in turn depends upon the objective conditions of production (and hence Marx preferred to use the term 'prices of production', rather than 'natural prices'), and consists in the cost of production, which includes wages, profits and rent.

The classical claim that prices tend to the cost of production presupposes that there is no full employment. If demand exceeds supply, the market price exceeds the natural price (that is, the cost of production). But since labour is available for further production (that is, there is no full employment of labour), more goods can be produced in order to satisfy existing demand and prices return to the cost of production, as Ricardo argued. If supply exceeds demand, in turn, the market price will be below the natural price, and a smaller quantity of goods will be produced (increasing the unemployment of labour) and the market price tends towards the natural price again. Supply and demand are not determinants of value, but rather forces that merely lead the market price to fluctuate around the natural price, that is, the cost of production, as Ricardo argued when elaborating upon Smith's perspective.

Walras criticised Ricardo's assumption that more goods can be produced when demand exceeds supply, thus presupposing full employment, as do the marginalist authors in general. But if supply cannot be increased in order to offset the increase in prices caused by an increase in demand, then we are left with supply and demand as the ultimate determinants of value, as Malthus argued in his exchanges with Ricardo. Vulgar economy developed a subjective explanation of supply and demand as exogenous factors, explained by biological and psychological laws, that is, by universal laws pertaining to land and the human mind.

If we follow Marx's interpretation of classical political economy, we find that the marginal revolution only consolidated the subjective supply and demand analysis that was already being developed within nineteenth-century 'vulgar economy'. The great break of continuity in economic theory does not occur in the marginal revolution, since the marginalist authors were merely continuing the supply and demand analysis of the classical authors. Rather, the great break within economic theory occurs when economists like Malthus argue that value is determined ultimately by supply and demand, and when costs start to be measured using subjective elements like 'abstinence' (a notion introduced by Senior) or 'sacrifice' (a notion used by Cairnes), in contrast to the classical approach where value is explained in terms of objective costs to be found in the process of production (such as the quantity of land necessary to sustain the labourer, or labour time).

Thus, the emphasis on subjective elements was already present in nineteenth-century vulgar economy, much before the marginal revolution. While 'vulgar' economists like Senior and Cairnes introduced notions such as 'abstinence' or 'sacrifice' when explaining costs and supply, the marginal revolution undertaken by Carl Menger, Stanley Jevons, Léon Walras and

Alfred Marshall led to the development of subjective elements pertaining to demand, which had already been developed before by Hermann Heinrich Gossen and Jules Dupuit.

Under Marx's conception, the term classical thus denotes a realist approach, concerned with underlying causes (consistent with a structured ontology such as the one advocated by Lawson). Marx, unlike Veblen, does not see the classical approach as a taxonomic approach to science in which the latter adopts natural laws. Such a description would fit more easily into what Marx called vulgar economy. In fact, the notion of 'natural law' appears especially in the nineteenth-century 'vulgar economy'. Veblen's characterisation of classical economy corresponds thus to what Marx called vulgar economy, which was indeed a taxonomic exercise aimed at identifying natural laws, which were seen as universal biological and psychological laws.

Effectively, Veblen refers often to the English: 'classical economists of the nineteenth century'. But the dominant school of economic thought in nineteenth-century England was the vulgar approach that runs from Malthus to Cairnes, which is often called classical political economy, under the assumption that it includes the work of Smith and Ricardo. But classical political economy, as defined by Marx, is not circumscribed to England since it includes Quesnay and the Physiocrats, and is essentially an eighteenth-century school, if we adopt an extended view of the period and include Petty's contribution in the late seventeenth century, and Ricardo's contribution in the early nineteenth century. Veblen's reference to the English classical economists of the nineteenth century can then be seen as a confirmation that he means by classical what Marx meant by vulgar.

Deductive economics and critical economics

Marshall claims to be developing Ricardo's framework. But when so doing, Marshall draws upon John Stuart Mill's development of Ricardo's perspective, which had replaced Ricardo's objective costs with subjective elements. Marshall's neoclassical approach attempted to develop the marginalist ideas while incorporating the subjective conception of cost of the vulgar economists within his notion of 'real cost', and illustrated well that there need be no great difference between the vulgar economists (who were called classical economists by Marshall) and the marginalists.

Effectively, when F. Y. Edgeworth (1881) argues that: 'the first principle of Economics is that every agent is actuated only by self-interest' (Edgeworth, 1881: 16), he is only restating Senior's (1836) first postulate of economics, according to which each economic agent: 'desires to obtain additional wealth with as little sacrifice as possible' (Senior, 1836: 138). After Senior, economics is already on course to become a theory grounded on subjective notions. Those subjective notions are, in turn, the basis for the deduction of economic laws. After the development of the vulgar conception, economics becomes not only a subjectivist science, but also a deductivist science.

The vulgar conception, and the marginalist developments it received, were much criticised by authors of the Historical Schools, not only in Germany but also in Britain. Cliffe Leslie criticised the subjectivist and deductivist approach of the vulgar economists and their attempt to explain economic reality in terms of the subjective desire for wealth stressed by Senior. Gustav von Schmoller, a leading member of the German Historical School who had a great influence on Veblen, also criticised (or in fact responded to the criticisms of) Carl Menger.

Marshall was sympathetic towards the 'inductive' approach defended by the Historical School, while arguing that the inductive method, defended by the Historical School, should be combined with the deductive method advocated by the vulgar economists and the marginalists. Thus, Veblen sees Marshall's contribution as part of the 'best work' done by authors who follow the neoclassical approach, which can be more aptly characterised as the 'neo-vulgar' approach if we adopt Marx's definition of classical political economy.

But even if Marshall's contribution is, according to Veblen, representative of the 'best work' done within neoclassical economics, it remains very much committed to the deductive methods of the vulgar economists, further developed by the marginalists. Indeed, Marshall himself stresses that his work is in continuity with the contributions of authors of the 'vulgar' period like John Stuart Mill, who in turn had interpreted Smith and Ricardo in subjective terms. Nineteenth-century vulgar economy engaged in generalisations of a teleological kind, in order to engage in deductive exercises grounded on those generalisations. This method was continued by the marginalists, while also focusing on subjective elements as the basis for the construction of economic theory.

We can then see why Veblen did not see too much of a difference between the vulgar economists (whom he called classical economists) and marginal utility theory, other than the fact that the latter sticks more consistently to teleological premises. The method used by the marginalists was the same method used by the vulgar economists, namely the *deductive* method. The basis for deduction was a series of universal postulates on the human mind and biological laws. In vulgar economy, Senior's contribution provides the more systematic account of the underlying postulates used for deduction. After the marginal revolution, the utility function becomes the most important basis for the deduction of economic laws, to which we may add as well the neoclassical production function.

The emphasis of the classical authors was not on deduction based on universal psychological and biological laws. Rather, the classical authors focused on the conditions of possibility for the reproduction of economic activity. The method of focusing on the conditions of possibility for a given activity can be designated as a *critical* (or transcendental) method – see Lawson (2003a: chapter 2) for a discussion. It is critical (or transcendental) in the sense that it does not consist in merely deducing based on given premises or postulates but rather in criticising (or transcending) those premises or postulates, in order to question their adequacy.

It was in this sense that Immanuel Kant (who also influenced Veblen) used the term critical when studying the conditions of possibility of the activity for the production of knowledge. Marx drew upon this critical method when studying classical political economy. But while Kant adopted a critical (or transcendental) *idealism*, by focusing on the human mind, Marx adopted a critical (or transcendental) *realism*, by focusing on the actual conditions for the reproduction of socio-economic activity. In this process, Marx defined classical political economy more clearly in terms of the conditions of possibility for the reproduction of socio-economic activity.

Marx drew not only upon Kant's critical method (while subjecting Kant's own idealism to a critique) but also upon Friedrich Hegel's philosophy, according to which everything is *internally related*. Lawson (1997, 2003a) defines an internal relation as a relation which is constitutive of the related entities. The problem raised by internal relations concerns our possibility of gaining knowledge of a reality which is deeply interconnected. Our mind can only grasp a part of reality, but each part is always related to the whole. So when studying any aspect of reality, we are always missing its relations to some other parts of reality, since it is impossible for our mind to grasp the whole *qua* whole.

In order to address this problem, Lawson (1997) distinguishes between abstraction and isolation. Abstraction consists in focusing on a given part of reality while taking into account that it is related to other parts of reality we are abstracting from. Isolation consists in focusing on a given part of reality without taking into account its relations to other parts of reality. Marshall (who was also influenced by Hegel) addressed the problem of internal relations by isolating the direct effects from the indirect effects, that is, focusing on a part of reality while assuming that it is not affected (for a time, at least) by the other aspects of reality, which are assumed to remain constant. In so doing, Marshall engaged in what Lawson calls isolation.

Marx, in contrast, addressed the problem of internal relations by engaging in abstraction, as Lawson (1997) notes. Because Marx's analysis is based on abstraction, Marx could not provide exact mathematical formulations, which are assumed to be independent from everything else, such as Marshall's supply and demand curves that are used to determine exactly prices and quantities. Rather, Marx provided only an analysis of the underlying tendencies of capitalism, and even his explanation of prices of production was only an approximation.

Marx had a firm grasp of differential calculus, as one can see by his mathematical manuscripts preserved by Friedrich Engels (who gave them great importance). But like the classical authors, Marx used only arithmetic in his economics. Arithmetic, unlike calculus, deals with aggregate magnitudes rather than with marginal changes. When focusing on marginal changes using differential calculus, Marshall and the marginalists were led to focus on the effect of a given variable X on another variable Y while assuming everything else remains constant. Notions such as the principle of substitution (of one variable by another) are based on this method of focusing on two variables while assuming everything else remains constant.

Marx, and the classical authors, did not focus on marginal changes between some variables while assuming everything else remains constant. Marx, like the classical authors, looked at the reproduction of the system as a whole. Thus, Marx and the classical authors simply focus on what happens on average, over a long period of time, while focusing on aggregate quantities, rather than looking at marginal changes. The method of focusing on aggregate quantities was the method that Marshall abandoned (and Kalecki and Keynes recovered afterwards), when Marshall decided to focus on incremental changes instead.

The normal position and the reproduction of economic activity

The classical method of focusing on an average, normal position, which is seen as the condition of possibility for socio-economic reproduction, is often seen as the key source of inconsistency between the classical approach and Veblen's approach. So much so that the notion of a 'normal position' is often seen as one of the key aspects of the classical approach maintained by Marshall, which prevented him from developing his own evolutionary vision.

However, this assessment springs from a failure to understand the notion of a normal position. The notion of a normal position refers merely to the conditions of possibility for the reproduction of socio-economic activity, in a context where the word 'normal' could be replaced by other words such as 'habitual', 'customary' or 'conventional'. As Lawson (1997, 2003a) explains when developing the (critical realist) transformational model of social activity, the conditions of possibility for the reproduction of human activity are the social structures, including social positions, each attaches to given social rules. Those social structures are not only the condition of possibility for the reproduction of human activity, which they facilitate and constrain, but are themselves also reproduced and transformed through human activity (just as the human agent is also transformed in this process).

Those conditions of possibility include the more persistent elements of socio-economic life, which provide a stable basis for human activity, without which human action is simply impossible. Thus, when the classical authors refer to the notion of a 'necessary' or 'natural' price (which could also be called a 'normal' price, as Marshall does), they are not referring to a teleological natural law, but only to the habitual, customary or conventional price, which enables the reproduction of the economic system. Thus Marx writes:

> The price of production includes the average profit. And what we call price of production is the same thing that Adam Smith calls 'natural price', Ricardo 'price of production' or 'cost of production' and the Physiocrats *'prix nécessaire'*, though none of these people explained the difference between price of production and value. We call it price of production because in the long term it is the condition of supply, the condition for the reproduction of commodities, in each particular sphere of production.
>
> (Marx, 1981 [1894]: 300)

The 'necessary' or 'natural' price is merely the ordinary or average price found ex post within the process of economic reproduction. When engaging in economic activity, human agents possess certain expectations as to what constitutes a natural or normal price, informed by habit and custom acquired in past transactions. Because human agents are creatures of habit, the price that persists on average reaches a significance of its own, as a conventional price set by habit and custom.

However, because economic reality is a continuous process of change, it cannot be ensured that the market price is always equal to the natural price. The market price will often deviate from what convention dictates. But the classical authors never believed that an exact account could be given of the way in which the market price oscillates around the necessary or natural price. Even notions such as gravitation refer only to a vague process of fluctuation around what convention dictates.

The same applies to categories such as wages, profits, rent or interest. The focus of the classical authors is on a customary level of these, which enables the reproduction of the economic process. For the classical authors, wages are at the subsistence level. But for the classical authors, subsistence meant more than merely biological survival. The subsistence level is the level that enables a level of consumption that is perceived by society as an acceptable standard of living, given existing customs and habits.

For Veblen, the level of consumption also depends upon social factors, which lead to a given wage set by social factors too. Furthermore, for Veblen, it is not only wages but also profits and interest that are set by habituation:

> It will be noted that the explanation here offered of depression makes it a malady of the affections. The discrepancy which discourages business men is a discrepancy between that nominal capitalization which

they have set their hearts upon through habituation in the immediate past and that actual capitalizable value of their property which its current earning-capacity will warrant. But where the preconceptions of the business men engaged have, as commonly happens, in great part been fixed and legalized in the form of interest-bearing securities, this malady of the affections becomes extremely difficult to remedy, even though it be true that these legalized affections, preconceptions, or what not, center upon the metaphysical stability of the money unit.
(Veblen, 1904: 114)

Habituation leads to expectations not only concerning what is a reasonable price but also concerning what is a reasonable wage, profit or interest, as Veblen notes in this passage. As Veblen explains here, and Keynes also argued afterwards (and as Marshall had argued before both of them), crises and depressions occur precisely when those expectations are not met.

Profits and interest are part of the surplus, which is a central concept within classical political economy. When studying the reproduction of socio-economic activity, the emphasis of the classical authors and Marx is on the creation, extraction, distribution and use of the social surplus, which takes place in this context. The social surplus is the part of production that is not used in the reproduction of the existing economic system, and can be used in order to expand the existing economic system (as investment) or in the consumption of luxury goods. The surplus is the central notion addressed by the classical authors and Marx.

As Quesnay (1759) argued long ago in his analysis of the circular process of reproduction, the dynamics of the economy depend on whether the surplus is used for productive activities or for the consumption of luxury goods. When the surplus is used in productive activities, the economy will grow, leading to socio-economic expansion (and, one may add, possibly transformation too, if there are technological or organisational innovations as a consequence of this expansion). If the surplus is used mainly in luxury, the economy will decline, leading to socio-economic contraction. The classical authors saw the economy as a dynamic entity, where the allocation of the surplus is the central aspect to explain. The case of simple reproduction at an unchanging scale is a particular case within classical analysis. The emphasis on a stationary state emerges only in vulgar economy, when the emphasis is placed on deduction based on unchanging biological and psychological laws.

Veblen's critique of the classical emphasis on a taxonomic exercise presupposing unchanging laws is an apt characterisation of vulgar economy, but not of classical political economy, where dynamic aspects are explained when addressing the reproduction and allocation of the surplus. In fact, once we interpret classical political economy properly (as an analysis of the reproduction and distribution of the surplus), we find that it is Veblen's own approach, rather than Marshall, which can be seen as a continuation of classical political economy.

The social surplus is also a central concept in Veblen's (1899, 1904, 1914, 1921) own contribution, which is centred on how the surplus is appropriated by a 'leisure class', which uses the surplus in luxury (a point which is also central to all the classical authors), in a context where the process of production is controlled by the 'captains of industry' who try to extract as much surplus as possible. The key to understanding the formation of a leisure class is the production and distribution of a surplus, as Veblen notes:

> [t]he technological basis for a pecuniary control of industry is given, in that the 'roundabout process of production' yields an income above the subsistence of the workmen engaged in it, and the material equipment of appliances (crops, fruit-trees, live stock, mechanical contrivances) binds this roundabout process of industry to a more or less determinate place and routine, such as to make surveillance and control possible. So far as the workman under the new phase of technology is dependent for his living on the apparatus and the orderly sequence of the 'roundabout process' his work may be controlled and the surplus yielded by his industry may be turned to account.
> (Veblen, 1914: 150)

Veblen (1908) criticised John Bates Clark (1891) for his attempt to explain distribution in terms of marginal productivity. For Veblen, the surplus is a social product, which depends upon the collective knowledge of the community and its technological state, and its distribution depends upon institutional aspects.

The same happens in classical theory, where the distribution of the surplus also depends upon institutional aspects, such as the social class where a given agent is positioned. As Avi Cohen and Geoffrey Harcourt (2003) explain, the critique of marginal productivity theory undertaken by Sraffa (1960) and Joan Robinson (1953) was not only in line with Marx's development of classical political economy but also with Veblen's own contribution, which consists of an analysis of the social and economic aspects surrounding the roundabout process of production and distribution of a surplus – see also Cohen (2014).

This process always presupposes a given technological phase, as Veblen stresses above. Changes in this technological phase will set into motion changes in the roundabout process of reproduction and distribution of the surplus. For this reason, authors like Clarence Ayres (1944, 1952) use the term 'Veblenian dichotomy' when identifying technology as the driving force of change in Veblen's conception, and institutions as the driving force of stability (within what we may term a 'normal position' is sustained by what Veblen calls the 'ceremonial' aspects of life).

Lawson (2003a, 2003b, 2005) characterises the institutionalist school associated with Veblen as an approach centred on the forces that cause stability and the forces that cause change, and sees institutions and technology as two possible causes of stability and change. But Lawson (2003b, 2005) sees the 'Veblenian dichotomy' as a result of a failure to distinguish between human agents and social structures. Drawing upon the transformational model of social activity, we can see more clearly that stability can be found at the level of social structures – I discuss the 'Veblenian dichotomy' in more detail in Martins (2009). But this stability at the level of social structures (which is implicit in the classical notion of reproduction through custom and habit, and in Veblen's account of institutions, habits and the ceremonial aspects of life) does not refer to teleological natural laws. It refers to the conditions of possibility of the process of reproduction and distribution of the surplus.

So there is nothing in Veblen's conception which makes it incompatible with classical political economy. Quite the contrary – Veblen's approach can best be interpreted as a further development of the surplus approach pioneered by the classical authors, an approach where economic transformation depends on whether the social surplus is used in productive activities, or in wasteful luxurious consumption, as argued by Quesnay, Smith, Marx and Veblen, among many others.

Should this school be called neoclassical economics?

The use of mathematico-deductivist methods was most successful in natural sciences like physics and is often identified with proper science. Thus, mathematico-deductivist methods are widely used in economics, in order to make economics appear to be a respectable science. Likewise, the term neoclassical commands a certain degree of respectability, and it suggests continuity with a classical and respected tradition. Terms like classical and neoclassical are also connected to contributions in other fields, which are much appreciated, and have thus a favourable semantic connotation.

But the truth is that mainstream economics is neither scientific nor classical in any sense. Science is essentially a critical exercise, where the conditions of possibility for a given phenomenon are questioned and scrutinised. It does not consist merely in the use of mathematico-deductivist methods, as Lawson (1997, 2003a) shows. Furthermore, the classical approach was very different from Marshall's interpretation of it. Marx used the term classical to denote a truly scientific endeavour, namely the explanation of the underlying structures behind the process of socio-economic reproduction and distribution of the surplus.

The reason why the term neoclassical economics is used in its contemporary sense is connected to the way in which classical political economy was reinterpreted in a different way than the way in which Marx defined it.

For Marx, classical political economy includes those who studied the objective causes of value and covers the period from Petty to Ricardo. Under such a description, Marx himself can also be seen as a classical economist, who indeed believed he had finally found the objective basis of value that the classical authors had been long searching for – see Martins (2013) on why Marx's description of classical political economy seems to be the more accurate description of the contributions of those authors.

Vulgar economy, in contrast, includes those who were concerned with subjective and superficial phenomena such as supply and demand, and covers the period from Malthus to Cairnes. Classical political economy was subsequently interpreted in terms of vulgar economy, which was believed to be its more advanced stage. Thus, the term classical is now used to designate the whole period from Petty to Cairnes, while interpreting all those contributions in line with vulgar economy and with its emphasis on supply and demand analysis and subjective preferences.

For this reason, Marshall sees no great difference between his own study of the equilibrium between supply and demand, where both demand curves and supply curves depend upon subjective preferences and the classical project so interpreted. Neither does Veblen, who uses the term neoclassical to designate the continuation of the classical project so construed, albeit already informed by an evolutionary vision such as the one that Marshall possessed.

Lawson (Chapter 1) is surely correct in pointing out that it is better to abandon the term neoclassical economics rather than using it in its present sense, which suggests a false idea of continuity with classical political economy. If we wanted to use the term neoclassical economics in an appropriate way, we would have to take into account the original meaning of the term classical, and the historical context in which the terms classical and neoclassical appeared within economics.

In Veblen's writings, the term neoclassical is meant to designate a combination of new evolutionary ideas (such as the ones of Spencer and Darwin) with a classical approach. But once we realise that the classical approach is concerned with the reproduction and allocation of the surplus, we must then reach the conclusion that the author who pioneered the combination of a new evolutionary perspective with the classical surplus approach was not Marshall. Marshall certainly possessed many new evolutionary insights. But Marshall's theory is essentially a continuation of the supply and demand analysis that was designated by Marx as vulgar economy, precisely in order to distinguish it from classical political economy. Thus, Marshall's approach can be more aptly characterised as 'neo-vulgar' economics, rather than neoclassical economics.

So who could be considered a neoclassical economist, in the sense of being an economist who combines the classical concern with the reproduction and distribution of the surplus on the one hand, with the new evolutionary insights brought by Spencer and Darwin on the other?

In light of what was argued above, it seems that no one fits better into this category than Veblen himself. That is, if we follow the original usage of classical as defined by Marx, and at the same time try to make this usage compatible with the original usage of neoclassical as defined by Veblen, we find that no one fits better into the definition of classical and neoclassical than the authors who coined each term. So if words such as classical and neoclassical are to be used in economics in any meaningful way, we reach the conclusion that Marx is the last classical economist and Veblen is the first neoclassical economist.

Concluding remarks

The claim that Marx is the last classical economist is not as contentious as the claim that Veblen is the first neoclassical economist. Furthermore, the latter claim is certainly contradictory with the subsequent use of the word neoclassical following Veblen's introduction of the term. As Lawson (Chapter 1, note 3: 67–68) notes, the term was not only identified with Marshall but also used by John Hicks and George Stigler to designate the orthodox research programme that emerged in the twentieth century. As Lawson (Chapter 1, note 3: 67–68) also notes, Maurice Dobb (who worked closely with Sraffa) thought that 'counter-classical' would be a better term, since the orthodox approach developed throughout the twentieth century is radically at odds with classical political economy as defined by Marx, and subsequently interpreted by Sraffa and Dobb following Marx's original usage of the term – see Martins (2013) for a discussion.

But the term neoclassical became associated with the orthodox approach throughout the twentieth century and was also used in this sense by critics of the orthodoxy, that is, by the heterodox economists. In such a context, Lawson (Chapter 1) suggests that the best strategy is to use the term to denote an inconsistency between reality and method, while pointing out how many economists who self-identify as heterodox economists (and thus see themselves as critics of neoclassical economics) fall into the same inconsistency and are thus neoclassical economists too.

As Lawson (Chapter 1: 56) notes, the term neoclassical can be used to denote such an inconsistency even if we follow Marx's original interpretation of the term, since 'classical' can be used in Marx's sense, in order to denote a scientific concern with underlying causes, and 'neo' can be used to denote a commitment to the new mathematico-deductivist methods that emerged after the marginal revolution (such as differential calculus), and especially throughout the twentieth century. Under such a view, neo no longer means what Veblen meant, but classical means what Marx meant.

I have, however, some reservations about using the term neoclassical as a form of criticism. As noted above, a term such as neoclassical commands respectability and suggests continuity with a classical tradition, which is also respected. Furthermore, as noted above, terms like classical and neoclassical are also connected to contributions in other fields which are much appreciated and have, thus, a favourable semantic connotation. In fact, I believe these are important reasons why the term neoclassical was strongly embraced by many orthodox economists as describing their own approach. The same happens with mathematico-deductivist methods: they are perceived as essential for proper science given their success in respected fields like physics and, thus, their use commands a certain degree of respectability.

Now, when studying any field with a certain degree of complexity, it is not possible to have a full command of all the relevant issues at stake. Rather, much information is processed at a non-conscious level, in which words, and their semantic connotation, play an important role as a signal that directs us in certain paths. For this reason, John Maynard Keynes (1936: 297–298) thought that words, rather than numbers, were more appropriate tools for studying socio-economic phenomena: words enable us to keep at the back of our heads important information which cannot all be processed at a conscious level – see Martins (2013: chapter 5) for a discussion. Thus, words such as classical and neoclassical are important assets, so to speak, which give a strategic advantage to anyone who adopts them and play an important role in establishing what Antonio Gramsci called 'hegemony'.

Of course, there is a psychological appeal in terms such as critical and heterodox too. They signal a non-conforming attitude, which should be encouraged by anyone concerned with free-thinking. But I believe that the history of economics shows that the tendency of the majority, not least students who are uncertain about the validity of competing approaches, is to side with whatever looks established and part of a respected tradition.

Furthermore, the monumental failure of mainstream economics did not change a context where important positions in the academia and other institutions are occupied by mainstream economists, not least because the heterodox traditions were not sufficiently organised around a common framework that can address the issues at stake. As Lawson (2003a) explains, the heterodox traditions share a common social ontology. But ontological commitments must be supplemented by more specific theories too, as Lawson also notes. The surplus approach is particularly appropriate for addressing problems, which were raised after the (2007–2008) crisis, such as problems of inequality and distribution, which have been increasingly in the public eye.

The classical surplus approach certainly helps to systematise many heterodox ideas, which are extremely relevant for understanding the contemporary crisis, not least because those ideas are in fact based on a surplus approach too – see Martins (2013: chapter 8) for a discussion. Terms such as heterodox are important to signal a critical attitude, but one must not give away a tradition, which is useful for theoretical and strategic reasons, such as the surplus approach. More importantly, doing so is also an exercise of intellectual honesty, for the surplus approach is actually more in line with the heterodox approaches than with the mainstream scarcity theory – see Martins (2013: chapter 8).

So I would argue that the more fruitful strategy would be to recover the word classical (as Sraffa tried to do) as part of the surplus approach shared by Marx and Veblen. As for the word neoclassical, ideally it should be recovered to and could be used to denote Veblen's project, as argued above. But if the context of its use throughout the twentieth century made the word neoclassical lose its proper meaning, the word neoclassical should then be abandoned, and there are persuasive arguments for doing so, as Lawson (Chapter 1) convincingly argues.

Acknowledgement

I am most grateful to Geoffrey Harcourt, Tony Lawson and Jamie Morgan for their helpful comments.

References

Ayres, C. (1944) *The Theory of Economic Progress*, 1st ed. Chapel Hill, NC: University of North Carolina Press.
Ayres, C. (1952) *The Industrial Economy: Its Technological Basis and Institutional Basis.* Cambridge, MA: Houghton Mifflin.
Clark, J. B. (1891) Distribution as determined by a law of rent. *The Quarterly Journal of Economics* 5(3): 289–318.
Cohen, A. J. (2014) Veblen *Contra* Clark and Fisher: Veblen-Robinson-Harcourt lineages in capital controversies and beyond. *Cambridge Journal of Economics* 38(6): 1493–1515.
Cohen, A. J. and Harcourt, G. C. (2003) Whatever happened to the Cambridge capital theory controversies? *Journal of Economic Perspectives* 17(1): 199–214.
Edgeworth, F. Y. (1881) *Mathematical Physics: An Essay on the Application of Mathematics to the Moral Sciences.* London, UK: Kegan and Paul & Co.
Fleetwood, S. (ed.) (1999) *Critical Realism in Economics.* London, UK: Routledge.
Fullbrook, E. (ed.) (2009) *Ontology and Economics: Tony Lawson and His Critics.* London, UK: Routledge.
Graça Moura, M. and Martins, N. (2008) On some criticisms of critical realism in economics. *Cambridge Journal of Economics* 32(2): 203–218.
Keynes, J. M. (1936) *The General Theory of Employment, Interest and Money.* London, UK: Routledge.
Lawson, T. (1997) *Economics and Reality.* London, UK: Routledge.
Lawson, T. (2003a) *Reorienting Economics.* London, UK: Routledge.
Lawson, T. (2003b) Institutionalism: On the need to firm up notions of social structure and the human subject. *Journal of Economic Issues* 37(1): 175–201.
Lawson, T. (2005) The nature of institutional economics. *Evolutionary and Institutional Economics Review* 2(1): 7–20.
Lawson, T. (2013) What is this 'school' called neoclassical economics? *Cambridge Journal of Economics* 37(5): 947–983. Also published in this book as Chapter 1, and page numbers cited refer to those in this book.

Lewis, P. (ed.) (2004) *Transforming Economics: Perspectives on the Critical Realist Project*. London, UK: Routledge.

Marshall, A. (1890) *Principles of Economics*. Available at: http://www.econlib.org/library/Marshall/marPCover.html (accessed 27 July 2015).

Marshall, A. (1919) *Industry and Trade*. London, UK: Macmillan.

Martins, N. (2009) A transformational conception of evolutionary processes. *Evolutionary and Institutional Economics Review* 6(1): 71–102.

Martins, N. (2013) *The Cambridge Revival of Political Economy*. London, UK and New York, NY: Routledge.

Marx, K. (1981 [1894]) *Capital*, vol. III. New York, NY: Pelican Books and (translated by Fernbach, D.) London, UK: Pelican Books.

Quesnay, F. (1759) *Tableau Économique* 3rd edition. Reprint (1972), edited by Kuczynski, M. and Meek, R. London, UK: Macmillan

Robinson, J. V. (1953) The production function and the theory of capital. *Review of Economic Studies* 21(2): 81–106.

Senior, W. N. (1836) *An Outline of the Science of Political Economy*. London, UK: W. Clowes and Sons.

Sraffa, P. (1925) Sulle relazioni fra costo e quantita prodotta. *Annali di economia* 2(1): 277–328.

Sraffa, P. (1926) The laws of returns under competitive conditions. *Economic Journal* 36(December): 535–550.

Sraffa, P. (1960) *Production of Commodities by Means of Commodities: Prelude to a Critique of Economic Theory*. Cambridge, UK: Cambridge University Press.

Veblen, T. (1898) Why is economics not an evolutionary science? *The Quarterly Journal of Economics* 12(4): 373–397.

Veblen, T. (1899) *The Theory of the Leisure Class*. New York, NY: Macmillan.

Veblen, T. (1900) The preconceptions of economic science: III. *The Quarterly Journal of Economics* 14(2): 240–269.

Veblen, T. (1904) *The Theory of Business Enterprise*. New York, NY: Charles Scribner's Sons.

Veblen, T. (1908) Professor Clark's economics. *The Quarterly Journal of Economics* 22(2): 147–195.

Veblen, T. (1909) The limitations of marginal utility. *Journal of Political Economy* 17(9): 620–636.

Veblen, T. (1914) *The Instinct of Workmanship and the State of the Industrial Arts*. New York, NY: Macmillan.

Veblen, T. (1921) *The Engineers and the Price System*. New York, NY: Macmillan.

7 Ten propositions on 'neoclassical economics'

John King

In this chapter I consider neoclassical economics as a piece of figurative speech that economists have borrowed, knowingly or otherwise, from art history and philosophy, and assert ten propositions about it. I discuss the diversity of meanings that have been attributed to neoclassical economics by lexicographers, historians of economic thought and economists, including Tony Lawson (Chapter 1). I conclude that the term need not be abandoned, as Lawson and others have maintained, and that some important and interesting questions about its use remain open for future research.

Proposition 1: Thorstein Veblen has no proprietary rights over the way in which 'neoclassical' is used in economics

This point can be made very briefly. Even if he were still alive, Veblen would have no particular ownership rights in the concept of neoclassical economics. What he intended when he invented the term is a very interesting question, but it is not decisive for its meaning, then or now. Usage varies in space and time, and there are no hard and fast rules – least of all, rules establishing property rights and rules of inheritance – to dictate the way in which any figure of speech is to be understood.

Proposition 2: 'neoclassical economics' is an example of figurative language

This, too, is stating the obvious, and it was (presumably) what Veblen intended when he invented the term. 'The ends of figurative language are achieved through repetitions, juxtapositions, contrasts and associations, by violating expectations, by evoking echoes of other people, places, times and contexts, and through novel, provocative imagery' (McArthur, 1998: 232). They have a rhetorical effect, even if there is no conscious persuasive intention. Veblen himself was famed for his use of figurative language, which either illuminated or obscured his underlying message, according to the tastes of the reader. While it is not a simple matter to distinguish figures of speech from the literal use of words, it seems pretty clear that neoclassical economics is an example of the former, which does indeed 'violate expectations' and 'evokes an echo' of a style of late nineteenth-century American art. Since it aims to persuade the reader by means of 'novel, provocative imagery', it is hardly surprising that the meaning of the imagery has proven controversial at times over the past century.

Proposition 3: if a definition of 'neoclassical economics' excludes Milton Friedman, there's something wrong with it

Ask 100 social science graduates to name just one neoclassical economist, and Milton Friedman would probably top the list. Ask them for the most important centre of neoclassical economics since 1945 and the University of Chicago would win, hands down. Any definition of neoclassical that excludes Friedman and the Chicago economists of his generation, just has to be wrong. Now Friedman was not a great mathematician or even a particularly accomplished formal theorist, and he would almost certainly fail Tony Lawson's 'mathematical deductivism' test. For the most part the Friedman-Stigler cohort of Chicago economists were not distinguished by their work in formal theory, which was done much better elsewhere in the United States (at MIT, for example, or Berkeley). Melvin Reder's well-known summary of the 'Chicago view' rightly emphasises their focus on 'tight prior equilibrium', not formalism (Reder, 1982), and I suspect that Friedman and Stigler would not have objected to their work being summarised in terms of David Colander's 'holy trinity' of rationality, greed and equilibrium (Colander, 2005: 930). All this suggests to me that there are serious problems with Lawson's definition of neoclassical economics, which I shall return to below.

Proposition 4: the way in which 'neoclassical' is used to refer to economics is rather odd

The rather odd use of the term neoclassical in the context of economics is not often remarked upon, but it strikes me as important. It can be seen from the definitions that are given in standard dictionaries. First, the *Concise Oxford Dictionary*, which defines the prefix 'neo' as: 'new, modern, later, revived', and neoclassical as: 'revival of classical style or treatment in art, literature, music, etc'. This is *not* what it means in economics: no-one has ever suggested that the work of Jevons, Walras or Menger, or for that matter Samuelson, involved a revival of Smith and Ricardo. Two of the examples that are provided of the use of the term outside art, literature and music confirm the association of neoclassical with 'revival': 'neo-Hellenism' is defined simply as 'revival of Greek ideas', and neo-scholasticism as: 'revival and restatement of teachings of medieval schoolmen'.

The *Shorter Oxford Dictionary* acknowledges the problem and gives two definitions of neoclassical, one general and one specific to economics. The general definition is similar to that of the *Concise Oxford Dictionary*: '1. of, pertaining to, or characteristic of a revival of classical style or treatment in the arts'. The specific definition follows: '2. *Econ.* of, pertaining to, or characteristic of a body of theory primarily concerned with supply and demand rather than with the source and distribution of wealth'. Two things should be noted here. First, this is the *only* usage of neoclassical for which a specific secondary definition is provided. Second, no reference is made in this definition of neoclassical economics to any revival of classical style.

The (almost) unique way in which the term has been used in economics is confirmed by reference to other dictionaries. Thus the entry on neoclassicism in the *Oxford Dictionary of American Art* defines it as a:

> [t]erm referring to enthusiasm for Greek and Roman forms and ideals ... Imitation of classical prototypes was most direct in architecture, sculpture and the decorative arts, but related concerns emerged in painting ... Narrative paintings in the neoclassical style often take subjects from classical literature.
>
> (Morgan, 2008: 336–337)

Again, no-one would accuse Léon Walras, John Bates Clark or J. R. Hicks of 'imitation of classical prototypes'. Their critics frequently complain of their *failure* to 'take subjects from classical literature', of *changing* the focus and the subject-matter of the discipline from that which prevailed in the era of classical political economy. Lawson himself quotes Maurice Dobb's description of neoclassical economics as being consciously intended as 'counter-classicism' (Lawson, Chapter 1, note 3: 67, citing Dobb, 1973: 248).

Proposition 5: we need to distinguish the use of 'neoclassical' by historians of economic thought and by others, in the past and now

One of the ways in which Lawson distinguishes meanings of the term neoclassical is by referring to its use by historians of economic thought and economic methodologists. He contrasts their careful employment of the term with the looser usage found in the work of economic theorists and political economists. As an historian of economic thought, I would have liked to believe that my fellow scholars in this branch of the discipline took a more reflective and more measured approach to the meaning of neoclassical economics than was displayed by textbook writers and policy analysts. I also expected, rather less confidently, to find somewhat more uniformity across space and time in the treatment of the term by intellectual historians than by economists with no great interest in the history of ideas.

I have not been able to conduct the substantial programme of research that would be needed to put these expectations to the test. A biased sample of history of economic thought texts, taken from my own library, offered only partial support. The variety is certainly there, but not (perhaps) the quality. I was surprised how many authors had managed to avoid the use of neoclassical altogether, judging by the indexes to their books. These include Joseph Dorfman (1949), who devotes many pages to a discussion of other aspects of Veblen's work; Eric Roll (1963), in a text first published in 1938 (but see Aspromourgos, 1986: 267, for a few scattered references in an earlier edition); Antal Mátyás (1980) in a substantial volume written in Communist-era Hungary; and Lionel Robbins (1998) whose posthumously published LSE lectures include seven chapters under the heading 'C19th Classicism', but make no reference to neoclassical economics. A quick scan of Robbins's three chapters on the 'Marginal Revolution' suggests that this is an accurate reflection of the content, and is not an omission by the indexer.

At the other extreme is the text by Kay Hunt and Mark Lautzenheiser (2011), where the index references extend over two pages and include a separate entry for 'neoclassical welfare economics'. In this volume the term neoclassical is used to cover not only the marginalist revolution but also subsequent developments, up to the mid-twentieth century. A similar treatment is provided in the recent text by Ernesto Screpanti and Stefano Zamagni (2005), where 'the neoclassical theoretical system' is briefly presented as the culmination of the marginalist revolution and then an entire chapter, entitled 'Neoclassical Economics From Triumph to Crisis', is devoted to twentieth-century controversies in general equilibrium theory, welfare economics and the theory of the firm (Screpanti and Zamagni, 2005: 165–168, 380–427).

Somewhere in between these two extremes are the authoritative history of thought texts by Mark Blaug, Joseph Schumpeter and Henry Spiegel. Schumpeter (1954) actually comments on: 'the habit, which has developed especially in the United States, of describing the "marginalist" theory as neo-classic'. On the whole he disapproves of the term: 'so far as pure theory is concerned, there is no more sense in calling the Jevons-Menger-Walras theory neo-classic than there would be in calling the Einstein theory neo-Newtonian' (Schumpeter, 1954: 919). Blaug makes only occasional use of the term in his chapter 'Marginal Revolution', but there is an extended and critical section in his 'methodological postscript' on 'falsifiability in neoclassical economics', where he offers no definition, but uses the word to denote the contemporary mainstream and takes aim at a passage from Samuelson's *Foundations* (Blaug, 1985: 699–702). Furthermore, Spiegel too has only a handful of references to neoclassical economics, one of which – a discussion of Marshall's ambivalence as to whether he wished to preserve the legacy of the classics or to undermine it – is of considerable interest (Spiegel, 1986: 565). Neil Hart (2012) has written on this theme with great insight.

Finally, here is an early use of the term by Terence Hutchison (1956), which I stumbled upon in the course of revising this paper, while seeking distraction by working on another project (Lawson has made me conscious of the need to interrogate all references to neoclassical, wherever they may be found, and this has been a valuable consequence of engaging with his essay). Hutchison is reviewing the three volumes of Jeremy Bentham's collected writings on economics:

> It has often been pointed out, obviously with much truth, that Bentham's development of, and emphasis on, the two concepts of maximisation and utility make him above all the ancestor of neo-classical economic theorising, and especially of Jevons and Edgeworth. But these ideas were developed in Bentham's political, legal and philosophical writings. As an *economist*, as to-day defined, Bentham made no attempt to develop an economic calculus or a theory of relative values and prices. His economic theorising, in fact, is of an exactly opposite pattern to that typical of the neo-classicals. It is *not* mainly abstract, deductive and 'micro-economic', tighly [sic] organised around the assumption of a 'maximising individual'; but, on the contrary, is rather practical, 'macro-economic', concerned with aggregate monetary problems, and if not statistical, at any rate concerned to exploit such crude statistics as were available, while being ready for and calling for more.
>
> (Hutchison, 1956: 298; original stress and hyphens)

For Hutchison, then, neoclassical means: 'abstract, deductive and "micro-economic"' theorising, tightly organised: 'around the assumption of a "maximising individual"'. Mathematical formalism is not explicitly specified, but it is implied by the reference to Jevons and Edgeworth.

Proposition 6: the use of 'neoclassical economics' by others now is somewhat varied

If the treatment of neoclassical economics by historians of economic thought varies considerably, in both quantity and quality, and it appears that it has always has done so, there is also considerable variety in the way in which the term is used by others today. This became apparent to me at the 25th anniversary conference of the *Review of Political Economy* in Great Malvern in July 2014 (which was also attended by Tony Lawson). Ed Nell saw the essence of neoclassical economics as a concern with *scarcity*, which he contrasted with the classical analysis of production and reproduction, above all the production of a surplus. For Susan Schroeder, the crucial distinction was between the neoclassical focus on the *individual* and the attention paid by classical economists to class relations. Neither of these viewpoints is inconsistent with David Colander's previously cited 'holy trinity' of rationality, greed and equilibrium, but the emphasis is rather different. Neither of them has much in common with Lawson's stress on mathematical formalism as the defining characteristic of neoclassical economics. This diversity of usage, which Lawson also explores before focusing on a revival of Veblen's definition, might be taken as an argument for avoiding the term altogether, though (as will be seen shortly) this is not a conclusion that greatly appeals to me.

Proposition 7: the distinction between 'neoclassical' and 'non-neoclassical' economics is a continuum, not a dual

Unlike neoliberal, the adjective neoclassical is not always used pejoratively. Some of my former colleagues at La Trobe University were proud to describe themselves as neoclassical. But it is not a black and white issue. To think otherwise would be to engage in what Sheila Dow describes as 'dualistic' thinking, which imposes 'either/or', 'A or not-A' mutually exclusive categories of thought on a reality that is generally much more complicated than this and needs to be conceived of in terms of a continuum rather than a dichotomy. The principle of the excluded middle – either neoclassical or not-neoclassical – is a feature of Cartesian-Euclidian thought, which Dow rightly rejects in favour of the more subtle and open-ended Babylonian mode of thinking (Dow, 1996, chapter 2).

Arranged on a scale from 0 to 100, the very best self-proclaimed neoclassicals would not score much above 90, since they were always careful to acknowledge their doubts and reservations. Think of Arrow, Debreu, Hahn or Samuelson. Presumably Pigou would score more than Marshall, Meade (a little) more than Harrod, Krugman (much) less than Lucas. There is scope for some animated after-dinner discussion here! Possibly you would have to be a thorough-going economics imperialist to go over 90, since a refusal to apply neoclassical methods and techniques to the subject-matter of the other social sciences would be viewed badly, at least in Chicago. While we are in the Windy City, how would you rate Deirdre McCloskey, with her deep hostility to formalism (and to the evil Samuelsonian genius known as 'Max U s.t.c.'), but equally profound admiration for the 'old Chicago' economics of Friedman and Stigler?

Where would you place yourself on this scale? I think I would rate myself at around 20 or 25, since for all my criticisms of neoclassicism I would not dispute the law of demand, or (to take just one important example) deny the case for increasing tobacco taxation to reduce smoking and save lives. I support a carbon emissions tax for similar reasons: it seems to be a necessary, though certainly not a sufficient, condition for saving the planet. Would *anyone* score zero? The more dogmatic Hegelian Marxists, perhaps, who view neoclassical economics as pure apologetics, with no scientific content whatsoever? Or the young Bob Rowthorn, who began his attack on 'neo-Ricardian' Marxism by declaring that he intended to use the terms neoclassicism and vulgar economy interchangeably (Rowthorn, 1974: 75). But then their critics might claim that they were 'not really economists' of any description and did not deserve to be awarded a score, even one of zero.

Proposition 8: a good working definition of 'neoclassical economics' is not, after all, very hard to find

For all that, even the fuzziest and most imprecise words do need to be defined; perhaps they are in even greater need of careful definition than less contentious terms. Sometimes that is just what they receive. Here, for example, is the definition of neoclassical economics offered by Oxford University Press's *Dictionary of Economics*:

> The analysis of economic activity based on the fundamental premises that economic agents have rational preferences, all consumers maximize utility, all firms maximize profit, and all choices are made taking into account relevant constraints. These components produce a variety of results, depending upon the assumptions on the economic environment in which the economic agents interact. For example, if all agents are assumed to be price-takers then a model of a competitive economy is obtained. Alternatively, if it is assumed that a firm is the only supplier of a product (and recognizes this fact) then the model is one of monopoly. Neoclassical economics is the accepted orthodox approach to economics.
>
> (Black *et al.*, 2013: 213)

What is wrong with this 109-word definition? It contains two of Colander's trilogy (rationality and greed, but not equilibrium) and hints at Nell's defining characteristic (scarcity) and, even more strongly, at Schroeder's 'individualism'. The missing elements could have been inserted, without contradiction, if another 30–40 words had been available. In my opinion, the final sentence is still an accurate description of economic orthodoxy, though this would be disputed by those who maintain that the new frontiers of the discipline are essentially non-neoclassical (Davis, 2008).

More subtle and more nuanced definitions can be found in the history of thought literature. By the 1920s, Roger Backhouse maintains, economics:

> [w]as genuinely pluralist, in that it was dominated by no single approach. The conventional way to view this pluralism is in terms of a split between 'neoclassicals' and 'institutionalists'. The neoclassicals ... emphasized individuals' maximizing behaviour and the role of competitive markets. Institutionalists ... denounced this approach and argued for a more holistic view in which economy and society

could not be separated. Such a characterization is, however, very misleading, for the picture was much more complicated. There was great diversity of approach within both neoclassical and institutional economics.

(Backhouse, 2009: 201)

Backhouse goes on to note that J. M. Clark occupied the boundary between the two schools, and that some neoclassicals (for example, Irving Fisher) were proud to be mathematical deductivists, while others (like J. B. Clark) took a: 'more traditional, non-mathematical and more ethical approach' (Backhouse, 2009: 201).

Ever since Doctor Johnson it has been recognised that lexicography is an imperfect science, but that is no reason for not attempting it. No definition of an interesting term like neoclassical will ever be perfect, or non-contentious, but I do not believe that this is a sufficient reason for abandoning the word. Its existence creates a focal point in terms of which ambiguity and difference can be explored to some effect, without the definition itself ever becoming entirely fixed.

Proposition 9: Tony Lawson's account of 'neoclassical economics' is questionable, for several reasons

And so I come back to Tony Lawson, who argues that abandonment is precisely what we should do with neoclassical economics. Lawson defines neoclassicism as: 'a form of mathematical deductivism in the context of economics', resulting in a reliance on laws based on event regularities (Lawson, Chapter 1: 32). He acknowledges that no-one else defines the term in this way (Lawson, Chapter 1: note 6: 70), but believes that it is consistent with Veblen's own intentions (Lawson, Chapter 1: 34). His criticism of the concept is equally idiosyncratic. Lawson maintains that the term neoclassical is 'not only productive of severe obfuscation' but is also: 'positively debilitating of the discipline not least through hindering effective critique' (Lawson, Chapter 1: 32). It does so by shifting attention towards: 'substantive theorising and policy formulation' and away from ontology, which he regards as more fundamental (Lawson, Chapter 1: 38). Thus the real problem is that the term neoclassical is a distraction.

As I have already suggested, no-one owns the term neoclassical, and Lawson is free to define it as he sees fit. He has written a great deal on these matters, and it seems likely that both his definition of neoclassical economics and his attitude towards formalism has shown some variation over time. In the preface to *Reorienting Economics*, for example, he states:

> I hope by now the highly conditional nature of my criticism is apparent. It is not, and has never been, my intention to oppose the use of formalistic methods in themselves. My primary opposition, rather, is

to the manner in which they are everywhere imposed, to the insistence on their being almost universally wielded, irrespective of, and prior to, considerations of explanatory relevance, and in the face of repeated failures.

(Lawson 2003: xix)

My fundamental problem is with his 2013 definition of neoclassical economics rather than the broader issues that he raised in earlier work. I simply do not regard 'mathematical deductivism' as either a necessary or a sufficient condition for a piece of economic theorising to count as neoclassical. It is not necessary, as otherwise we should have to exclude Milton Friedman from the school (and other eminent Chicagoans, such as Ronald Coase). It is not sufficient, as otherwise we should have to include mathematical models which are explicitly anti-neoclassical in nature, like the well-known 'classical' growth model developed by the otherwise impeccably neoclassical John von Neumann (1945–6).

Lawson tends to conflate 'mathematical deductivism' with 'formalism', and does not clearly distinguish the latter from mere theoretical abstraction. These concepts should, I think, be regarded as nesting like Russian dolls, one inside the other, with all three requiring the existence to some degree of the 'event regularities' that Lawson repudiates in his work on social ontology. Marx practised formalism on occasion (for example in volumes II and III of *Capital*) and theoretical abstraction in almost everything he wrote (the *Grundrisse*, for example, or volume I of *Capital*), and he tried (unsuccessfully) to learn algebra in order to undertake mathematical deductivism in the writing of *Capital*. Much the same could be said of Keynes. There are equations in three chapters of the *General Theory*, and a number of mathematical symbols in a fourth (Keynes, 1936: chapters 4, 19 and 20; Keynes, 1936: chapter 3). As regards the Cambridge Post Keynesians, Joan Robinson's (1956) *Accumulation of Capital* is a deeply 'formalist' work, though proudly devoid of mathematics, while it is sometimes forgotten that Geoff Harcourt's great book on the capital controversies includes a large number of equations (Robinson, 1956; Harcourt, 1972, especially chapters 2 and 5). But it would be perverse to describe any of these works as a piece of neoclassical economics. Lawson's third division in his (2013) essay seems to imply that they are.

Finally, I am not convinced that the use of the term neoclassical does serve to hinder effective critique, at least not to inhibit criticism of the 'substantive theorising and policy formulation' of mainstream economists who operate within (and identify themselves as part of) that intellectual tradition. Take as an example the entry on neoclassical economics in the *Collins Dictionary of Sociology*, which describes it as the approach to economics associated with Walras and Marshall that dominated economics between 1870 and 1930 (with the interesting and contentious implication that it no longer does so). The criticisms that follow are worth quoting at some length:

It replaced the explicitly socio-political analysis, in terms of land, capital, and labour, which characterized the work of CLASSICAL ECONOMISTS, including Marx ... with a more formal analysis of the conditions for the optimal allocation of scarce resources. The approach can be described as 'subjectivist', since its central concept, *utility* ... cannot be measured directly but can only be inferred from market behaviour. The approach is also known as *marginal analysis* ... While earlier theories of VALUE based on the 'costs of production' found room for notions such as EXPLOITATION, no place exists for these in neoclassical theory. Thus it has been suggested that neoclassical economics be seen as involving special pleading on behalf of CAPITALISM AND THE CAPITALIST MODE OF PRODUCTION. Others, however, argue that the 'marginalist revolution' in economics can be accounted for by the inherent superiority of this mode of analysis.

(Jary and Jary, 1991: 420–421; original stress and capitalisation, the latter referring to other entries)

One can argue with the details of this entry. The young Joan Robinson, for one, would have been most unhappy with the claim that 'exploitation' had no place in neoclassical economics (for her own use of the term, see Robinson, 1962: chapter 4). But hindering criticism does not appear, at least to me, to be one of its defects.

Proposition 10: a lot of work remains to be done

However, Lawson is to be thanked for reminding us of the importance of methodology, which is sometimes denied by heterodox economists who really ought to know better (Fontana and Gerrard, 2006), and for pointing to the many things that we still need to know about neoclassical economics. Rather than abandoning the term, a great deal of work remains to be done. This includes a detailed analysis of the use of neoclassical in the past, both in accounts of the history of economic thought and in contemporary discussions of the state of 'economics now', both at the time when Veblen first used the term and subsequently. Tony Aspromourgos (1986) has made a good start on this project, but his brief paper was written before computer search technology was available and contains only a small sample of the pre-1950 literature. Is it really the case that it was 'only with Hicks and Stigler, in the 1930s and 1940s, that the term was extended' from the work of Alfred Marshall 'to embrace marginalism in general'? (Aspromourgos, 1986: 266). It would be interesting to know the full details of the usage of neoclassical circa 1930, just before the Keynesian revolution; circa 1970, at the onset of the monetarist counter-revolution and the abortive radical rebellion of the time; and again today, when maybe (or maybe not) it is again becoming a matter of contention. The use of the term in textbooks and works of reference would be a good starting point, and '"Neoclassical economics" in economic dictionaries and encyclopaedias' might be a good working title (see Besomi, 2012).

Such a project would also require a detailed analysis of the use of the prefix 'neo-' outside economics, in art, music and literature, but especially in philosophy. I have to confess that my citations from the *Concise Oxford Dictionary* under proposition 4 above were deliberately selective. I omitted the definition of 'neo-Platonism', which is sufficiently different from that of the other examples, cited above, to suggest that philosophers have also taken liberty with the 'neo' prefix, beginning at the end of classical antiquity: 'neo-Platonism, 3rd-c. mixture of Platonic ideas with Oriental mysticism, similar doctrine in medieval and later times'. Evidently Veblen cannot be blamed for this. It would be good to know who can, and why.

In conclusion, neoclassical economics is, like love, a many-splendoured thing. Like love, it sometimes induces frustration bordering on despair, and it always needs careful attention. But I think it would be a shame to renounce its pleasures.

Acknowledgement

I am grateful to Jamie Morgan for helpful comments on an earlier draft, but the usual disclaimer does of course apply.

References

Aspromourgos, T. (1986) On the origins of the term 'neoclassical'. *Cambridge Journal of Economics* 10(3): 265–270.

Backhouse, R. (2009) *The Ordinary Business of Life: A History of Economics from the Ancient World to the Twenty-First Century*. Princeton, NJ: Princeton University Press.

Besomi, D. (ed.). (2012) *Crises and Cycles in Economics Dictionaries and Encyclopaedias*. Abingdon, UK and New York, NY: Routledge.

Black, J., Hashimzade, N. and Myles, G. (2013) *A Dictionary of Economics*. Oxford, UK: Oxford University Press.

Blaug, M. (1985) *Economic Theory in Retrospect*, 4th ed. Cambridge, UK: Cambridge University Press.

Colander, D. (2005) The future of economics: the appropriately educated in pursuit of the knowable. *Cambridge Journal of Economics* 29(6): 927–941.

Davis, J. B. (2008) The turn in recent economics and the return of orthodoxy. *Cambridge Journal of Economics* 32(3): 349–366.

Dobb, M. H. (1973) *Theories of Value and Distribution since Adam Smith: Ideology and Economic Theory*. Cambridge, UK: Cambridge University Press.

Dorfman, J. (1949) *The Economic Mind in American Civilization. Volume Three: 1865–1918*. New York, NY: Kelley, 1969.

Dow, S. C. (1996) *The Methodology of Macroeconomic Thought*. Cheltenham, UK and Northampton, MA: Edward Elgar.

Fontana, G. and Gerrard, B. (2006) The future of Post Keynesian economics. *Banca Nazionale del Lavoro Quarterly Review* 59(236): 49–80.

Harcourt, G. C. (1972) *Some Cambridge Controversies in the Theory of Capital*. Cambridge, UK: Cambridge University Press.

Hart, N. (2012) *Equilibrium and Evolution: Alfred Marshall and the Marshallians*. Basingstoke, UK: Palgrave Macmillan.

Hunt, E. K. and Lautzenheiser, M. (2011) *History of Economic Thought: A Critical Perspective*. Armonk, NY: M. E. Sharpe.

Hutchison, T. W. (1956) Bentham as an economist. *Economic Journal* 66(262): 288–306.

Jary, D. and Jary, J. (1991) *Collins Dictionary of Sociology*. London, UK: Harper Collins.

Keynes, J. M. (1936) *The General Theory of Employment, Interest and Money*. London, UK: Macmillan.

Lawson, T. (2003) *Reorienting Economics*. London, UK and New York, NY: Routledge.

Lawson, T. (2013) What is this 'school' called neoclassical economics? *Cambridge Journal of Economics* 37(5): 947–983. Also published in this book as Chapter 1, and page numbers cited refer to those in this book.

Mátyás, A. (1980) *History of Modern Non-Marxian Economics*. Basingstoke, UK: Macmillan.

McArthur, T. (1998) *Concise Oxford Companion to the English Language*. Oxford, UK: Oxford University Press.

Morgan, A. L. (2008) *Oxford Dictionary of American Art and Artists*. Oxford, UK: Oxford University Press.

Reder, M. W. (1982) Chicago economics: Permanence and change. *Journal of Economic Literature* 20(1): 1–38.

Robbins, L. (1998) *A History of Economic Thought: The LSE Lectures*. Princeton, NJ: Princeton University Press.

Robinson, J. (1956) *The Accumulation of Capital*. London, UK: Macmillan.

Robinson, J. (1962) *Economic Philosophy*. Harmondsworth, UK: Penguin.

Roll, E. (1963) *A History of Economic Thought*. London, UK: Faber.

Rowthorn, B. (1974) Neo-classicism, neo-Ricardianism and Marxism. *New Left Review* 86: 63–87.

Schumpeter, J. A. (1954) *History of Economic Analysis*. London: Allen & Unwin; reprinted London, UK: Routledge, 1994.

Screpanti, E. and Zamagni, S. (2005) *An Outline of the History of Economic Thought*, 2nd ed. Oxford, UK: Oxford University Press.

Spiegel, H. W. (1986) *The Growth of Economic Thought*, revised ed. Durham, NC: Duke University Press.

Von Neumann, J. (1945–6) A model of general economic equilibrium. *Review of Economic Studies* 13(1): 1–9.

8 Neoclassical economics
An elephant is not a chimera but is a chimera real?

Ben Fine

Opening sallies

Tony Lawson's (Chapter 1)[1] dual commitment to a critical realist social ontology for economics (CRE) and the specification of mainstream economics by its deterministic ontology, are both well-known and have been heavily debated.[2] I find it difficult to contribute further to such debate, especially in light of his contribution under review for two separate, but closely related reasons.[3] The first is that his position tends to close off progress in debate even if exchange of fire continues. As, for him, the mainstream[4] is (defined by) its ontology, its substantive theoretical content might be of interest, but is rendered somewhat irrelevant and need not be discussed as central in defining our discipline ('ontology rules ok'). Without wishing to tar all followers of CRE with the same brush, the failure to engage substantively both with economic theory and economic analysis has been particularly striking and observed as such. So, whilst my own position is that the mainstream is primarily defined by the content of its theoretical core and practices (together with a heavy and increasing dose of flexible and flexibly attached econometrics), and Lawson may even agree (but probably does not) with the corresponding characterisation and critique of that substance, he pays it little attention as presumably contributing no more than the epiphenomena of, or illustrative form taken by, our discipline relative to its ontological core.[5] Thus, p. 32, emphasis added:

> Certainly the contemporary discipline is dominated by a mainstream tradition. But whilst the concrete substantive content, focus and policy orientations of the latter are highly heterogeneous and continually changing, the project itself is <u>adequately</u> characterised in terms of its enduring reliance, indeed, unceasing insistence, upon methods of *mathematical modelling*. In effect it is a form of *mathematical deductivism* in the context of economics.

Or, even more bluntly, p. 35, emphasis added: 'Modern mainstream economics, if to repeat, is *just a form* of mathematical deductivism'.

The second difficulty in debating Lawson is that, despite his main message or debate closure through extreme definition of the mainstream as mathematical deductivism, he does engage with the substance of mainstream theory from time to time, but in ways that are not necessarily essential to his position and which are often more or less casual even if framed by his position, and, to be frank, might be perceived to be arbitrary and even opportunistic in promoting his main message and higher priority in hitting the ontology target. In my previous, I repeat, reluctant commentaries, I have been provoked by how Lawson has (mis)conceived heterodox economics and interdisciplinarity, possibly the better for him to be able to promote (in his own view) social ontology in which he has been both remarkably and commendably successful (Fine, 2004 and 2006b, respectively). In a sense, given single-minded emphasis on ontology, substantive content does become arbitrary or amenable to other purpose. His position on interdisciplinarity is particularly disturbing from the perspective of my own emphasis on the significance of mainstream economics as a separate discipline with its historical logic underpinning economics imperialism. For me, this is characteristic of its own inner content and of its relationship to other social sciences.[5]

This is the vein in which I understand his latest sortie beyond ontology, the denial that neoclassical economics exists except in the minds of its heterodox critics and, it might reasonably be added, legions of neoclassical, oops, mainstream economists themselves. There are an awful lot of deluded economists out there who pull the wool over their own eyes by neglecting not the ontological determinants, but the ontological determination of their discipline. Somewhat perversely for Lawson's hypothesis (although it is not clear how it might be refuted), in the wake of the global crisis (of economics), mainstream economists, especially those critical of neo-liberalism have been lining up to reassert their commitment to neoclassical economics, even if in a more rounded, realistic version of what Lawson deems not to exist.

Lawson is kind enough to opine that I am closest of all to his own position. It is churlish of me to repay this kindness by adopting entirely the opposite stance to his own on his main message. I do consider that neoclassical economics exists; it is well-defined insofar as an evolving discipline or school can be (indeed, it is more so than most), and, as such, it is of the most compelling strategic imperative to specify and critically deconstruct neoclassical economics rather than somewhat casually dismiss it as ephemeral. Further, heterodox economics, whilst multidimensional and multi-layered, is equally well-defined by, not despite, its varieties and variations. It must, at least in part, thrive by taking neoclassical economics as its central critical point of departure, whilst also (re)constructing economic analysis of its own either as a consequence of such departure or in parallel in light of its continuing and independent traditions.[7]

These introductory remarks aside, let me begin, though, with a confession. I was a reviewer, for the *Cambridge Journal of Economics*, for Lawson's submission. I suggested that the piece falls into two parts. The one on Veblen's take on neoclassical is of considerable interest within the history of economic thought and I did not have the expertise to assess its originality, but it could well have formed a publishable piece. The second part, on the non-existence of neoclassical economics, I judged to be purely opportunistic in promoting Lawson's position, adding little to what had been contributed already in the CRE critique of the mainstream and its specification. The novel attachment to Veblen's historical invention and use of the term is neither here nor there in terms of determining whether neoclassical economics exists or not today, nor what is the nature of the contemporary mainstream?[8] Indeed, the contribution is notably weak on any discussion of the substantive (theoretical) content of the mainstream, something that might be thought to be important (beyond ontology) in deciding whether neoclassical economics exists or not. What are the new developments? What has happened to the old? What is being taught? What is the content of the journals? How does this all influence economic ideology and the making of policy? Lawson is primarily silent on these questions other than to observe that there are (relatively minor) differences over what neoclassical economics is amongst mainstream practitioners and critics alike.

These differences across those who deploy the moniker 'neoclassical' and more substantial differences with, even departures from, Veblen's original conception, lead Lawson to abandon the term as either inconsistent in what it represents or, even stronger, falsely to represent the ontologically determined mainstream. This argument, though, is transparently almost unimaginably weak as far as it is taken (no doubt it could be taken further) and does not stand up even to superficial scrutiny. Whether something is defined consistently or not, or is itself consistent, is neither proof nor denial of its existence (all humans have two legs; no, so humans do not exist?). Our definitions of things may require them to be variable and shifting across users at one time and over time.[9]

Of course, Lawson may still be right and I may be wrong. How far may variability or even inconsistency go before we call it a day and accept that something does not exist or needs to be named differently? But Lawson's position effectively precludes that categories allow for variability and inconsistency whereas this can be a defining characteristic of things. Indeed, my position is that neoclassical economics does exist, is correctly named as such, and the meagre evidence of non-existence or whatever offered by Lawson is nothing of the sort. Indeed, it reflects the very nature of neoclassical economics itself as it is wrought by continual, if evolving and shifting, tensions.

Now, presumably, it could be countered that my position is equally unassailable for allowing any degree of flexibility in the mainstream whilst still allowing it to remain neoclassical. But this is not the case. We need to examine the weight of evidence within a framed understanding and debate it. But, as suggested in my very first point above, Lawson's ontological determination of the mainstream (handily supported by the antediluvian Veblen) precludes framed assessment of the sort I consider essential both to assess the mainstream (whatever it is called) and whether to dub it neoclassical or not.

In this light, I am reminded of the infamous story of Baudrillard who claimed that the Gulf War did not exist and was purely a creation of the media, such is the nature of the media in creating rather than reflecting the news. On being offered to be taken to the frontline, he gallantly refuses on the grounds that, sorry, he is a theorist. It would surely be the height of irony for Lawson, the leading proponent of CRE, to have become so close to the postures of one of the leading representatives of postmodernism. Neoclassical economics does not exist, he says. Mainstream economics is purely a creation of ontology. We say, please come to the classroom, the journals and even the pluralist movements on whom you have exercised so much influence, to see otherwise. Sorry, I am an ontologist.

As already mentioned, what Lawson does provide, with a few cursory illustrations, is the suggestion that definitions of so-called neoclassical economics differ from one another, undermining the credibility of its existence (and, to re-spoof, demonstrating the irregularity of outcomes from underlying ontology?). During the course of the paper, he even seems to find it necessary to convince himself of his own conclusions, with his hypothesis gathering pace from mild suggestion to established truth like a growing indignation. Initially, the term neoclassical: 'is invariably employed rather loosely and somewhat inconsistently across different contributors' (p. 30). Subsequently: agreement is harder to find and significant variety creeps in' (p. 31). Also, just one page later:

> If current use of the term 'neoclassical' has lost touch with its original meaning, does not live up to its billing of signalling continuity with a classical school and is not consistently or usefully interpreted even by those who seek internal coherence, it seems to be additionally the case that there is no real need for such a term anyway, at least not for capturing major developments and/or approaches within the modern economics academy.
>
> (p. 31)

And, after one further page, we are reminded of the earlier reference to the 'loosely', if as 'looseness', but it has become identified with wide disparity:

> However, in the current situation the manner in which, and the wide disparity in the ways, the term 'neoclassical' is applied is not only productive of severe obfuscation, and seemingly increasingly so, it is

also, or so I shall argue, positively debilitating of the discipline not least through hindering effective critique. Indeed, a major motivation of this article is precisely an assessment that the looseness with which this central term is interpreted (along with the toleration of this looseness) is a major factor inhibiting progress in economic understanding.

(p. 32)

In between, the evidence in support of this trajectory from loose to wide disparity is primarily provided in a lengthy note 4, with reference to how neoclassical economics is understood by Hahn (a neoclassical rogue), Arnsperger and Varoufakis, Becker, Hodgson and myself. Read this for yourself and you will find considerable complementarity as opposed to variety other than in this sense.[10]

Just to hammer home the point of the weakness of Lawson's argument in which looseness/wide disparity is perceived to indicate non-existence, by chance, just after the invitation to write this piece, I passed the two stadia in Athens in one of which the first modern Olympiad was held in 1896, and in the other was held the 2004 Games. They are, of course, miles apart in all respects. Yet, we might ask ourselves whether Olympics or Olympic sports still exist or not. I suspect that Veblen did not attend the 1896 Games, but it would have been fascinating to have known his views on the Olympics. Interestingly, we do know something about Veblen's views on sport, for example:

> Thorstein Veblen said that 'religious zeal' and the 'sporting element' derived from similar sources: the need to distinguish oneself and the urge to believe in divine beneficence or good luck. In the arcane academic terms of his day, Veblen insisted that 'the habitation to sports, perhaps especially to athletic sports, act to develop the propensities which find satisfaction in devout observances'.
>
> (Baker, 2000: 68)

The quotes from Veblen are from *The Theory of the Leisure Class: An Economic Study of Institutions* (1912), where there is much more besides on sport and religion. I did think to use, as an alternative to Olympics and sports, the parallel with religion. Does it exist given how many different religions there are, each with different definitions? Even within each religions there are closely contested sects with differences, so Christianity, Islam, etc. do not exist? Of course, we can reasonably argue that gods do not exist, just as the neoclassical economy does not exist (in whatever version it is projected), but that neoclassical economics does not exist is surely a step, even a staircase, too far – at least without going to the frontline of its high priests and cathedrals (the few overwhelmingly influential US universities)?

Whether (and how) Veblen's views would shed light on the nature of the Olympics (and religion) today, as much as neoclassical economics, is a moot point. It certainly would not help us understand, other than most indirectly, how the Olympic spirit (whatever that is) has been broken or transformed, not least from amateur to professional, and through commercialisation, professionalisation (*Chariots of Fire!*) and the media. Furthermore, the included sports themselves have been expanded (synchronised swimming, female boxing). Over all the issues involved in defining the spirit of the Olympics and even what an Olympic sport is, we would all disagree to a greater or lesser extent (clay pigeon shooting, anything involving horses and so on are out as far as I am concerned although others might want to include motor racing and darts, and something like chess straddles the game/sport divide as well).[11] Can we safely assume, therefore, that the Olympics and Olympic sports do not exist? Summer events in Rio in 2016 might suggest otherwise, let alone the relics of stadia scattered around the world (from Athens to London)!

In some respects, this is to point to the extent that precise definitions in our context are inappropriate by virtue of the nature of what is being defined – without, thereby, being laid open to the charge that it is impossible for neoclassical economics ever to disappear or fail to exist.[12] For the latter, there is some fuzzy boundary just as when spring becomes summer where a rigid definition by date might not suit weather conditions.[13] At issue in the case of neoclassical economics is a combination of the shifting variability both of the nature of the world and how we create, perceive and contest it. Consequently, in this framing (as opposed to a precise definition), Lawson's rejection of the existence of neoclassical economics is nothing of the sort and serves more as evidence not just of its existence but just how omniscient and pervasive it is within the discipline, once account is taken of its substantive and evolving theoretical content. Furthermore, it should be added, it is so dominant without, in general, exhibiting any regard whatsoever to its own ontology of which it is blissfully unaware – take the sponsorship and never mind the spirit except for corresponding pragmatic or commercial purposes (publish or perish, research grant or die); the winning not the taking part has become the thing.

Hitting the target

So, if neoclassical economics does exist but is subject to evolving variability, what is it? As argued at length in Fine and Milonakis (2009) and Milonakis and Fine (2009) and elsewhere,[14] such questions are not addressed primarily by ontology but by the technical apparatus (TA1) of the mainstream (reducible to production and utility functions), and the technical architecture (TA2) focused on optimisation, efficiency and equilibrium, giving rise to TA^2 for short. In brief, the passage from the marginalist revolution of the 1870s to the formalist revolution of the 1950s (the latter establishing the use of mathematics within economics as increasingly standard and ultimately de rigueur) witnessed the single-minded development of TA², culminating in general equilibrium and the Hicks-Slutsky-Samuelson conditions for individual optimisation. This was done through an extraordinary reductionism in which all else was sacrificed in order to obtain the desired results, an implosion of *homo economicus* upon itself.

One result, though, was to develop the TA² only at the expense of allowing other approaches to and within economics to prosper, not least (Keynesian) macroeconomics but also any other number of applied fields. TA² was restricted to *one* aspect of individual economic behaviour in the context of *market* supply and demand. Everything else tended to belong to other fields of economics or other disciplines. A second, paradoxical result was to have developed the TA² in this way but with a substance, both ahistorical and asocial, that remains universal in application (as most notable in its entirely abstract mathematical and conceptual formulation in terms of utility and production functions, and the pursuit of self-interest in the context of efficiency and equilibrium). Such a historical logic – market, at the time, in practice as the historical, and application to everything in principle as the logic – gave rise to the potential for economics imperialism, that is the expansion and extension of TA² both within the discipline and to other disciplines, the latter most notable in the 1950s with cliometrics, public choice theory and human capital theory.

Such economics imperialism was limited until the 1970s, after which it was consolidated by the rise of the new classical economics microfoundations of macroeconomics (and much else) and by the reaction against this in the limited form of the market imperfection (especially asymmetric information) approach. Initially, especially with Becker, economics imperialism had been based on treating the non-market as if market. Subsequently, it treated the non-market as if a response to market imperfections. Whilst this difference in the nature and understanding of the workings of markets, and the consequences of them, are significant, especially to their proponents, they share in common the commitment to TA² even, paradoxically and perversely, when it is modified, absent or rejected (as with increasing returns to scale, endogenous preferences, or whatever – see below on suspension).

Not surprisingly, with the rise of microeconomics in and of itself and over macroeconomics over the past 50 years, the same has applied to the use of mathematics as the form in which neoclassical theory has been cloaked. Consequently, prior to the current global crisis, but strengthened by it, so secure has been TA² that it has increasingly been applied incoherently and inconsistently with any other number of approaches, especially through various forms of behavioural economics. It is a beautiful irony that so much that was taken out in the implosion to establish TA² is now being brought back in on terms dictated by its presence. This can even involve suspension of, not break with, core elements of TA² itself, allowing for other motivation or behaviour, increasing returns, and so on.[15]

Having now suggested that neoclassical economics today might best be described as it were as TA² plus or minus, with scope covering the social sciences plus or minus, and with heavy reliance upon mathematical form, it is relatively easy to see why neoclassical economists themselves should see the discipline as sound despite its overwhelming failings. Tell us what you want and we will incorporate it whether studying the economy or otherwise. It is also possible to understand why those such as Colander should see the discipline as disintegrating from without. Furthermore, of course, it is equally understandable for Lawson to draw the conclusion on ontology alone that neoclassical economics does not exist, whilst setting substantive theory aside especially when this is put in terms of benefitting from a precise and common definition.

Indeed, that this is clearly the case is revealed by his explicit commentary on my own position in his article where he claims that my position 'comes closest' to his own (p. 63).[16] He also identifies where we differ in terms of: 'where Fine's analysis proves *deficient*', emphasis added. As already argued here, and confirmed by his commentary on me, he sees deviations from TA² as undermining the existence of neoclassical economics. Furthermore, he sees me as deficient for interpreting these as: '*merely* "wrinkles or complexity"', emphasis added to indicate that he adds 'merely' to my account.

But, as is apparent in my contribution at the time, and certainly in that offered here, whilst wrinkles (if not complexity) might have been an unfortunate choice of expression, this is no 'merely', not least with my immediately preceding comment that: 'institutions, history, path dependence, aggregation now matter, glorifying previous inconveniences as the way forward to add wrinkle or complexity', reproduced by Lawson himself in divorcing the wrinkle *and complexity* from the broader point being made about the very nature of neoclassical economics in its latest, and possibly last, form of economics imperialism.[17] Also, of course, this was almost a decade ago during which precisely the phenomenon that I have highlighted (wrinkling and complexity then, but dubbed suspension here) has gathered scale and scope. Furthermore, far from being close to Lawson other than in acknowledging the pervasive presence of wrinkling, we interpret it in diametrically opposite, or mirror image ways. For him, it is the end of neoclassical economics (not unlike Colander), whereas for me it is the very nature of twenty-first-century neoclassical economics.

As shown, then, in terms of the historical logic of economics imperialism, beginning with Veblenesque (and Marshallian) tensions around core technical content and evolutionary commitments, the nature of neoclassical economics is exactly to have evolved and come to display the features that lead Lawson to suggest that it does not exist. Contemporary neoclassical economics is a chimera comprised of TA², other elements being brought back in and mathematical form. But, unlike the equally monstrous and fire-breathing creature of Greek mythology, composed out of a lion, a snake and a goat, neoclassical is alive, well and real, and far from fictional, wildly imaginative or implausible.[18]

It should be added, as highlighted by Lawson, that the mathematical form in which neoclassical economics is now habitually presented can itself become suspended from the core content and, to that extent, become independent of TA². As is apparent, we both agree on this even if drawing opposite conclusions for its implications for whether neoclassical economics exists or not. From my perspective, he may be right, if for the wrong reasons, contingent upon the evidence. But the question of whether such suspension, whether mathematical or otherwise, is so extensive in scale and scope that it leads to the dissolution of neoclassical economics is an empirical question that surely cannot be answered at the level of ontology as opposed to the practices of the discipline itself in research, teaching and inter- and intra-disciplinary (and broader) contexts, on which Lawson seems to have little to say (and my own evidence is admittedly casual and personal, relating to my own experience of the strengthening of the mainstream around its core *and* its suspension).[19]

From my perspective, what would neoclassical economics look like if indeed moving beyond a state of suspension to one of euthanasia? Lawson and I might even agree on this with economics having morphed into mathematical social science (with Lawson possibly suggesting this has already happened with a bit of a lag on its ditching reference to the economy and economic concepts, and TA², in deference to a generally applicable deductive ontology). This is, however, questionable or at least incomplete, without explaining who then does the economic analysis itself and how – explaining the determinants of employment, growth, inflation, etc. Also, it is more than plausible to suggest that such economics would remain much as it is now, dependent upon a more or less suspended version of neoclassical economics that is much more deeply rooted than Lawson would appear to allow, both within academia and outside.

How can two mathematicians come to opposite conclusions?[20]

Further, from this discussion, it does follow that one of the major propositions adopted by Lawson on neoclassical is necessarily wrong and ill-conceived, although possibly arbitrary through the prism of his take on neoclassical ontology. For Lawson, explanation of why economics is the way it is derives from the triumph of mathematics as the arbiter of scientific reasoning. Unfortunately, though, this raises serious problems over the timing (why not earlier?, for example) and content of that mathematics (why primarily confined to the third rate stuff, as one of my colleagues insists, of algebra and calculus?). Why should one sort of mathematics prevail as opposed to another? And why is mathematics so powerfully privileged in economics as opposed to many other social science disciplines? These sorts of questions cannot be answered without descending (ascending?) to consider the substantive content of economic theory *and* its institutionalisation in the broadest sense (although somewhere between the shifting character of capitalism and the role of select US universities makes for a grand starting point).

Significantly, Lawson (2003) does address the reason for the triumph of mathematics within economics. But his continual posing rather than answering of the question is totally unsatisfactory if not as weak as that provided in his article under review. His explanation is also doubly perverse. It relies upon an abstract, universal deterministic *model* of evolutionary self-selection in which once mathematics, if historically identified,[21] acquired a foothold it benefitted from a self-sustaining momentum of its own including exclusion of others. In other words, we are offered an explanation conforming to the sort of mathematical model of precisely the sort that would be entirely acceptable to the mainstream, in terms of collective response drawn out of atomised individuals pursuing disciplinary self-interest.[22]

Equally, if not more perverse, is the appeal to institutions in general, and McCarthyism in particular (both politically and anti-intellectually), as the conveyor belt for mathematical deductivism within economics. But, if these are influential factors, as indeed they are, if not decisive on their own, why is there no space for the substantive content of economic theory to have an affect (and to be affected) not least, to be self-indulgent, along the lines laid out in my own previous account according to the theoretical goals that neoclassical economics set itself, how it achieved them and with what consequences. Of course, even if in the extreme, McCarthyite, Americanisation of the discipline, and so on, may have been the conductors of the economics orchestra, the instruments still had to be played by the economists!

Moreover, what Lawson is seeking to explain, and takes as self-evident, is false once moving beyond a specification of the mainstream in terms of its mathematically deterministic ontology. For, it is not simply that economics is impoverished and selective in its mathematics from the standards of that discipline, but that the mathematics is itself of second-order significance for neoclassical economics.

What I mean by this is that the results of mathematical reasoning are discarded by the mainstream if they are unpalatable to its core, or suspended, content. The leading examples are as well-known, at least to heterodoxy, as they are subject to absolute neglect by the mainstream itself (except for the purposes of being brought back in and suspension, with Krugman receiving a Nobel prize for applying increasing returns to trade theory and the new economic geography), such as the existence, uniqueness, stability and efficiency of general equilibrium, Arrow's impossibility theorem, the theory of the second best, factor reversals, aggregation problems (including Cambridge capital theory), and so on. The mathematics suggests one proposition, rejection of the mainstream economists' working vision of the economy, but in practice they assume the opposite, that it should remain, often as unexamined and implicit, a conventional wisdom.[23]

In short, the triumph of mathematical reasoning is observed more in the breach in its application in mainstream economics. This is a longstanding and endemic characteristic, certainly distinguishing it from the deployment of mathematics in the natural sciences and more broadly. Moreover, far from mathematical reasoning strengthening its hold over the discipline, the paradox is the more that mathematics has been deployed the less influence it has had, precisely because of the triumph of TA^2 and its incoherent extension against the thrust of mathematical reasoning (revisit previous paragraph). From this, it follows that we ought to welcome the triumph of mathematical reasoning within mainstream economics (although not at the expense of other forms of reasoning), because paradoxically, this would be almost entirely destructive of so many of its key conventional wisdoms.

Presumably Lawson does recognise, unlike most mainstream practitioners, that mathematical reasoning has only won a pyrrhic victory within economics in establishing itself in impoverished form and with overlooked implications. Far from mathematical reasoning ruling as triumphant as it is pervasive, this is the exact opposite of the truth. What, however, is more challenging for Lawson's position, given this dependence on bad maths and bad application of maths, is to address what maths prevails and how and why in its badness. Furthermore, defining the mainstream in terms of its ontological deductivism alone precludes an answer to these questions. In short, neither the maths nor the ontology define or determine the nature of the mainstream, important elements though they may be in and of themselves and to be highlighted (thank you, CRE). For the mainstream has its own evolving character (Veblen would be pleased at this), even at times, even all the time, in contradiction with those of its determinants preferred by Lawson. Moreover, of course, such considerations lead Lawson to deny neoclassical economics exists rather than to specify its evolving and contradictory content and forms.

At most, then, it might be argued that mathematical reasoning within economics is the main form taken by the theory (as well as the maths being selective and abused) and this is why neoclassical economics does not exist. My position is different: yes, mathematics is the form, it continues to have TA^2 at its core, but this is so strong that it can be violated with the form prevailing over, or in conjunction, with the core. Now, as already indicated, as argued by Colander and others, possibly the suspension of the core has become so prevalent and potentially destructive of the core that neoclassical economics is in a state of dissolution.[24] I am not sure whether this would be a welcome development or not as most behavioural economics and the like, for example, look little better across most criteria than what they are putatively displacing. But, as already suggested, this is first and foremost an empirical question, albeit one framed by how the mainstream is understood. Lawson's denial of neoclassical economics would appear to refuse to investigate what is happening substantively within the discipline (Baudrillard meets CRE?) and even to deny that this is relevant. Neoclassical economics does not exist – that is until we go to the real world of textbooks, journals and so on.

Heterovexology

Of course, Lawson's position on neoclassical economics, and how he obtains it, has had profound implications for his take on heterodox economics, which has, to his credit, hardly made him popular with its proponents. He has equally raised the vexed question – I shall term it heterovexology – of what is heterodox economics and how should we define it, comprised as it is of numbers of competing and complementary schools to various degrees. For most, not unreasonably, I suspect heterodoxy is defined by its departure from the mainstream, closely identified with neoclassical economics. Given neoclassical economics does not exist for Lawson, the same must surely apply to heterodoxy. By the same token, my own position is different.

As is apparent, so legion are the deficiencies of the mainstream – across ontology, *and* methods, concepts and theory, let alone 'realism' – that the scope for heterodoxy is extraordinarily variegated. Indeed, this is so much so that the deviations from the norms within the mainstream can offer some legitimate claim to heterodoxy – Krugman with increasing returns, Stiglitz with asymmetric information, or Colander with dissolution from without. Here, there are multi-dimensional boundaries, not a single frontier, and my own definition of heterodoxy is generous to the extreme in encompassing those contributions that depart from TA^2 in a way that contributes to further critical departure from, and reconstruction of, the discipline (as is not the case with Krugman and Stiglitz and only marginally with Colander, although Austrianism is a different kettle of interesting, if rotting, fish).

By contrast, Lawson adopts a much harder, uncompromising and, what might be thought to be as much less refined, perspective. All economics is seen through the 2x2 matrix of social ontology (yes or no) and mathematical deductivism (yes or no) with the option of no and no casually omitted without comment, see pp. 63–64. So just as the pure neoclassical mainstream is yes and yes, he is himself yes and no, so heterodoxy is simply yes and yes as is the impure forms of mainstream itself (starting with Veblen's definition). As a result, both of the terms neoclassical and heterodoxy should presumably be abandoned for Lawson, the better to focus upon and expose the underlying and determining weaknesses of both in relying upon mathematical deductivism.

Significantly, then, Lawson chooses to reject the term neoclassical, and presumably heterodoxy, as its anti-thesis, because it does not allow for coherence in the definition of either to the extent that:

> I do not really think it reasonable to distinguish or identify any group on the grounds of a shared fundamental inconsistency. My aim here, in reporting my findings, is, in the end partly rhetorical, namely, to point out that if coherence in use is required, then according to the seemingly most sustainable conception, many of those who use the term 'neoclassical' as an ill-defined term of abuse can be viewed ultimately as engaged in unwitting self-critique. But I am hoping, more fundamentally, that it is enough in this manner to communicate (in a yet further way) that in modern economics there prevails largely unrecognised a basic tension between ontology and method, one that hinders serious attempts to overcoming the real problems of the discipline.
> (p. 65)

There is something approaching original sin (mathematical deductivism) and virtue (social ontology) in this posturing, in which both must be identified and rooted out at the expense of, and in determining, all other sins and virtues which are merely their bi-products.[25] For Lawson:

> A factor that contributes to the preservation of this confused situation is a constant if uncritical repetition of the refrain, at least within heterodoxy, that neoclassical (substantive) theorising is the cause of the problems, even though there is the noted lack of clarity over the meaning of such a term. This activity serves to focus attention on conflicts at the level of substantive theorising and policy formulation, and thereby away from the deeper fundamental tensions at the level of ontology that inhibit systematic progress on all sides of modern debate.
> (p. 40)

But even the Garden of Eden had snakes, trees and apples, and let us not forget Cain and Abel, the Tower of Babel, and so on. What of these, let alone other religions? So, in contrast to reducing heterovexology to social ontology versus mathematical deductivism, my position is to acknowledge that both neoclassical and heterodoxy are inconsistent and should be acknowledged as such, but across the multiplicity of factors by which they are defined, of which Lawson's original sin and virtue are purely and simply, just two.

In other words, Lawson has discovered, or at least highlighted, a methodological logic in mainstream economics to accompany its historical logic (as discussed above, unlimited domain of application in principle, confined to market historically). This is that the application of mathematical deductivism inevitably brings it into contact and conflict with the social (wages, prices, profits, capital, labour, property, etc.) and this creates tensions, recognised or not, addressed or not. Lawson reduces this methodological logic to one of tension with social ontology alone, purely and simply. But that tension is much more complex and wide-ranging and, inevitably, can only reveal itself in practice through how it is applied in method, concept and theory where Lawson fears to tread lest the source of the sin and virtue be lost to the sinner and the virtuous in a cascade of detail. Indeed, he confesses this is his goal: 'to bring repeatedly to the fore a [for him this should be the] basic tension that lies at the core of the discipline's problems' (p. 64).

There is, however, a much deeper point to be made here that necessarily escapes Lawson in his aim to under-labour for a more relevant academic economics discipline, by finessing his dualism between social ontology and mathematical deductivism without addressing substantive content. First, as observed and probably fully accepted by Lawson, the mainstream predilection for a purely mathematical deductive methodology cannot be realised in practice as even, for example, the Bourbakian general equilibrium theory of Debreu necessarily incorporates conceptual content concerning markets, prices and the like.[26] Second, such deviations from purity necessarily have substantive (theoretical) content that is not reducible to social ontology and mathematical deductivism, even if examining along these two dimensions alone.

Third, and this is the killer punch, the smallest deviations from mathematical deductivism in general (and from TA^2 in particular) can lead to extraordinarily insightful outcomes, whereas larger deviations and, in this sense, lesser consistency that Lawson values, can be totally lacking in illumination, although these outcomes depend on how such deviationism is deployed and interpreted. Thus, for example, the need to extend general equilibrium to all markets and all activities reveals both the fragility of how the economy is understood and the need to incorporate time and place appropriately. The model of Walrasian general equilibrium depends upon a fictional auctioneer and points to the absence of a price-setting mechanism (let alone allowing for Hicksian false trading during the 'tâtonnement' when we need a cup of tea whilst waiting upon the groping to finish). Adam Smith's components theory of price is invalid if each component is taken as independent, but brilliantly poses the problems of how prices are determined whilst technology is changing and allows for the presence of absolute rent. Furthermore, Ricardo's deductivist labour theory of value falters over price determination when composition of capitals or circulation times differ, but, from a Marxist perspective, identifies the appropriate category, value, for understanding the capitalist mode of production.[27]

Fourth, then, and this is the knock-out blow for gold, especially but not necessarily departing Lawson's sin/virtue dualism, the relationship between mainstream and heterodoxy is contingent on how they are combined with two crucial features. On the one hand, such combinations can only be engaged at the substantive level of which methods, concepts and theories are deployed. On the other hand, almost a parody of the theory of the second best, the outcomes of such interactions are unrelated to the greater or lesser proximity to purer forms of the two extremes, reinforcing the immediately previous point. As a result, quite apart from rejecting Lawson's criterion of coherence for defining neoclassical and heterodox schools on the basis of his dualism or otherwise, it is necessary to consider substantive content of method, concepts, theory, etc. in delineating them. His three-way categorisation is simply a punch drunk given its reductionism to dualistic defences.

Back to the frontline contest

This, though, is not simply some academic exercise, or pub debate, over what is or is not an Olympic sport/neoclassical economics. By defining away neoclassical economics by virtue of a single (and falsely applied) criterion of ontology (reducing economics to its mathematical form and disregarding its substantive if shifting theoretical content and scope of application), Lawson is equally discarding what has proven to be the single most important strategic aspect of the struggle against mainstream economics. Again, in this he seems to waiver in his position if also building up a froth of indignation. For him, for neoclassical: 'the looseness with which this central term is interpreted (along with the toleration of this looseness) is a major factor inhibiting progress in economic understanding (p. 32–33). He immediately continues:

> Not only is the economy in crisis but, as is now widely recognised, so is the discipline of economics itself. Yet the debate over the nature of the latter's problems, weaknesses and limitations has so far been mostly fairly superficial; indeed, it is apparent that within the academy there has been very little if any significant progress. A major reason for this, I will be arguing, is that loose and varying interpretations of neoclassical theorising, especially when standing in as forms of criticism and dismissal, actually serve to distract sustained reflective attention from the real, or more systematic, causes of the discipline's failings.
>
> (p. 33)

Unfortunately, *pace* the favoured Colander, the idea that the mainstream is in crisis might be thought to be exaggerated or even the opposite of the case, but clearly Lawson believes the use of the term neoclassical is to some degree to blame for failing to highlight its key weaknesses for other, less compelling and derived, causes.

Nonetheless, on the next page, he is willing to concede: 'that [although] theorising and policy stances labelled neoclassical are not the primary causes of the discipline's problems, I accept (below) they may often be manifestations of it (p 33). Indeed: 'my aim is to help remove certain significant obstacles that obstruct the path of seriously addressing those factors that are the more fundamental causes of the modern discipline's increasingly widely recognised and indeed very widespread problems' (p. 34). But, turn on one more page, p. 35, and we are told in no uncertain terms:[28] 'Modern economics, as has already been noted, is dominated by a mainstream tradition that insists on the repeated application of methods of mathematical modelling ... That, in summary, is the real cause of the discipline's problems'. Furthermore, by the final paragraph, this is reiterated:

> The contemporary discipline of economics, most now agree [I don't think so], has lost its way. It is easy enough to demonstrate that this is due largely to the widespread contemporary persistence with methods of mathematical modelling (whether through mainstream insistence or through heterodox confusion/optimism) in conditions where this persistence is unwarranted.
>
> (p. 67)

Such is to blame both perpetrators (mainstream economists) and their victims (heterodox economists, both bold and accommodating).[29] Causes relating to institutionalised disciplinary monopoly, neo-liberalism or whatever, have simply faded away in Lawson's account and been substituted by a failure to acknowledge original sin and virtue.

The alternative offered here is to insist that neoclassical economics is alive and well, prospering despite all of its multifarious contradictions and, as such, has attracted overwhelming critical attention from an increasingly vibrant heterodoxy targeting the substantive content of neoclassical economics including not only its reduction to mathematical reasoning but also methodological individualism, lack of realism, lack of history of economic thought, lack of pluralism, lack of methodology, policy failures, etc.

Consequently, rightly or wrongly on whether neoclassical economics exists, the strategic disregard for these issues in emphasising mathematical reasoning alone as the core character of the mainstream is devastatingly debilitating for the most welcome tsunami of critical reflection that has been targeted at neoclassical economics, particularly in the wake of the global crisis. Even so, turning round the discipline remains an Olympian task. Should we tell our students to give up fighting an neoclassical enemy that does not exist for an ontological cause that the ontological enemy does not even (care or need to) acknowledge, let alone engage? As we teach our students alternatives to neoclassical economics, it is hard enough for their morale in critically undermining what they have spent so much hard time learning. Are we also to tell them that what they have learnt does not even exist?

Acknowledgement

Thanks to those who made comments on an initial draft, especially Andy Brown and Jamie Morgan.

Notes

1 This article is published in this book as Chapter 1, and page numbers cited here refer to those in this book, unless otherwise indicated.
2 My own, somewhat reluctant, contributions on the grounds that my enemy's enemy is my friend, can primarily be found in Fine (2004, 2006a, 2007). But, as with Lawson's denial of the neoclassical moniker, one's 'friends' can go too far (as can the neoclassical 'enemy', but neoliberal stalwart, neo-Austrianism for example).
3 Another reason is that in our longstanding, if occasional and alcohol-laced, amicable relations, we never seem to find anything on which to disagree (as he always says he agrees with me, but possibly not with this contribution!).
4 I tend and am more or less pleased to use the terms neoclassical, mainstream and orthodoxy more or less interchangeably, as do many others (apart from select market imperfection economists, such as Stiglitz, who seem to believe that not being neoliberal is a sufficient condition for not being neoclassical). Mainstream/orthodox might, though, reasonably be thought to be more general than neoclassical as such, depending on how much is allowed in departing from the neoclassical core (especially in light of the 'suspended' nature of the latest phase of economics imperialism). Throughout, as a friendly gesture, I use mainstream wherever possible.
5 It is hard to avoid the parody that ontology under-labours to reveal the irregularities of the mainstream (in addition to those of the economy).
6 Here, there are two different, if closely related, issues. The first, covered here, is in specifying mainstream economics (as neoclassical or not) and its current relations to the other social sciences. The second is what ideally would constitute an appropriate 'economics'. I suspect Lawson and I would agree that its content would range across that currently attached to other social sciences, although this raises a third issue of whether economics, political economy or whatever would continue to constitute a separate discipline.
7 See Lee (2012) for a similar view, with Colander as critical point of departure, but with whom Lawson would appear to be sympathetic; hardly surprising in view of the titles of Colander (2000) and Colander et al. (2004) and the 'changing face', if not 'death', of neoclassical economics and a corresponding aversion to heterodoxy and its strategic thrust against the dead or dying.
8 Although, of course, the tensions highlighted by Veblen (and Lawson) between the embryonic determinism of neoclassical and an evolutionary commitment are telling. The same applies even more, or sharply so, to Alfred Marshall.
9 Of course, this also applies to the notion of a 'school' that graces the title to Lawson's piece. What school of thought, or anything else for that matter, ever had a consistent, unchanging definition or characterisation?
10 There is also considerable misinterpretation of my position as depending upon its technical apparatus, TA1, alone in defining neoclassical economics. I allow for both a fuller box of tricks and for them to be suspended.

11 I also considered using the more general notion of a game/sport (in the tradition of Wittgenstein) to demonstrate that variability, even vagueness, in definition of type is essential, as opposed to not being a recipe for non-existence.
12 Note that Lawson does not seem to recognise this issue since he is of the view that: 'in most contexts of human interaction more clarity is preferable to less' unless: 'a contributor may have something to hide' (p. 32). He also explains:

> [a]n author does not want to reveal too much early on in a text ... [or] is unable to weigh up the arguments and seeks to avoid making a commitment prematurely... In addition the meanings of many (if not most) categories do evolve to an extent over time, and in any case may, in part at least, be determined (and so revealed only) in use.
>
> (p. 32)

But he simply does not seem to recognise that the nature of the beast is that it is, to varying degrees, imprecise.
13 Of course, the metaphors could proliferate, and possibly Venn diagrams could help. Neoclassical economics might be construed as core content with optional, possibly unspecified or open, overlapping variation or even as a chain of overlapping content (so that two definitions might not overlap at all, but they are connected through other definitions with which they both ultimately indirectly overlap). I feel embarrassed to make these elementary points about the nature of things, but it seems necessary in light of Lawson's apparent requirement of a single, uniform characterisation of neoclassical economics by its practitioners and its critics alike.
14 Most recently, see Fine (2013).
15 Consider neuroeconomics which, whatever its own other madnesses, takes utility function as the point of departure, and often basis, for bringing back in the brain as proxy for determinants of choice. See Fine (2011a, Appendix).
16 He is referring to Fine (2006b), a comment on Lawson (2006) that was rejected for publication by the *Cambridge Journal of Economics* despite Lawson's encouragement otherwise. This piece is already suggesting that maths is not the defining characteristic of economics.
17 Where do you go after you have already gone from as if perfect markets, through as if market imperfection, to market and behavioural imperfections?
18 See entry in Wikipedia, http://en.wikipedia.org/wiki/Chimera_(mythology). As heterodox economists and pluralists know only too well, neoclassical economists do not allow for rival siblings, in contrast to the chimera!
19 Thomas Piketty, the new darling of the discipline at the time of writing, uses a Cobb-Douglas production function, sending us back 50 years in the evolution of the discipline in light of the Cambridge Critique.
20 Both Tony and I delight in sharing having first degrees in mathematics.
21 Somewhat inevitably given it happened, and the French did it. But what about the routes not chosen, not least Keynes' antipathy to such analytical foundations to the discipline even as his own ideas came to the fore.
22 Not mentioned in his account, Lawson seems to be drawn at least implicitly once more to a notion of path dependence for which I have previously criticised him, as this has itself been increasingly incorporated into the mainstream, Fine (2004). Is the latter's obsessive mathematics due to which ball was drawn out of a Pólya urn?

23 I have also argued that methodological individualism is essentially incompatible with the philosophical foundations of mathematics in light of Russell's paradoxes, see Fine (2011b). But such foundations are of no interest to economists despite, according to Lawson, their commitment to mathematics.
24 The weaknesses of its intellectual foundations become more exposed, the stronger neoclassical economics is in its scope of application and as it potentially confronts other methodologies, theories and conceptualisations. My view is that the strengths have unambiguously prevailed over the weaknesses, as is evidenced by the monolithic nature of the discipline (and yet the prospering of heterodox economics analysis within other disciplines is at least as much as within economics itself).
25 It is tempting to suggest this pastiche with original sin and virtue is warranted by the transhistorical social ontology adopted by Lawson. Barring all the detail in between, ultimately, my differences with him might be reduced to this at one extreme (for me, the same social ontology is not universal, i.e. equally applicable to capitalism as other modes of production, etc.) and, at the other extreme, my insistence on the need to engage with substantive content both in and of itself and to reflect historically-specific social ontology itself.
26 Essentially, I first made this point in Fine (1980) in suggesting, against Maurice Dobb, that mathematical equations are not neutral (in application) as they carry overtones of structure, causation and meaning.
27 See Fine (1982) and Milonakis and Fine (2009) for elaboration.
28 Even immediately above this, we have the more diluted position – right or wrong, is it to hinder effective critique or is it the cause of the problem:

> a widespread loose usage of the phrase 'neoclassical economics' or 'neoclassical theorising', especially in criticism, has tended to deflect from the real source of the discipline's problems, so I had better indicate here what the latter is and how the slack use of the category neoclassical economics hinders effective critique.
>
> (p. 35)

29 Once again, very Colanderesque.

References

Baker, W. (2000) *If Christ Came to the Olympics*. Sydney, Australia: University of New South Wales Press.
Colander, D. (2000) The death of neoclassical economics. *Journal of the History of Economic Thought* 22(2): 129–143.
Colander, D., Holt, R. and Rosser, J. (2004) The changing face of mainstream economics. *Review of Political Economy* 16(4): 485–500.
Fine, B. (1980) *Economic Theory and Ideology*. London, UK: Edward Arnold.
Fine, B. (1982) *Theories of the Capitalist Economy*. London, UK: Edward Arnold.
Fine, B. (2004) Addressing the critical and the real in critical realism, in Lewis, P. (ed.) *Transforming Economics: Perspectives on the Critical Realist Project*. London, UK: Routledge.
Fine, B. (2006a) Debating critical realism in economics. *Capital and Class* 89: 121–129.
Fine, B. (2006b) Critical realism and heterodoxy. Mimeo, SOAS. Available at: https://eprints.soas.ac.uk/7024/1/lawsonono.doc (accessed 27 July 2015).

Fine, B. (2007) Rethinking critical realism: Labour markets or capitalism? *Capital and Class* 91.

Fine, B. (2011a) Prospecting for political economy. *International Journal of Management Concepts and Philosophy*, 5(3): 204–217.

Fine, B. (2011b) The general impossibility of neoclassical economics. *Ensayos Revista de Economía* 30(1): 1–22.

Fine, B. (2013) *Economics – Unfit for Purpose: The Director's Cut*. SOAS, Department of Economics Working Paper Series, no. 176, longer version of 'Economics: Unfit for purpose'. *Review of Social Economy* 71(3): 373–389.

Fine, B. and Milonakis, D. (2009) *From Political Economy to Freakonomics: Method, the Social and the Historical in the Evolution of Economic Theory*. London, UK: Routledge.

Lawson, T. (2003) *Reorienting Economics*. London, UK: Routledge.

Lawson, T. (2006) The nature of heterodox economics. *Cambridge Journal of Economics* 30(4): 483–505.

Lawson, T. (2013) What is this 'school' called neoclassical economics? *Cambridge Journal of Economics* 37(5): 947–983. Also published in this book as Chapter 1, and page numbers cited refer to those in this book.

Lee, F. (2012) Heterodox economics and its critics. *Review of Political Economy* 24(2): 337–351.

Milonakis, D. and Fine, B. (2009) *From Political Economy to Economics: Method, the Social and the Historical in the Evolution of Economic Theory*. London, UK: Routledge.

Veblen, T. (1912) *The Theory of the Leisure Class: An Economic Study of Institutions*. New York, NY: Macmillan.

9 The state of nature and natural states

Ideology and formalism in the critique of neoclassical economics

Brian O' Boyle and Terrence McDonough

Introduction

Tony Lawson's latest contribution to economics is deliberately provocative. Since the marginal revolution of the 1870s, critics of the capitalist system have understood neoclassical economics as an ideological support for the defence and preservation of capitalist class relations.[1] Instead of investigating the social dynamics of an existing economy, neoclassical economics examines a fantasy realm of individual decision making. From here, it constructs deductive-nomological (D-N) models, which justify the superiority of laissez-faire capitalism. In order to sustain its hegemony, neoclassical economics has developed into a *multifaceted system* made up of: (1) a particular object of investigation; (2) an underlying philosophy of science; (3) a set of analytical techniques; and (4) a series of substantive theoretical positions. Lawson wants to dispute all of this, arguing that neoclassical economics is a signifier that we can best do without. In Lawson's estimation, the normal criterion for defining a *neo*classical school is historical continuity with something classical and/or internal coherence around a shared set of analytical features (Lawson, Chapter 1: 30). Assessing a number of contributions on the historical lineage of the discipline, Lawson argues that any sense of theoretical continuity (with classical economics) is nowhere to be found. Meanwhile, even 'cautious interpreters' have struggled to come up with a description of any internal coherence (Lawson, Chapter 1: 31). Why does any of this matter? Lawson ultimately wants to jettison all talk of neoclassicism on the basis that it hinders effective critique of the economic mainstream.

Before he does so, however, he wants to offer a novel interpretation of the historical usage of the term neoclassical economics, which is radically at odds with that outlined above. Drawing on the work of Thorsten Veblen, Lawson argues that neoclassical economics signifies a group of theorists defined by their common inconsistency. Specifically, neoclassical economists are that subset of the discipline who recognise the historicity of social reality and yet persist with methods of analysis that presuppose ahistorical (closed) environments (Lawson, Chapter 1: 55). According to

Lawson, the advantage of Veblen's categorisation is that it sustains a sense of historical continuity (in methods) within an overall context of difference (in ontological perspective) (Lawson, Chapter 1: 55–56). This is then used to legitimate Lawson's long-term project to redefine economics in terms of its methods. Hitherto, commentators have predominantly understood schools of economic thought in terms of a vertical integration running from philosophy and methodology to techniques and substantive positions. Lawson wants to overturn this perspective in favour of a bifurcation of the discipline into two broad ontological camps, each with an attendant set of analytical methods. In one camp, Lawson situates those schools such as Post-Keynesianism, Marxism and Feminist Economics, which can reasonably be seen to follow the strictures of realist philosophy. In the other camp, he places all attempts to model the world in terms of deductive-nomological techniques.

Lawson's redefinition of neoclassical economics supports this taxonomy by indicting economists with an evolutionary (realist) ontology for failing to apply the proper (realist) methods. This is then used to buttress a series of familiar Lawsonian assertions: (1) academic economics is best understood as an orientation in method; (2) the mainstream is defined *exclusively* in terms of mathematical modelling techniques; (3) this project is far from healthy; (4) the reason for any ill-health is that mainstream methods are not appropriate to the object they are (purportedly) investigating; and (5) developments associated with mathematics are key to explaining the persistence of these methods. We wish to dispute this analysis in the strongest possible terms. Rather than rejecting the current use of the neoclassical signifier on the basis of Veblen's methodological writings, we seek to uphold its integrity by rooting mainstream theory squarely within the capitalist economy. From our perspective, neoclassical economics must be understood as an integrated theoretical problematic made up of metaphysics (naturalism, utilitarianism and methodological individualism), substantive positions (rational behaviour, optimisation and equilibrium states) and analytical techniques (utility and production functions). Together, these attributes constitute the hard core of the paradigm, with mathematics used for legitimation and protection. Based on this understanding we acknowledge the cogency of Lawson's ontological critique of mainstream methods, whilst strongly resisting his attempts to sever these methods from within their theoretical context. This is because the move towards closed-system modelling took place within a totalising paradigm shift of the object of economic investigation, the scientific procedures used for this investigation, the substantive questions that were deemed legitimate and the analytic techniques used to answer them. Lawson's latest contribution renders all of this complexity theoretically invisible. Moreover, by focusing his analysis on developments within the twentieth century, Lawson also misses the formative period of the neoclassical school in the decades following the 1870s. The upshot is greater confusion than would otherwise be the case. Rather than accurately identifying the problems in current economic science, Lawson's work is increasingly becoming a block to uncovering the ideological nature of neoclassical economics. For this reason, we will remain faithful to the question that Lawson poses (What is this 'school' called neoclassical economics?) without working blow by blow through the limitations of his answer. Instead, we will use the rest of this piece to subject his overarching project to define economics in terms of its methods to a Marxist-realist critique.

In the opening section we dispute the nature of Lawson's application of critical realism to academic economics. Since the early 1990s, Lawson's primary concern has been with assessing the *epistemological adequacy of mainstream techniques* using ontological insights from realist philosophy. This largely accurate analysis has come at the expense of investigating the ideological efficacy of D-N modelling, as Lawson has chosen to argue the centrality of either modelling *or* ideology.[2] This places the critical realism in economics project (CRE) in tension with the Marxist-realism of the Bhaskarian tradition and renders Lawson's analysis insufficiently critical and insufficiently real (Fine, 2004; O'Boyle and McDonough, 2011). Once this has been established, we turn to the *conceptual nature* of the neoclassical school, arguing that the current signifier can be rendered intelligible by seeing neoclassical economics as an integrated paradigm linked to capitalism through Hobbesian state of nature theory. Like its classical predecessor, neoclassical economics naturalises what are historically specific social relationships. This provides a level of *ideological continuity* within an overall context of *conceptual change*, as the means by which this naturalisation is achieved is different in the respective paradigms. Finally, we look at the *historical development* of neoclassical economics, arguing that Lawson's neglect of the marginal revolution is an important anomaly that needs to be challenged. Lawson places significant explanatory burden on the mathematisation of economics without investigating the birth of formalised economics in any great detail. We will argue that Lawson's historical narrative is necessarily selective. Neoclassical economics was born in the marginal revolution of the 1870s and has sustained its institutional dominance ever since. Far from hampering an effective critique of the mainstream discipline, this suggests that neoclassical economics is the proper signifier for a multifaceted theoretical problematic built within and alongside efforts to legitimise the capitalist economy.

Lawson's selective use of the realist tool-kit

Critical realism emerged in the 1970s as a powerful antidote to the twin dangers of post-modernism and empirical realism. Through a ground-breaking analysis of the natural sciences, Roy Bhaskar developed a realist philosophy aimed at 'reclaiming reality' for emancipatory social movements (Bhaskar, 1989: vii). This entailed underlabouring for the genuine sciences at two discrete levels. On the one hand, Bhaskar deployed ontological weapons to undermine the epistemological assertions of his philosophical rivals. On the other, he appealed to the nature of capitalist society to explain why these rivals often sustained their legitimacy in the face of obvious theoretical deficiencies (O'Boyle and McDonough, in press). Working transcendentally from the historic significance of experiments, Bhaskar initially demonstrated that the world must be characterised by ontological depth, processual change and internally related structured relationships (Bhaskar, 2008). Despite this, most existing philosophy of science presupposed surface events, atomistic connections and methodological individualism. Within empiricism, Bhaskar explains how reality gets collapsed into sensory experience through an *epistemic fallacy* (Bhaskar, 2008: 16). This procedure ensures that positivism can sustain neither the idea of an independent reality nor the idea of a socially produced science (Bhaskar, 1989: 51). So how did such an impoverished perspective maintain its hegemony for so long? To explain this phenomenon, Bhaskar moves beyond strictly theoretical considerations to a critique of the relations between positivist theory and capitalist society. In an explicit account of *ideology critique*, Bhaskar argued that: 'there is something about the market and what Marx called the value and wage forms that makes empirical realism the account of reality or ontology spontaneously generated therein' (Bhaskar, 1989: 192). The predominance of instrumental logic combined with the individualisation of capitalist exchange relations helps to make atomistic social theory intuitively appealing. This, in turn, legitimates a conception of individual sensors observing sequences of (atomistic) events in order to record the existence of natural (nomological) laws.

From the early 1990s onwards, Lawson broke new ground in the field of economic methodology by applying critical realism to the various schools within the academy. As a leader of the CRE project, Lawson aspired to reconstruct economics along the lines of a realist social science (Lawson, 2003: xxii). In order to achieve this objective, he applied Bhaskarian insights to the central traditions within economics. Reflecting on the nature of economic heterodoxy, Lawson asserted that any substantive theoretical differences were secondary to a common adherence to realist analysis (Lawson, 2006: 493). This conception of 'unity within difference' was well received and it helped to give philosophical coherence to a movement that is much maligned institutionally. Turning to the question of economic orthodoxy, Lawson developed an argument that was as parsimonious as it was effective. Stated succinctly, Lawson utilised Bhaskarian realism to demonstrate a debilitating mismatch between the methods of investigation applied by the mainstream and the nature of the object that is (purportedly) under investigation. Mainstream methods are built to examine an object that is radically at odds with the world we inhabit and this is enough to preclude these methods from ever delivering. Why would any discipline continue to use methods of analysis that are stubbornly unproductive? In his more recent contributions, Lawson has placed the explanatory burden for this 'anomaly' on a supposed doxa around the use of mathematics:

> The reason why mainstream economists may indeed be blind to the possibility that their methods of mathematical modelling are inappropriate to social analysis . . . is simply that mathematics has been so successful in the history of human endeavour, and especially within (non-social) natural science, that its centrality to all science . . . is, throughout wide sections of society, taken as an article of faith.
> (Lawson, 2012: 15)

Lawson's argument rarely goes any further than this today. Yet in his earlier writings he was keen to discuss an attendant influence from positivist philosophy. Reflecting on the predominance of D-N modelling in the 1990s, Lawson argued that a specifically positivist conception of scientific knowledge was responsible for the widespread application of deductive reasoning within the mainstream, alongside a generalised reluctance to engage in reflection (Lawson, 1994: 509). According to Lawson, positivism is first and foremost: 'a theory of knowledge, its nature and its limits' (Lawson, 1994: 510). Epistemological considerations have conceptual primacy, but positivism also presupposes an empirical realist ontology, an individualistic sociology and a Humean conception of nomological laws (Lawson, 1994: 510). Working collectively, these attributes result in an overwhelmingly 'conservative philosophy' as knowledge becomes naturalised, monistic and incorrigible (Lawson, 1994: 511). Meanwhile, methodological reflection is actively discouraged as part of an epistemological project to 'defend' the sciences from 'metaphysical speculation'. Mainstream methods cannot do the jobs expected of them, but those that wield these tools are comfortable in their methodological ignorance. This leaves mainstream theory doubly depleted, as it becomes impossible to explain the world with D-N tools *and* inadvisable to investigate the reasons for this failure. Indeed, mainstream economics seems to be simultaneously obsessed with (formal) method and totally disparaging of (all) methodology (Colander et al., 2004: 492). In these early offerings, Lawson was even willing to countenance a causal sequence from deficient philosophy to the individualist orientation of mainstream theory:

> I think with a bit of reflection . . . it can be seen that most of orthodoxy's standpoints – its individualist orientation including its stress on rationality, concern for equilibrium, assumptions about knowledge and foresight [and] significance upon exchange activities rather than those of production and distribution . . . can be shown to be rooted in results or conceptions [associated with positivism].
> (Lawson, 1994: 507–509)

Had he subsequently also considered the persistence of these attributes in terms of their ideological efficacy, Lawson would have gone a long way towards tying the deficiencies of the mainstream project to its role in sustaining the capitalist economy. As it was, Lawson made the crucial decision to establish the 'mainstream as ideology thesis' as an *explanatory rival* of the disciplines deficiencies (Lawson, 2006, 2012). What was worse was that he subsequently redefined the nature of academic economics to suit this argument. Lawson argues that defective methods are the real source of the discipline's problems, with any focus on ideology serving to draw attention away from the use of D-N modelling (Lawson, Chapter 1: 35). Meanwhile, the rise of these methods itself gains a questionable explanation based around the general standing of mathematics in the Western Academy (outlined above). In order to defend this position, Lawson has increasingly severed substantive economic theory from its philosophical moorings (Fine, 2006: 121). Instead of assessing the complex levels within the neoclassical system, Lawson splits and fractures his opponent illegitimately. First off, mainstream economics becomes *either* an orientation in method *or* an orientation in substantive theorising. Secondly, mainstream failings are rooted *either* in apologetics *or* in mathematical modelling (Lawson, 2006: 20).[3]

Arguing explicitly in either/or categories, Lawson misses the ideology that resides within the mathematisation of mainstream economics itself.[4] Earnest scientists, unable to break with society-wide 'mathematics envy' (Lawson, 2012: 11), stands in for a critical analysis of conservative methodology. Moreover, Lawson merely compounds these difficulties by truncating his detailed historical analysis to the formalist revolution (in the 1950s). We believe that the crucial shift occurred more than a half-century earlier during the marginal revolution. We also believe that marginalism was so revolutionary precisely because it managed to shift the *entire focus of the discipline* away from the class relations of a capitalist society towards a Hobbesian style logical construct. Above everything, marginalism involved a transformation in the *object of investigation* and the *narrative structure* of the analysis. It was only once this meta-shift had been established that the formal tools could be safely deployed. Far from introducing much needed rigour into economic science, marginalism effectively severed *Newtonian mathematics* from the *scientific method* (O'Boyle, 2015). Lawson is therefore mistaken to counterpose *mainstream methods* to *neoclassical ideology*. Neoclassical economics is, first and foremost, an orientation in ideology – with the formal methods facilitating a move away from science. In order to establish this, we shall initially outline the (methodological/conceptual) architecture of classical political economy, before doing the same for its *neo*classical successor. Arguing in this way will hopefully reveal the ideological continuity between the respective systems, alongside the different internal coherences within each problematic. This will help to establish the specific role that mathematical methods played in the course of this transition.

The Newtonian roots of classical political economy

One difficulty in discussing the nature of 'classical political economy' is the disagreement around what it actually defines. For thinkers like Veblen and Keynes, the classical school is a 'catch-all category' for economists who today might best be defined as neoclassical. In the *General Theory*, Keynes (1997) attributes the dogmas of Say's Law and market clearing equilibrium to a classical school rooted in the precepts of supply and demand (Keynes, 1997: 18). This clearly denotes something very different to Marx's division (which we accept) of classical from vulgar economy, developed from the 1840s onwards. Marx wanted to reconstruct political economy along the lines of an historical, dialectical and realist social science. As part of this project he separated what he felt was the genuine, if one-sided, analysis of thinkers like Adam Smith and David Ricardo, from the vulgar economy of the likes of Thomas Malthus and Nassau Senior. These latter theorists accepted the capitalist economy as it appeared to the senses, subjectivising its key relationships and mystifying its class dynamics (Marx, 1972). Smith and Ricardo were far superior in this regard. Starting with a genuine attempt to unearth the structural dynamics of the capitalist system, Smith and Ricardo bequeathed a (partly) scientific analysis rooted in the methodological precepts of Isaac Newton.

What exactly are these precepts? In both his *Principia* (1995) and his *Opticks* (1979), Newton developed a method of analysis/synthesis that works across five key stages. First, the theorist chooses a set of real world phenomena to investigate. If these objects are amenable to experimentation, detailed investigation can proceed. If not, repeated observations will have to suffice. This observational phase allows the theorist to generate data that serve as the entry point to the investigation. From here the theorist constructs hypothetical *causes* that can potentially bring order to the phenomenal *effects* that have been recorded. This is the second phase, as the causes or hidden connections that potentially lie behind observed reality are brought into focus. For Newton, such causes are natural, law-like and amenable to mathematical manipulation/generalisation. Once this is achieved, the third phase can begin as tentative hypotheses are tested against further observations. If hypotheses are still found to be empirically defensible, a series of novel phenomena can potentially be brought under the auspices of 'natural laws'. This is the fourth stage of the Newtonian system as mathematics are used to deduce the workings of a whole range of secondary phenomena. Finally, the fifth and ultimate stage occurs when all of the phenomena under investigation can be deduced from the workings of the causes discovered. Newton captures the essence of his method in the following terms:

> From Effects to their Causes, and from particular Causes to more general ones ... This is the Method of Analysis: And the Synthesis consists

in assuming the causes discover'd and establish'd as Principles, and by them explaining the Phenomena proceeding from them, and proving the Explanations.

(Newton, 1979: 404–405)

Adam Smith was so taken by Newton's achievements as to proclaim his system: 'the greatest and most admirable improvement that was ever made in the history of philosophy' (Smith, 1982: 98). Newton's laws reigned supreme in the educated mind of the eighteenth century. Yet how was Smith to emulate the master? In the *Wealth of Nations* (1999 [1776]), Smith begins by observing the enormous increase in productivity occasioned by the rapidly developing division of labour (Smith, 1999 [1776]: 109). The division of labour is itself created by the burgeoning market, but what foundational force could account for these phenomena? Smith argues that the: 'principle that gives occasion to the division of labour' is a transhistorical propensity rooted within human *nature*: 'The division of labour . . . is the *necessary* though very slow and gradual consequence of a certain *propensity in human nature* . . . to truck, barter and trade one thing for another (Smith, 1999 [1776]: 117, emphases added).

Riveting observable changes on the surface of capitalism to the immutable laws of human nature proved the hallmark of classical political economy (Rubin, 1979: 171). Like Newton, Smith observes real world phenomena, before retroducing natural causes from visible effects (Montes, 2003: 741).[5] This methodological procedure ensured that the subsequent analysis was thoroughly realist in its orientation (Montes, 2003: 741). Moreover, it immediately involved Smith in detailed substantive analysis, as hypotheses had to be created before being tested. In Newton's case, the theory of gravity is a workhorse hypothesis designed to bring observations of celestial phenomena under the auspices of a single force. In Smith's case the *labour theory of value* is designed in analogous fashion to capture the movements of commodities under the forces of self-interest. Working under the assumption that the labour theory of value is an appropriate analogue for the forces of nature, Smith reasons that in precapitalist societies, commodities can only be exchanged on the basis of the amount of labour embodied within them (Smith, 1999 [1776]: 151). Smith also understands that the mere act of hiring someone has no effect on the value of a commodity and yet he fails to square this with the observed reality of capitalist profits. To remain consistent with Newton's procedure, Smith should be able to sustain an invariable relationship between the *immutable* laws of human nature and his value analysis. If labour creates all of a commodity's value, then how can anyone not labouring secure any of its income? The value embodied should go entirely to the labourer, whilst in capitalism commodities generate incomes for workers *and* capitalists alike. Instead of realising that the value produced by the labourer can be (partly) appropriated by the capitalist, Smith assumes a world of harmonious order and shifts his value analysis to cope with appearances. Smith's *labour command theory* seems to tally with observable experience in capitalist distribution relations. However it leaves a debilitating contradiction within the central categories of his value analysis. Where Newton managed to bring all of his observations under the rubric of his central laws, Smith had discontinuous value theories underpinned by continuity in natural behaviour.

The idea of universal laws generating different rules for different societies was predictably seized upon by some of Smith's vulgar opponents. David Ricardo's chief merit was to attempt to solve this 'anomaly' by situating the source of profits in the unpaid work of the working classes (Marx, 1968: 106). In Ricardo's estimation, Smith: 'had accurately defined the original source of exchangeable value' with his labour embodied concept (Ricardo, 2004: 7). Throughout his *Principles*, Ricardo therefore inquires how far this foundational hypothesis can be squared with the observed reality of wages, rents and profits. Ricardo's deduction basically starts at the third phase of Newton's method insofar as he assumes the data from Smith's analysis before working to make the Smithian system internally consistent. This procedure helped Ricardo to unearth the *hidden connections* between the various classes in a capitalist society. Yet his own proclivity to naturalise capitalism soon resulted in theoretical anomalies (around the rate of profit). The upshot was a theory that could sustain empirical validity at the cost of conceptual confusion or conceptual clarity at the cost of empirical confusion. Unsurprisingly this proved meat and drink for Ricardo's theoretical opponents. From the early 1830s, a raft of theorists from Malthus and Torrens to Bailey and Longfield attacked the empirical anomalies of the Ricardian system (Henry, 1990: 127). Collectively, these assaults seriously weakened the standing of classical political economy, but they proved insufficient to actually unseat it. This changed dramatically during the marginal revolution of the 1870s.

The Hobbesian roots of Neoclassical Economics

The attempt to apply Newton's scientific method to capitalist social relations characterised classical political economy. Moving from observed phenomena to underlying causal forces, Smith and Ricardo developed a value category that laid the basis for genuine economic science (Marx, 1968, 1978). This would have been inconceivable had they not been trying to root social phenomena in human nature, and yet this very procedure ultimately proved the undoing of the classical system. Naturalising what are historically specific social relations ensured that neither Smith nor Ricardo had the ability to follow Newton successfully. It is simply not possible to explain capitalist phenomena with a labour theory unless the latter is reconstructed to take account of exploitation and value transfers. Marx successfully achieved this reconstruction via his conceptions of labour power and intraclass competition. However, this meant moving his value analysis in a thoroughly historical direction (Marx, 1972, 1981). Marginalism, meanwhile, moved neoclassical economics in entirely the opposite direction. Instead of sustaining the classical value theory on the basis of historicised social relations, Stanley Jevons and Leon Walras jettisoned the labour theory of value whilst claiming to uphold the legitimacy of natural scientific methods. On the surface, their attempt to deduce the mechanical laws of human behaviour seemed remarkably Newtonian. Matter-in-motion is written into the DNA of the neoclassical paradigm, and yet the narrative structure of the marginalist argument is far more Hobbesian than Newtonian.

Writing during the period of the English Civil War, Thomas Hobbes devised a scientific method that attempted to outline the political arrangements that men on either side would rationally assent to. In the first phase of his investigation, Hobbes laid out what he believed to be the immutable laws of human nature (Hobbes, 1985: 85). Once this nature was established, Hobbes famously moved into a *hypothetical state of nature* – deducing the dystopian outcomes that would exist in the absence of any social rules and the contractual agreements needed to create them (Hobbes, 1985: 183). Hobbes founds his model on axioms of human behaviour before entering into his logical construct. The subsequent deduction stands or falls on the basis of its initial assumptions, and this marks an important distinction with the empirical method of the classical theorists. In the classical system, the phenomena of a capitalist economy are the benchmark against which hypothesis testing is actually carried out (though using historical evidence rather than quantitative measurement). Indeed, it is only because Smith and Ricardo test their hypotheses that the weaknesses in their value categories can come to light. In the marginalist system this is no longer the case. Instead of beginning with observations of an actual economy, marginalism assumes *homo economicus* operating in a conceptual space designed to deduce the optimality of idealised capitalism. An appeal to human nature marks an important theoretical continuity with the classical system, except that now the psychological laws of human self-interest make up the very object of the investigation. Like Hobbes, Jevons begins his enquiry by abstracting the laws of human nature from their social surroundings. In his estimation, economics must become an axiomatic-deductive science based exclusively on first principles intuited from self-reflection:

> [In science] possessing certain facts of observation, we frame an hypothesis as to the laws governing these facts; we reason from the hypothesis deductively to the results to be expected; and we then examine these results in connection with the facts in question ... *The science of economics, however, is in some degree peculiar, owing to the fact ... that its ultimate laws are known to us immediately by intuition* ... That every

person will choose the greater good, that human wants are more or less quickly satiated ... from these axioms we can deduce the laws of supply and demand, the laws of that difficult conception, value, and all the intricate results of commerce.

(Jevons, 2013: 18, emphasis added)

Jevons builds legitimacy for his new economics on the basis of the analytical tools of the infinitesimal calculus (Jevons, 2013: xxviii). To this end, he writes repeatedly of the need to mathematise the discipline in line with the natural sciences. However, it is vitally important to keep the primacy of the narrative structure firmly in focus. Jevons's most important task involves a shift in the *object of economic investigation* (from capitalist society to the 'natural laws' of individual human wants) alongside a shift in the nature of his *scientific procedure* (from Newtonian empiricism to Hobbesian deductivism). It is only once this meta-transition has been achieved, that he can present a new set of economic questions, alongside an attendant set of innovative mathematical procedures. Taking on J. S. Mill, Jevons writes that economics must move away from its traditional focus on production and distribution for a formalised account of rational consumption. According to Jevons: 'economics must be founded upon a full and accurate investigation of the conditions of utility, and to understand this element we must necessarily examine the desires of man' (Jevons, 2013: 39). This move has extremely important *substantive implications*, as Jevons can now formalise his system as the study of rational calculators tasked with distributing scarce resources so as to achieve the highest degree of personal utility (Jevons, 2013: 71). Crucially moreover, it is only at this stage that the Newtonian mathematics can be safely deployed, as Jevons deduces an isomorphism between nineteenth-century physics, the mechanics of utility maximisation and rational exchange in laissez-faire capitalism (Jevons, 2013: 140).

Turning to Walras, we find much the same conceptual pattern, as science begins with ideal-type constructs far removed from the messy world of empirical reality (Walras, 2003: 61). Unlike Jevons who merely forestalls the day of empirical reckoning, Walras has no time for empirical verification of any description. The validity of his arguments flows exclusively from the 'truth' of their initial assumptions, alongside the rigour of his deductive procedure (Walras, 2003: 71). This ensures that his pure economics begins and ends within a: 'hypothetical realm of perfect competition' (Walras, 2003: 40). Walras's main aim is to deduce the existence of a set of hypothetical prices that are capable of bringing all markets into equilibrium simultaneously. The mathematics he employs are more algebraic than geometric, but the metaphysics are virtually identical to those of Jevons and Carl Menger (Walras, 2003: 44). Behind Walras's demand and offer curves is the same hedonistic maximiser determining prices on the basis of marginal utility calculations (rareté) (Walras, 2003: 38).

Moreover, once Walras has specified his model in terms of: (1) atomistic utility calculations; (2) perfect competition; and (3) decentralised price information, his deduction of the superiority of laissez-faire capitalism becomes axiomatic.

> We have, perhaps, reached the place where we can see the importance of a scientific formulation of pure economics. From the viewpoint of pure science, all that we needed to do, and all that we actually have done . . . was to treat free competition . . . as an hypothesis, for it did not matter whether or not we observed it in the real world, since strictly speaking it was sufficient that we should be able to form a conception of it. It was in this light that we studied the nature, causes and consequences of free competition. We know now that these consequences may be summed up as the attainment within certain limits, of maximum utility . . . the equations we have developed do show [that] freedom procures the maximum utility; and since factors that interfere with freedom are obstacles to the attainment of this maximum, they should . . . be eliminated as completely as possible.
> (Walras, 2003: 255–256)

Here we see the ideology in full display, as a metaphysical defence of capitalist society is presented as the endpoint of a scientific deduction. Aspects of the neoclassical system had actually been handed down from Bentham (utilitarianism) and Ricardo (deductive theorising) (Milonakis and Fine, 2009: 94). However, the manner in which the conceptual framework was brought together was radically unique. Marginalism represented a paradigm shift in every sense of the term. It involved nothing less than a revolution in the object of investigation, the narrative structure of the investigation, the types of questions being addressed and the sorts of techniques available to answer them. Each of the facets hangs together as an integrated whole, but there can be little doubt that the principle change was in the overall structure of the problematic. By shifting the focus of the discipline towards the rational mechanics of assumed behaviour, neoclassical economics successfully severed Newton's mathematics from the scientific method. Far from using mathematics to increase the rigour of a natural science, the marginalist deployment of the calculus was always in the service of utilitarian ideology. This suggests that the architecture of the mathematised model cannot be divorced from the substantive theory, as every step in the deductive sequence is designed to produce the desired correspondence with a set of ideological presuppositions. Contra Lawson, the use of D-N modelling is not an error perpetrated on the basis of a cultural illusion. Rather the mathematical formalism is a consequence of the prior utilisation of the Hobbesian method and the joining of this method with a set of ideological propositions. The procedure is not mistaken; it is apologetic.[6] Moreover, the propositions are linked with (and developed to be consistent with) Newtonian mechanics in order to give the impression that the maths are the result of the Newtonian method, when in fact the entire project is fundamentally Hobbesian.

Understanding this helps to explain the peculiar nature of neoclassical empirical practice. Whilst claiming adherence to a strict Popperian conception of scientific method, the actual practice of mainstream economic journals renders falsification impossible. Models are constantly being constructed on the basis of neoclassical assumptions and tested against available empirical data. All practitioners know these models frequently fail the test of the data. Yet these are deemed negative results and unpublishable. They are thus discarded before being subjected to collective scientific scrutiny. In the physical sciences a similar suppression of negative (that is, falsifying) results would be regarded as a scandal. Ordinarily, this might be viewed as a failure to consistently apply scientific ideals, which could be rectified through a stricter privileging of negative results. This assumes, however, that neoclassical practice is actually Newtonian in its initial concern with real world phenomena. On the contrary, the initial step is the assumption of first principles, which do not have their origin in the physical world. They cannot therefore be falsified. They can only be rendered more plausible by those instances where empirical data exhibits a correspondence with the deduced behaviour. These correspondences are thus what is deemed legitimately publishable from the neoclassical perspective. Indeed, Milton Friedman has famously argued that the existence of these correspondences is enough to render even admittedly unrealistic assumptions scientifically useful (Friedman, 1953).

Neoclassical economics in historical context

One way to think about the marginal revolution is as the turning point in a 'war of position' against the classical system. Classical political economy emerged alongside the bourgeoisie and reflected their need to unearth the workings of the capitalist economy (Henry, 1990: 64). The scientificity of Smith and Ricardo was intimately tied to the progressive nature of the class they supported – with the labour theory of value erected as part of a theoretical assault on feudal privilege. By the 1830s, however, the class dynamics of the capitalist system had been altered decisively. Following the Corn Laws, capital increasingly worked with a weakened aristocracy to hold down the power of the proletariat. Meanwhile, the revolutions of 1848 merely confirmed that it was now the working classes that had to be vanquished. In this environment it was inevitable that reactionary doctrines would get a hearing, particularly as the Ricardian system had run its course as an effective ideology for bourgeois society. Ricardo's scientific integrity meant that the further he moved into the architecture of capitalist relations, the more he exposed the inherent conflict between capital and wage labour. This left his theory open to being appropriated by the political left and critiqued by the political right. From the early 1830s, most of the prominent political economists predictably lined up against the classical system. Yet why did it take until the 1870s for the tide to turn decisively? Essentially this can be explained on the basis of the changing nature of capitalist society, alongside the growing professionalisation of the academic discipline. By the 1870s, the capitalist classes across Europe were faced with three interlocking challenges. First was the growth of large-scale trade unionism combined with the emergence of various nascent socialist organisations (including the First International in 1864). This advance in working class organisation was also bolstered theoretically as the publication of *Capital* (originally published in 1867, but see Marx, 1972, 1981) marked a definitive transformation in the class character of the classical system and rendered it unusable (by the bourgeoisie) from that point onwards. Added to this, was a rise in working class militancy, exemplified by the workers revolt during the Paris commune (1871) (Henry, 1990: 177). Finally, there was the Great Depression of 1873 as capitalism began a long period of monopolistic reconstruction and consolidation (Dobb, 1963: 300). The fact that the commune was drowned in blood proved the willingness of the ruling classes to engage in barbarity. However, they were also keen to develop transmission mechanisms for their most important ideas. The professionalisation of economic theory provided one such mechanism. From the early 1870s, the success of the marginalist reconstruction of political economy moved in lock-step with its professionalisation (Stigler, 1973: 10). This in many ways reflects the evolutionary tale that Lawson has developed (about the 1950s), as thinkers who would previously have been neglected, gradually found themselves with professional advantages (see Lawson, 2003: 247).

The great strength of the marginalist system lay in its ability to present bourgeois ideology as scientific progress. Prior to the 1870s, reactionary thinkers had successfully pinpointed anomalies within classical political economy, without managing to shift the terrain upon which they were generated. Marginalism was successful precisely because it managed to achieve this feat. Synthesising vulgar economy with Hobbes' method, the marginalists isolated bourgeois characteristics from their social context before presenting them as human nature. This emptied political economy of its socio-historical specificity, as class and crises were gradually banished from the core of the discipline (Milonakis and Fine, 2009: 109). It might seem like simple apologetics to remove such foundational categories from economic theory. Yet for Jevons and Walras it was precisely this stripping away of social phenomena that provided the basis for their 'scientificity'. Following the precepts of Newtonian philosophy, marginalism argued that science must be built on natural laws that are universal in their scope and precision (Walras, 2003: 47). Within the realm of pure economics these laws were subsequently secured through the simple procedure of *assuming* the universality of rational decision making at the margins. This appeal to universal truths eventually allowed neoclassical economics to become hegemonic, but in the early phase of its development both Walras and Jevons saw the need to strategically narrow the scope of their enquiries. According to Jevons, his *abstract economics* would sit alongside statistics and various other aspects of the newly constructed economics (Jevons, 2013: xxxviii). Walras meanwhile argued that his *pure economics* was restricted to exchange relations, leaving ample space for the art of production and the moral science of institutions (Walras, 2003: 63). The (seemingly) limited aspirations of these systems was part of their initial appeal, particularly in the hands of Alfred Marshall. Marshall wrote the definitive textbook of the late nineteenth century replete with the caveats around method that Lawson refers to (Lawson, Chapter 1: 53). As a cautious thinker, Marshall was undoubtedly concerned about the overly static/mechanistic nature of the new economics, and yet – for all of his equivocations – he insisted that human nature was permanent enough to become the proper object of economic investigation:

> The fundamental substance of economic organization ... depends mainly on such wants and activities such as preferences and aversions as are *found in man everywhere*; they are not indeed always in the same form, nor even quite the same in substance *but yet they have a sufficient element of permanence and universality to enable them to be brought in some measure under general statements.*
>
> (Marshall, 2012: 468, emphasis added)

Marshall also argued that any: 'individual peculiarities of character ... are a less hindrance to the general application of the deductive method than at first sight appears (Marshall, 2012: 464). The key is to forge short chains of deductive reasoning (partial equilibrium analysis), rather than long ones. With Marshall, the system of neoclassical concepts was diffused throughout the profession in a form that would not seem overly threatening to other modes of economic reasoning. From here it was a short step to constructing the hard core of the discipline around the new theoretical concepts and a protective belt made up of mathematics and empirics. Moscati notes that the history of neoclassical demand theory has been littered with instances of protecting the integrity of this theoretical core at the expense of mathematical rigour and/or empirical validity. When Edgeworth championed a general utility function to replace the additive function of Jevons and Walras, increasing realism would have come at the cost of introducing indeterminateness between prices and demand. Instead of accepting this indeterminateness, neoclassical economics ignored the real world utility interdependence of goods in order to protect the integrity of their conceptual framework (Moscati, 2005: 9).Similar instances occurred with the mathematical gymnastics needed to find determinate solutions to general equilibrium. The mathematics used to solve Walras' system show that the result is: 'not liable to exist, to be unique and stable, or to display efficiency properties' (Milonakis and Fine, 2009: 293). Despite this, general equilibrium remains the workhorse model at the textbook level, where unsuspecting students are imbued with the virtues of the fundamental welfare theorems. When mathematics exposes the untenably of its working models, neoclassical economics has consistently protected its central principles. The most famous example of this is probably the Cambridge controversy of the 1960s. However, the post-war shift towards axiomatics also exhibits these priorities just as readily.

According to Lawson, the emergence of relativity theory and quantum mechanics at the turn of the twentieth century undermined confidence in the Newtonian insistence on viewing mathematics as the language of nature (Lawson, Chapter 1: 57). Around the same time, David Hilbert was inspiring his Göttingen School to axiomatise branches of mathematics, including geometry. Drawing on the work of Hilbert, mainstream economists gradually began to bury the question of empirical validity ever deeper under layers of conceptual rigour. Instead of worrying about real world applicability, mainstream theorists began to see their models as self-contained systems comprising sets of axioms and their deductive consequences (Lawson, Chapter 1: 57). This so-called formalist revolution apparently supports Lawson's attempt to redefine economics in terms of its methods. It actually shows how far neoclassical economics has gone to protect its central core. There is powerful ideological resonance in the Newtonian ideal of balanced equilibrium that cannot be replicated by chaos theory or quantum mechanics. Instead of moving with their physical counterparts, neoclassicism therefore relied upon a *highly selective* deployment of mathematics to insulate their models from unwelcome intrusion. Whereas physics jettisoned its Newtonian metaphysics in order to accommodate the latest science, neoclassical economics sustained its Newtonian metaphysics on the basis of a (further) move away from reality. Von Neumann and Debreu may have argued that their mathematical frameworks were devoid of content, but the fact remains that both of them worked within the rational individualistic framework of the neoclassical mainstream. Game theory and axiomatic general equilibrium accept the basic principles of marginalist economics even as they extend its boundaries in different directions. By the 1950s it was widely known that both Frege and Russell had failed in their attempts to ground mathematics in formal logic. More importantly, Gödel had demonstrated the impossibility of grounding mathematics in axiomatic set theory, whilst Quine was just showing the impossibility of positivistic verification (D-N modelling). Axiomatic formalism and logical positivism have taken scarcely less philosophical damage than classical Newtonianism and yet the mainstream has remained blissfully aloof from *these particular* philosophical challenges. What did occur in the second half of the twentieth century was a rebooting of the central core of the discipline alongside an imperialist expansion into other areas (Milonakis and Fine, 2009: 303).

Since the 1970s, the implosion of Keynesianism has opened the field to a virulent strain of neoclassical orthodoxy. This so-called *new classical economics* assumes perfectly efficient markets populated with representative agents with complete rationality. Armed with this omnipotent calculator, neoclassical economics has forayed into all manner of adjacent disciplines (Milonakis and Fine, 2009: 303). Scientifically, the mainstream is undoubtedly in very bad shape, but from its own viewpoint it remains fundamentally healthy. Even the latest economic crisis has barely shaken the discipline's confidence and, for us, this can only be a sign that mainstream concepts (including its methods) are doing the jobs expected of them. Whatever else they may be, mainstream methods are particularly effective in their ability to package bourgeois ideology as rigorous science. This is the real reason that they have been retained and only a new paradigm, which does the same ideological duty or a radical challenge to capitalist dominance will see them relinquished.

Conclusion

Tony Lawson has based his influential critique of mainstream economics in the disjunction between the open character of economic and social reality and the closed world needed for the application of mathematical models. He has argued that its commitment to mathematical modelling is what defines the mainstream and, consequently, discussion of a specifically neoclassical tradition is a misspecification which detracts attention from this methodological Achilles Heel. In the course of his argument he has dismissed the importance of ideology in understanding the constitution of mainstream theory. Whilst accepting Lawson's fundamental argument about the inappropriateness of closed models being used to investigate open systems, we have questioned his contention that mainstream economics cannot be characterised as an ideologically driven neoclassicism. There is no shortage of specific instances of the appearance of ideology in economics. However, these can be countered, at least rhetorically, by citing instances of its apparent absence. We have chosen instead to confront Lawson's overarching argument on its own ground by trying to understand the specific role that mathematics has played in the history of neoclassical economics and the specific relationship of that role to its ideological character. Having adopted this strategy we have little to say one way or the other about Lawson's claims about heterodox economics. There are undoubtedly theorists who accept a processual ontology alongside closed-system modelling, but whether any progress can be made through shifting longstanding signifiers seems questionable at best. What we are concerned with disputing is Lawson's claim that the current use of the neoclassical signifier risks an analysis that is superficial and insufficiently radical (Lawson, Chapter 1: 38). On the contrary, we have argued that any analysis that fails to root the mathematisation of economics in the wider shift of the mainstream problematic will essentially let neoclassical ideology off the hook (O'Boyle and McDonough, 2011: 19). The role of mathematics in the neoclassical tradition emerges along with its successful break with the classical tradition of Smith and Ricardo. This break had the character of a paradigm shift in that it was not confined to differences over the proper description of economic phenomena. The break also involved questions of philosophy, the nature of the object of investigation, the questions which were posed and the analytical techniques used to address these questions, including mathematical modelling. Practitioners on both sides of this break claimed an allegiance to science and inspiration in the Newtonian tradition. Lawson is correct to emphasise that a claim to continued scientificity was central to the success of the new programme. We have argued that the exact nature of this claim, as made by the emerging neoclassical tradition, was of central importance. Rather than the Newtonian procedure of moving from reality to scientific laws before testing these hypothetical laws against further observations of reality, the new neoclassical paradigm chose an essentially Hobbesian procedure of starting not with reality but with assumed first principles. Neoclassicism essentially maintained its claim to scientificity by redefining science. This claim was buttressed by pointedly retaining Newton's mathematics whilst abandoning his scientific procedure.

The abandonment of Newton's procedure is essential to the retention of his mathematics. As Lawson continually points out, the chances are minimal that an examination of an open human system would generate tight analogies with the closed world of nineteenth-century physics. Neoclassical economics changed the subject of economics from production and distribution to the study of rational calculators, maximising personal utility in free exchange relations. This object of study already embodies a set of assumed principles and is already amenable to modelling based on Newtonian mechanics. There is a direct line of connection between a priori assumptions, the object of study, the questions asked and the analytical technique deployed. This direct line is there from the beginning of neoclassical economics. The mathematical techniques are indeed used by the neoclassical mainstream as a warrant of their claim to science. But this does not mean that the mathematics can be separated out from the neoclassical framework and considered in isolation. Neoclassical economics shifted the object of investigation away from class and exploitation to the beneficent effects of free market capitalism. To the extent that this move was ideological, so too was the adoption of the accompanying mathematical analysis. Far from the problem with mainstream economics being *either* ideology *or* inappropriate maths, the inappropriate maths were always part and parcel of neoclassical ideology.

Acknowledgement

The authors would like to thank Jamie Morgan for valuable comments on an earlier draft of this paper. The usual proviso applies.

Notes

1 Throughout this piece we follow Marx in framing ideology in materialist terms. In *Capital*, Marx developed a triple critique of: (1) bourgeois political economy (in both its classical and vulgar guises); (2) the everyday ideas and experiences that this theory worked to formalise; and (3) the underlying social relations that render these experiences and ideas necessary and appealing. This is the template for our forthcoming analysis as we analyse the nature of the conceptual defence of capitalist society erected by the neoclassical school. This is not to suggest malign intent on behalf of all neoclassical economists, merely that their system of concepts works as an ideology whether they are conscious of it or not.

2 In an article under the title 'Mathematical modelling and ideology in the economics academy: competing explanations of the failings of the modern discipline', Lawson (2012) explicitly argues against traditional views of neoclassical ideology in order to legitimate his own perspective. Below is an excerpt that makes this clear:

> My own view is that explanations of the state of modern economics [in terms of political economic ideology] are unsustainable. It is one thing to suggest that mainstream economists mostly suppose that capitalism, as a market centred system, is somehow natural or normal or the best that can be achieved; but it is quite another thing to suppose that much of the output of these economists is even mainly concerned with such issues of political economy . . . In short, the modern mainstream is not a project whose emphases and explanatory failures are mainly direct manifestations either of intentions to maintain attachment to the existing economic system, or of a blindness to its real nature.
>
> (Lawson, 2012: 8 and 10)

3 This is clear in both 'The nature of heterodox economics' (Lawson, 2006) and 'mathematical modelling and ideology in the economics academy' (Lawson, 2012) as he criticises the efficacy of traditional ideology critique in order to make the theoretical space for his own ontological critique of the mainstream.

4 Although Lawson has consistently argued against attempts to understand the economic mainstream as an orientation in ideology and has sought to position his own interpretation as a rival explanation of mainstream failings, he has accepted that there are ideological effects associated with the use of D-N models (Lawson, 2012: 17). Specifically, Lawson has accepted that the use of D-N modelling serves to render analysis of power, exploitation and oppression almost impossible (Lawson, 2012: 17). For our part, we believe that any discussion of these ideological effects must be situated *within the complex levels of the neoclassical problematic*. This disrupts Lawson's attempt to argue in terms of either ideology or methods as we seek to show in the rest of this chapter.

5 In Montes (2003, 2008) and Kim (2012) Lawson's work is credited with providing the philosophical resources to define both Newton and Smith in critical realist

terms. This is a positive inheritance of the CRE project, which we are happy to acknowledge.
6 Once again it is important to stress that we are analysing the structural nature of the problematic, rather than the conscious intentions of those using it.

References

Bhaskar, R. (1989) *Reclaiming Reality: A Critical Introduction to Contemporary Philosophy*. London, UK: Verso.
Bhaskar, R. (2008) *A Realist Theory of Science*. London, UK: Verso.
Colander D., Holt, R. P. and Rosser, J. B. Jr. (2004) The changing face of mainstream economics. *Review of Political Economy* 16(4): 485–500.
Dobb, M. (1963) *Studies in the Development of Capitalism*. New York, NY: International Publishers.
Fine, B. (2004) Addressing the critical and the real in critical realism, in Lewis, P. (ed.) *Transforming Economics*. London, UK: Routledge.
Fine, B. (2006) Debating critical realism in economics. *Capital & Class* 30(2): 121–129.
Friedman, M. (1953) The methodology of positive economics, reprinted in Caldwell, B. (ed.) (1984) *Appraisal and Criticism in Economics: A Book of Readings*. London, UK: Allen and Unwin.
Henry, J. (1990) *The Making of Neoclassical Economics*. London, UK and Boston, MA: Unwin Hyman.
Hobbes, T. (1985) *Leviathan*. London, UK: Penguin Classics.
Jevons, W. S. (2013) *The Theory of Political Economy: Fourth Edition*. London, UK: Palgrave and Macmillan.
Keynes, J. M. (1997) *The General Theory of Employment, Interest and Money*. New York, NY: Prometheus Books.
Kim, K. (2012) Adam Smith's 'History of Astronomy' and view of science. *Cambridge Journal of Economics* 36(4): 799–820.
Lawson, T. (1994) The Nature of Post Keynesian economics and its links to other traditions: A realist perspective. *Journal of Post Keynesian Economics* 16(4): 503–538.
Lawson, T. (2003) Reorienting Economics. Oxford, UK: Routledge.
Lawson. T. (2006) The nature of heterodox economics. Cambridge *Journal of Economics* 30(4): 483–505.
Lawson, T. (2012) Mathematical modelling and ideology in the economics academy: Competing explanations of the failings of the modern discipline. *Economic Thought: History, Philosophy and Methodology* 1(1): 1–20.
Lawson, T. (2013) What is this 'school' called neoclassical economics? *Cambridge Journal of Economics* 37(5): 947–983. Also published in this book as Chapter 1, and page numbers cited refer to those in this book.
Marshall, A. (2012) *Principles of Economics*. Boston, MA: Digireads.com Publishing.
Marx, K. (1968) *Theories of Surplus Value: Part Two*. Moscow, Russia: Progress Publishers.
Marx, K. (1972) *Capital: A Critique of Political Economy, Volume One: The Process of Capitalist Production*. New York, NY: International Publishers.
Marx. K. (1978) *Theories of Surplus Value: Part One*. London, UK: Lawrence and Wishart.
Marx, K. (1981) *Capital: A Critique of Political Economy, Volume Three*. London, UK: Penguin Classics.

Milonakis, D. and Fine, B. (2009) *From Political Economy to Economics: Method, the Social and the Historical in the Evolution of Economic Thought*. London, UK: Routledge.
Montes, L. (2003) Smith and Newton: Some methodological issues concerning general economic equilibrium theory. *Cambridge Journal of Economics* 27(5): 723–747.
Montes, L. (2008) Newton's real influence on Adam Smith and its context. *Cambridge Journal of Economics* 32(4): 555–576.
Moscati, I. (2005) *History of Consumer Demand Theory 1871–1971: A Neo-Kantian Reconstruction*. Università Bocconi, Milan, Italy, mimeo. Available at: http://econpapers.repec.org/paper/wpawuwpmh/0506002.htm (accessed 2 June 2014).
Newton, I. (1979) *Opticks: Or, a Treatise of the Reflection, Refractions, Inflections and Colours of Light*. London, UK: William Innys.
Newton, I. (1995) *The Principia*. Amherst, NY: Prometheus Books.
O'Boyle, B. (2015) *From Newton to Hobbes: The Shifting Roots of Mainstream Economics*. National University of Ireland Working Paper.
O'Boyle, B. and McDonough, T. (2011) Critical realism, Marxism and the critique of neoclassical economics. *Capital and Class* 35(1): 3–22.
O'Boyle, B. and McDonough, T. (in press) Critical realism and the Althusserian legacy. *Journal for the Theory of Social Behaviour*.
Ricardo, D. (2004) *The Principles of Political Economy and Taxation*. Mineola, NY: Dover.
Rubin, I. I. (1979) *A History of Economic Thought*. London, UK: Ink Links Ltd.
Smith, A. (1982) The principles which lead and direct philosophical enquiry: Illustrated by the history of astronomy, in Wightman, W. P. D. and Bryce, J. C. (eds) *Essays on Philosophical Subjects*. Indianapolis, IN: Liberty Fund.
Smith, A. (1999 [1776]) *The Wealth of Nations* Books I–III. London, UK: Penguin Classics.
Stigler, G. (1973) The adoption of marginal utility theory, in Collison Black, R. D., Coats, A. W. and Goodwin, C. (eds) *The Marginal Revolution in Economics*. Durham, NC: Duke University Press.
Walras, L. (2003) *Elements of Pure Economics: Or the Theory of Social Wealth*. London, UK: Routledge.

10 Heterodox economics, social ontology and the use of mathematics

Mark Setterfield

Introduction

According to Lawson (Chapter 1), based on his reading and advocacy of Thorstein Veblen's original use of the term (Veblen, 1900), many heterodox economists (as much if not more so than most mainstream economists) are properly categorized as "neoclassical." This is obviously a provocative claim, not least because heterodox economists see themselves as being in opposition to neoclassical economics. It may even appear reckless, given that heterodoxy is sometimes characterized by its critics as amounting to little more than a general opposition to neoclassical economics.[1] But on closer inspection, Lawson's claim deserves more careful attention. An important part of its substance is that heterodox economists' widespread use of mathematics in economic theory is contradictory to their (implicit) open-systems ontology (Lawson, Chapter 1: 37–40).[2] The purpose of this chapter is to address this criticism directly and suggest that it need not be correct: there need be no contradiction between the use of mathematics and adherence to the ontological postulate that the economy is an open system.

The remainder of the chapter is organized as follows. The next section briefly reviews Lawson's recent assessment of neoclassical economics and criticisms of heterodox economics. Thereafter, we describe an open systems, *ceteris paribus* (OSCP) approach to mathematical modeling that addresses these criticisms. The final section concludes.

What is this "school" called neoclassical economics?

Lawson on neoclassical economics: are heterodox economists neoclassical?

According to Lawson (Chapter 1: 30–35), the term neoclassical has lost touch with its original meaning, does not reflect continuity with classical economics, and is used inconsistently even by those who seek to give it a coherent meaning. Ultimately, Lawson argues that it would be best to abandon use of the term altogether. As a second-best alternative to this strategy, he suggests that a better and more coherent account of the term be furnished—a task to which he subsequently applies himself.

The motivation for this project is the claim that the loose and contested use of the term neoclassical that is currently prevalent hinders critique and reform of orthodox or mainstream economics, a project that can be successfully characterized without recourse to the term neoclassical. This is because the dominant characteristic of mainstream economics is mathematical modeling. For Lawson (Chapter 1: 35–37), the identification of this dominant characteristic points immediately to what is wrong with the mainstream project that demands critique and reform: it is a project that is at odds with the intrinsic nature of its object of analysis. Hence mathematical modeling is "deductivist," postulating "event regularities" characteristic of closed systems, whereas social systems are (in general) open. It follows that:

> [t]he sorts of conditions under which the modelling methods economists have employed would be useful are found to be rather uncommon, and indeed unlikely, occurrences in the social realm. Alternatively put, the ontological presuppositions of the heavy emphasis on mathematical modelling do not match the nature of the "stuff" of the social realm.
>
> (Lawson, Chapter 1: 35)[3]

So what does any of this have to do with heterodox economics? In the first instance, Lawson (Chapter 1: 37–40) notes that while heterodox economists frequently criticize the mainstream's insistence on mathematical modeling, this criticism stems only from a desire for pluralism in the methods of economic inquiry. Heterodox economists seldom identify mathematical modeling as the quintessence of the mainstream project and seldom object outright to mathematical modeling per se. This, Lawson argues, creates something of a tension. On the one hand, heterodox economists do not unequivocally reject mathematical modeling as a tool for the development of social science. On the other, they frequently (if often only implicitly) identify with the open-systems ontology that is incompatible with the deductivism of mathematical modeling. For example, Post-Keynesian emphasis on fundamental uncertainty (implicitly) recognizes the openness of the social realm (Lawson, Chapter 1: 38).

In his subsequent ruminations on the meaning of the term neoclassical, Lawson (Chapter 1: 40–56) identifies this same tension, "a tension of ontological perspective and method (or the latter's ontological presuppositions)" (Lawson, Chapter 1: 40), with Veblen's original characterization of neoclassical economics. He goes on to identify Veblen's usage as: "the most appropriate and coherent use of the category." The result of all this is straightforward: for Lawson, many self-described heterodox economists are properly described as modern-day neoclassicists. As Lawson himself puts it:

> So is it really the case that I am suggesting that all mathematical modellers in modern economics, who at some level appear to subscribe to the causal-processual [open-systems ontology] worldview, including those who self-identify as heterodox, are appropriately characterised as (modern-day) neoclassical economists? . . . I certainly think this is the most coherent rendering of neoclassical economics.
> (Lawson, Chapter 1: 59)

An initial (heterodox) response

As should be clear from the above, Lawson's Veblenian interpretation of the term neoclassical provides a basis for both: (a) furnishing a coherent interpretation of the term that, by virtue of its coherence, makes the term useful once again in economic discourse; and (b) identifying a particular swathe of economists—a swathe that includes many who would self-identify as heterodox—as neoclassical economists.

An initial (heterodox) response to all this might be to respond dismissively. For several decades now, Lawson has attempted to draw the attention of heterodox economists to issues that link ontology and methodology and that in so doing, call into question the methodology of heterodox economics—at least as it is practiced in some quarters—given its (apparent) ontological presuppositions. What better way to call attention to this project than to label heterodox economists neoclassical, associating them at a stroke with the *bête noire* of their own project! But make no mistake: Lawson's is no idle rhetorical strategy in a meaningless war of words and should not be treated as such. He raises real issues of substance that demand to be engaged.

Looking beyond his preferred use of the term neoclassical, the key issue on which Lawson seeks to focus is mathematical modeling and its (in)appropriate use in the articulation of social theory. Rejections of mathematical modeling are not new, of course. At the same time, there exist many practical defenses of the use of mathematics that have been advanced in response to rejections of its use. In general, these express the view that while some economists have so elevated the importance of mathematical modeling that it has become an end in itself, once it is recognized that mathematics is merely a means to an end—a tool for expressing ideas about how the economy functions—appropriate use of mathematical modeling can be retained as part of the economic theorist's toolkit. In short, mathematics is a "good servant but a bad master." One need not look to the mainstream project for this sort of defense: such sentiments are alive and well among heterodox economists. Consider, for example, the following from Geoff Harcourt:

> First, the vexed question of mathematics. This is a red herring. My own stance was influenced by Keynes. He argued that in a subject like economics there is a spectrum of appropriate languages, running from intuition and poetry through lawyer-like arguments to formal logic and mathematics. All have a role, depending upon the issue (or the aspects of an issue) being discussed. Mathematics is a good servant but a bad master, that is to say, always pose the economics of an issue first, then see whether some form of mathematics may be of use in solving the problems thrown up. This approach also has the blessing of von Neumann, Michał Kalecki and Josef Steindl, a worthy Trinity if ever there was one.
>
> (Harcourt, 2003: 70)

Although her comments are ostensibly more critical of mathematical modeling (since her purpose is to critique the "hegemony of formalists" and to advocate for pluralism in economic methodology),[4] Victoria Chick expresses sentiments that are essentially similar to those of Harcourt when she writes:

> In my view, economics is a subject so complex and interwoven that the achievement of cogent knowledge by any single method is impossible; therefore there is scope and need for a variety of approaches. Formal methods cannot claim to be the only valid approach, at least in their present forms. Formal techniques are powerful tools, but they can also be dangerous; the problem is to identify applications where they can be used safely.
>
> (Chick, 1998: 1859)

In other words—and to quote the title of Chick's paper—the use of mathematical modeling in economics boils down to a question of "knowing one's place."[5]

Lawson's rejection of mathematical modeling is by no means absolute. Indeed, on the face of it, his concerns appear quite compatible with the sentiments of Harcourt and Chick outlined above. Hence he writes:

> I hope by now the highly conditional nature of my criticism is apparent. It is not, and never has been, my intention to oppose the use of formalistic methods in themselves. My primary opposition, rather, is to the manner in which they are everywhere imposed, to the insistence on their being almost universally wielded, irrespective of, and prior to, consideration of explanatory relevance, and in the face of repeated failures.
>
> (Lawson, 2003: xix)

Lawson's objections to mathematical modeling are, however, more pointed than mere concern with the possibility that it has become a "bad master."

The essence of his argument concerns ontology and the (in) consistency of mathematical modeling, with the (implicit) conception of the economy as an open system that many heterodox economists appear to entertain (Lawson, 2006). The premise in what follows is that any truly compelling defense of mathematical modeling must engage this alleged inconsistency and in so doing, show that mathematical modeling is not (or at least need not be) inconsistent with open-systems ontology.

An OSCP approach to mathematical modeling[6]

Methodology and ontology

The crux of Lawson's objection to mathematical modeling is that mathematical models are "deductivist," meaning that in such models, causality is understood in terms of constant conjunctions of events or "event regularities" of the form "wherever event x, then event y." Consider, for example, a simple aggregate consumption function of the form:

$$C = cY \qquad (10.1)$$

where C denotes aggregate consumption, Y is aggregate income, and c is the average (and marginal) propensity to spend. In equation (10.1) whenever there is an increase in aggregate income, then there is an increase in aggregate consumption. In other words, causality is precisely of the "whenever event x, then event y" or event regularity form. But systematic observation of constant event conjunctions is properly understood as a feature of systems characterized by both extrinsic closure (as a result of which effects always have the same causes) and intrinsic closure (as a result of which causes always have the same effects). The problem is that if social reality is structured but open, event regularities will be rare in social systems. This means that mathematical models, premised on closed systems in which event regularities are common, must be unsuitable vehicles for expressing economic theory.

Mathematical models need not fall prey to this problem, however. What Setterfield (2003, 2007) calls the open systems, *ceteris paribus* (OSCP) approach to mathematical modeling is designed to avoid it altogether by explicitly confronting ontological concerns with the openness of social systems.

As its name suggests, the OSCP approach is based on explicit recognition that one of the essential properties of social systems is that they are open. Mathematical models constructed in accordance with the OSCP approach should themselves, therefore, either be open, or else embody only conditional closures. Conditional closures are introduced into a model by describing as constant variables and/or structural relations that are understood to be transmutable and are therefore known to be capable of change over time. The artificial or temporary nature of the resulting closure is then explicitly acknowledged—a process akin to what Kregel (1976) describes as "locking up without ignoring" certain dynamic features of a system in the methodology of Keynes and Post-Keynesian economics.[7] Note that it is the use of conditional closures that introduces the ceteris paribus limiter into the OSCP approach. Hence in this context, the term ceteris paribus draws attention to the fact that a model is a partial representation of reality, not simply because it abstracts from some features of reality (all models do this by definition) but rather in a strictly dynamic sense. Specifically, within the temporal frame of reference of the model itself, some things that are transmutable and known to be capable of change over time (including things that are understood to be subject to novel change and for which there does not exist, in principle, any foreclosed rule (equation) of inter-temporal motion) are held constant.[8] As will become clear, there are two different types of conditional closure and it is as a result of this that such closures may be either artificial or temporary, as suggested above.

The type of functional relations used to articulate formal models of the OSCP genus specify transmutable, conditional relations of the form:

$$y = f_t(\mathbf{x}_t) \qquad (10.2)$$

where y is the dependent variable, $\mathbf{x}$ denotes a vector of independent variables, and the precise meaning of the t-subscripts will be discussed in due course. Detailed examination of equation (10.2) reveals why Lawson's claim that mathematical models are deductivist is true only some of the time, and problematic only some of the time that it is true. First, the time subscripts in equation (10.2) denote that the precise form of the function f together with the contents of the vector $\mathbf{x}$ (not just the magnitudes of the scalar quantities of which it is comprised) are time-dependent. Causes need not always have the same effects or effects the same causes, i.e., the system lacks both intrinsic and extrinsic closure. But this does not mean that there are simply "missing equations." Rather, f and $\mathbf{x}$ are understood to be transmutable in novel ways. Their change over time cannot be "endogenized" in the conventional manner (i.e., reduced to foreclosed explanation in terms of given and immutable data), thus re-imposing system closure as the result of a successful search for Lucasian "deep parameters" that are invariant with respect to changes introduced into the system from without (such as a new tax, or a new strategy to match competitors' prices) by parties public or private.[9] Instead, by virtue of the innate openness of social systems, deep parameters are hypothesized not to exist, and the functional relation in equation (10.2) remains open. Moreover, because equation (10.2) is open, it will not (in general) generate event regularities and therefore cannot be considered a form of deductivism. Any conjunction of events expressed by the model in one period will likely cease to obtain in the next and does not, therefore, constitute an enduring event regularity. In other words, the very purpose of an expression such as equation (10.2), based on the OSCP approach to mathematical modeling, is to explicitly capture and emphasize the fact that any particular conjunction of events today should not be expected to rematerialize in the future, because of the lack of intrinsic and/or extrinsic closure characteristic of the data generating process from which observed outcomes emanate.

As noted earlier, the OSCP approach does allow for the introduction of conditional closure into mathematical models, as a result of which certain dated variables that are known to be transmutable and capable of change over time (such as the precise form of f or the composition of x in equation (10.2)) are held constant. Conditional closures can be introduced in two ways, both of which entail a process of "locking up without ignoring" the openness that is believed to characterize social systems (Setterfield, 2003: 76–78). Hence, "pure" locking up without ignoring involves introducing closure as an analytical device, in order to illuminate more clearly some particular principle or feature of an economic system.[10] Although properly conceived as convenient fictions, the resulting closures can serve important pedagogic purposes—indeed, their introduction is conditional on the fact that they do—even when they involve locking up without ignoring an essential feature of a system's dynamics. This is exemplified by Keynes's assumption of a constant state of long-run expectations in order to demonstrate the principle of effective demand (Kregel, 1976). By making this assumption, Keynes ruled out any effect of disappointed short-term expectations on the state of long-run expectations—a potential source of indeterminacy in the principle of effective demand. The resulting system is conditionally closed by the assumption just noted, but nevertheless serves an important purpose: it suffices to demonstrate the relative autonomy of aggregate demand conditions in the determination of output and employment. It is interesting in the current context to note Kregel's conclusion that:

> [i]t would appear to be a disservice to both Keynes's methodology and that of the Post-Keynesian writers to accuse them of some other parentage or . . . to bracket their writings with orthodox approaches . . . Their basic methodology is distinctly different.
> (Kregel, 1976: 222–223)

Apparently, not all closed systems are created equal.[11]

Conditional closure can also be introduced by means of "empirically grounded" locking up without ignoring. This is based on the observation of actually existing, relatively enduring institutions (norms, conventions, rules, etc.) within the system that is being modeled. These institutions can be expected to arise in response to the very openness of social systems which, by rendering the future fundamentally uncertain, and hence future-oriented (consequentialist) decision making difficult to practice, can have a debilitating effect on ends-oriented behavior.[12] Institutionalized behavior, which involves a deliberate and reasoned abandonment of consequentialism in favor of proceduralism, provides a practical escape from this dilemma.

Furthermore, by routinizing behavior, institutions lend greater regularity to the flux of events than would otherwise be observed in the potentially kaleidic environment of an open system—at least, as long as they endure.[13] In this case, then, the validity of the closure introduced into a model is conditional on the purposive reproduction over time by human agents of an actually existing institution within the system that is being modeled, it being understood that one of the properties of institutions is to create greater regularity in actions and events than would otherwise be observed in their absence.[14] To summarize, the argument is essentially that: (a) the logic of social theory consistent with an open-systems ontology suggests the capacity for episodes of conditional closure over restricted spatio-temporal regions, as individuals create and maintain institutions in response to fundamental uncertainty; and (b) these restricted spatio-temporal regions are non-trivial—on the contrary, their identification and study is an important and useful part of social science and can inform the construction of ontologically sensitive mathematical models consistent with the OSCP approach.

Two final points remain to be made about empirically grounded conditional closures. First, just as such closures will apply only to restricted spatio-temporal regions, so, too, will any event conjunctions to which they give rise. Because the underlying system is open and its very structure is ultimately transmutable in novel ways, it will display no propensity to generate constant conjunctions of events. These observations draw attention to the fact that a conditionally closed system is fundamentally non-atomistic, even as it may temporarily appear to display the properties of an atomistic system.

Second, when they are empirically grounded, conditional closures are not just a pragmatic modeling strategy. Instead, a mathematical model based on empirically grounded conditional closures can claim fidelity to the social material it purports to represent. Indeed, the nested or hierarchical "closure within an open system" characteristic of such a model seems perfectly congruent with Lawson's own preferred "agency/structure interaction" view of society. Hence as Davis (2016) argues:

> [w]hile indeed it is a property of social reality that it is processual and highly transient, since this is what seeing the agency/structure pair as interaction requires, it is also . . . a property of social reality that it is recurringly stable and temporarily unchanging. That is, when we adopt an agency/structure interaction view, social reality has both the property of change and the property of stability . . . Put in terms of

Lawson's agency/structure interaction view, human action presupposes social structures, so social structures must be stable enough to provide a basis for human action. Yet human action also transforms social structures, demonstrating their changing character. That is . . . there is not only change *but importantly also stability within a process of change.*

(Davis, 2016; emphasis added)

As Davis goes on to note:

Thus it is not accurate to simply say that social reality is processual and highly transient, as this is an incomplete characterization of the properties of social reality . . . the emphasis in "What is this 'school' called neoclassical economics?" is too strong on the side of social reality seen as changing, and too weak on the side of social reality seen as in some manner unchanging.

(Davis, 2016)

On this view, from both the OSCP perspective advanced in this chapter and on the basis of Lawson's own agency/structure interaction view of social reality, the fault that Lawson (Chapter 1) finds with heterodox mathematical modeling is, in general, incorrect, by virtue of its getting the ontology wrong: it puts too much emphasis on openness and change in social systems, and not enough on stability and inertia rooted in actually existing conditional closures.[15]

Whether pure or empirically grounded, the process of locking up without ignoring is ontologically sensitive to the innate openness of social systems and can result in conditional closures that have some validity—albeit of a spatio-temporally or analytically limited nature—in the analysis of what are ultimately understood to be open systems. Hence mathematical models generated by the OSCP approach to formalism, that display conditional closures by virtue of proper application of the process of locking up without ignoring, must also share the same validity in the analysis of social systems. It follows that even when mathematical models do generate event regularities and thus seemingly resemble deductivist laws, this is not always a problem. To be more specific, mathematical models that describe universal, immutable event regularities are problematic, but those that appear deductivist only by virtue of the proper introduction of conditional closures into expressions, such as equation (10.2), are not.[16]

An example

Examples of (implicit) appeal to OSCP methodology in economic theory can already be found in existing literature. Hence, elements of the OSCP approach are implicit in the mathematical characterizations of hysteresis due to Katzner (1998) and Setterfield (1998), the contrast between models of economic dynamics consistent with either logical or historical time in Harris (2005), and in the model of cycles due to Setterfield (2000). But the OSCP methodology outlined in the previous subsection can be made more concrete by detailed discussion of an example of its explicit application. The example developed below is that of the dynamic credit supply curve developed by Setterfield (2014), designed to reconcile the horizontalist and structuralist positions regarding the shape of the credit supply curve in endogenous money theory (on which see Lavoie (2007) and Dow (2007), respectively). We begin by writing:

$$r_t = (1 + \theta_t)\delta_t \tag{10.3}$$

Equation (10.3) relates the value of the commercial interest rate (r) to the value of the discount rate (δ) and commercial banks' mark up (θ). The equation explicitly purports to describe the behavior of the commercial rate over time, as a result of inter-temporal variations in the discount rate and/or the mark up and has a basic structure that is immediately recognizable as being akin to that of equation (10.2). Now let θ_0 and δ_0 denote the values of θ and δ, respectively, in some initial instant, and write:

$$\theta_t = f_t(Y_t) \tag{10.4}$$

$$\delta_t = g_t(Y_t) \tag{10.5}$$

where $f'_t, g'_t \geq 0$. These expressions are once again compatible with the structure of equation (10.2). Equations (10.4) and (10.5) express the possibility that θ and/or δ will vary over time with nominal income (Y), the assumption being that increases/decreases in Y are accompanied by increases/decreases in the demand for credit arising from the finance motive.[17] Note that equations (10.4) and (10.5) express only the possibility that θ and/or δ will vary with Y, because the first derivatives of these equations may be either greater than or equal to zero. More importantly, f_t and g_t (and hence their derivatives) are time varying, so that we can have $f'_t, g'_t \neq 0$ even if $f'_{t-1}, g'_{t-1} = 0$ (or vice versa). Moreover, note that the precise evolution of f_t and g_t (and hence their derivatives) remains deliberately unspecified. This is because f_t and g_t are understood to be transmutable in novel ways—there are no "missing equations" that can be introduced to close the system in equations (10.4) and (10.5) so as to give rise to a determinate relationship between r_t and Y_t expressed in terms of Lucasian deep parameters. Instead, the system remains intrinsically open, and the relationship between r_t and Y_t will not be characterized by event regularities since the causal event $\dot{Y}_t$ will not always have the same effect (as measured by $\dot{r}_t$). In other words, it is impossible to make "whenever x then y" statements of the form "whenever nominal income expands, commercial interest rates rise" (structuralism) or "whenever nominal income expands, commercial interest rates remain the same" (horizontalism).

The point established by this analysis is that Post-Keynesians should not attempt to substantiate either horizontalist or structuralist arguments as a matter of a priori logic and thus seek to establish that the dynamic credit supply schedule in equation (10.3) is either horizontal or upward sloping in principle. To do so would involve insisting that "missing equations" can be introduced into the analysis that render the resulting relationship between the commercial interest rate and nominal income closed, i.e., equations (10.3) to (10.5) would express an event regularity of the form "whenever nominal income increases, the commercial interest rate rises" or, alternatively, "whenever nominal income increases, the commercial interest rate stays the same." This would permit the drawing of a dynamic credit supply schedule that is either upward sloping or horizontal. But in the process, it would rule out the possibility that there is, in fact, no foreclosed relationship between nominal income and the commercial interest rate, and that this relationship is, instead, open. Furthermore, since it is open systems that are congruent with the Post-Keynesian conception of historical time while closed systems belong in the domain of logical time (see, for example, Lang and Setterfield (2007)), this would be tantamount to providing a logical time account of an economic process unfolding in historical time. As such—and per Lawson—it would violate one of the first principles of Post-Keynesian economics: that economic processes unfold in historical time and that economic analysis must be congruent with this fact.

Consider now how the dynamic credit supply curve does, in fact, work. On the basis of equations (10.4) and (10.5), we can write:

$$\dot{\theta}_t = f'_t \dot{Y}_t \tag{10.6}$$

$$\dot{\delta}_t = g'_t \dot{Y}_t \tag{10.7}$$

Combining this information with the initial conditions θ_0 and δ_0 and equation (10.3), it follows that over any time horizon $t = 0, \ldots, n$ that is longer than an "instant,"[18] the dynamic credit supply schedule is given by:

$$r_t = (1 + \theta_0 + \int_{t=0}^{n} f'_t \dot{Y}_t \, dt)(\delta_0 + \int_{t=0}^{n} g'_t \dot{Y}_t \, dt) \tag{10.8}$$

Note that if $f'_t = g'_t = 0$ for all t, then we will observe $r_t = r_{t-1}$ for all t and the dynamic credit supply schedule will be horizontal. But if $f'_t \neq 0$ or $g'_t \neq 0$ for some t, then we will observe $r_t > r_{t-1}$ for some t and the dynamic credit supply schedule will be an upward-sloping step function. In short, the dynamic credit supply schedule in equation (10.8) encompasses both horizontalist and structuralist positions regarding the shape of the credit supply schedule, and does so by embracing what is understood to be the intrinsic openness of the monetary relations from which observed behavior of the nominal interest rate is derived.

Conclusions

According to Lawson (Chapter 1), the best available definition of a neoclassical economist is one who fails to recognize an unresolved tension between their methodology and their ontological presuppositions. This means that many economists who self-identify as heterodox are, in fact, modern-day neoclassicists, because they employ mathematical modeling techniques while (implicitly) entertaining an open-systems ontology. The unresolved tension to which this combination gives rise emanates from the fact that mathematical modeling is deductivist: it presupposes system closure and is therefore incompatible with an open-systems ontology.

The arguments advanced in this chapter involve several key points of departure from Lawson's position. Each of these emanates from an OSCP approach to mathematical modeling, which promises to contribute to the Lawsonian goals of better economic theory and explanatory success by embracing the Lawsonian notion that proper economic method and theory must be derived from (and consistent with) an explicit social ontology. The first point of departure concerns Lawson's identification of mathematical modeling with deductivism (Lawson, Chapter 1: 32, 35). For Lawson: "mathematical methods and techniques of the sort employed by economists (functions, calculus and so forth) presuppose regularities at the level of events" (Lawson, Chapter 1: 35). The OSCP approach to mathematical modeling denies this, claiming instead that mathematical expressions of causal relations need not involve closure and event regularities.

The second point of departure is Lawson's (implicit) notion that closure, because it represents an unrealistic portrayal of the intrinsic nature of social material, is always and everywhere undesirable in the formulation of economic theory. The position taken in this chapter is that some invocation of closure may serve a limited, but useful, pedagogical function—akin to the method adopted by Keynes in *The General Theory* for outlining the principle of effective demand (Kregel, 1976), and the use of provisional or conditional equilibrium as organizing constructs for theory development advocated by Chick and Caserta (1997) and Setterfield (1997).

The final point of departure is Lawson's conception of closure in social systems as being uncommon to the point of being negligible. The OSCP approach to mathematical modeling posits, instead, that closures are socially constructed (through institutions created in response to the anxiety/anomie that the indeterminacy of an open social reality creates) and that although transient, may be sufficiently durable to be worth taking into account in social theory. Lawson acknowledges this approach when writing:

> [w]here within heterodoxy, a continuing faith in, and/or resources allocated to, exercises in mathematical modelling are not accounted for by an inattention to ontological preconceptions of methods, the explanation is seemingly that the individuals in question entertain hopes of identifying certain contexts in which local closures (facilitating the appropriate use of mathematical methods) do, temporarily, obtain.
> (Lawson, Chapter 1: 39)

But as the general tenor of this quotation suggests, he does not set much store in the approach. The commonality and durability of local closures is not something that can be resolved as a matter of logic and is worthy of empirical investigation as an outgrowth of the methodological debate over the use of mathematical modeling in economics.

To summarize, for Lawson:

> [a] good deal of sustained heterodox research is couched in conceptual frameworks consistent with ... [a] causal-processual ontological conception ... All too often, however, this goes hand in hand with a lack of realisation that methods of mathematical modelling require formulations that are in severe tension with this ontology.
> (Lawson, Chapter 1: 39)

The position advanced in this chapter, meanwhile, is that mathematical modeling does not require such formulations and, where the noted tension does arise, explicit acknowledgment of the tension is as if not more important than the tension itself. In other words, the argument that mathematical modeling must always describe closed systems that generate event regularities is:

a   true only some of the time, depending on the approach to [mathematical modeling] that advises the author; and
b   problematic only some of the time that it is true, again depending on the approach to [mathematical modeling] that advises the author.
(Setterfield, 2007: 204)

It follows that as long as heterodox economists are explicitly mindful of ontological concerns when constructing mathematical models and engage in mathematical modeling accordingly (under the auspices of the OSCP approach), their use of mathematics in the development of economic theory does not mean that they necessarily fall victim to a mismatch between ontology and methodology. The Veblenesque charge of "neoclassicism" is thereby avoided, revealing that Lawson's critique of heterodox practice, while true in some cases, need not be in all.

Notes

1 Even proponents of heterodox economics are wont to identify opposition to neoclassical economics as one of heterodoxy's key unifying themes. To take the example of Post-Keynesian economics, see the various references cited by Lawson (1994: 503).
2 On the implicit acceptance of openness in heterodox economics, see Lawson (2006).
3 For extensive elaboration on this theme, see Lawson (1997, 2003).
4 When referring to the hegemony of formalists, Chick treats "formalism" or "formal modeling" as synonymous with mathematical modeling. In general, however, she argues that mathematics is only one way of expressing arguments "formally."
5 It should be noted that according to Chick's analysis there are limitations to the use of mathematical modeling, because of the open and organic nature of economic reality. Unlike many contributions to the "good servant, bad master" doctrine, Chick is therefore sensitive to the ontological issues identified below with Lawson's critique of mathematical modeling. Ultimately, her analysis implies that mathematics can only usefully be used to illuminate some parts of the economy and is never a sufficient tool for economic analysis. Although it is not the purpose of this chapter to argue that mathematical modeling is a sufficient tool for economic analysis, it can nevertheless be thought of as extending Chick's argument by suggesting that even open systems can (although need not be) represented by mathematical models, if the latter conform to the OSCP methodology described below.
6 The analysis in this and the following section borrows extensively from Setterfield (2007) and Setterfield (2014).
7 Conditional closures might also be referred to as provisional closures in the nomenclature of Chick and Caserta (1997).
8 The astute reader will note the generalization of the Lucas critique (Lucas, 1976), resulting from the hypothesized absence of "deep parameters." that is implicit in this last statement (see also Lawson, 1995). We will return to this theme immediately below.
9 See Lawson (1995) on the generalization of the Lucas critique implicit in this interpretation of equation (10.2), and in particular Lawson (1995: 266–271) for detailed criticisms of the mainstream project of "solving" the problems raised by the Lucas critique by means of extending and re-fashioning models in the search for eventual system closure. Note that, for Lucas (1976), the problems posed by the Lucas critique are specific to public policy interventions. As the above characterization of deep parameters suggests, however, once social systems are conceived as open and the substance of the Lucas critique is thereby generalized, the problems that the critique poses are found to confront all decision makers whose behavior is conditioned upon a characterization or "model" of the social system in which they wish to intervene. See also Lawson (1995: 271).
10 A mathematical model involving "pure" locking up without ignoring may be likened to what Hodgson (2004) identifies as a "formal heuristic," the purposes of which are to "identify possible causal mechanisms that form part of a more complex and inevitably open system" and thus "to establish a plausible

segment of a causal story, without necessarily giving an adequate or complete explanation of the phenomena to which they relate" (Hodgson, 2004: 7).

11 Of course, this example also illustrates a potential pitfall of models based on OSCP methodology: they can all too easily be misinterpreted. Hence, witness the countless examples of "hydraulic" Keynesianism that lack fidelity to Keynes's methodology (at least as it is identified by Kregel (1976)). See also Louçá (2001) on the correspondence between Frisch and Schumpeter regarding Frisch's model of the cycle for a telling account of how deductivism can both colonize and misrepresent the economic theories it claims to be articulating.

12 The frustration of consequentialist decision rules (such as the comparison of marginal cost and expected marginal benefit) by fundamental uncertainty might give rise to anxiety. Alternatively, the seemingly limitless possibilities of an uncertain future might give rise to anomie. Either of these conditions can be thought of as debilitating in the sense that they thwart action.

13 Institutions are transmutable in novel ways and the expectation must be that this transmutability will eventually assert itself.

14 See also Crotty's discussion of "conditional stability" in macroeconomic systems for a similar account of the role of institutions in both actual economic systems and in macroeconomic models (Crotty, 1994).

15 I am grateful to John Davis for drawing this last point to my attention.

16 See also Chick and Dow (2001: 711–714) for a similar conclusion.

17 As will become clear below, $f'_t \geq 0$ expresses the possibility that (for example) variations in loan demand are accompanied by changes in lenders' risk; $g'_t \geq 0$ expresses the possibility that the central bank will react (by changing the discount rate) to nominal expansion/contraction of the economy. In other words, there are well-specified behavioral foundations in monetary macroeconomics for both $f'_t, g'_t > 0$ and $f'_t, g'_t = 0$: the mathematical structure of equations (10.4) and (10.5) is representative of plausible monetary behavior that can be extracted from the structuralism versus horizontalism debate in endogenous money theory (see Setterfield, 2014).

18 During an "instant" institutional features of the banking system make equations (10.4) and (10.5) conditionally closed. Specifically, we observe $f'_t = g'_t = 0$, for $t = 0, \ldots, k$ (this last expression defining the interval of the instant, during which both the mark-up and the discount rate are always constant). We therefore have $r_t = (1 + \theta_0)\delta_0$ from equation (10.3), where θ_0 and δ_0 are historically given data.

References

Chick, V. (1998) On knowing one's place: The role of formalism in economics. *Economic Journal* 108(451): 1859–1869.

Chick, V. and Caserta, M. (1997) Provisional equilibrium and macroeconomic theory. In Arestis, P., Palma, G. and Sawyer, M. (eds) *Markets, Employment and Economic Policy: Essays in Honour of G. C. Harcourt*. London, UK: Routledge, pp. 223–237.

Chick, V. and Dow, S. (2001) Formalism, logic and reality: A Keynesian analysis. *Cambridge Journal of Economics* 25(6): 705–721.

Crotty, J. (1994) Are Keynesian uncertainty and macrotheory compatible? Conventional decision making, institutional structures and conditional stability in Keynesian macromodels. In Dymski, G. and Pollin, R. (eds) *New Perspectives in Monetary Macroeconomics*. Ann Arbor, MI: University of Michigan Press, pp. 105–139.

Davis, J. (2016) Lawson on Veblen on social ontology. In this volume.

Dow, S. (2007) Endogenous money: Structuralist. In Arestis, P. and Sawyer, M. (eds) *A Handbook of Alternative Monetary Economics*. Cheltenham, UK: Edward Elgar.

Harcourt, G. C. (2003) A good servant but a bad master. In Fullbrook, E. (ed.) *The Crisis in Economics*. London, UK: Routledge, pp. 70–71.

Harris, D. (2005) Robinson on 'history versus equilibrium'. In Gibson, B. (ed.) *Joan Robinson's Economics: A Centennial Celebration*. Cheltenham, UK: Edward Elgar, pp. 81–108.

Hodgson, G. (2004) On the problem of formalism in economics. *Post-Autistic Economics Review* 28, Article 1.

Katzner, D. (1998) *Time, Ignorance and Uncertainty in Economic Models*. Ann Arbor, MI: University of Michigan Press.

Keynes, J. M. (1936) *The General Theory of Employment, Interest and Money*. London, UK: Macmillan.

Kregel, J. A. (1976) Economic Methodology in the Face of Uncertainty: The Modelling Methods of Keynes and the Post-Keynesians. *Economic Journal* 86(342): 209–225.

Lang, D. and Setterfield, M. (2007) History versus equilibrium? On the possibility and realist basis of a general critique of traditional equilibrium analysis. *Journal of Post Keynesian Economics* 29(2): 191–209.

Lavoie, M. (2007) Endogenous money: Accommodationist. In Arestis, P. and Sawyer, M. (eds) *A Handbook of Alternative Monetary Economics*. Cheltenham, UK: Edward Elgar.

Lawson, T. (1994) The nature of Post Keynesianism and its links to other traditions: A realist perspective. *Journal of Post Keynesian Economics* 16(4): 503–538.

Lawson, T. (1995) The 'Lucas critique': A generalisation. *Cambridge Journal of Economics* 19(2): 257–276.

Lawson, T. (1997) *Economics and Reality*. London, UK: Routledge.

Lawson, T. (2003) *Reorienting Economics*. London, UK: Routledge.

Lawson, T. (2006) The nature of heterodox economics. *Cambridge Journal of Economics* 30(4): 483–505.

Lawson, T. (2013) What is this 'school' called neoclassical economics? *Cambridge Journal of Economics* 37(5): 947–983. Also published in this book as Chapter 1, and page numbers cited refer to those in this book.

Louçá, F. (2001) Schumpeter and the pendulum: how evolution was whipped out in the construction of canonical economics. In Garrouste, P. and Ioannides, S. (eds) *Evolution and Path Dependence in Economic Ideas: Past and Present*. Cheltenham, UK: Edward Elgar, pp. 71–90.

Lucas, R. E. (1976) Econometric policy evaluation: A critique. *Carnegie-Rochester Conference Series on Public Policy* 1(1): 19–46.

Setterfield, M. (1997) Should economists dispense with the notion of equilibrium? *Journal of Post Keynesian Economics* 20(1): 47–76.

Setterfield, M. (1998) Adjustment asymmetries and hysteresis in simple dynamic models. *The Manchester School of Economic & Social Studies* 66(3): 283–301.

Setterfield, M. (2000) Expectations, endogenous money, and the business cycle: An exercise in open systems modeling. *Journal of Post Keynesian Economics* 23(1): 77–105.

Setterfield, M. (2003) Critical realism and formal modelling: Incompatible bedfellows? In Downward, P. (ed.) *Applied Economics and the Critical Realist Critique*. London, UK: Routledge, pp. 71–88.

Setterfield, M. (2007) Are functional relations always the alter ego of Humean laws? *Review of Political Economy* 19(2): 203–217.

Setterfield, M. (2014) An essay on horizontalism, structuralism and historical time. Working Paper 14-02, Trinity College. Available at: http://internet2.trincoll.edu/repec/WorkingPapers2014/WP14-02.pdf (accessed 20 August 2015).

Veblen, T. (1900) The preconceptions of economic science III. *Quarterly Journal of Economics* 14(2): 240–269.

11 Is neoclassical economics mathematical?
Is there a non-neoclassical mathematical economics?

Steve Keen

Introduction

A critical and realistic response to Lawson's "What is this 'school' called neoclassical economics?" boils down to answering two related questions: Is neoclassical economics truly "mathematical" in the genuine sense of that word?; and can there be a mathematical economics which is not neoclassical, using an augmented form of Arnsperger and Varoufakis' definition of neoclassical? I argue that the answers to these questions are respectively a resounding "No" and a qualified "Yes."

Lawson's position

Lawson disputes that the term neoclassical has any meaning apart from the use of mathematics by economists, where that use presupposes the existence of a closed social reality, which in turn is defined as "a world of isolated atoms," where "the term 'atom'":

> [r]efers to anything that (if triggered) has the same independent effect whatever the context. Formulations couched in terms of atomistic factors allow the deduction and/or prediction of events. Or rather, they do so if nothing is allowed to interfere with the actions of the atoms. So to guarantee that at the theory level outcomes are truly predictable and/or deducible, the atoms must be assumed to act in isolation from any countervailing factors that could interfere with the outcomes.
> (Lawson, Chapter 1: 35)

Lawson contrasts this to the methodology that he believes economics must adopt to understand social reality. Here, causal relations dominate over correlations, and social reality is an emergent phenomenon of non-atomistic human interaction. He describes this as a "causal-processual or causal-historical ontology":

> Once, however, we change tack and give primary attention not to mathematical modelling but to studying more directly the actual nature of

Is neoclassical economics mathematical? 239

> social reality, a quite different and clearly more explanatorily powerful or superior conception emerges. According to this alternative social ontology, causality always matters, and a more complex, processual account tends to dominate. The conception of social ontology I have in mind is processual in that social reality, which itself is an emergent phenomenon of human interaction, is recognised as being (not at all atomistic in the sense just noted but rather) highly transient, being reproduced and/or transformed through practice; social reality is in process, essentially a process of cumulative causation. Furthermore, social reality is found to be composed of emergent phenomena that (far from being isolatable) are actually constituted in relation (that is, are internally related) to other things, and ultimately to everything else (for example, students and teachers, qua students and teachers, are constituted in relation to each other; so are employers and employees, landlords/ladies and tenants, creditors and debtors and so forth.
> (Lawson, Chapter 1: 36)

Lawson's position—that mathematical formalism alone is the problem, rather than a particular usage (or abusage) of it that can be characterized as neoclassical—also necessarily criticizes economists who agree with Lawson on ontology, but who believe there is a distinctive neoclassical methodology, which they themselves reject, and yet who also employ a mathematical methodology. Lawson therefore sees a paralyzing tension between their (valid) ontology and their (allegedly invalid) methodology:

> In fact, a good deal of sustained heterodox research is couched in conceptual frameworks consistent with the sort of causal-processual ontological conception just described. All too often, however, this goes hand in hand with a lack of realisation that methods of mathematical modelling require formulations that are in severe tension with this ontology. This lack of realisation both underpins a misapprehension of the source of the unrealistic nature of many competing claims, as well as the recourse of many heterodox economists to using mathematical modelling methods in seeking to advance insights obtained by other means.
> (Lawson, Chapter 1: 39)

Lawson finally divides economists into three categories, which can be parodied as "The Bad, The Good, and the Ugly": those who are strictly mathematical in their approach and do not take ontology seriously; those who do take ontology seriously and do not do mathematics; and those who take ontology seriously but still do mathematics:

> In short, I am suggesting that there are three basic divisions of modern economics that can be discerned in the actual practices of modern economists. These are:

1) those who both (i) adopt an overly taxonomic approach to science, a group dominated in modern times by those that accept mathematical deductivism as an orientation to science for us all, and (ii) effectively regard any stance that questions this approach, whatever the basis, as inevitably misguided;

2) those who are aware that social reality is of a causal-processual nature as elaborated above, who prioritise the goal of being realistic, and who fashion methods in the light of this ontological understanding and thereby recognise the limited scope for any taxonomic science, not least any that relies on methods of mathematical deductive modelling; and

3) those who are aware (at some level) that social reality is of a causal-processual nature as elaborated above, who prioritise the goal of being realistic, and yet who fail themselves fully to recognise or to accept the limited scope for any overly taxonomic approach including, in particular, one that makes significant use of methods of mathematical deductive modelling ...

members of group 1 ... more or less reduce to the contemporary mainstream; and those in group 2 constitute the coherent core of modern heterodoxy; it is members of group 3, again mostly made up by those that utilise mathematical methods, that most qualify as modern neoclassical economists.

(Lawson, Chapter 1: 63–64)

Whereas most critics of neoclassical economics would regard the mainstream (Lawson's first group) as coextensive with neoclassical economics, Lawson thus argues that his last "ugly" (my word, not his) group epitomises neoclassical economics—and this necessarily consists primarily of self-described heterodox economists who employ mathematical methods.

[t]he defining feature of all neoclassical economics is basically an inconsistent blend of the old and the new; it is in effect an awareness of the newer metaphysics of processual cumulative or unfolding causation, combined with a failure to break away from methods of the older taxonomic view of science that are in tension with this modern ontology.

(Lawson, Chapter 1: 53)

There are aspects of Lawson's position for which I have great sympathy. However, overall I find his thesis dramatically overstated at best, and false at worst, for two reasons. First, I reject his characterization of what I define as neoclassical economics as truly "mathematical," in the genuine sense of that word. Second, I reject his implicit assertion that there are no mathematical methods that can model the causal-processual or causal-historical ontology we actually inhabit. This second issue is more easily tackled than the first, since it is simply a matter of fact that mathematical methods exist that are not atomistic, as Lawson defines the term.

Mathematics, atomism, and nonlinearity

Lawson's characterization of mathematical methods as presupposing the existence of discrete atoms, which: "must be assumed to act in isolation from any countervailing factors" is true of linear systems only. A linear system is one in which the interactions between its variables are additive (even if the variables themselves are transformed in some nonlinear fashion), so that the contribution of one variable to a systemic outcome is not influenced by the value of any other variable. The technical term for this property is "superposition," the colloquial is that "the whole is precisely the sum of its parts."

A nonlinear system is one in which the entities in a system interact in ways that breach superposition, so that: "the whole is not the sum of its parts," but rather is dependent upon the interactions between its components. In particular, given Lawson's definition of "atom" as: "anything that (if triggered) has the same independent effect," in a nonlinear system the impact of a system variable can be dramatically altered by the values of other system variables.

Any nonlinear dynamic system can therefore be characterized as non-atomistic, in Lawson's sense of the word, and mathematical models of such systems abound. A simple instance of this is the classic Lotka-Volterra predator-prey model, in which the growth rates of the prey and predator depend on the current values of both populations and not just on each other's level. This violates Lawson's definition of an atomistic system, and yet is a perfectly valid mathematical model—see Equation (11.1) and Figure 11.1:

$$\frac{1}{\text{Prey}}\frac{d}{dt}\text{Prey} = a - b \times \text{Predator}$$
$$\frac{1}{\text{Predator}}\frac{d}{dt}\text{Predator} = -c + d \times \text{Prey} \tag{11.1}$$

The same value for the prey population can make a negative or a positive contribution to its own rate of growth (and that of the predator), because its effect is not independent of the value of the predator population. Thus, as Figure 11.1 illustrates, the same value for the prey population (say 200) is associated with either a rising or a falling prey population, depending upon the value of the predator population at the same time (roughly 7,

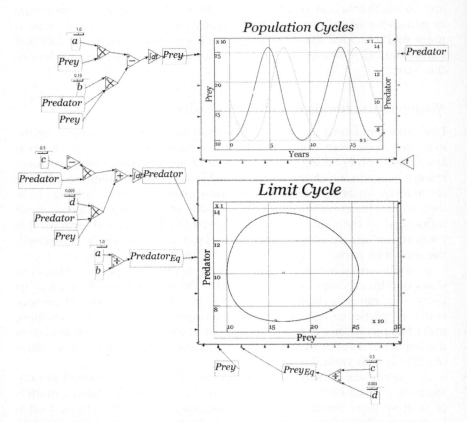

Figure 11.1 A predator–prey model in the system dynamics program Minsky.

which is consistent with a rising number of prey, and roughly 13, which is consistent with a falling number of prey).

Within nonlinear systems there are further subsets which are even more emphatically non-atomistic: *complex systems* and (within these) chaotic systems, and complex *adaptive* systems. All of these systems manifest emergent properties—behaviors which cannot be reduced to that of an isolated atom (or system state) within the system, but originate in the interactions between entities. Only the last-mentioned is not susceptible to mathematical treatment—but it is an active area of research in computer simulation modelling (see, for example, Barr *et al.*, 2008; Dosi *et al.*, 2008; Ussher, 2008).

Such systems are also normally (though not necessarily) open systems, both in the technical meaning of the word and in Lawson's usage of it (p. 35), and non-ergodic. The first highly influential such model was Lorenz's chaotic model of turbulent flow in a heated fluid (Lorenz, 1963). Figure 11.2 illustrates one aspect of this mathematical model that contradicts Lawson's definition of an atomistic system: a tiny difference

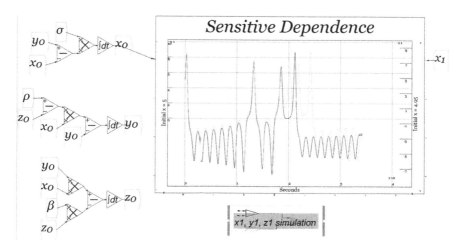

Figure 11.2 Lorenz's model illustrating sensitive dependence on initial conditions.

between initial states results very rapidly in an inability to predict its future course, so that: "deduction and/or prediction of events" becomes impossible past a very limited time window.

Since then, many complex system economic models have been produced by an active but largely neglected subset of economists (see, for example, Lorenz, 1987; Goodwin, 1990; Keen, 1995; Lux, 1995; Chiarella and Flaschel, 2000; Asada et al., 2010; Grasselli and Costa Lima, 2012; Costa Lima et al., 2014). Almost all these mathematical systems have unstable equilibria as well, so that rather than equilibrium defining the end states of such systems, they instead define where the system will never be. Figure 11.3 demonstrates one such example.

There is, therefore, a mathematics which is non-atomistic, capable of modelling emergent properties, and suitable for open systems. Economists who work in this area are in fact keenly aware of the methodological issues that Lawson raises. They are aware: "of the newer metaphysics of processual cumulative or unfolding causation," and therefore reject: "the methods of the older taxonomic view of science that are in tension with this modern ontology" (Lawson, Chapter 1: 53). They use instead mathematical methods that are consistent with this modern ontology, and are also normally conscious of the limits of these methods.

So the use of mathematics per se does not define an economist as neoclassical as Lawson uses the term. Instead, I concur with (and slightly extend) Arnsperger and Varoufakis to argue that the neoclassical school is characterized by a set of meta-axioms that are based upon a teleological rather than scientific vision of capitalism (Arnsperger and Varoufakis, 2006).

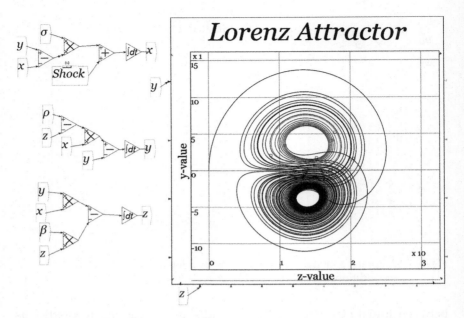

Figure 11.3 The dynamic path of the Lorenz model around its three unstable equilibria.

What is this "school" called neoclassical economics?

Arnsperger and Varoufakis (2006) note three "meta-axioms" which they see as defining the neoclassical approach: (1) methodological individualism ("the idea that socio-economic explanation must be sought at the level of the individual agent"); (2) methodological instrumentalism ("all behaviour is preference-driven or, more precisely, it is to be understood as a means for maximising preference-satisfaction"); and (3) methodological equilibration ("they pose the standard question: What behaviour should we expect in equilibrium? The question of whether an equilibrium is likely, let alone probable, or how it might materialise, is treated as an optional extra; one that is never central to the neoclassical project").

I would add a fourth meta-axiom: methodological barter. In neoclassical theory, economic interaction is treated as primarily involving the exchange of two commodities by two agents, in which the determination of relative prices plays the central role, and where the role of money is assistive of barter rather than crucial to commerce.

While I regard these four meta-axioms as the defining features of neoclassical economics, it is still possible for one or more of these axioms—but not all at once—to be tested by individual authors or papers without taking them outside the confines of that school. Thus, there have been papers by neoclassical authors considering chaos theory—see Rosser (2013) for example. This provides neoclassical stalwarts with a handy defence of the neoclassical core: though the vast majority of neoclassical papers will not consider chaos, the existence of a handful that do provides a riposte to criticisms that chaos is not considered. However, such papers never lead to the phenomenon being integrated into the neoclassical core, and they cannot because they would require the rejection of all three meta-axioms as defined by Arnsperger and Varoufakis (2006).[1]

Thus though mathematical modelling is a hallmark of the neoclassical approach, the mathematics that is employed is largely consistent with these meta-axioms. This, in turn, rules out a genuine engagement with complex systems within the neoclassical school, since complex systems undermine these meta-axioms. Firstly, as Anderson put it so well in "More is different" (Anderson. 1972), the behavior of complex systems cannot be extrapolated from the characteristics of its constituent parts alone:

> The behavior of large and complex aggregates of elementary particles, it turns out, is not to be understood in terms of a simple extrapolation of the properties of a few particles. Instead, at each level of complexity entirely new properties appear, and the understanding of the new behaviors requires research which I think is as fundamental in its nature as any other.
>
> (Anderson, 1972: 393)

Consequently, the properties of a complex system cannot be derived by extrapolating from the properties of an isolated entity—which is the essence of methodological individualism. The theory of demand, for example, attempts (and fails—an issue I return to later) to derive the phenomenon of a downward-sloping market demand curve from the properties of a single isolated consumer. This is equivalent to attempting to derive the features of water by studying the properties of an isolated molecule of H_2O. This of course cannot be done: a single molecule of water is not "wet," neither can it turn into ice or snow. All those phenomena are the product of the interaction of water molecules with other water molecules, in what are known as "emergent properties." Economics is unique among intellectual disciplines in its insistence upon deriving upper level phenomena (market and macroeconomy) by extrapolation from lower level phenomena (individual consumer, firm or investor). The source of the insistence is the neoclassical school (as Arnsperger and Varoufakis (2006) define it) and no other.

Complex systems are also normally characterized by unstable equilibria and far from equilibrium dynamics. The standard neoclassical question of: "What happens in equilibrium?" returns the answer "Nothing" for most complex systems models, since the instability of these models' equilibria guarantees that the systems will never be in equilibrium.

This is not a problem for the actual sciences, since methods for analyzing non-equilibrium systems have flourished since the development of computers. Only in economics is equilibrium analysis dominant, and axiomatically imposed on mathematically unstable systems—as in the case of neoclassical growth theory (Ramsey, 1928) and its derivative DSGE macroeconomics. This again is predominantly—but unfortunately not exclusively, as I discuss below—a phenomenon confined to the neoclassical school.

Is neoclassical economics mathematical?

Lawson characterizes the essence of his "ugly" definition of neoclassical economics as the use of (linear) mathematical methods where they are ontologically inappropriate. However, I would dispute that neoclassical economics as Arnsperger and Varoufakis (2006) and I define it, is worthy of the label of "mathematical." Mathematics, when used to explore a concept deductively, can have an inexorable logic (I say "can" because the vast majority of mathematical problems do not have a deductive solution). If neoclassical economics were truly mathematical, it would accept those logical conclusions even when they clash with cherished neoclassical priors. But this is not what has happened. When mathematical logic has led to a result that clashes with neoclassical priors, the result has been ignored or dismissed.

There are many such examples—for surveys of the mathematical fallacies that pepper neoclassical economics, see Blatt's masterful, but out of print, *Dynamic Economic Systems* (Blatt, 1983), or my *Debunking Economics* (Keen, 2011). I therefore believe that it does a disservice to mathematics to describe neoclassical economics as mathematical. A more apt term is that it is "mythematical": it preserves the a priori beliefs of the neoclassical school in the face of mathematical contradictions of these beliefs, while concealing this practice beneath a welter of superficially mathematical formalisms.

My favorite piece of neoclassical mythematics is one Lawson alludes to in a specious attempt (I'm sorry Tony, but that's the only way to describe it!) to argue that neoclassical economics cannot be characterized by Arnsperger's and Varoufakis' meta-axioms (Lawson, 2006): the Sonnenschein-Mantel-Debreu (SMD) theorem on the impossibility of deriving downward-sloping market demand curves from heterogeneous agents in a multi-commodity economy (Sonnenschein, 1972, 1973a, 1973b, 1974; Mantel, 1974, 1975, 1976).

This theorem can be regarded as a proof by contradiction. Starting from the proposition that the economy consists of numerous agents with different (or "heterogeneous") utility functions, each with a different initial relative endowment of qualitatively different goods, and each of whom has a downward-sloping Hicksian-compensated demand curve for every good, the SMD theorem shows that the only conditions under which market demand curves will also be downward-sloping is if agents have homogeneous utility functions and all commodities are qualitatively identical (so that all Engels curves are parallel straight lines). This means that aggregation is possible only if consumers are homogeneous and goods are qualitatively identical (so that neither luxury goods nor necessities exist: all commodities are consumed in the same ratio by an individual regardless of that individual's income). This contradicts the starting point of assuming that consumers are heterogeneous and goods are qualitatively different.

Mathematical logic thus leads to the result that a market demand curve cannot be derived by extrapolating from the properties of an isolated consumer—and equally, that an entire economy cannot be represented by a single "representative agent." This in turn implies, not that empirically observed market demand curves can have any (polynomial) shape at all, but that neoclassical theory cannot explain the empirical regularity of demand falling with rising price without including factors that are not deducible to a single agent—such as the distribution of income between individuals.

This, as Alan Kirman eloquently argued, should have forced economists to begin their analysis at the level of social classes:

> If we are to progress further we may well be forced to theorise in terms of groups who have collectively coherent behaviour. Thus demand and expenditure functions if they are to be set against reality must be defined at some reasonably high level of aggregation. The idea that we should start at the level of the isolated individual is one which we may well have to abandon.
> (Kirman, 1989: 138)

Lawson uses this as an example of the mainstream being willing to transcend methodological individualism:

> Moreover, some mainstream economists are prepared to abandon the individualist framework entirely if this will help make the 'economic theory' framework more productive in some way. As the 'economic theorist' Alan Kirman writes:
>
> 'The problem [of mainstream theorising to date] seems to be embodied in what is an essential feature of a centuries-long tradition in economics, that of treating individuals as acting independently of each other' (Kirman, 1989: 137). Kirman adds 'If we are to progress further we may well be forced to theorise in terms of groups who have collectively coherent behaviour' (Kirman, 1989: 138). So it is not obvious that even assumptions of individualism and rationality are ultimately essential to the mainstream position.
> (Lawson, 2006: 488)

In fact (a) Alan Kirman cannot be characterized as a representative of the mainstream since he is a critic of and developer of alternatives to it (Kirman, 1992, 2010, 2011); and (b) the mainstream failed to do anything like what Kirman called for in the early 1990s, but instead remained wedded to methodological individualism, and was willing to make patently absurd and fundamentally anti-mathematical "deductions" in order to do so.

The first neoclassical economist to realise the essence of this result reacted to it in a quintessentially anti-deductive way. Rather than concluding that this meant that an entire economy could not be represented by a single "representative agent," Gorman described the patently ridiculous assumptions needed to do so as "intuitively reasonable":

> [w]e will show that there is just one community indifference locus through each point if, and only if, the Engel curves for different individuals at the same prices are parallel straight lines . . . The necessary and sufficient condition quoted above is intuitively reasonable. It says, in effect, that an extra unit of purchasing power should be spent in the same way no matter to whom it is given.
> (Gorman, 1953: 63–64)

When the result was rediscovered in the context of trying to determine whether a market demand curve necessarily had the downward-sloping property of a Hicksian-compensated individual demand curve, its restatement was far less sanguine, though still delusional, in asserting that only "strong restrictions" were needed: "to justify the hypothesis that a market demand function has the characteristics of a consumer demand function":

> First, when preferences are homothetic and the distribution of income (value of wealth) is independent of prices, then the market demand function (market excess demand function) has all the properties of a consumer demand function . . .
>
> Second, with general (in particular non-homothetic) preferences, even if the distribution of income is fixed, market demand functions need not satisfy in any way the classical restrictions which characterize consumer demand functions . . .
>
> The importance of the above results is clear: strong restrictions are needed in order to justify the hypothesis that a market demand function has the characteristics of a consumer demand function. Only in special cases can an economy be expected to act as an 'idealized consumer'. The utility hypothesis tells us nothing about market demand unless it is augmented by additional requirements.
> (Shafer and Sonnenschein, 1993: 671–672)

These "strong restrictions" and "special cases" are logically equivalent to assuming that there is just one agent and one commodity—in which case, the whole concept of a curve relating demand for a commodity to *relative* price becomes farcical. This result should have ended any attempt to derive macroeconomics from microeconomics by simple extrapolation of the properties of an individual consumer, but instead this practice flourished *after* this result was discovered, as the "microfoundations revolution" took hold. Rather than accepting the mathematical result that this was impossible, the profession's mendacious texts assured students that (for reasons they could not understand) this practice was acceptable:

> it is sometimes convenient to think of the aggregate demand as the demand of some 'representative consumer'... The conditions under which this can be done are rather stringent, but a discussion of this issue is beyond the scope of this book.
> (Varian, 1984: 268)

This is not mathematics, but mythematics.

Is neoclassical an accurate descriptive term?

Lawson notes that the term neoclassical implies continuity with the preceding classical school, and also that it is frequently used as a pejorative and critical label. Here I am in agreement. Though there is some continuity in belief if one sources the neoclassical emphasis upon self-equilibrating markets to Smith's "invisible hand" remark, there is no continuity in methodology between the two schools. The classical school had an objective theory of value; the neoclassical theory of value is fundamentally subjective. Classical theorists frequently reasoned in terms of social classes, not from methodological individualism. Furthermore, although equilibrium was a common concept in the classical school, a form of dynamic reasoning was also commonplace—as with Ricardo's explanation for rent, or Marx's explanation of wage-profit cycles in capitalism.

A more accurate characterization of the neoclassical school is that it is the anti-classical school—not the least because its rise to dominance was partially in reaction to Marx's takeover of the classical approach and his use of it to criticize the capitalist order, rather than to defend it as Ricardo had done. The irony is that the true mathematical results of this anti-classical school have in fact supported the classical approach. The SMD theorem is indicative here since, as Kirman observed, it argues that economists: "may well be forced to theorise in terms of groups who have collectively coherent behaviour," which is precisely what the classical school did when it analyzed society as the outcome of the struggle between competing social classes.

From my perspective, the label "anti-complexity" economics is more apt, but we are stuck, for better or worse, with the term neoclassical as the label by which this anti-mathematical and anti-classical school is known.

Is heterodox economics completely free of mathematical error?

Though in general I reject Lawson's characterization of neoclassical as any group that, while aware of ontology, uses mathematics anyway, there are ways in which part—but not all—of his criticism does apply to some heterodox mathematical modelling. Lawson claims that much heterodox research accepts the need for a "causal-processual" ontology, but then uses methods which are inconsistent with it:

> In fact, a good deal of sustained heterodox research is couched in conceptual frameworks consistent with the sort of causal-processual ontological conception just described. All too often, however, this goes hand in hand with a lack of realisation that methods of mathematical modelling require formulations that are in severe tension with this ontology.
>
> (Lawson, Chapter 1: 39)

Post-Keynesian modellers clearly differ from neoclassical modellers on several of the points by which Arnsperger and Varoufakis (2006) define neoclassical economics. They reject methodological individualism and methodological instrumentalism, and they also reject methodological barter, since a defining feature of the modern Post-Keynesian school is an insistence on modelling monetary flows within the overall rubric of stock-flow consistency.

However, many papers in this non-neoclassical tradition overlap with neoclassical practice in the use of "methodological equilibration." Two indicative papers here are Dos Santos and Zezza (2008) and Dallery and van Treeck (2011). Dallery and van Treeck (2011) argue that Post-Keynesian economists should: "not abandon long-run analysis to orthodox economists," and associate the long-run with a state of equilibrium:

> While we appreciate the general proposition by Chick & Caserta (1997: 233) that equilibrium is not necessarily 'a state of perfect harmony', we contend that Post-Keynesians should not abandon long-run analysis to orthodox economists, who routinely resort to it to deny any relevance to Keynesian ideas.
>
> (Dallery and van Treeck, 2011: 192)

Dos Santos and Zezza assert that there is nothing wrong with assuming that: "the economy is always in long-period equilibrium":

Skott (1989: 43), for example, criticizes this Asimakopulos-Kalecki-Robinson view on the grounds that, when coupled with the usual Keynesian assumption that firms' short-period expectations are roughly correct, it implies—given constant animal spirits—that the economy is always in long-period equilibrium, as defined by Keynes in chapter 5 of the General Theory. While this last point is certainly correct, we do not see it as a bad thing. In fact, we argue in section 3 that a careful analysis of Keynes' long-period equilibrium is much more useful than conventional wisdom would make us believe.

(Dos Santos and Zezza, 2008: 443)

Here the problem arises from not too much mathematics, but too little. Many Post-Keynesian modellers lack an appreciation of the mathematics needed to analyze complex systems and the central role of structural nonlinearities in that mathematics. They therefore impose equilibrium as a frame of reference in the modelling process, or in the belief that the end product of any dynamic process is a state of long-run equilibrium. The former practice is not necessary—nor even necessarily useful—given modern nonlinear dynamical technique, and the latter belief is simply wrong (Cvitanovic et al., 2011). Long-run methodological equilibrium analysis should indeed be abandoned to neoclassicals, since it is a waste of time—though the study of the stability or otherwise of equilibria in genuinely dynamic models remains a valid enterprise (Costa Lima et al., 2014) which, as Arnsperger and Varoufakis (2006) note, neoclassical economists rarely if ever undertake.

Conclusion

Lawson's identification of neoclassical economics with mathematical formalism is correct only insofar as Lawson's presumption that mathematical methods imply "a world of isolated atoms" is correct, but this applies to linear economic models only—and these are the hallmark of the neoclassical approach as defined by Arnsperger and Varoufakis (2006). Individualism, instrumentalism, and equilibration are essential methodological components of the neoclassical school, and these in turn bias this school toward linear methods, as Blanchard (2014)—in what can be seen as a *mea culpa* article, albeit one in which in the end he still adheres to the neoclassical canon—makes clear:

> However, these techniques made sense only under a vision in which economic fluctuations were regular enough so that, by looking at the past, people and firms (and the econometricians who apply statistics to economics) could understand their nature and form expectations of the future, and simple enough so that small shocks had small effects and a shock twice as big as another had twice the effect on economic activity. The reason for this assumption, called linearity, was technical.

Models with nonlinearities – those in which a small shock, such as a decrease in housing prices, can sometimes have large effects, or in which the effect of a shock depends on the rest of the economic environment – were difficult, if not impossible, to solve under rational expectations.

Thinking about macroeconomics was largely shaped by those assumptions. We in the field did think of the economy as roughly linear, constantly subject to different shocks, constantly fluctuating, but naturally returning to its steady state over time. Instead of talking about fluctuations, we increasingly used the term 'business cycle'. Even when we later developed techniques to deal with nonlinearities, this generally benign view of fluctuations remained dominant.

(Blanchard, 2014)

Lawson's critique of mathematical methods in economics is thus valid if confined to critiquing linear models, but it is invalid when extended to mathematics in general, especially since the major strides in modelling in the last 50 years have come from the development of techniques to handle nonlinear systems.

What economics needs is not to abandon mathematical methods, but to catch up with the last half-century of progress in mathematics and computing that has made it possible to model non-atomistic, emergent, complex systems. Economic modelling of these processes will never be as complete as, for example, meteorological modelling can be in its domain, given the self-referential and evolutionary nature of the economy when compared to the weather. But it will enable us to construct an economics which transcends the ontologically inappropriate methodological choices made by the neoclassical school.

Note

1 Methodological barter could survive the acceptance of a complex systems approach. Conversely, however, rejecting methodological barter also leads to rejecting Arnsperger and Varoufakis' (2006) three "meta-axioms"—since modelling endogenous money leads to non-equilibrium systems in which bank behavior plays a primary role that makes it impossible to base economic analysis solely upon individualism and instrumentalism.

References

Anderson, P. W. (1972) More is different. *Science* 177(4047): 393–396.
Arnsperger, C. and Varoufakis, Y. (2006) What is neoclassical economics? *Post-Autistic Economics Review* 38: 1–8.
Asada, T., Chiarella, C., Flaschel, P., Mouakil, T., Proano, C. R. and Semmler, W. (2010) Stabilizing an unstable economy: On the choice of proper policy measures. *Economics: The Open-Access, Open-Assessment E-Journal* 4.

Barr, J. M., Tassier, T. and Ussher, L. (2008) Symposium on agent-based computational economics: Introduction. *Eastern Economic Journal* 34(4): 421–422.

Blanchard, O. (2014) Where danger lurks. *Finance & Development* 51(3): 28–31.

Blatt, J. M. (1983) *Dynamic Economic Systems: A Post-Keynesian Approach*. Armonk, NY: M. E. Sharpe.

Chiarella, C. and Flaschel, P. (2000) *The Dynamics of Keynesian Monetary Growth*. Cambridge, UK: Cambridge University Press.

Costa Lima, B., Grasselli, M. R., Wang, X. S. and Wu, J. (2014) Destabilizing a stable crisis: Employment persistence and government intervention in macroeconomics. *Structural Change and Economic Dynamics* 30(1): 30–51.

Cvitanovic, P., Artuso, R., Mainieri, R., Tanner, G. and Vattay, G. A. (2011) *Chaos: Classical and Quantum*. Atlanta, GA: Gone with the Wind Press.

Dallery, T. and Van Treeck, T. (2011) Conflicting claims and equilibrium adjustment processes in a stock-flow consistent macroeconomic model. *Review of Political Economy* 23(2): 189–211.

Dos Santos, C. H. and Zezza, G. (2008) A simplified, 'benchmark', stock-flow consistent post-Keynesian growth model. *Metroeconomica* 59(3): 441–478.

Dosi, G., Fagiolo, G. and Roventini, A. (2008) The microfoundations of business cycles: An evolutionary, multi-agent model. *Journal of Evolutionary Economics* 18(3–4): 413–432.

Goodwin, R. M. (1990) *Chaotic Economic Dynamics*. Oxford, UK: Oxford University Press.

Gorman, W. M. (1953) Community preference fields. *Econometrica* 21(1): 63–80.

Grasselli, M. and Costa Lima, B. (2012) An analysis of the Keen model for credit expansion, asset price bubbles and financial fragility. *Mathematics and Financial Economics* 6(3): 191–210.

Keen, S. (1995) Finance and economic breakdown: Modeling Minsky's 'financial instability hypothesis'. *Journal of Post Keynesian Economics* 17(4): 607–635.

Keen, S. (2011) *Debunking Economics: The Naked Emperor Dethroned?* London, UK: Zed Books.

Kirman, A. P. (1989) The intrinsic limits of modern economic theory: The Emperor has no clothes. *Economic Journal* 99(395): 126–139.

Kirman, A. P. (1992) Whom or what does the representative individual represent? *The Journal of Economic Perspectives* 6(2): 117–136.

Kirman, A. P. (2010) The economic crisis is a crisis for economic theory. *CESifo Economic Studies* 56(4): 498–535.

Kirman, A. P. (2011) The crisis in economic theory. *Rivista Italiana degli Economisti* 16(1): 9–36.

Lawson, T. (2006) The nature of heterodox economics. *Cambridge Journal of Economics* 30(4): 483–505.

Lawson, T. (2013) What is this 'school' called neoclassical economics? *Cambridge Journal of Economics* 37(5): 947–983. Also published in this book as Chapter 1, and page numbers cited refer to those in this book.

Lorenz, E. N. (1963) Deterministic nonperiodic flow. *Journal of the Atmospheric Sciences* 20(2): 130–141.

Lorenz, H.-W. (1987) Strange attractors in a multisector business cycle model. *Journal of Economic Behavior and Organization* 8(3): 397–411.

Lux, T. (1995) Herd behaviour, bubbles and crashes. *Economic Journal* 105(431): 881–896.

Mantel, R. R. (1974) On the characterization of aggregate excess demand. *Journal of Economic Theory* 7(3): 348–353.

Mantel, R. R. (1975) *Implications of Microeconomic Theory for Community Excess Demand Functions*. Cowles Foundation, Yale University, Cowles Foundation Discussion Papers: 409: 24 pages. Available at: http://cowles.yale.edu/cfdp-409 (accessed April 2015).

Mantel, R. R. (1976) Homothetic preferences and community excess demand functions. *Journal of Economic Theory* 12(2): 197–201.

Ramsey, F. P. (1928) A mathematical theory of saving. *The Economic Journal* 38(152): 543–559.

Rosser, J. B. (2013) *From Catastrophe to Chaos: A General Theory of Economic Discontinuities*. New York, NY: Springer.

Shafer, W. and Sonnenschein, H. (1993) Market demand and excess demand functions. In Arrow, K. J. and Intriligator, M. D. (eds) *Handbook of Mathematical Economics*. Amsterdam: Elsevier, (2): 671–693.

Sonnenschein, H. (1972) Market excess demand functions. *Econometrica* 40(3): 549–563.

Sonnenschein, H. (1973a) Do Walras' identity and continuity characterize the class of community excess demand functions? *Journal of Economic Theory* 6(4): 345–354.

Sonnenschein, H. (1973b) The utility hypothesis and market demand theory. *Western Economic Journal* 11(4): 404–410.

Sonnenschein, H. (1974) An axiomatic characterization of the price mechanism. *Econometrica* 42(3): 425–433.

Ussher, L. J. (2008) Symposium on agent-based computational economics: A speculative futures market with zero-intelligence. *Eastern Economic Journal* 34(4): 518–549.

Varian, H. R. (1984) *Microeconomic Analysis*. New York, NY: Norton.

12 Neoclassicism forever

Don Ross

Introduction

Like Tony Lawson, I have avoided using the phrase 'neoclassical economics' in my work, because it has never seemed to me to pick out any definite school of thought distinguished by either a clear doctrine or method. Instead, it has tended to be used to refer to any economics that is not deemed 'heterodox'. Furthermore, even that negative classification is generally unhelpful, because the boundaries of heterodoxy can reasonably be drawn differently by different commentators (e.g. Davis, 2009). Most recently, the cluster of research activity in mainstream literature most frequently rhetorically contrasted with neoclassicism by those who regard themselves as orthodox has been behavioural economics. But the majority of economists who embrace the label of heterodoxy do not regard typical behavioural economists as members of their club. In its assumptions and objectives most behavioural economics more closely resembles the early marginalist, Benthamite, economics of Jevons and Edgeworth than it does the post-war orthodoxy of Samuelson, Debreu and Arrow; but in that comparative context, orthodoxy is further from rather than closer to the classicism of Smith and Ricardo, which renders the semantics of neoclassicism peculiar. In the face of such confusion Lawson is well motivated to seek clarity in the original coinage of the term neoclassicism by Veblen. The results of Lawson's (2013) philosophically sophisticated exercise in the history of thought, as also presented in Chapter 1 of the present volume, are a revelation. In light of it we can conclude that the meaning of neoclassical economics has likely never been fully clear and coherent in any usage since Veblen's own, at least until Lawson's paper. A neoclassicist, according to Veblen and Lawson, is one who appreciates that the world is more causally complex, context-sensitive and dynamic than their own modelling strategy would seem to presume, but who persists with the modelling strategy in question anyway.

Lawson ultimately concludes that the term neoclassical economics: 'should be dropped from the literature' on the grounds that if we continue to apply it, now intending Veblen's original meaning, on each application we will refer to a (huge) group of economists on the negative basis of an analysis they would not themselves accept. Furthermore, I would add, the boundaries of the group will be fuzzy, because the extent to which an economic model is, in Veblen's terms, 'genetic' rather than 'taxonomic' will vary continuously and be subject to interpretation. Many useful concepts of course have blurred edges; but that *is* a problem when, as with neoclassical economics, almost the entire interest of the idea concerns the placement of its boundaries. It contributes no insight to say that Tony Lawson or Ben Fine are not neoclassicists. But is Herbert Simon? Douglass North? Vernon Smith? In each of these cases I think that the answer, if we went to the trouble of carefully testing out the question using Lawson's reconstruction of the term's meaning, would be 'up to a point'.

What I will argue here is that that is the answer that an economist who aims at objective understanding of the world should *expect*, without the slightest grounds for embarrassment or apology, to apply to their work. Lawson thinks that the neoclassical tension between modelling technology and ontology that he identifies is something we should seek to overcome and, indeed, could escape from immediately by adopting the philosophy of critical realism. I will argue by contrast that such tension is the social scientist's fated condition. My view is that *if* there is any representational technology that would be fully adequate to the actual structure of social reality, it will be mathematical rather than linguistic; but I am doubtful that, even if it exists, a moment will ever dawn when we will recognize that we have found it. In fact my pessimism, as Lawson would understand it, goes deeper. Following the philosopher of science Paul Humphreys (2004), I expect that powers of prediction will steadily expand with the capacity of computers to identify ever more patterns in ever larger data sets. Such machine learning about society will implicitly discover structures that humans will not be able to make explicit, because the structures in question will increasingly resist representation in the folk ontological category spaces underlying natural language and, in addition, will be too complex to be captured by sets of closed-form equations. From the point of view of purely epistemic values, then, as opposed to engineering values, my view of the economist's situation is tragic. With respect to prospects for improved sophistication of policy responses, however, my stance allows for, though of course it does not imply, optimism.

Ontology

Like Lawson (Chapter 1), I base my view of the philosophy of economics on a more general philosophy of science that is realist rather than empiricist. Thus, also like Lawson, I begin from ontology. The philosopher of science, James Ladyman, and I have articulated and defended a specific approach to ontology (which we refer to as 'metaphysics') in Ladyman and Ross (2007), adding elaboration and stressing its affinities with the philosophy of C. S. Peirce in Ladyman and Ross (2012). Ross (2014) reviews some of its implications for economics. The position in question combines Ladyman's ontic structural realism (Ladyman, 1998) with a modified version of Daniel Dennett's (1991) thesis that: 'to be is to be a real pattern'. Our name for this conjunction, 'rainforest realism' (RR), is based on metaphorical contrast with W. V. O. Quine's (1969) physicalist/reductionist preference for austere 'desert landscapes' cleared of 'jungle foliage' by philosophical analysis. The ontology of real patterns, we argue, is far more lush than all the science performed in a finite galaxy will ever be able to fully catalogue. While still at the level of general metaphors and slogans, I can additionally mention the conclusion stated in Ladyman and Ross (2012), riffing on Wittgenstein, that: 'the world is the totality of non-redundant statistics'. The point of this slogan is to stress our view, following Peirce, that most relationships among real processes are nondeterministic.

RR has much in common with Lawson's critical realism. First, both views insist that the world is irreducibly dynamic. Second, both agree that, on the (fallible) ontology most consistent with contemporary science, what Lawson calls 'atoms', and Ladyman and Ross call 'individuals' do not exist outside of pragmatically delimited contexts. That is, the world is not composed of entities that exhibit consistent intrinsic properties, including causal capacities, as they shift across dynamical settings. Third, both views acknowledge that although it is sometimes useful, for practical and limited purposes, to model specific processes as though they were causally isolated from the rest of reality, conclusions drawn from such isolations tend not to reliably generalize.

Though these two versions of scientific realism thus agree on much, they are derived very differently and their respective proponents draw sharply different implications from them. Lawson's philosophy of science is broadly Kantian.[1] That is, he surveys the actual progress and state of various sciences and then performs what he (rightly) calls a 'transcendental deduction'. In Peircean terms, he reasons abductively, inferring the ontological conclusions that would explain the overall pattern of scientific successes and failures. By contrast, Ladyman and Ross's most basic ontological thesis, their anti-individualism, derives directly from fundamental physics, specifically from quantum mechanics and quantum field theory. By 'fundamental' physics they do *not* refer, as the majority of philosophers do, to the parts of physics to which the patterns studied by the special sciences (including the non-fundamental parts of physics) allegedly reduce or on which they allegedly supervene. Ladyman and Ross indeed argue that the recent history of science is inconsistent with both general reductionism and with the weaker thesis that domains of special sciences supervene on the domain of fundamental physics. In this respect their anti-reductionism goes deeper than Lawson's: in polar contrast to Lawson, they deny that science reveals a layered structure to reality. The parts of physics that are fundamental, according to Ladyman and Ross, are fundamental only in the sense that they constrain all measurements – meaning, generally, all statistical estimations – taken anywhere in the universe. (One such constraint emerges as a limitation on the possible categorical stability of real patterns at any scale.) This is reflected in the following methodological asymmetry observed in the institutional practice of science: where tensions arise between models in fundamental physics and models in special sciences, there is pressure to revise the latter, but no pressure to revise the former. This is not without ontological or epistemological implications – for one thing, it is the source of the provisional acceptance by special scientists of 'laws of nature' – but these implications are much more modest than reductionists or believers in physicalistic supervenience suppose.

The reader might at this point form the idea that Ladyman and Ross's philosophy is simply a more ontologically cautious version of dynamical realism than Lawson's. Dialectical relations are in fact significantly more complicated than that. Like Lawson, Ladyman and Ross emphasize that special sciences generally aim to identify causal relationships. Unlike Lawson, however, they regard causation as an approximation, essential for human engineering and other practical purposes, of more general influence transmission relations studied by the physical theory of information processing. At the scale of fundamental physics such information processing respects the constraints of quantum rather than classical computation. These constraints are not consistent with the axioms of classical logic or set theory that structure causal concepts. Thus the general structure of the world, which furnishes the modal background for all special structures, can only be represented mathematically. Characterizing the relationships between general and special ontological structures – developing, in other words, the ontology consistent with science – thus consists in examining relationships among bodies of mathematics. For example, following suggestions of French (2014), we can work with the fact that classical set theory approximates quasi set theory, which can in turn be used to model the mathematical structure that currently appears to literally characterize the fundamental physical scale viz group theory. Then if quasi set theory can also be used to represent the structures studied by non-fundamental sciences, it provides a possible mathematics in which the unity of the scientific worldview – which is to say, metaphysics – can be expressed.

Lawson is a realist about everyday structures and processes, including those studied by social sciences. In one – important – sense Ladyman and Ross agree: most of what people track as individuals, for example Napoleon, the table in front of me, a biological species or Miles Davis's last recorded trumpet solo, are real patterns. What this means, ontologically, is that they are statistically non-redundant: they cannot be identified from analysis of more general data structures. Which patterns are real in the sense of being non-redundant cannot be inferred from human practice or language, but can only be affirmed with more or less confidence on the basis of statistical modelling.

A crucial difference between Ladyman and Ross's philosophy of science and Lawson's is that the former make deeper concessions to empiricism, of the specific contemporary form ('constructive empiricism') defended by Bas van Fraassen (1980, 1989, 2002). In general, as van Fraassen insists, special scientists are content with aiming for empirical adequacy in their models. Ladyman and Ross's objection to the constructive empiricist's rejection of all metaphysics (i.e. rejection of objective ontology) is that it also forces van Fraassen to deny that inductive inferences are soundly motivated by any modally interpreted generalizations. But scientists do believe in laws in the limited sense of over-arching generalizations that they take as non-revisable *except by fundamental physicists*. In RR this realism manifests in the account of statistically non-redundant patternhood: a pattern is not real merely because it *is* used by someone for inferential projection, but because if it were not identified then some information that is in fact available through sound data transformations *would not* be accessible, as a matter of physical information-theoretical fact. These modally inflected facts need not be expressed in classical modal logic; mathematics that is powerful enough to include group theory can represent them, and if French (2014) is correct then mathematics that includes quasi set theory may suffice.

Ladyman and Ross and Lawson, then, agree with respect to the second-order description of scientific practice and share rejection of individualistic, non-dynamical ontologies. Notwithstanding so much agreement, Lawson's confidence in the power of natural language to describe fundamental ontology leads him to both a philosophy of science and a metaphysic that are diametrically at odds with Ladyman and Ross's on just the point that matters most to his philosophy of economics: his view of the ontological significance of mathematical modelling.

Ladyman and Ross follow Lakoff and Johnson (1980) and Lakoff (1987) in viewing natural language as largely structured by deep metaphors,[2] which in turn encode a folk metaphysics that serves the practical challenges of environmental manipulation faced by humans in their four-dimensional world of medium-sized objects and causal influence that is most saliently exemplified by pushing, pulling, pounding and cutting things. The metaphorical structuring of social relationships in the folk ontology draws on these same metaphors. However, the actual ontology in which human lives and actions are embedded is much more complex than this. Just as classical mechanics is false if interpreted as an objective account of physical laws, because it fails to generalize, so the folk ontology largely claws the air in the face of real complexity. Its categories and restrictive assumptions simply fail to generally apply.

This, according to Ladyman and Ross, is why mathematics is the essential idiom for the attempted formulation of objective knowledge by scientists. The reader might object, however, that even if it were conceded that ontology/metaphysics must be expressed mathematically, it does not follow that a special science arguably focused on everyday-scale processes such as economics cannot be conducted entirely using the resources of natural language. This is a possible, indeed natural, position for an empiricist who denies that scientists in general are accountable for aiming to establish facts about a single unified ontology. A realist, however, and most emphatically a critical realist such as Lawson, must insist on identifying the target ontology of all sciences from the metaphysical point of view; and that point of view, according to Ladyman and Ross, requires mathematical formulation. More directly, the constraints on influence transmission relations that govern all sciences come from mathematical information theory. In consequence, we should expect the economic concepts that can be stitched into a unified scientific worldview to be technical and to fail to straightforwardly match concepts from folk social ontologies (Ross, 2009). Thus, economic agents are not coextensive with either biological or socially individuated people; an economic agent's income is not a person's salary in money, but rather the maximum exchange value of resources the agent could have consumed in a time interval and been as wealthy at the end of the interval as they had been at the beginning of the interval; a game (in extensive form) is a vector of strategies in a directed graph or (in normal form) a set of such vectors, rather than an instance of a loosely related family of activities people pursue for amusement.

Like Lawson, Ladyman and Ross avoid conceiving of mathematics as a language. It is, rather, the science of general patterns, some of which are real in the sense of being empirically manifest as transformation groups and quasi sets. Institutionally, mathematics is an evolving practice governed by rules that prevent its users from thinking that they are reasoning soundly when they slip into reliance on folk ontological assumptions built into natural language. According to Ladyman and Ross, an advantage of requiring scientists to rely on mathematical representations is that such discipline consistently forces genuinely new insights to be coupled with representational innovations. Of course, most scientists never produce mathematical innovations; most merely apply already discovered structures to new data. A whole discipline might conceivably fall into doing this and doing no more. That is what we would expect to observe with economics if Lawson is right that (mainstream) economists have been stuck for a century in an ontological cul-de-sac. I turn now to that issue, the main topic of the present essay.

Mathematical modelling in economics

As briefly explained above, Ladyman and Ross view natural language as, for the scientist, a kind of trap, which tends to confine thought to the categories of the familiar, practical, often body-centred (Johnson, 1987), folk ontology, whereas the actual structure of reality is more complex. Lawson seems to acknowledge that mathematics can sometimes have the effect of forcing conceptual innovation. For example, he celebrates the example of Newton inventing the calculus in order to be able to express the relationships that became the foundation of classical mechanics (Lawson, 2009). But Lawson alleges, throughout his work, that economists have institutionally restricted themselves to a specific style and province of mathematics that blocks their ability to represent dynamical relationships among, using Ladyman and Ross's language, patterns that exhibit different influence transmission properties – or, henceforth, relaxing Ladyman and Ross's 'strictly speaking' voice for ease of dialectics, different causal powers – in different contexts. 'Mathematical methods and techniques of the sort employed by economists (use of functions, calculus and so forth)' Lawson argues: 'presuppose regularities at the level of events' (Lawson, Chapter 1: 35). By this he means that the modelling style forces the economist to search for classes of recurring event types, where the types in question are based on classifications of the alleged context-free causal powers of the atoms (which may be objects or closed processes).

Much economics, like much of any regular human activity, is derivative, unimaginative and unambitious. When economics has that character, it indeed typically takes the form that Lawson describes. For example, cross-country growth rates are frequently regressed on macroeconomic policy variables as if it were sensible to expect that (say) 10% reductions of average marginal tax rates would have similar effects on growth across all countries over (say) a 20-year period. Or, to take another example, impacts of increases in consumer spending on medium-term interest rates are sometimes estimated without regard to how many of the consumers are spending from increased real earnings and how many are running down savings. Every economist has sat through seminars in which presenters walk through such naïve estimations and are criticized by their audiences for doing so – but on the basis of instance-specific objections that are not methodologically, let alone ontologically, generalized. It is a useful insight of Lawson's to point out that one example after another of wayward economic reasoning instantiates a common philosophical mistake: overlooking the context-sensitivity of causal effects of types of economic events and processes. When the economists in a seminar room are quick to spot the specific errors but do not see them as resulting from a persistent misfit between the common style of analysis and the structure of the world, then they reveal, in Lawson's terms, their neoclassicism.

That boring economics tends consistently to be boring in just this way supports Lawson's contention that the form of mathematical modelling that has become common encourages economists to under-generalize the context-sensitivity of economic causes. But 'the form of mathematical modelling' in question has a number of parts. In the quotation reproduced above, Lawson casually gestures at: 'use of functions, calculus and so forth'; elsewhere he stresses the baleful effects of standard econometric methods. In still other moments he complains about the use of axioms and deductive operations to impose artificial 'closure' on models of a world that is actually 'open'.

As sources of boring economics, I do not think that these elements of standard methodology are on all fours with one another. So as to keep the review on the ontological plane, I will consider the respective blameworthiness of the modelling elements in a somewhat oblique way, by comparative reference to use of mathematical methods in fundamental (quantum) physics. This comparison may be fruitful for two reasons. First, it directs us to a domain where Lawson's general ontological picture is *clearly* accurate: there are no individual entities in quantum physics (French 1989, 1998; French and Krause 2006; Ladyman and Ross 2007, chapter 3), and physicists can produce what Lawson calls 'atomic event regularities' only by literally sealing off systems in which they engineer relative context-freedom from the rest of the world using particle accelerators and ingenious experimental designs.[3] On the other hand, in quantum physics mathematical modelling is obviously not optional, since it is the exemplary case of a domain where the representational adequacy of natural language, and the folk ontological categories that structure such language, unambiguously break down. One cannot come close to accurately describing quantum reality without mathematics. Indeed, as argued in Ladyman and Ross (2007), using natural language *at all* to represent the content of quantum physics invariably has the effect of 'domesticating' it, in other words concealing the radicalism of its implications for the accuracy of folk ontology.

In this context, let us consider whether economists unduly crimp their potential ontological insights by relying on 'functions, calculus and so forth'. The most charitable way of interpreting this is as directing our attention to the fact that most models and proofs in mainstream economics papers manipulate sets and assume the axioms of set theory. This indeed encourages a modeller to conceptualize the domain of application as involving individual objects or modular processes that carry their causal powers with them, as they are considered in the contexts of different sets linked by mapping functions. Quantum phenomena, by illustrative contrast, generally cannot be modelled set-theoretically; the crucial physical symmetries that constitute the most important generalizations are defined using group theory.

So, should economists start developing group-theoretic models? This seems to be an institutional reform that Lawson's arguments suggest would be valuable.[4] If economists used group theory as the basis for stating and proving theorems and building models, this might well help them to see economies as transformations of path-dependent processes, with important influence transmission channels that are evidently not based on transportable causal powers of individuals. It seems unlikely that there are major institutional barriers to a development of this kind; the most prestigious economics journals are hardly known for looking askance at mathematics that is more sophisticated than usual. Would Lawson then regard these hypothetical group-theoretic economists as no longer neoclassicists in his and Veblen's sense? This question might make him a bit uncomfortable. Clearly the imagined development is nothing at all like the kind of reform that Lawson and his institutional allies in the 'post-autistic' economics lobby have in mind. But it is hard to see why the development should not have the effect of significantly reducing the tension between mathematical methods in economic modelling and the real structure of the modelled world. But I can conjecture a plausible riposte here on Lawson's behalf. He might contend that the adoption of group theory in *formal* modelling would likely have little impact unless it were accompanied by a corresponding transformation in *empirical* modelling methods. I will consider the implications of this imagined retort, which I regard as a sound one, in the next section of the paper.

Among the elements of neoclassical modelling Lawson criticizes as ill-suited to the economic realm, I am least persuaded by his conviction that 'deductivism', that is, the use of axiomatic systems in stating and proving theorems and, more importantly, in defining the elements of models, forces economists to regard 'open' (that is, network embedded, dynamical and structurally fluid) systems as if they were 'closed' (that is, modular, static and structurally fixed).

Some economists' rhetoric, especially from what one might regard as the golden age of neoclassicism (again, in Veblen's and Lawson's sense of that label), supports Lawson's interpretation. The most important promoter of axiomatic economic theory was Samuelson; indeed, such promotion is the main point of Samuelson's (1947) monumental *Foundations of Economic Analysis*. Samuelson frequently claims that the main motivating value of axiomatic constructions is that they allow for exact determinations of the testable predictions of models defined in terms of them. To contemporary philosophers of science this attitude will seem strikingly naïve, skating blithely over the enormous complications involved in moving from formal to empirical modelling.[5] In fairness to Samuelson, ideas of this kind were standard fare in mid-twentieth-century philosophy, but they collapsed in the 1960s and 1970s under critical assaults from Kuhn, Quine and others.[6] The consequence in philosophy of science was the rise of so-called semantic (as opposed to syntactic) theories of the relationships between theories, models and empirical domains, which is accepted even by empiricists such as van Fraassen. Indeed, this was the transformation in mainline philosophical thinking that made realism the dominant philosophy of science; van Fraassen's initial challenge was precisely to show that it is possible to adopt the semantic view of theories and remain an empiricist anyway. Only a minority of philosophers of science think that he has met the challenge successfully.

Can the case be made that economists failed to notice all of this? Of course economists have seldom paid much attention to philosophy, and one can still find echoes of Samuelson's rhetoric in contemporary texts – for example, Caplin and Dean (2009) and Glimcher (2011) reproduce it exactly when promoting the project of building an axiomatic neuroeconomics. However, it seems to me that economists' *practice*, at least since the explosion of computational resources allowed them to meaningfully estimate the fit of structural models with data beginning in the 1980s and 1990s, is almost universally to take an implicitly semantic view of their models. Why, then, is axiomatic construction still so popular among them? Returning to the comparison with quantum physics, we may note that axiomatic construction is long extinct among physical theorists, who simply write down sets of field equations and argue later over their 'interpretations', or indeed over whether trying to 'interpret' them at all constitutes productive scientific activity (Ladyman and Ross, 2012).

The most plausible explanation of economists' continuing fondness for axiomatic constructions is particularly interesting in light of Lawson's reconstruction of neoclassicism. When I read a verbal story that sketches out a causal account of an economic event or cluster of events, no matter how sophisticated, factually alert and well considered the reasoning in the story seems to me to be, I typically feel less than wholly satisfied if I am not given a formal representation of it. The reason for this dissatisfaction is precisely that the network of economic causal relationships is complex and that these relationships almost invariably have varying boundary conditions that intuition cannot identify. Only a naïve consumer of economic models should imagine that a model is likely to actually locate the relevant boundary conditions in actual, empirical magnitudes. But the model should show me *which* empirical measurements I should focus on critically and carefully if I am thinking of advising someone, or myself, to take the proposed causal story seriously in choosing or advocating policy. In other words, I take naturally and without explicit philosophical reflection exactly the stance that Lawson's neoclassicist should be expected to take. Knowing that an actual economy is complex, dynamic and 'open', I know better than to simply 'believe' a model – including, I must add in the present dialectical context, a verbal, narrative, causal model – that inevitably imposes some false closures. To critically apply the model I want to see where the closures in question are, and I want to see this more precisely than a verbal model can typically show.

Even if this much is conceded, it does not indicate why, lurking behind the empirical model, I might also expect some axiomatic structure. But this too can be explained by appeal to neoclassical sophistication. The neoclassicist expects that a real economic phenomenon of any complexity can typically be modelled in multiple empirically adequate ways. But this is not simply a matter of 'one damn model after another'; models come in *families*, distinguished from one another by 'hinge' relationships that drive their main intended insights. For example, two models of an equities market might both link price movements to choices of monetary policy, but one might do so by way of instantaneous or lagged changes in the money supply, while another might do so by way of asymmetric effects on expectations of heterogeneous investors.[7] It is often not obvious from a verbal explanation which of these two families a model falls into – consider, for example, the widespread partial attribution of the recent world financial crisis to global imbalances in capital stocks and flows. Setting models in the context of theories deduced from axioms forces economists to disambiguate in such cases. On the account I am giving here, such disambiguation contributes nothing to the persuasiveness of a model as an empirical hypothesis; it simply helps everyone to be clear about just *which* empirical hypothesis it is. That is surely important. On the other hand, Lawson is right that a sequence of papers on a topic that consisted *solely* in the production of new axiomatic theories and derivation of their 'results' would remain disengaged from reality.

In my experience this is very widely recognized by economists. Effort may have been disproportionately allocated to abstract theory production and manipulation for a few decades during which scarcity of computational power made serious empirical applications of complex models impractical. For example, McFadden (1974) persuaded most economists of the importance of allowing for distributions of heterogeneous utility structures in modelling population-scale demand; but then for about 20 years this insight was filtered through use of conditional logit designs that imposed severe restrictions on distributions, because more general econometrics were computationally intractable. It speaks to economists' neoclassical attitude – that is, to their recognition that reality about market demand is more complex than a conditional logit estimation can typically capture – that when powerful computational resources *did* become cheap and widely available there was an immediate and massive shift of emphasis in the discipline towards econometric innovation.

This point, I think, brings us to the true core of Lawson's critique. His analysis of neoclassicism clearly signals his recognition – which he has always expressed, but sometimes with less emphasis – that mainstream economists understand that formal models of economic phenomena are typically extreme simplifications. But there is a new optimism abroad – from Lawson's point of view one might call it 'rampant' – according to which economists at last have the tools they need to get seriously to grips with empirical complexity (Coyle, 2007). Lawson vigorously declines to join this celebration, because according to him it is in relying on econometrics as their toolbox for relating theory to observation that economists most clearly express the neoclassicist cul-de-sac, that is, their commitment to searching for event regularities in a world that they (sort of) know to be too complex and context-sensitive to manifest them.

Econometrics

According to Lawson (Chapter 1): 'the atomistic condition for a closure requires only that the (atomistic) factors in question have the same separate and independent effect whatever the context' (Lawson, Chapter 1: 61). He is correct that this expectation must underlie all efforts to produce causal generalizations from linear regression models. Of course all users of such models recognize that magnitudes of effect coefficients of right-hand variables, with the dependent variable held constant, vary from one application to another. Furthermore, no one practises empirical economics for long before they encounter coefficients that change signs between applications. This need not disturb the modeller's ontological sangfroid if they assume that the variable in question has intrinsic causal dispositions that are simply unobservable in some contexts. But Lawson's point is that that assumption is not itself grounded anywhere in the 'official' methodology of mainstream economics, and that is in turn the mark of the neoclassical tension.

I will draw a simple example from my own work on gambling behaviour. Suppose I draw a random sample of middle-class South Africans and record their scores on an instrument intended to measure risk for developing pathological gambling[8] (PG). If I linearly regress that variable on a set of right-hand variables that includes a binary dummy for 'regularly patronizes licensed casinos' then in every middle-class sample I have encountered I will find that a positive value for the dummy is a significant predictor of a higher score on the PG risk instrument. If, on the other hand, I draw a random, representatively weighted sample of South African adults in general, I will find that a positive value for the dummy significantly predicts *reduced* risk of PG. I do not regard this sign change as at all mysterious. It results from the fact that poor South Africans have far higher frequency of high PG risk scores than middle-class South Africans, along with the fact that the overwhelming majority of poor South Africans do all of their gambling outside licensed casinos. It is harder than one might expect to make the negatively signed coefficient go away by carefully selecting the other independent variables in the model, because of such further complications as the fact that many poor South African women have no access to games that involve stakes high enough to reveal PG-indicative behaviour, and the fact that no one has yet found a cluster of demographic variables that reliably selects the subset of poor South Africans with the highest PG risk except geographical variables – and then, as fate would have it, the areas where the high-risk poor South Africans live are also the areas where the licensed casinos they do not visit are concentrated. Again, though, I am at no loss for understanding here; I just explained why not, by reference to actual facts about relationships among distributions of variables. When I write policy reports based on PG risk prevalence studies in the general population, which include some linear regression tables, I typically include a warning, which rhetorically is a sort of joke, to the effect that: 'the reader should not conclude that a policy encouraging people to patronize casinos would reduce the prevalence of PG in South Africa'. This of course reflects my confidence that regular participation in gambling, including legal casino gambling, increases the risk of PG for any set of people, despite the fact that vanilla survey data econometrics will not show me this causal relationship.[9]

I expect that most economists will react to this little example without any surprise; almost all of them could relate similar experiences. I have underlying confidence in a causal relationship that I rely upon to explain away a statistical peculiarity. But that is just Lawson's point: context-specific belief in a real causal relationship is allowed to come to the rescue when the econometrics generate a result that would otherwise be puzzling. I am not troubled by this in my everyday scientific or policy work because I am an expert on gambling and am institutionally allowed to invoke that expertise to, as it were, ignore what the rules would require me to conclude if I were truly a strict, robotic, empiricist. The generality of this kind of situation among economists can partly explain the resilience of the neoclassical tension. Because I need not be professionally troubled by the failure of fit between modelling strategy and reality in the domain with which I am familiar through multiple knowledge-generating channels, I may not be led to notice the methodological implications of the fact that *everybody* regularly proceeds this way within their own areas of specialization. Therefore, I assume the neoclassical position: I know that the world is more richly causally structured than linear regression will reveal, indeed I can rely on that knowledge to avoid believing crazy things, and so can comfortably go on running linear regressions. But then the following question must be confronted: why, when I *do not* have underlying causal knowledge in which I am confident, do I take the regression results as pointing me towards the truth?

In my view, reflections of the above kind, which I take to express a Lawsonesque critique, should motivate serious disquiet about some leading current trends not only in economics but in the social sciences generally. I join Leamer (2010), Keane (2010) and Rust (2010) in observing that increasing numbers of young economists are trained to be experts in Stata, and in experimental or survey design, but are only shallowly educated in economic theory and are not taught how to construct structural models. Ironically, this enculturates them well for interdisciplinary work, because they will encounter sociologists and other social scientists who have similar technical preparation and methodological orientations. Furthermore, their approach will not seem esoteric to the consumers of their work among non-academic policy makers and curious non-specialists. It is only very recently that DIY regression packages have become standard parts of the educated person's desktop and pocket equipment kit; but already we are seeing a proliferation of linear regression exercises in blogs and popular books by political and social commentators. The commercial success of the 'freakonomics' volumes and blogs by Levitt and Dubner (2006, 2009) testifies to the market power of econometric studies that are devoid not only of ontological self-awareness but of economic and social theory too (see Fine and Milonakis, 2009).

To be sure, this econometric hyper-empiricism has its sophisticated methodological expositors. Angrist and Pischke (2009) stress the importance, in non-experimental settings, of finding critically considered instrumental variables if one hopes to try to derive insights into causal relationships from linear regressions. But this should be fuel that is maximally incendiary for Lawson's critical fire; attempting to arrive at causal generalizations by adding instrumental variables to simple regression models is *exactly* the project of seeking event regularities in Lawson's sense. It is deeply regrettable that while many graduate students will be directed to read Angrist and Pischke (2009), few will encounter Lawson's contrary perspective (or even, for that matter, Leamer's (2010) or Keane's (2010)).

I find little basis for optimism that widespread ability to build structural models by hand, informed by rich immersion in economic theory, will make a comeback. But it seems equally unlikely that social science will become permanently trapped in wandering aimlessly among proliferating linear regression models. What I expect will happen is that statistical estimation software will become steadily more sophisticated, especially when it is set inside the powerful learning systems that artificial intelligence researchers and engineers are at last delivering. Let us just imagine one such probable thread of development. At the present time, when an economist who acknowledges heterogeneity of structural utility functions – either static or dynamic – in a sample of agents responding to a shared incentive structure wants to econometrically estimate this structure using a maximum likelihood mixture model (Andersen *et al.*, 2008), in which choice probabilities are assigned based on vectors of demographic conditioning variables, they must hand code the estimation algorithm in Stata. As this methodology becomes more common, we can expect the Stata developers, with guidance from economists, to eventually build it in. Such heterogeneity is both pervasive and dynamic. There is no reason in principle why a neural network could not operate on the new canned Stata code to track evolving mixtures of response functions in populations. Since this would be extremely useful for marketers, political parties and others with strong incentives to predict population-scale response patterns and changes in such patterns, the technology can be expected to arise.

The evolution of such technology will make it less, rather than more, likely that graduate students in economics and other social sciences will learn how to produce structural models. Their software, after all, will know how to do it, and will soon enough be able to *discover* structural models too subtle and complex to be written even by a master. On this scenario we would expect to see escalating improvements in the accuracy of prediction of social phenomena, but the theoretical knowledge underlying these improvements would only be implicit in the evolving computer models and would increasingly elude explicit representation by social scientists. This merely applies Humphreys's (2004) general prediction about science to the particular circumstances of economics.

The ineliminable neoclassical tension

Let me now weave together all of the strands developed to this point. I have indicated the philosophical basis on which I share Lawson's view that the world studied by social scientists is one of dynamic, open, causally structured processes that cannot be accurately captured by representing them as produced by modular, context-insensitive systems. In technical metaphysical terms, such modular systems are *individuals*; but on the metaphysics most compatible with the recent history of science, there are no such things.

The neoclassical economist, as depicted by Veblen and Lawson, may not realize just how radically false atomism and individualism are, but they at least understand that the world they aim to model is dynamically complex. Lawson urges them to respect this understanding by becoming (much) less reliant on mathematics. This is disastrous advice. The alternative representational technology, natural language, is systematically ill-suited to characterizing objective ontology, because its most basic function is to coordinate social expectations by associating confusing novelties with familiar, shared metaphors.[10] It thus naturally leads its users away from, rather than towards, recognition that the real patterns of the world involve forms of influence transmission that go beyond classical causation and that are not limned by the axiomatic restrictions of logic and set theory. The only technology that can be *increasingly* adequate to their representation is *more* powerful mathematics.

We will likely never achieve a level of mathematical power that is *fully* adequate to the deep strangeness, to folk ontology, of the structure of the world. I say this not because I have a belief about the in principle impossibility of reaching a limiting convergence between mathematics and reality – how could any such belief be justified? – but because I expect that increasingly powerful computational technology will deprive us, as a species, of the motivation and the capacity to keep seriously trying to reach for such a limit. All philosophers, and many or most scientists, are 'truth freaks', but most people in the societies that fund them are not. They mainly want improved prediction and control, and more powerful technology is likely to deliver that much more effectively and rapidly than more powerful understanding that depends upon achievements of mathematical genius.

All economists, therefore – or, at least, those who do not *deny* that the world is open and complex – will forever remain neoclassical up to a point.

That is, the mathematics they use for expressing their understanding – including of the predictions churned out by econometric machines – will always fall somewhat short of the complexity they acknowledge. Indeed, we may now find ourselves in a time of regression (pun intended). Machines available to anyone – economists, other social scientists and non-specialists – encourage a style of 'lowest common denominator' economics that might be characterized as 'Lawson's nightmare': we are swamped with atheoretical linear regression models that are pathetically unlikely to contribute to general insights, because they are perfect embodiments of thoughtless ontological atomism. I predict that the nightmare will be temporary, because models of this kind will be recognized as being not much good for anything except, sometimes, rejecting retrodictive causal stories that should have been viewed as implausibly simple in the first place. Better technology will be developed that will implicitly discover the structures of real economic patterns. Of course, people will go on theorizing about the performance of these machines and trying as best they can to strategically position themselves as use of the machines restructures the social and economic environment. But then the inescapability of the neoclassical position will be obvious: we will all know that our best theories are shadow play. For some temperaments this will make the activity of constructing them seem hollow; for other temperaments it will reduce the weight of responsibility and make economics more fun. Certainly there will then be *less* economics, because there will be little money to be earned from doing it. There, at least, is one economic prediction about which, humble neoclassicist though I am, I feel confident.

Notes

1 This statement should be read very literally. Neither critical realism nor the general epistemology Lawson associates with it are Kantian. My claim is that Lawson philosophizes about science in a Kantian manner, which is by asking what general structures that cannot be directly empirically derived would best account for the content of the actually successful scientific explanatory programs.
2 I am grateful to Jamie Morgan for reminding me that according to Lakoff and Nuñez (2001), mathematics is also built up on the basis of metaphors. I would argue, however, that natural languages invariably conserve and enrich the metaphorical structures on which their semantics are constructed, whereas the history of mathematics has involved systematic transcendence of the metaphorical foundations people used, and that children still use, to grasp concepts such as number and set. Maddy (1990) argues that this transcendence is what the fierce controversies around the axiom of choice were all about.
3 The powerful effectiveness of technology for sealing off experimental physical systems explains the fact that quantum physicists obtain empirical predictions that are statistically accurate to a degree unachievable in any other part of science.
4 Group theory is not entirely absent from economics. There is a tradition of modelling in game theory, for example, that considers game solutions as

topological features of optimization landscapes and then directly studies classes of transformations across such landscapes. I do not think that such game theorists can accurately be characterized as trying to represent event regularities in Lawson's sense.
5 One could fairly say, from the perspective of 2015, that Samuelson's confidence here involves ignoring most of the current content of philosophy of science.
6 Quine often credits Carnap with inspiring the insights behind his critique, which is borne out in Creath (1991), so knee-jerk disdain for 'positivism' here should be suppressed.
7 This is the approach, for example, of Frydman and Goldberg (2007).
8 It is becoming more common in the literature to refer to 'gambling addiction' rather than 'pathological gambling'. But as I am using this as an example I will stick with the more standard, though fading, terminology here.
9 Structural econometric analysis of (lab and field) experimental data are another matter in this respect.
10 Of course, people are entranced by new metaphors, both those that are produced by artists and those that evolve collectively. But there is no reason to believe that the evolution of human metaphorical culture follows the kind of progressive direction that we crucially want from science. I apply a different significance metric to perceptions of human relationships than Aristotle or Shakespeare did, but I doubt there is any justification for regarding my twenty-first-century rich liberal person's metric as *more accurate* than theirs. Excellent art is not the road to excellent science.

References

Andersen, S., Harrison, G., Lau, M. and Rutström, E. (2008) Eliciting risk and time preferences. *Econometrica* 76(3): 583–618.
Angrist, J. and Pischke, J.-S. (2009) *Mostly Harmless Econometrics*. Princeton, NJ: Princeton University Press.
Caplin, A. and Dean, A. (2009) Axiomatic neuroeconomics. In Glimcher, P., Camerer, C., Fehr, E. and Poldrack, R. (eds) *Neuroeconomics: Decision Making and the Brain*. London, UK: Elsevier, pp. 21–31.
Coyle, D. (2007) *The Soulful Science*. Princeton: Princeton University Press.
Creath, R. (ed.) (1991) *Dear Carnap, Dear Van: The Quine-Carnap Correspondence and Related Work*. Berkeley, CA: University of California Press.
Davis, J. (2009) The nature of heterodox economics. In Fullbrook, E. (ed.) *Ontology and Economics*. London, UK: Routledge, pp. 83–92.
Dennett, D. (1991) Real patterns. *Journal of Philosophy* 88(1): 27–51.
Fine, B. and Milonakis, D. (2009) *From Economics Imperialism to Freakonomics*. London, UK: Routledge.
French, S. (1989) Identity and individuality in classical and quantum physics. *Australasian Journal of Philosophy* 67(4): 432–446.
French, S. (1998) On the withering away of physical objects. In Castellani, E. (ed.) *Interpreting Bodies: Classical and Quantum Objects in Modern Physics*. Princeton, NJ: Princeton University Press, pp. 93–113.
French, S. (2014) *The Structure of the World*. Oxford, UK: Oxford University Press.
French, S. and Krause, D. (2006) *Identity in Physics: A Historical, Philosophical and Formal Account*. Oxford, UK: Oxford University Press.

Frydman, R. and Goldberg, M. (2007) *Imperfect Knowledge Economics.* Princeton, NJ: Princeton University Press.
Glimcher, P. (2011) *Foundations of Neuroeconomic Analysis.* Oxford, UK: Oxford University Press.
Humphreys, P. (2004) *Extending Ourselves.* Oxford, UK: Oxford University Press.
Johnson, M. (1987) *The Body in the Mind.* Chicago, IL: University of Chicago Press.
Keane, M. (2010) Structural vs. atheoretic approaches to econometrics. *Journal of Econometrics* 156(1): 3–20.
Ladyman, J. (1998) What is structural realism? *Studies in History and Philosophy of Science* 29(3): 409–424.
Ladyman, J. and Ross, D. (2007) *Every Thing Must Go.* Oxford, UK: Oxford University Press.
Ladyman, J. and Ross, D. (2012) The world in the data. In Ross, D., Ladyman, J. and Kincaid, H. (eds) *Scientific Metaphysics.* Oxford, UK: Oxford University Press, pp. 108–150.
Lakoff, G. (1987) *Women, Fire and Dangerous Things.* Chicago, IL: University of Chicago Press.
Lakoff, G. and Johnson, M. (1980) *Metaphors We Live By.* Chicago, IL: University of Chicago Press.
Lakoff, G. and Nuñez, R. (2001) *Where Mathematics Comes From.* New York, NY: Basic Books.
Lawson, T. (2009) On the nature and role of formalism in economics. Reply to Hodgeson. In Fullbrook, E. (ed.) *Ontology and Economics.* London, UK: Routledge, pp. 189–239.
Lawson, T. (2013) What is this 'school' called neoclassical economics? *Cambridge Journal of Economics* 37(5): 947–983. Also published in this book as Chapter 1, and page numbers cited refer to those in this book.
Leamer, E. (2010) Tantalus on the road to asymptopia. *Journal of Economic Perspectives* 24(2): 31–46.
Levitt, S. and Dubner, S. (2006) *Freakonomics.* New York, NY: Morrow.
Levitt, S. and Dubner, S. (2009) *Superfreakonomics.* New York, NY: Morrow.
Maddy, P. (1990) *Realism in Mathematics.* Oxford, UK: Oxford University Press.
McFadden, D. (1974) Conditional logit analysis of qualitative choice behavior. In Zarembka, P. (ed.) *Frontiers in Econometrics.* New York, NY: Academic Press, pp. 105–142.
Quine, W. V. O. (1969) *Ontological Relativity and Other Essays.* New York, NY: Columbia University Press.
Ross, D. (2009) Ontic structural realism and economics. *Philosophy of Science* 75(5): 732–743.
Ross, D. (2014) *Philosophy of Economics.* Basingstoke, UK: Palgrave Macmillan.
Rust, J. (2010) Comments on 'Structural vs. atheoretic approaches to econometrics' by Michael Keane. *Journal of Econometrics* 156(1): 21–24.
Samuelson, P. (1947) *Foundations of Economic Analysis.* Enlarged edition (1983) Cambridge, MA: Harvard University Press.
Van Fraassen, B. C. (1980) *The Scientific Image.* Oxford, UK: Oxford University Press.
Van Fraassen, B. C. (1989) *Laws and Symmetry.* Oxford, UK: Oxford University Press.
Van Fraassen, B. C. (2002) *The Empirical Stance.* New Haven, CT: Yale University Press.

13 Reflections upon neoclassical labour economics

Steve Fleetwood

Introduction[1]

Whilst Lawson (Chapter 1) explores possible meanings of the term 'neoclassical', primarily, via the work of Veblen (who first coined the term), the lessons Lawson offers extend not only beyond the history of economic thought but also beyond the meaning of the term neoclassical. The main lesson, as I read it, is Lawson's insistence on locating the discussion *not* at the level of *substantive* theory, but at the level of *meta-theory*. Attempts to label this or that substantive theory neoclassical are problematic: (a) because it encourages critics to identify limitations solely at the level of *substantive* theory; and (b) because it encourages critics to dismiss substantive theories without attending to the more fundamental meta-theoretical nature of their limitations. So, for example, some economists find themselves rejecting the so-called neoclassical theory of value, whilst accepting an identical meta-theoretical approach to value theory, i.e. one rooted in mathematical modelling.[2] Instead, and following Veblen, Lawson argues that the real limitations lie at the level of *meta-theory*. More specifically, he argues that if neoclassical economics can be characterised by anything, then it is the following:

- a commitment to the view (at some superficial level) that social reality is causal-historical or causal-processual;
- a commitment to realisticness;
- a commitment to modelling economic phenomena mathematically; and
- a failure to recognise that a commitment to the first two simultaneously is contradictory.

In this chapter I elaborate upon, and extend, Lawson's arguments in three ways. First, I shift the discussion from economics in general, to *labour* economics in particular. Second, I show the limitations of attempts to define neoclassical labour economics at the level of *substantive* theory. I do this by, third, shifting the focus to the level of *meta-theory*. Here I show that, whilst the substantive theoretical concepts used to identify neoclassical labour economics come and go, the following remain:

1   a commitment to the view (at some *very* superficial level) that labour markets are emergent, causal, processual, historical and open;

   (1.1) an inability to deliver on this commitment.

2   a commitment to realisticness;

   (2.1) an inability to deliver on this commitment.

3   a commitment to modelling labour markets mathematically; and
4   a failure to recognise that the commitment to 1 and 2 simultaneously with 3 is contradictory.

The next section elaborates upon, and extends, Lawson's key arguments, relocating them in the specific context of *labour* economics. Then I focus on the level of *substantive* theory. It identifies attempts made to define neoclassical labour economics in terms of five concepts (labour supply and demand, methodological individualism, rational maximisation, equilibrium and Pareto efficiency) before showing that even this definition has been overtaken by events. The next section shifts the focus to the level of *meta-theory* and considers the way developments in mathematics, logic and philosophy of science encouraged a commitment to modelling labour markets mathematically. The following section shifts the focus once more, introducing the searching and matching approach that has marginalised, and may even have replaced, the supply and demand approach. There are two reasons for introducing the searching and matching approach. First, it means that supply and demand (and Pareto optimality) cannot be included in the core concepts that have been said to define neoclassical labour economics. Second, it shows that the commitment to mathematical modelling remains. I then go on to establish claims 1 to 4 above. A final section concludes.

Two notes of caution. First, when I present various attempts to define neoclassical labour economics at the level of substantive theory, and in terms of five core concepts, note that they are others' attempts: I am simply reporting them. Second, I will use the term 'mainstream' instead of neoclassical when I want to use a less evocative term to refer to the most common school of contemporary economics.

Augmenting Lawson's key ideas

This section elaborates upon Lawson's key insights, hopefully, without changing their meaning.

Causal-processual or causal-historical

Let us start by elaborating upon what Lawson refers to as a causal-processual or causal-historical ontology.

The conception of social ontology I have in mind is processual in that social reality, which itself is an emergent phenomenon of human interaction, is recognised as being . . . highly transient, being reproduced and/or transformed through practice; social reality is in process, essentially a process of cumulative causation . . . Furthermore, social reality is found to be composed of emergent phenomena that . . . are actually constituted in relation (that is, are internally related) to other things, and ultimately to everything else (for example, students and teachers, qua students and teachers, are constituted in relation to each other; so are employers and employees . . . Constitutive social relations in short are a fundamental feature of social reality. So, social reality consists of emergent phenomena, constituting highly internally related causal processes. For ease of exposition in what follows I often simply refer to this alternative worldview as a causal-processual or causal-historical ontology or some such.

(Lawson, Chapter 1: 36)

This causal-processual or causal-historical ontology is a potted version of the social ontology Lawson has elaborated upon at length elsewhere. Because my arguments require a little more elaboration than this, I take the liberty of augmenting this along lines that I am sure Lawson would accept and, furthermore, placing them in the specific context of labour economics.

Social systems as causal, emergent, processual, historical and open

To get underway, let me introduce the term 'socio-economic phenomena', by which I have in mind things like agreements, codes, conventions, (proper) institutions, laws, mores, norms, obligations, precedents, procedures, regulations, (official and unofficial) rules, social structures, organisations and values. Most labour economists use the term 'institutions' to refer to things like these, but I prefer to conceive of institutions as part of socio-economic phenomena (Fleetwood, 2006, 2008a, 2008b).[3] The following is a more elaborated version of Lawson's (potted) social ontology.

- Labour market agents (e.g. workers selling labour services or searching for jobs, and firms demanding labour services or searching for workers[4]) enter into a pre-existing environment replete with socio-economic phenomena specific to labour markets. In order to formulate and initiate labour market orientated plans and actions, labour market agents have no option but to draw upon these socio-economic phenomena.
- By drawing unconsciously, implicitly and tacitly upon socio-economic phenomena like institutions, rules, norms, values and mores; and consciously, explicitly and non-tacitly upon socio-economic phenomena

like agreements, codes, conventions, laws, obligations, precedents, procedures, regulations, social structures and organisations, labour market agents reproduce or transform these socio-economic phenomena.
- Labour markets are, or are constituted by, these socio-economic phenomena. Indeed, labour markets emerge from, but are irreducible to, those socio-economic phenomena reproduced or transformed by labour market agents.
- As labour market agents reproduce or transform these socio-economic phenomena, they simultaneously reproduce or transform themselves as labour market agents, e.g. as job searchers, demanders of labour services, unemployed, skilled, low-paid, discouraged, etc. Via this reproduction or transformation, both labour markets and labour market agents continue their existence into the future.
- Labour market agents are not isolated atoms, driven by 'immaculately conceived' preferences, as Hodgson (2003: 160) puts it, and pre-programmed with one and only one imperative: to maximise some objective function. Labour market agents act, or more accurately *interact*, with other agents and do so only via social phenomena. The latter causally govern, but do not determine, agents' preferences.
- Because the socio-economic phenomena that constitute labour markets are *transformed*, not just reproduced, by labour market agents, then labour markets are transient, i.e. they evolve and change. The way a specific category of workers search for jobs in one time period can be transformed due to (a) changes in the socio-economic phenomena they engage with; and/or (b) changes in their thinking, i.e. changes in their evaluations, interpretations, expectations, not just changes in preferences.
- This transformation, evolution and change make it most unlikely that labour markets will display event regularities, laws or law-like relationships. Labour markets are, therefore, likely to be characterised by lack of event regularities, laws or law-like relationships. Labour markets are likely to be open, not closed, systems.
- This transformation, evolution and change make it most unlikely that causality will be based upon event regularities, as in the regularity view of causation and the regularity view of law. In open systems causality is based upon powers and tendencies, where the latter does not mean (something like) a 'rough and ready' event regularity, or a probabilistic or statistical law (Fleetwood, 2009, 2011a, 2011b, 2012). Lawson's use of the term 'causal' then is a reference to causality as power or tendency.

This, or something very close to it, is what Lawson means by 'causal-processual or causal-historical'. I will, henceforth, refer to social systems, including labour markets, as being emergent, causal, processual, historical and open and variations on this theme.

The failings of mainstream economics

From here, Lawson goes on to what he considers to be the failing of mainstream economics:

> the failings of the discipline arise just because economists everywhere are seeking to provide analyses of a social system that is, amongst other things, open (in the sense of not consisting in event regularities), processual and highly internally related, in terms of formulations that require that the social realm be treated as if made of closed systems of isolated atoms.
>
> (Lawson, Chapter 1: 37)

The failings arise because mainstream labour economists are seeking to provide an analysis of a system that really is causal, emergent, processual, historical and open in terms of formulations that require the system to be theorised as if it has none of these properties.

Attempts to define neoclassical labour economics

It is not clear if the term neoclassical refers to a set of ideas, concepts, tools, techniques, theories and models, or to a more general view, hypothesis, paradigm, perspective or approach. All of these terms appear in the literature. To get some consistency into the discussion I will use the following phraseology. I will consider the attempts made by others to define a neoclassical *approach* to labour economics in terms of a set of *core concepts*.

Virtually all attempts to define the neoclassical approach to labour economics have focused upon the level of substantive theory, and five core concepts have been identified. The central concept is labour supply and demand (curves or functions), which is then analysed using methodological individualism, rational maximisation, equilibrium and Pareto efficiency.

Many mainstream labour economists feel no need to even mention the term neoclassical. Examples are labour economics textbooks by Bosworth *et al.* (1996), McConnell *et al.* (2006), Ehrenberg and Smith (2009), Smith (2009) and Borjas (2010). Other textbooks, by contrast, do feel the need to *mention* the term, but they offer little or no elaboration. Examples include Addison and Siebert (1979), Killingsworth (1983), Fallon and Verry (1988), Elliott (1991), Hamermesh (1993), Coleman (2010), Hyclack *et al.* (2013) and Sloane *et al.* (2013). Cahuc and Zylberberg's (2004) textbook is a little curious because, although they mention the term and have a chapter dedicated to the neoclassical theory of labour supply, they have no chapter dedicated to neoclassical theory of demand. Indeed, none of their other chapters have the term neoclassical in their titles. To simply mention the term neoclassical without feeling the need to elaborate, I have the following kind of thing in mind:

> [t]he neoclassical paradigm [is] grounded in a view of rational maximising behaviour on the part of the individual, a group of individuals or a firm [that] provides a logical framework with which to interpret and to predict behaviour in labour markets.
>
> (Elliott, 1991: xvii)

Most intermediate level books hardly mention the term neoclassical either. Examples are Killingsworth (1983), Hamermesh (1993), Booth (1995), Marsden (1999), St Paul (2000), Manning (2003), Garibaldi (2006) and Boeri and van Ours (2008). The same goes for the prestigious *Handbook of Labour Economics* (Ashenfelter and Layard, 1986a, 1986b; Ashenfelter and Card 1999a, 1999b, 1999c, 2011; Card and Ashenfelter, 2011) and Borjas's (2014) collection, *The Economics of Labour*. Combined, these two texts constitute around 170 papers. The term neoclassical crops up throughout, but the more important point is that the editors feel no need to include even one paper defining the term.

There are, however, a handful of labour economists who have attempted to identify the core concepts that might define neoclassical labour economics, such as King (1990), Tilly and Tilly (1998), Petridis (1999), Kaufman and Hotchkiss (2006) and Laing (2011).[5] These authors identify the following as core concepts: methodological individualism, rational choice/maximising behaviour, equilibrium and Pareto efficiency.

There is, however, something very strange about these four core concepts, namely, the absence of any reference to the labour supply and demand. Discussing developments in neoclassical theory, Cahuc and Zylberberg (2004) note that the seminal textbook authored by the institutionalist Reynolds, which appeared in 1949, was still in use in the 1970s, despite the fact that it contained no analysis of supply and demand. Things then started to change.

> The first textbooks to build on a theoretical foundation, neoclassical in inspiration, saw the light in the 1970s. In [these] books, the descriptive aspect was considerably reduced, and the chapters were organized around topics that claimed to apply general principles of economic theory.
>
> (Cahuc and Zylberberg, 2004: xxvi)

Mortensen makes a similar point about theorising before the late 1960s: 'The prior theoretical lens used to view the labour market was the "supply and demand" framework of neoclassical economics' (Mortensen, 2011: 1074–1075). This had been the case ever since Hicks (1932) synthesised various existing economic concepts into the model of labour markets recognisable today. Pick up any contemporary labour economics textbook and similar sentiments to Hick's can be found, for example:

The most pervasive theory of the labour market is the neoclassical theory of labour supply and labour demand interacting to determine an optimal combination of wages and employment. This theory represents a good starting point for a textbook of labour economics because it is consistent with the microeconomic analysis found in the traditional theory of the firm and the analysis of consumer behaviour.

(Smith, 2009: 2)

This sentiment can be found in journal articles too:

Neoclassical models refer to concepts of the supply and demand model and predictions on the degree to which wage increases reduce demand for labour ... Wages, it is assumed, are determined by the marginal productivity of labour in the competitive labour market. In the basic neoclassical model, the price of labour is determined at the equilibrium of labour supply and demand.

(Kwon, 2014: 62)

Addison and Siebert (1979: 2) refer to this as the: 'central core of thought in labour economics'. This makes perfect sense. Labour economics is the sub-discipline of economics dedicated to the analysis of labour markets, that is, to the analysis of both labour *and* markets. Furthermore, in the discipline of economics, markets are universally understood (or misunderstood) as places where suppliers and demanders come together to determine prices and quantities.[6]

Now, whilst King (1990), Tilly and Tilly (1998), Petridis (1999) and Kaufman and Hotchkiss (2006) try, they do not succeed in identifying a consistent core of neoclassical labour economics, because each of them goes on to add other concepts. King adds the principle of substitution. Tilly and Tilly (1998: 6–8) consider the neoclassical view to be based upon a commitment to 'a naturalistic framework' (a kind of ahistorical universalism); a lack of attention to coercive structures; given, stable and consistent preferences, determined outside of the world of work; a commitment to rational expectations; a belief in the symmetry of (Walrasian) power; and a belief that marginal productivity theory solves the problem of income distribution between workers and between workers and capitalists. Whilst Kaufman and Hotchkiss (2006: 28–30) have a section entitled 'The neoclassical school', they note that recent developments within the school means that: 'whether this new approach is still neoclassical, at least as far as this term was originally conceived, is a matter of debate' (Kaufman and Hotchkiss, 2006: 28). They see neoclassical labour economics in terms of Becker's idea that the economic approach is not the study of markets per se, but the application of a model of rational maximising behaviour to all aspects of human life. A corollary of this involves the mathematical technique of constrained optimisation. For them, central to neoclassical theory, is the belief that labour markets are, some unique features notwithstanding, similar to all other markets and can be studied with the same theoretical model. They also believe that neoclassical economics, whether in price-theory or choice-theory, adheres to a general version of the invisible hand. Unlike most commentators, Kaufman and Hotchkiss (2006) also believe neoclassical economics has certain methodological commitments. There is a preference for deductive over inductive reasoning. Because deductivism requires the use of a few general assumptions, it invites problems when these assumptions do not accord with real-world labour markets. There is heavy reliance on marginal decision rules. The final distinctive aspect of neoclassical methodology (which seems to me to be *three* aspects) is: 'a commitment to a uni-disciplinary, heavy formalistic (mathematical) and imperialistic approach to theorizing' (Kaufman and Hotchkiss, 2006: 30). Petridis (1999) also includes the concept of the margin, substitution and competitive markets. He adds: 'In methodology there is a strong tendency to abstraction and a reliance on deductive reasoning, which invariably involves the application of mathematical techniques' (Petridis, 1999: 788–789). Petridis also mentions the 'Marshallian cross (supply and demand curves)'. Laing (2011) is a little harder to fathom. His introduction has a 14-page section entitled 'The supply and demand framework', concluding with the observation that: 'In fact it is probably fair to say that most labour economists first don their supply-demand spectacles when they wish to examine a new phenomenon . . . Yet despite its strengths, the framework suffers from several limitations (Laing, 2011: 22).

He then goes on to offer five pages explaining the: 'four main pillars of the neoclassical approach' (noted above) without any mention of the supply and demand framework he has just discussed at length. It seems to me, however, that if labour economists 'first don their supply-demand spectacles' before turning to methodological individualism, rational choice/maximising behaviour, equilibrium and Pareto efficiency, then they ought to identify supply and demand as part of this core.

Pause to take stock

Attempts to define the neoclassical approach to labour economics have focused upon the level of substantive theory, and five core concepts have been identified. Unfortunately, this definition has been overtaken by events, as the following section will show.

Change and evolution in the discipline of mainstream labour economics

Let us consider how the discipline of labour economics has changed and evolved since the 1970s.

Since then, labour economics has undergone the same evolution as many other fields. Economic theory has made strides in the analysis of strategic relations and information asymmetries, and dynamic behaviour; data of the most various kinds are accessible, and statistical techniques have improved, along with the calculational capacities of modern computers; all these factors led to a profound restructuring of labour economics in the last three decades of the twentieth century.
(Cahuc and Zylberberg, 2004: xxvi)

Mortensen makes a similar point:

The prior theoretical lens used to view the labour market was the 'supply and demand' framework of neoclassical economics . . . [T]his approach assumes exchange in a centralized market in which information about the goods and services traded as well as the price are perfect . . . In the late 1960s a group of economists . . . started to think about a more nuanced conception of the labour market based on observations regarding the actual experiences of individual workers over time . . . Early on, theorists realized that a dynamic 'flows approach' was needed for an adequate analysis of unemployment fluctuation.
(Mortensen, 2011: 1074–1075)

The term neoclassical might have been appropriate once, so the argument goes, but it has been overtaken by events. Kwon (2014: 61) refers to 'neoclassical, labour monopsony, and Harris-Todaro models', as well as the 'efficiency wage model' and 'dual labour market theory'. This makes the neoclassical approach (model or theory) just one of several. D'Auria et al. (2010) express a similar sentiment when, drawing upon a paper by Pissarides, they write: 'there are broadly four different hypotheses which try to describe the labour market: the neoclassical view, the efficiency wage approach, the wage bargaining theory and the search model (D'Auria et al., 2010: 66).[7]

So, in addition to the neoclassical approach (model, theory, hypothesis, framework or lens) there is also labour monopsony, Harris-Todaro, efficiency wages, dual labour market, wage bargaining and search approaches. But why stop here? There has been a proliferation of new ideas in the last 30 or 40 years, such as transitional labour markets; assimilation (vis-à-vis migration) theories; dual and segmented labour markets; efficiency wage theories; insider-outsider theories, principle-agent theories; the searching and matching approach to labour markets involving job creation, job destruction/separation, job flows, job searches and job matches; theories of pre-market and in-market discrimination and prejudice including discrimination by gender and race (but not, strangely, by class); human capital theories with various concepts of education, training and learning; hedonic theories; theories of screening and signalling; theories of tournaments; theories of different wages and payment systems; and theories of unions and union-employer bargaining. Then there are ideas and concepts, such as: job and worker churning, explicit, implicit, psychological, relational, self-enforcing and deferred payment contracts; asymmetric and imperfect information; monopolistic competition; free-riding; high performance work and work-places; incentives; job attributes; job ladders; job networks; job security; job stability; job shopping; low, middle and high ability workers; moral hazard; stigma effects not to mention concepts like lemons, fattism and good looks.

Changes and evolution in mainstream thinking have contributed to the difficulty in finding a definition of neoclassical labour economics at the level of substantive theory. But what about at the level of meta-theory, especially developments in mathematical modelling?

Mathematical modelling

Recall D'Auria *et al.* who set out four different hypotheses describing the labour market. Despite differences in these hypotheses, they spot a 'generic wage rule covering all four hypothesis'.

$$w_t - p_t^e = a_0 + (1-\mu)b_t^e + \mu pr_t^e - \beta\mu_t + a_t^w \tag{13.1}$$

Workers/trade unions negotiate a nominal wage w_t at time t conditional on the price expectation p_t^e, on the expected level of the reservation wage b_t, on expected productivity $pr_t = y_t - l_t$, and on the unemployment rate u_t. The term a_t^w is a shock to the wage-setting rule (D'Auria *et al.*, 2010: 66).

The important thing here is *not* to focus on the particular variables in the equation, but to focus on the *equation itself*. Despite neoclassical, efficiency wage, wage bargaining and search theories all being different theories, involving different concepts, they are always modelled mathematically. Indeed, if I went on to add other theories (e.g. human capital theories); to change the assumptions about the degree of competition (e.g. from perfect to imperfect or monopolistic competition); and to include this or that labour market institution and/or friction, all this could be, and indeed is, modelled mathematically. The upshot of this is simple, but this should not be interpreted to mean it is unimportant: far from it. Various theoretical concepts can come and go, including labour supply and demand (as we will see later), but mathematical modelling remains. Let us have a closer look at Lawson's ideas on mathematical modelling.

Lawson and mathematical modelling

Let me start with a sketch of Lawson's argument. The belief that economics (and maybe all social sciences) could, and should, be mathematised, emerged with the Enlightenment. By the late nineteenth and early twentieth century, economists with a mathematical bent were under pressure to adopt methods similar to those of some natural sciences, especially physics. Indeed, the classical reductionist programme advocated the reduction of all mathematics-based disciplines to the strictly deterministic approach of mechanics, with its emphasis on techniques of infinitesimal calculus. For various reasons, especially the emergence of relativity and quantum mechanics, this programme eventually withered and was replaced by a new orientation deriving from the work of Hilbert and the Bourbaki School. Lawson goes on to claim that mathematics came to be conceived of as a discipline or practice, properly concerned with providing a pool of frameworks for *possible realities*; and concerned with formulating systems comprising sets of axioms and their deductive consequences, with these systems in effect taking on a life of their own. This influenced mathematical economists who: came to regard the task of finding applications as being of secondary importance at best, and not of immediate concern; postponed the day of interpreting their preferred axioms and assumptions; no longer regarded it as necessary, or even relevant, to consider the nature of social reality; and were potentially oblivious to any inconsistency between the ontological presuppositions of adopting a mathematical modelling emphasis and the nature of social reality. In sum, *reality* ceased to be a major concern for mathematics and, more importantly, mathematical (labour) economics.

> Certainly the contemporary discipline [of economics] is dominated by a mainstream tradition. But whilst the concrete substantive content, focus and policy orientations of the latter are highly heterogeneous and continually changing, the project itself is adequately characterised in terms of its enduring reliance, indeed, unceasing insistence, upon methods of *mathematical modelling*. In effect it is a form of *mathematical deductivism* in the context of economics.
> (Lawson, Chapter 1: 32)

I am, largely, in agreement with Lawson's historical argument vis-à-vis the drive to mathematise economics. Indeed, Cahuc and Zylberberg (2004) probably speak for most labour economists when they write:

> Today, labour economics, like many other areas of economic analysis gives pride of place to teaching methods based upon mathematical models . . . But the domination of formalized economics is not the outcome of a random draw from among several possible equilibria. For one thing, economic science lends itself to formalization, since it deals with quantified magnitudes . . . A mathematical model allows us to clearly establish a linkage between hypothesis and results. It proves particularly effective, indeed indispensable, when the mechanisms studied are complex and involve the relations among a number of variables. Formal models of economic activity are entirely unavoidable.
> (Cahuc and Zylberberg, 2004: xxviii)

I also accept that mathematical economics was influenced by the work of Hilbert and the Bourbaki School. I differ only in the sense that I believe that the desire to mathematise was (and still is) part of a *wider intellectual milieu* that has shaped contemporary (labour) economics. This milieu includes developments in logic and philosophy of science.

Philosophy of science witnessed a complex shift from logical-positivism, with its syntactic view of theories (where theories are sets of uninterpreted statements presented in a formal language) to post-positivism and a shift of focus from theories to models, culminating in the semantic view of models, often referred to as the model-theoretic view, or structural view. Part of this shift, however, involved developments in logic, especially the work of Tarski and logical operations, the further establishment of a logico-mathematic language and developments in set theory. The interconnected nature of the developments in mathematics, logic and philosophy of science makes it difficult for them to be 'unpicked', as it where, and causal efficacy attributed to them independently (Backhouse 1998: 1848).

These developments in mathematics, logic and philosophy of science have, arguably, encouraged a similar lack of concern for reality in economics. As Boumans and Davis (2010: 28) put it, in this genre: 'one plays with symbols devoid of any meaning according to certain formal rules that are agreed upon in advance'. They go on to cite the 'punch line' delivered by the Nobel Prize laureate, Debreu: 'Allegiance to rigor dictates the axiomatic form of analysis where the theory, in the strict sense, is logically entirely disconnected from its interpretations' (Boumans and Davis, 2010: 29).[8]

Pause to take stock

That contemporary (labour) economics is preoccupied with mathematical modelling, is not doubted by anyone. What is doubted, however, is whether or not this commitment to mathematical modelling is consistent with: (a) a commitment to the view (at some *very* superficial level) that labour markets are emergent, causal, processual, historical and open; and (b) a commitment to realisticness. These, and other, issues will be explored in the next section, using the example of the search and matching approach.

The searching and matching approach to labour markets

Since about 1995 mainstream labour economics has undergone a seismic shift. The searching and matching approach now competes with the labour supply and demand approach and may even have replaced it at the centre of mainstream labour economics. The searching and matching approach, schematised in Figure 13.1, can be summarised thus:

Reflections on neoclassical labour economics 285

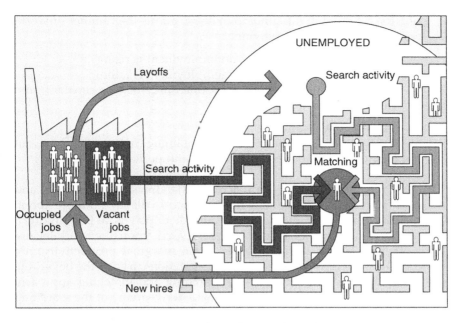

Figure 13.1 A schematic overview of searching and matching.

- jobs are continually being created;
- jobs are continually being destroyed;
- workers (both employed and unemployed) are continually searching for jobs;
- firms are continually searching for workers;
- when jobs are created, some searching workers find these jobs;
- when these workers find these jobs, some workers accept these jobs;
- when searching workers find and accept jobs, then workers are matched to jobs and their state changes from unemployed to employed or from being employed in firm a to being employed in firm b;
- when matching occurs, workers flow out of unemployment;
- when jobs are destroyed, workers flow into unemployment;
- there are three types of flows into unemployment:

    i   flows involving those currently not in the labour force at all;
    ii flows involving those in the labour force but unemployed;
    iii flows involving those who are currently employed.

- there are two types of flows out of unemployment:

    i   flows involving those who gain employment;
    ii those who drop out of the labour force.

- any change in the level of unemployment is equivalent to the number of workers flowing into unemployment, minus the number of workers flowing out of unemployment:
    i   if inflows exceed outflows, unemployment is rising;
    ii if outflows exceed inflows, unemployment is falling;
    iii if inflows equal outflows, then unemployment is constant, in a steady state.
- all of this occurs in time;
- all of this occurs in a labour market containing 'frictions' such as, but not restricted to, imperfect information and perhaps 'institutions'.

The searching and matching approach has abandoned labour supply and demand curves – and Pareto efficiency, which I will say no more about. Any role labour supply and demand continue to play is, at best, indirect. Moreover, the *theories* of labour supply (based upon the work-leisure trade-off) and labour demand (based upon marginal productivity) are unnecessary to derive the wage curve, job creation curve or the Beveridge curve, i.e. the theoretical core of the searching and matching approach. These theories *may not* even be necessary to derive many of the searching and matching approach's other concepts – much depends upon the details of the particular model. I say 'may not' because the searching and matching approach is notoriously lacking in 'micro-foundations', so it is often difficult to see what micro-concepts are, and are not, used or presumed.

I am not aware of anyone actually stating, clearly and unequivocally, that the searching and matching approach has actually replaced the supply and demand approach. Most comments make the less controversial point that the searching and matching approach can deal with important concepts and address important questions, which the supply and demand approach cannot, as the following comment shows:

> While the usual paradigm of supply and demand in a frictionless labour market is useful for discussing some issues, many important questions are not easily addressed with this approach... From its inception, search [and matching] theory has provided a rigorous yet tractable framework that can be used to address these and related questions.
> (Rogerson *et al.*, 2005: 959)

There is no canonical searching and matching model, and many could serve as examples, so I have chosen the following model from Pissarides, because it is well known. Pissarides comes close to saying that the searching and matching approach has replaced the labour supply and demand approach. Indeed, he cites Hall (2005) favourably because his analysis: 'implies that there are no conventional supply and demand functions' (Pissarides, 2011: 1101). Moreover, Pissarides actually states that his model:

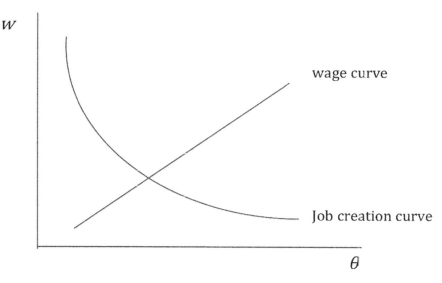

Figure 13.2 Equilibrium wages and market tightness (Pissarides, 2000: 19).

[r]eplaces the conventional demand and supply diagram for labour with a new diagram with the Beveridge curve as its centerpiece ... [The] Figure [13.2] shows the equilibrium for tightness and wages. Recall that (1.22) [equation 13.5 in this text] is the job creation curve, and in tightness-wage space, it slopes down: Higher wage rate makes job creation less profitable and so leads to a lower equilibrium ration of jobs to workers. It replaces the demand curve of Walrasian economics. Equation (1.23) [equation 13.2 in this text] is the wage curve and it slopes up: At higher market tightness the relative bargaining strength of market participants shifts in favour of workers, it replaces the supply curve. Equilibrium (θ, w) is at the intersection of the two curves.

(Pissarides, 2000: 19)

The wage curve

The wage curve is given by:

$$w = (1-\beta)z + \beta p\,(1+c\theta) \qquad \text{(13.2 [Pissarides' equation 1.23])}$$

- w cost of labour
- θ tightness of the labour market, i.e. the vacancies to unemployment ratio (v/u)
- β worker bargaining power

z   unemployment benefits
p   output of the job
c   hiring cost

Job creation curve or condition

Pissarides first derives the asset value of a *vacant* job: Let J be the present discounted value of expected profit from an occupied job and V the present discounted value of expected profit from a vacant job. With a perfect capital market, an infinite horizon and when no dynamic changes in parameters are expected, V satisfies the Bellman equation:

$$rV = -pc + \theta q(\theta)u \qquad (13.3)$$

He then derives the asset value of an *occupied* job: The flow capital cost of the job is rJ. In the labour market, the job yields net return p-w where p is real output and w is the cost of labour. The job also runs the risk of λ of an adverse shock, which leads to the loss of J. Hence J satisfies the condition:

$$rJ = p\text{-}w - \lambda J \qquad (13.4)$$

With a little manipulation, he derives the job creation curve:

$$p - w - \frac{(r+\lambda)pc}{q(\theta)} = 0 \qquad (13.5 \text{ [Pissarides' equation 1.22]})$$

w   cost of labour
r   rate of interest
pc   vacant job cost
p   output of the job
θ tightness of the labour market
$q(\theta)$ rate at which workers arrive at vacant jobs
λ rate of an idiosyncratic, adverse, shock that destroys jobs

In equilibrium, the zero profit condition holds. Output is assumed to remain constant. The (discounted) rate of job destruction is exogenous. The hiring costs change state with rate $q(\theta)$. A fall in the wage rate is offset by an increase in the rate at which vacancies are filled. The job creation curve is downward sloping.

Beveridge curve

The Beveridge curve is derived from two flows and expresses these two flows as follows:

1. Job creation takes place when firm and worker search, meet and agree to form a match, causing a flow out of unemployment.
2. Job destruction takes place when an exogenous, negative, idiosyncratic shock to occupied jobs arrives at the Poisson rate λ, causing a flow into unemployment.

The evolution of mean unemployment is given by the difference between the two flows:

$$\hat{u} = \lambda(1-u) + \theta q(\theta)u \qquad (13.6)$$

In the steady state, the mean rate of unemployment is constant, so:

$$\hat{u} = \lambda(1-u) + \theta q(\theta)u \qquad (13.7)$$

Pissarides rewrites this equation as an equation determining unemployment in terms of two transition rates, which is the Beveridge curve.

$$u = \frac{\lambda}{\lambda + \theta q(\theta)} = 0 \qquad (13.8 \text{ [Pissarides' equation 1.21]})$$

Pissarides goes on to show the steady state equilibrium with a second diagram in vacancy and unemployment space (Figure 13.3). He transposes the job creation curve into a straight line through the origin with slope θ. The steady state condition for unemployment (equation 13.8 [Pissarides' equation 1.21]) is the Beveridge curve.

Pause to take stock

Marginalising, or even abandoning labour supply and demand, leaves the definition of neoclassical labour economics based on just three concepts: equilibrium, methodological individualism and rational maximisation. More important, however, is the following observation. The searching and matching approach, just like the supply and demand approach, is rooted in mathematical modelling. One set of curves, or one set of mathematical functions, has been swapped for another set, but the commitment to mathematical modelling remains.[9] Even equilibrium, methodological individualism and rational maximisation are retained not because they are requirements of theory, but because they are requirements of mathematical modelling. I will come back to this later in the chapter.

Reflecting upon the searching and matching approach

Are advocates of the searching and matching approach committed to: (a) the view that labour markets are emergent, causal, processual, historical and open systems; and (b) realisticness? Let us consider these questions in turn, starting with the latter.

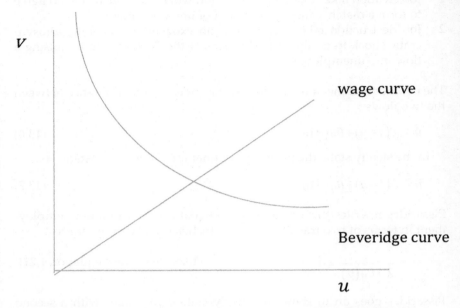

Figure 13.3 Equilibrium vacancies and unemployment (Pissarides, 2000: 20).

Searching, matching and realisticness

The issue of realisticness is highly problematic within mainstream labour economics. On the one hand, a series of passing comments seem to suggest a commitment to realisticness, i.e. models should be realistic; it would be better if models were more realistic; or realistic assumptions are preferred to unrealistic ones – and variations on this theme. On the other hand, more specific methodological claims suggest that theories and models *cannot* be realistic.

Passing comments indicating a commitment to realisticness

> One of the appeals of early search theory was that it appeared realistic... A process whereby both workers and firms search for each other and jointly either accept or reject the match seemed to be closer to reality.
>
> (Pissarides, 2011: 1093)

> Keynes's famous statement that the unemployment of workers between jobs can be ignored... is unverified conjecture. *Descriptively it is false*: With the exception of a few 'discouraged' workers,

unemployed workers are always between jobs, or between some other state and a job.

(Pissarides, 2000: xv, emphasis added)[10]

The model [in this chapter] *does not yet claim to be realistic* or empirically implementable. At this stage many of the variables that are likely to be important in an empirical analysis of unemployment are left out.

(Pissarides, 2000: 3, emphasis added)[11]

We extend the NK [New Keynesian] model by introducing a more realistic labour market, with frictions similar to those found in the Diamond-Mortensen-Pissarides searching and matching model of unemployment.

(Blanchard and Galí, 2010: 1)

The matching function . . . encapsulates searching and matching frictions, allowing a more realistic description of the labour market, and of unemployment.

(Stevens, 2007: 847)

There are several reasons why it is important to know the actual matching pattern in the market. First, it allows us to test different economic models that predict distinct matching equilibrium patterns, and this gives insights into the realism of the assumptions on which the models rely.

(Mendes *et al.*, 2010: 929)

The incorporation of wage stickiness makes employment realistically sensitive to driving forces . . . I conclude that a realistic model of the labour market needs to invoke a market-wide force that has powerful effects on the recruiting efforts of employers.

(Hall, 2005: 50 and 53)

The simple supply and demand approach is ill suited for discussing questions such as those raised in the previous paragraph . . . Traditional frictionless models assume that a worker can costlessly and immediately choose to work for as many hours as he wants at the market wage. By relaxing these extreme assumptions, search models allow us to think about unemployment and wages in a different light.

(Rogerson *et al.*, 2005: 963)[12]

It would probably be more realistic to incorporate some degree of wage stickiness in the model . . . To make the model more realistic, it is often calibrated to replicate the results given by Calvo . . . I make this assumption because it is more realistic.

(Zanetti, 2011: 646)

Comments like these seem to illustrate a commitment to some kind of realisticness – although, it is worth noting that the terms 'realisticness' and 'unrealisticness' are never defined. What about specific methodological claims?

Comments indicating that models cannot be realistic

> Any time we attempt to explain a complex set of behaviours and outcomes using a few fundamental influences, we have created a *model*. Models are not intended to capture every complexity of behaviour; instead they are created to strip away random and idiosyncratic factors so that the focus is on the general principles.
>
> (Ehrenberg and Smith, 2009: 4–5)

> We could, of course, create a more complex model of the . . . labour market that incorporates every single one of these omitted factors. Now that would be a tough job! A completely realistic model would have to describe how millions of workers and firms interact and how these interactions work themselves out throughout the labour market. Even if we knew how to accomplish this difficult task, this 'everything-but-the-kitchen-sink' approach would defeat the whole purpose of having a theory. A theory that mirrored the real-world labour market . . . down to the most minute detail might indeed be able to explain all the facts, but it would be as complex as reality itself, cumbersome and incoherent, and thus would not at all help us understand how the . . . labour market works.
>
> (Borjas, 2010: 8)

> There has been a long debate over whether a theory should be judged by the realism of its assumptions or by the extent to which it finally helps us understand and predict the labour market phenomena we are interested in. We obviously have a better shot at predicting labour market outcomes if we use more realistic assumptions. At the same time, however, a theory which mirrors the world too closely is too clumsy and does not isolate what *really* matters. The 'art' of labour economics lies in choosing which details are essential to the story, and which are not. There is a trade-off between realism and simplicity, and good economics hits the mark just right.
>
> (Borjas, 2010: 8)

> If a model exactly mirrored the reality of a given situation, then it would be too complicated for anybody to comprehend it . . . Consequently, models must entail simplifications in order for them to be useful . . . The

process of simplification necessarily entails making choices about what to include in the analysis and what to exclude from it.

(Laing, 2011: 3–4)

They [economists] thus argue that the theory underlying positive economics should be judged on the basis of its *predictions*, not its assumptions.

(Ehrenberg and Smith, 2009: 4)

The more important point, however, is that economists do not judge a theory by its descriptive content but rather by its ability to predict. The strength of neoclassical theory is that it yields a number of testable predictions regarding the demand for factors of production. It is on the empirical performance of these predictions that theory should be judged.

(Fallon and Verry, 1988: 99)[13]

Of course, economic models do not have to be realistic to be useful, and the supply and demand paradigm is obviously useful for studying many issues in labour economics.

(Rogerson et al., 2005: 963)

The argument contained in these comments can be summarised as: Because labour markets are complex phenomena, all models must simplify and idealise, meaning that models of labour markets will always, strictly speaking, be unrealistic. This is not a problem because, as Friedman taught, the objective of building models is to derive predictions.

This argument only *works* by trading on an illicit, and illegitimate, opening gambit. Realsticness is equated to something like *detailed description*, i.e. where the model: 'mirrors the real-world labour market . . . down to the most minute detail' as Borjas (2010) puts it. Detailed description is treated as a mixture of impossibility and absurdity and, thereby, rejected. The way is then paved for existing models of labour markets to be accepted as legitimate, irrespective of how unrealistic they are. Friedman's Instrumentalism then delivers the *coup de grâce*, by prioritising prediction over realisticness.

There are several problems with this argument that cannot pass without comment, I want to mention four. First, I am not aware of any critic of the unrealisticness of mainstream economics, who goes on to advocate the use of descriptively detailed models. Second, as the above passing comments indicate, any commitment to Instrumentalism is 'honoured in the breach'. Mainstream labour economists are *not* committed to Friedman's Instrumentalism – this doctrine is 'wheeled out' by the authors of textbooks who (understandably) feel the need to say something to students about the unrealisticness of mainstream models. Third, it ignores other mainstream methodological defences of unrealisticness, such as the concept of 'successive approximation', i.e. the successive relaxation of assumptions in order that models come to approximate reality.[14] Fourth, this reasoning is, arguably, an 'evasive justification' (Mäki, 2001: 73).[15] It *evades* serious criticism, whilst *justifying* the continued use of unrealistic models. As a result, *quite literally*, any degree of unrealisticness could be justified. There would, for example, be no way to argue against the use of a concept like 'matching angels' who descend from heaven and bring workers and employers together.

How, then, to proceed? Establishing more sophisticated definitions of realisticness and unrealisticness, and using them to evaluate searching and matching models is, clearly, beyond the scope of this chapter. But, fortunately, there is a simpler way to proceed, based upon the fact that mainstream economists themselves accept that their models are unrealistic, irrespective of the definition. The late Hahn, himself an ardent mathematical economist, put matters succinctly:

> When a mathematical economist assumes that there is a three good economy lasting two periods, or that agents are infinitely lived ... everyone can see that we are not dealing with any actual economy. The assumptions are there to enable certain results to emerge and not because they are taken descriptively.
> (Hahn, cited in Lawson, 1997: 110)

Consider the following:

> Workers differ not only in age, but also in their level of general human capital or skill, x_h. Workers enter the labour market with the lowest skill, x_1, and have chances to accumulate it up to x_H, where $0 < x_1 < x_2 < \cdots < x_H$. While employed, human capital appreciates by one level during each period with probability $\rho \in [0, 1]$.
> (Esteban-Pretel and Fujomoto, 2014: 579)

To say workers differ in age or skill levels is realistic even if we cannot measure these skill levels. To say that human capital appreciates by one level during each period with probability $\rho \in [0, 1]$ is unrealistic in several senses: (a) even if the concept of human capital makes sense,[16] it is impossible to measure *meaningfully*;[17] (b) even if it was measurable, it might well decrease as well as increase, and/or oscillate between increasing and decreasing over successive periods; (c) the precision underlying the idea that a precise unit of this human capital 'stuff' accumulates in precise units of time is an unrealistic (and spurious) precision; and (d) the idea that human capital accumulates at a rate somewhere between complete improbability and complete certainty is totally vacuous.

To be fair, Esteban-Pretel and Fujomoto probably know this is unrealistic. They assume it for reasons of tractability, i.e. without it (or something like it) human capital appreciation cannot be modelled mathematically. The fact is all mathematical models require the use of unrealistic assumptions that are made solely to ensure mathematical tractability. I cite one example:[18]

> The search literature has implicitly assumed a memory loss assumption because all separations are modelled to be permanent. This implicit assumption is not completely relaxed here for tractability reasons. If agents kept full records of their employment histories, the setup would become highly intractable as workers could be rehired by potentially infinitely many firms. Likewise, the time elapsed since a separation is not recorded for tractability reasons.
> (Ferandez-Blanco, 2013: 888)

Pause to take stock

How, then, should we interpret these views on realisticness? First, mainstream views on this matter are deeply problematic in the sense that they are under-elaborated, philosophically unsophisticated, confused, confusing and contradictory Second, irrespective of passing comments indicating a commitment to realisticness, mainstream models are unrealistic, and everyone knows this, including mainstream economists. As a result, we end up with three plausible interpretations:[19]

1. Interpretation one (i) takes the passing comments seriously; (ii) *rejects* the methodological claim that models cannot be realistic; (iii) interprets mainstream economists as being committed to realisticness; meaning (iv) that mainstream economists cannot deliver on this commitment.
2. Interpretation two (i) does *not* take the passing comments seriously (i.e. takes them as mere 'lip service'); (ii) *rejects* the methodological claim that models cannot be realistic; and (iii) interprets mainstream economists as *not* being committed to realisticness.
3. Interpretation three (i) does *not* take the passing comments seriously; (ii) *accepts* the methodological claim that models cannot be realistic; and (iii) interprets mainstream economists as *not* being committed to realisticness.

Which of these interpretations can be defended? I reject the second interpretation on the grounds of a *reductio ad absurdum*: a commitment to the construction of knowingly unrealistic models, without even the pretence of a methodological justification, would be self-evidently absurd. Whilst this could be an example of labour economics influenced by the developments in mathematics, logic and philosophy of science discussed earlier,

I cannot find any comments, not even in passing, indicating that mainstream economists are *not* committed to realisticness. I reject the third interpretation on the grounds that the methodological claim that models cannot be realistic is something mainstream economists 'wheel out' when put on the spot. The claim, only 'works' because it evades, and it evades only insofar as it is not examined too closely. It is not a defensible claim. By default, then, I accept the first interpretation, and conclude thus: mainstream labour economists, exemplified by advocates of the searching and matching approach, are committed to realisticness; their problem is that they cannot deliver on this commitment.

Before leaving this section I want to mention an important issue. Some labour economists, especially econometricians committed to empirical research, appear to avoid the obvious unrealisticness of mathematical modellers. Lawson makes the argument and the counter-argument succinctly:

> If there are exceptions to the latter sorts of formulations, these arise in the few exercises where the emphasis on mathematical modelling is retained but the modellers seek to avoid the usual unrealistic (atomistic and isolationist) conceptions by downgrading the role of theorising almost entirely. In such cases attempts are usually made to avoid theorising in terms of causal factors altogether as the emphasis is placed more on data information than theorising, as or where faith is placed, as with some modern approaches to econometrics, is more or less simply uncovering event regularities.
> (Lawson, Chapter 1: 36)

It is, then, a pyrrhic victory that avoids the criticism of unrealisticness by retreating to various forms of ultra-empiricism that downgrade the role of theorising almost entirely.

Searching and matching, and emergent, causal, processual, historical and open systems

In order to consider whether advocates of the searching and matching approach are committed to the view that labour markets are emergent, causal, processual, historical and open systems, it will be helpful to add a further example. Whilst Pissarides' model is useful in exploring the centrality of wage and Beveridge curves, I want to add an example showing how the process of searching is modelled mathematically. Consider the following from Rogerson *et al.* (2005: 961–962) who model a single agent looking for a job: Consider an individual searching for a job in discrete time, taking market conditions as given. The person seeks to maximise $\mathbb{E}$ where $\mathbb{E} = \beta^t x_t$, where $\beta \in (0,1)$ is the discount factor, x_t is income at t and $\mathbb{E}$ denotes the expectation. Income is $x = w$ if employed at wage

w and $x = b$ if unemployed. Although we refer to w as the wage, more generally it could capture some measure of the desirability of the job, depending on benefits, location, prestige, etc. and although we refer to $b > 0$ as unemployment insurance, it can also include the value of leisure or home production.

We begin with the case where an unemployed individual samples one independently and identically distributed offer each period from a known distribution $F(w)$. If an offer is rejected, the agent remains unemployed for that period. For now, we assume that if a job is accepted the worker keeps it forever. Hence, we have the Bellman equations[20]

$$W(w) = w + \beta W(w) \tag{13.9}$$

$$U = b + \beta \int_0^\infty \max \{U, W(w)\} \, dF(w) \tag{13.10}$$

where $W(w)$ is the payoff from accepting a wage w (W stands for working) and U is the payoff from rejecting a wage offer, earning b, and sampling again next period (U stands for unemployed). Since $W(w) = w/(1 - \beta)$ is strictly increasing, there is a unique w_R, called the *reservation wage*, such that $W(w_R) = U$, with the property that the worker should reject $w < w_R$ and accept $w \geq w_R$ (we adopt the convention that he accepts when indifferent). Substituting $U = w_R/(1 - \beta)$ and $W(w) = w/(1 - \beta)$ into (13.10), we have:

$$w_R = T(w_R) \equiv (1 - \beta)b + \beta \int_0^\infty \max \{w, w_R\} \, dF(w) \tag{13.11}$$

The function T is easily shown to be a contraction, so there is a unique solution to $w_R = T(w_R)$. This implies that if one fixes w_0 and recursively defines $w_{N+1} = T(w_N)$, the sequence converges to w_R as $N \to \infty$. If the initial wage is $w_0 = b$, the worker's reservation wage in the final period of a finite horizon problem, w_N has the interpretation of being the reservation wage when N periods of search remain, after which the worker receives either b or the accepted wage w forever. The optimal search strategy is completely characterised by (13.11).

So, can the searching and matching approach be interpreted as demonstrating a commitment, even at a very superficial level, to the view that labour markets are causal, emergent, processual, historical and open systems? The most straightforward answer would be to say 'no' and leave it at that. Furthermore, as we will see below, there would be good reasons for saying this. If, however, we deploy a more charitable interpretation, we end up with a different, and more sophisticated, answer. Let us, then, be a little more charitable.

Two things are immediately worth noting. First, advocates of the searching and matching approach do not use phraseology like: 'causal, emergent, processual, historical and systemically open'. Second, it is possible to be committed to something, even if this commitment is based upon a very superficial level of understanding. Consider some, typical, comments:

> Early on, theorists realized that a dynamic 'flows approach' was needed for an adequate analysis of unemployment fluctuation.
> (Mortensen, 2011: 1074–1075)

> A basic tenet of the searching and matching approach is that to explain the current stock of unemployment it is necessary to fully account for both the inflows into the unemployment pool and the outflows from it ... The hallmark of much of this revolutionary new literature is the emphasis placed on the frictions that inhere in the process of trade between workers and firms. A natural source of these frictions is imperfect information.
> (Laing, 2011: 801)

> The matching function is the lynchpin of searching and matching models of the labour market. But when workers and firms have to engage in a costly and time-consuming process of search to find each other, the matching function captures the technology that brings them together.
> (Stevens, 2007: 847)

> One feature shared by all these [i.e. non-searching and matching] models is that they are static. They explain how real wages and employment respond to shocks in a comparative-static framework but say nothing about the adjustment path from one equilibrium to the next. Also, the models say nothing about job vacancies, either in equilibrium or during the adjustment process. By contrast, this paper takes the view that by modelling job vacancies explicitly, one can learn more about the behaviour of unemployment and real wages, both in equilibrium and during the adjustment to equilibrium. Thus, the model developed below is explicitly dynamic, and in it job vacancies play a critical role in the transmission of output shocks to real wages and unemployment.
> (Pissarides, 1985: 676)

> The idea is that the job search underlying unemployment in the official definitions is not about looking for a good wage, but about looking for a good job match. Moreover, it is not only the worker who is concerned to find a good match, with the firm passively prepared to hire anyone who accepts its wage offer, but the firm is also as concerned with locating a good match before hiring someone.

The foundation for this idea is that each worker has many distinct features, which make her suitable for different kinds of jobs. Job requirements vary across firms too, and employers are not indifferent about the type of worker that they hire, whatever the wage. The process of matching workers to jobs takes time, irrespective of the wage offered by each job.

(Pissarides, 2011: 1093)

As the models above (Rogerson *et al.*, 2005; Pissarides, 2011) illustrate, agents are engaged in a continual process of searching, finding, accepting and being matched; all this is subject to frictions generated (presumably) by 'institutions'; models are set in discrete or continuous time; agents transform their state, e.g. from unemployed to employed or from unskilled to skilled; unemployment stocks and rates evolve; even a steady state unemployment rate is based upon continual changes in inflows and outflows; jobs are interpreted as assets, delivering an income stream over time; Bellman equations deal with dynamic decision problems by expressing the value of a decision at time t, in terms of the payoff from initial choices plus the values created by the future decisions resulting from initial choices. Advocates of the searching and matching approach constantly compare their 'dynamic' models to other 'static' models.

I interpret advocates of the searching and matching approach, therefore, as being committed to something approaching the view that labour markets are causal, emergent, processual, historical and open systems, albeit at a very superficial level. Their problem is not that they are not so committed, but that they cannot deliver on this commitment. To see why not, let us revisit the summary of social systems as emergent, causal, processual, historical and open from the introduction and work through it, establishing why advocates of the searching and matching approach cannot deliver on their commitment point by point. This section will also explain why methodological individualism, rational maximisation and equilibrium are retained.

Revisiting emergent, causal, processual, historical and open systems

To avoid any confusion, the following (italicised) sentence precedes all the following bullet points. *In mainstream labour economics, exemplified by the searching and matching approach*:

- Labour market agents are *not* engaged in an on-going process of drawing unconsciously and/or consciously upon socio-economic phenomena, and in the process, reproducing or transforming it. There are two reasons for this. First, rational economic man cannot act unconsciously, only consciously, i.e. maximising choices are fully conscious choices. Second, labour economic agents cannot, even when acting consciously, draw upon socio-economic phenomena (or 'institutions') because these phenomena do not, or should not exist in models based upon methodological, and thereby ontological, individualism. I will say more about this below.

- Without socio-economic phenomena to engage with, mainstream labour economists cannot explain how labour market agents actually manage to take any social action whatsoever. A language speaker could not, for example, string even a couple of words together to form an intelligible sentence without engaging (typically unconsciously) with socio-economic phenomena in the form of the rules of grammar. A job-searcher could not even buy a newspaper to look for job vacancies without interacting with the newsagent and, therefore, engaging (consciously and/or unconsciously) with socio-economic phenomena.

Mainstream labour economists half grasp this. For example, they accept the existence of socio-economic phenomena such as the decision rule 'whenever $w \geq w_R$, accept job offer'. Notice, however, that these are *precise rules, consciously understood and precisely followed*. There may be rare cases where real agents really do deliberate over rules like this, but they do not engage in this kind of conscious deliberation constantly, because they would be paralysed by the sheer number of decisions. This is why the use of precise decision rules is defended not on the grounds of realisticness, but on the grounds of tractability – they form the basis for algorithms. Mainstream labour economists invoke the 'as if' assumption: it is 'as if' agents follow a decision rule. This assumption is, of course, (knowingly) unrealistic. But what about those cases where agents follow what we might call 'rules of thumb'? Rules of thumb may be *unconsciously understood* and *loosely followed*, like norms, mores and values. Or they may be *consciously* understood and loosely followed, like agreements, codes, conventions, obligations, precedents and procedures. No-one seriously doubts the existence of these social phenomena, not even mainstream labour economists. Unfortunately for them, however, the commitment to rational economic man, who cannot act unconsciously, leaves mainstream labour economists unable to explain how agents interact with social phenomena, other than by reducing them to precise rules, consciously understood, and precisely followed.

Why, then, do mainstream labour economists not simply alter their conceptual apparatus and include things like rules of thumb, unconsciously understood and loosely followed. The answer is because these rules are not mathematically tractable. Consider two examples. First, let us allow an agent to act on the basis of something like a semi-conscious habit. Imagine that the job-searcher is a young woman, and one of the jobs on offer is for a bricklayer. It is highly likely that this young woman will reject this job without even giving a second thought to whether $w \geq w_R$. This is because of the largely semi-conscious, gendered habits, caused by her internalising stereotypes about 'men's jobs' and 'women's jobs'. In this case, the decision rule would have to be restyled along the following lines: '*sometimes* when $w \geq w_R$, accept job offer'. The problem this raises for mathematical modelling is that it is impossible to apply deductive logic to a model containing the term 'sometimes'. Introduction of the term 'sometimes' (or something similar) would transform the closed system into an open system.[21]

Second, let us abstract from unconscious habit, and allow the agent the power or capacity to reflect and the freedom to choose *not* to follow the fixed rule. Let us allow the agent to reflect upon what Rogerson *et al.* (2005: 3) refer to as the 'desirability of the jobs' on offer and use this reflection as part of the decision to accept or reject the offer. In this case, the decision rule would have to be restyled along the following lines: 'when $w \geq w_R$, *and when the job is desirable*, accept job offer'. The problem this raises for mathematical modelling is that it is impossible to apply deductive logic to a model containing the phrase 'when it is desirable'. Introduction of this phrase (or something similar) would transform the closed system into an open system.

In both of these examples, the presumption that all decision rules are precise rules, consciously understood and precisely followed, is a necessary requirement of the assumption that agents are rational maximisers. This presumption and this assumption, prevent problems for mathematical modelling from arising in the first place.

> The feature in all this that warrants emphasis (and tends to be overlooked) is that the primary purpose of any rationality axiom is just to fix individual behaviour in some way to render it atomistic and so tractable. The precise (set of) assumption(s) whereby this is done is secondary to this requirement.
> (Lawson, Chapter 1: 61)

- The presumption that all decision rules are precise rules, consciously understood, and precisely followed, and that agents are rational maximisers: (a) illustrates a failure to display a commitment to labour markets as causal, emergent, processual, historical and open; (b) illustrates a failure to deliver on their commitment to realisticness; and (c) are necessary consequences of mathematical modelling and cannot be abandoned without abandoning mathematical modelling.
- Without socio-economic phenomena, mainstream labour economists are unable to explain what kind of 'stuff' labour markets are made of, or *constituted* by, other than to say that they are made of, or constituted by, curves or functions. Neither can they explain how labour markets emerge in the first place – a set of curves of functions did not just materialise one day. Without socio-economic phenomena it is unclear how

labour market agents reproduce or transform themselves as labour market agents (e.g. as job searchers, worker-searchers, unemployed, skilled, low-paid, discouraged, etc.) and continue their existence into the future.

- Without socio-economic phenomena that *transform*, not just reproduce labour markets, mainstream labour economists cannot explain transience, evolution or change other than in terms of change or evolution of the *magnitude of variables*. There is no way in which a specific category of workers searching for jobs in one time period can be transformed: (a) due to changes in the socio-economic phenomena they engage with, because either there are none or because they cannot influence agents (immaculately conceived) preferences; and/or (b) due to changes in their thinking, i.e. evaluations, interpretations, expectations, because rational maximising agents do not evaluate or interpret, and any changes in expectations are assumed to be already known.
- Without socio-economic phenomena labour markets have to be modelled without transformation, evolution and change. We have to tread carefully because, as noted above, the searching and matching approach appears to allow transformation, evolution and change. Agents are engaged in a continual process of searching, finding, accepting and being matched; all this is subject to frictions generated by 'institutions'; models are set in discrete or continuous time; agents transform their state, e.g. from unemployed to employed, unskilled to skilled, or from young to old; unemployment stocks and rates evolve; even a steady state unemployment rate is based upon continual changes in inflows/outflows into/out of unemployment. The technique of asset evaluation makes the present values of key variables dependent upon the expected future value stream, allowing for historical changes. The use of Bellman equations allow economists to deal with dynamic decision problems, i.e. they keep track of future developments by expressing the value of a decision at time t, in terms of the payoff from initial choices at t, plus the values created by the future decisions resulting from the initial choices. The snag with these kinds of conception of transformation, evolution and change is that they are one-dimensional: they are all quantitative. Variables increase or decrease in magnitude, over time, but they do not undergo *qualitative* transformation, evolution and change.

Consider the example given by Rogerson et al. (p. 301 above) of the present value of a payoff U resulting from rejecting the job and earning only unemployment insurance b. Including the discounted value of unemployment insurance over multiple periods looks, superficially, like it is being modelled in time. But nothing about unemployment insurance changes qualitatively as time passes, apart from its magnitude. Things like eligibility criteria, coverage or political discourse

that influence decisions about claiming unemployment insurance cannot be allowed to change in the model. Unemployment insurance at the end of the modelling period is qualitatively no different to what it was in the first period. Important developments in political power or political discourse cannot therefore, be (meaningfully) addressed. The various mathematical techniques used to make variables comparable over time simply collapse the future values of variables into the present values of variables, presuming, therefore, that the things these variables represent undergo no qualitative transformation, change or evolution. This example: (a) illustrates a failure to display a commitment to labour markets as causal, emergent, processual, historical and open; (b) illustrates a failure to deliver on their commitment to realisticness; and (c) are necessary consequences of mathematical modelling and cannot be abandoned without abandoning mathematical modelling.
- A caveat. Labour markets can be modelled with transformation, evolution and change, but only if knowingly unrealistic assumptions are made. For example, qualitative changes in unemployment insurance (e.g. changes in eligibility criteria, coverage or political discourse) could be modelled, by making assumptions about the future states and fixed decision rules appertaining to them. The problem is that fixed decision rules are problematic for the reasons discussed above.[22] It is against this that rational expectations, assumed in almost all searching and matching models, should be interpreted. The innocuous expectations operator $\mathbb{E}$ is slipped in and (depending upon the version of rational expectations assumed) effectively takes care of any future unforeseen transformation, evolution and change.
- Generally speaking, mainstream labour market models must be devoid of transformation, evolution and change in order to ensure that they display event regularities, laws or law-like relationships and, therefore, systemic (theoretical) closure (Fleetwood, 2001, 2014).
- Mainstream labour market models without transformation, evolution and change 'fit' with the conception of causality based upon event regularities, as in the regularity view of causation and the regularity view of law. Not only is there no need to introduce conceptions of causality based upon powers and tendencies, they could not be accommodated anyway due to the commitment to mathematical modelling.
- Labour market agents cannot be modelled as *interacting* with other agents *via social phenomena*, which causally govern but do not determine, their preferences. Rather, labour market agents have to be modelled as isolated atoms, driven by immaculately conceived preferences and pre-programmed with one and only one imperative: to consciously maximise some objective function.[23] This explains the commitment to methodological individualism. According to one mainstream labour economist:

> *Methodological individualism.* This is the view that human social behaviour can be explained by understanding the behaviour of the individual decision makers within a group ... Given that methodological individualism is a central pillar of the approach, it is evident that a satisfactory model of human behaviour must be furnished in order to make further progress.
>
> (Laing, 2011: 23)

- The basic tenet of methodological individualism is that reasoning should proceed from the (rational) individual, with 'given' preferences, who formulates plans and initiates actions. Methodological individualism is, however, intelligible *only* on the presupposition of *ontological* individualism, the basic tenet of which is that *all* that exists are individuals, their preferences and their actions. Any social phenomena or 'institutions' (e.g. trade unions) are merely the outcome of individuals acting or interacting. Taken together, methodological and ontological individualism imply that the basic unit of analysis, along with the *well-spring, the initial urge, the motive force, the first cause, the uncaused cause* or *ultimate cause*, of all labour market activity are individuals' preferences. Labour market institutions are not causally efficacious, but are themselves ultimately caused by individuals' preferences.

    The moment mainstream labour economists allow things like institutions (or socio-economic phenomena) into the model, they introduce the possibility that these institutions might influence agents' plans and actions in ways that cause agents to take unpredictable, and therefore, not deducible, actions. Consider the following entirely realistic example. Suppose we allow *social stigma* into the model. We can no longer ensure that all agents will reject the job offer if $w < w_R$. An agent might accept the job even if $w < w_R$ because they believe they will be stigmatised if they reject it, due to the government attacking 'dole scroungers'. In this case, the decision rule would have to be restyled along the following lines: 'if $w < w_R$, reject the job offer – unless you feel this might stigmatise you. The problem this raises for mathematical modelling is that it is impossible to apply deductive logic to a model containing the phrase 'unless you feel this might stigmatise you'. Introduction of this phrase (or something similar) would transform the closed system into an open system. By ignoring all socio-economic phenomena (like social stigma) and building a model *containing only agents themselves*, methodological and ontological individualism ensures systemic closure.

    Methodological and ontological individualism are necessary consequences of mathematical modelling, and cannot be abandoned without abandoning mathematical modelling. Laing is entirely correct to say that: 'a satisfactory model of human behaviour must be furnished

in order to make further progress'. But the commitment to methodological and ontological individualism, with agents as isolated atoms, (as noted above) unable to engage with social phenomena, is a most unsatisfactory model of human behaviour.
- For the concept of equilibrium, Lawson makes the point succinctly and without the need for much elaboration.

In the context of modern economics especially, equilibrium is basically a solution concept, given a system of equations. Where such a system is generated under deductivist thinking, a question that can in some contexts be meaningfully addressed is whether the resulting set of equations are mutually consistent. Is there a vector of values consistent with them all? The solution concept, especially where prices are involved, is often called an equilibrium state; when economists enquire whether an equilibrium state exists, they are merely inquiring as to whether a set of equations has a solution. In this manner we can understand why, at least from a mathematical point of view, such a concern may be of interest, and thereby we can explain the (former) high frequency of appearance of the category equilibrium in the economics literature.

Demonstrating that a set of equations has a solution is, clearly, not the same as demonstrating that real labour markets are in equilibrium. Given that mainstream labour economists do not, typically, set out to construct a set of equations that do *not* have a solution and, therefore, equilibrium, then the latter must be considered to be a necessary consequence of mathematical modelling and cannot be abandoned without abandoning mathematical modelling.

Pause to take stock

Whilst advocates of the searching and matching approach are committed to something approaching the view that labour markets are causal, emergent, processual, historical and open systems, albeit at a very superficial level, their problem is they *cannot deliver on this commitment*.

Conclusion

This chapter has demonstrated the value of following Lawson's (Chapter 1) lead and insisting upon relocating discussion of the term neoclassical from the level of *substantive* theory to the level of *meta-theory*. This allowed me to reveal the mismatch between the desire to be realistic at the level of substantive theory and the inability to be realistic, because of particular meta-theoretical commitments. More precisely, I used the search and matching approach to show that contemporary mainstream labour economics is characterised by: (a) a commitment to the view (at a very superficial level) that labour markets are emergent, causal, processual, historical and open systems, but they cannot deliver on this commitment; and (b) a commitment to building realistic models, but they cannot deliver on this commitment either. The reason they cannot so deliver is due to their commitment to mathematical modelling. If we want to build realistic models of labour markets as emergent, causal, processual, historical and open systems, then we will have to abandon the commitment to mathematical modelling.

Notes

1 I want to thank Jamie Morgan for insightful comments on a previous draft of this chapter.
2 The paradigm case is Sraffian value theory. For the record, I reject both neoclassical and Sraffian theories of value.
3 From personal correspondence I know Lawson would not use the terms 'institution' and 'habits' as I do here. I am currently trying to develop these concepts so perhaps it is best to treat them with some caution. Nothing of significance in this chapter depends upon them.
4 For simplicity I am using the term 'labour market agents' here to exclude those (agents) who, for example, work in a job centre, or who administer web-pages advertising vacancies. A job centre worker might become a labour market agent if they actively sought another job in another organisation.
5 It is curious that the textbook by Institutionalists, Reynolds *et al.* (1998), does not mention the term.
6 Note that sometimes references are made to the 'Walrasian' approach or to the analysis being 'perfectly competitive'. These are oblique references to approaches and analyses using specific forms of labour supply and demand curves.
7 D'Auria *et al.* do not define the term neoclassical. They refer to 'an atomistic labour market without any market power for workers such as in the neoclassical model' without defining the term 'atomistic'. Nor do they clarify what they mean by a *hypothesis* that *describes* the labour market. Pissarides does *not* use the term neoclassical but rather 'competitive'.
8 A good example of this is Sutton's (2000) book on economic models, which seems to implicitly presume a model-theoretical approach to economic modelling without feeling the need to make it clear. For historical accounts, see Boumans and Davis (2010) and Morgan (2012).
9 I have left the mathematics and the curves in the following section, to emphasise the point that the commitment to mathematical modelling is as central to the search and matching approach as it is to the supply and demand approach. I thank Tony Lawson for raising this point.
10 This implies that Pissarides prefers claims that are not descriptively false, but perhaps descriptively true.
11 It only seems worth mentioning this if, in later chapters, Pissarides intends to add some important variables and makes the model *realistic*. He does not do this.
12 I take the reference to 'extreme assumptions' as a reference to unrealistic assumptions. It cannot pass without comment that Rogerson *et al.*'s paper is replete with assumptions that are extreme and unrealistic, yet he chooses not to mention them.

13 They refer the reader to Friedman's 1953 *Essays in Positive Economics* in a footnote (15).
14 Lest there be any misunderstanding, note that I do *not* think this is a plausible defence. It is possible that Rogerson et al. (above) have this in mind when they refer to 'relaxing these extreme assumptions'.
15 I should point out that Mäki is dealing with falsity, not unrealisticness, but I cannot elaborate here.
16 See Hodgson (2014) for critical comments on human capital.
17 Quite literally, *anything* can be measured if we are prepared to make enough assumptions and to accept extremely dubious proxies. But what really matters is whether or not the resulting measures are sensible, informative or meaningful. See Fleetwood and Hesketh (2010: circa 160).
18 Pissarides (above on p. 288) assumes: 'a perfect capital market, an infinite horizon and when no dynamic changes in parameters are expected ...'.
19 I address some of these issues in the case of the economics of trade unions in Fleetwood, (1999).
20 The Bellman equations are simplified by removing time subscripts.
21 Attempts to deal with this via fuzzy logic and Boolean approaches create their own problems vis-à-vis probability. In any case, probabilistic or statistical event regularities, causality, laws and closed systems are all still event regularities, causality, laws and closed systems.
22 Again we come across the issue of *meaningful* measurement of something like political discourse – see note 15.
23 This raises the issue of rational choice and game-theoretic models, which claim precisely to model inter-agential action. I cannot elaborate here, except to say that they too cannot get beyond assuming decision rules are conscious rules, precisely understood and followed, and are caught in the contradiction of committing to both the existence of rules and to methodological individualism where rules should not exist.

References

Addison, J. and Siebert, W. S. (1979) *The Market for Labor: An Analytical Treatment*, Los Angeles, CA: Goodyear/Scott Foresman.
Ashenfelter, O. and Layard, R. (1986a) *Handbook of Labour Economics*, Vol 1. Amsterdam, The Netherlands: Elsevier.
Ashenfelter, O. and Layard, R. (1986b) *Handbook of Labour Economics*, Vol 2. Amsterdam, The Netherlands: Elsevier.
Ashenfelter, O. and Card, D. (1999a) *Handbook of Labour Economics*, Vol 3, part A. Amsterdam, The Netherlands: Elsevier.
Ashenfelter, O. and Card, D. (1999b) *Handbook of Labour Economics*, Vol 3, part B. Amsterdam, The Netherlands: Elsevier.
Ashenfelter, O. and Card, D. (1999c) *Handbook of Labour Economics*, Vol 3, part C. Amsterdam, The Netherlands: Elsevier.
Ashenfelter, O. and Card. D (2011) *Handbook of Labour Economics*, Vol 4, part A. Amsterdam, The Netherlands: Elsevier.
Backhouse, R. (1998) If mathematics is informal, then perhaps we should accept that economics must be informal too. *Economic Journal* 108(451): 1848–1858.

Blanchard, O. and Galí, J. (2010) Labour markets and monetary policy: A new Keynesian model with unemployment. *American Economic Journal: Macroeconomics* 2(2): 1–30.

Boeri, T. and Van Ours, J. (2008) *The Economics of Imperfect Labour Markets*. Princeton, NJ: Princeton University Press.

Booth, A. (1995) *The Economics of Trade Unions*. Cambridge, UK: Cambridge University Press.

Borjas, G. (2010) *Labour Economics*, 10th edition. New York, NY: McGraw-Hill.

Borjas, G. (2014) *The Economics of Labour*. London, UK: Routledge.

Bosworth, D., Dawkins, P. and Stromback, T. (1996) *The Economics of The Labour Market*. Harlow, UK: Addison Wesley Longman.

Boumans, M. and Davis, J. (2010) *Economic Methodology: Understanding Economics as a Science*. Basingstoke, UK: Palgrave Macmillan.

Cahuc, P. and Zylberberg, A. (2004) *Labour Economics*. Cambridge, MA: MIT Press.

Card, D. and Ashenfelter, O. (2011) *Handbook of Labour Economics*, Vol 4, part B. Amsterdam, The Netherlands: Elsevier.

Coleman, W. (2010) *The Political Economy of Wages and Unemployment: A Neoclassical Exploration*. Basingstoke, UK: Edward Elgar.

D'Auria, F., Denis, C., Havik, K., McMorrow, K., Planas, C., Raciborski, R., Roger, W. and Rossi, A. (2010) The production function methodology for calculating potential growth rates and output gaps. *European Commission, Economic and Financial Affairs*, economic papers 420, July. Available at: http://ec.europa.eu/economy_finance/publications/economic_paper/2010/ecp420_en.htm (accessed 14 August 2015).

Ehrenberg, R. and Smith, R. 2009. *Modern Labour Economics: Theory and Public Policy*. Boston, MA: Pearson, Addison Wesley.

Elliott, R. (1991) *Labor Economics: A Comparative Text*. London, UK: McGraw-Hill.

Esteban-Pretel, J. and Fujomoto, J. (2014) Life-cycle labour research with stochastic match quality. *International Economic Review* 55(2): 575–599.

Fallon, P. and Verry, D. (1988) *The Economics of Labour Markets*. New York, NY: Phillip Allen.

Ferandez-Blanco, J. (2013) Labour market equilibrium with rehiring. *International Economic Review* 54(3): 885–914.

Fleetwood, S. (1999) The inadequacy of mainstream theories of trade unions. *Labour* 13(2): 445–480.

Fleetwood, S. (2001) Conceptualising unemployment in a period of atypical employment: A critical realist analysis. *Review of Social Economy* 59(1): 211–220.

Fleetwood, S. (2006) Re-thinking labour markets: A critical realist-socioeconomic perspective. *Capital and Class* 30(2): 59–89.

Fleetwood, S. (2008a) Institutions and social structures. *Journal for the Theory of Social Behaviour* 38(3): 241–265.

Fleetwood, S. (2008b) Structure, institution, agency, habit and reflexive deliberation. *Journal of Institutional Economics* 4(2): 183–203.

Fleetwood, S. (2009) The ontology of things, powers and properties. *Journal of Critical Realism* 8(3): 343–366.

Fleetwood, S. (2011a) Sketching a socio-economic model of labour markets. *Cambridge Journal of Economics* 35(1): 15–38.

Fleetwood, S. (2011b) Powers and tendencies revisited. *Journal of Critical Realism* 10(1): 80–99.

Fleetwood, S. (2012) Laws and tendencies in Marxist political economy. *Capital and Class* 36(2): 235–262.
Fleetwood, S. (2014) Do labour supply and demand curves exist? *Cambridge Journal of Economics* 38(4): 1–27.
Fleetwood, S. Hesketh, A. (2010) *Explaining the Performance of Human Resource Management*. Cambridge, UK: Cambridge University Press.
Garibaldi, P. (2006) *Personnel Economics in Imperfect Labour Markets*. Oxford, UK: Oxford University Press.
Hall, R. (2005) Employment fluctuations with equilibrium wage stickiness. *The American Economic Review* 95(1) 50–65.
Hamermesh, D. (1993) *Labour Demand*. Princeton, NJ: Princeton University Press.
Hicks, J. (1932) *The Theory of Wages*. London, UK: Macmillan.
Hodgson, G. (2003) The hidden persuaders: Institutions and individuals in economic theory. *Cambridge Journal of Economics* 27(2): 159–175.
Hodgson, G. (2014) What is capital? Economists and sociologists have changed its meaning: Should it be changed back? *Cambridge Journal of Economics* 38(5): 1063–1086.
Hyclack, T., Johnes, G. and Thornton, R. (2013) *Fundamentals of Labour Economics* 2nd edition. Mason, OH: South Western.
Kaufman, B. and Hotchkiss, J. (2006) *The Economics of Labour Markets and Labour Relations*. Mason, OH: Thompson South Western.
Killingsworth, M. (1983) *Labour Supply*. Cambridge, UK: Cambridge University Press.
King, J. (1990) *Labour Economics*. Basingstoke, UK: Macmillan.
Kwon, H-S. (2014) Economic theories of low-wage work. *Journal of Human Behavior in the Social Environment* 24(1): 61–70.
Laing, D. (2011) *Labour Economics: Introduction to Classic and the New Labour Economics*. New York, NY: Norton.
Lawson, T. (1997) *Economics and Reality*. London, UK: Routledge.
Lawson, T. (2013) What is this 'school' called neoclassical economics? *Cambridge Journal of Economics* 37(5): 947–983. Also published in this book as Chapter 1, and page numbers cited refer to those in this book.
Mäki, U. (2001) Models, metaphors, narrative and rhetoric: Philosophical aspects. In N. Smelser, N. and Baltes, B. (eds) *International Encyclopedia of Social and Behavioural Science* 15–9931.
Manning, A. (2003) *Monopsony in Motion: Imperfect Competition in Labour Markets*. Princeton, NJ: Princeton University Press.
Marsden, D. (1999) *A Theory of Employment Systems: Micro-Foundations of Societal Diversity*. Oxford, UK: Oxford University Press.
McConnell, C., Brue, S. and Macpherson, D. (2006) *Contemporary Labour Economics*. Boston, MA: McGraw-Hill, Irwin.
Mendes, R., Van den Berg, G. and Lindeboom, M. (2010) An empirical assessment of assortative matching in the labour market. *Labour Economics* 17(6): 919–929.
Morgan, M. (2012) *The World in the Model: How Economists Work and Think*. Cambridge, UK: Cambridge University Press.
Mortensen, D. (2011) Markets with search friction and the DMP model. *American Economic Review* 101(4): 1073–1091.
Petridis, R. (1999) Neoclassical economics. In O'Hara, P. *Encyclopaedia of Political Economy* Volume 2. London, UK: Routledge.

Pissarides, C. (1985) Short-run equilibrium dynamics of unemployment, vacancies, and real wages. *The American Economic Review* 75(4): 676–690.
Pissarides, C. (2000) *Equilibrium Unemployment Theory*. Cambridge, MA: MIT Press.
Pissarides, C. (2011) Equilibrium in the labor market with search frictions. *American Economic Review* 101(4): 1092–1105.
Reynolds, L., Masters, S. and Moser, C. (1998) *Labour Economics and Labour Relations*. Upper Saddle River, NJ: Prentice-Hall.
Rogerson, R., Shimer, R. and Wright, R. (2005) Search-theoretic models of the labour market: A survey. *Journal of Economic Literature* 43(4): 959–988.
Sloane, P., Latreille, P. and O'Leary, N. (2013) *Modern Labour Economics*. London, UK: Routledge.
Smith, S. (2009) *Labour Economics*. London, UK: Routledge.
Stevens, M. (2007) Microfoundations for the aggregate matching function. *International Economic Review* 48(3): 847–868.
St Paul, G. (2000) *The Political Economy of Labour Market Institutions*. Oxford, UK: Oxford University Press.
Sutton, J. (2000) *Marshall's Tendencies: What Can Economists Know?* Cambridge, MA: MIT Press.
Tilly, C. and Tilly, C. (1998) *Work under Capitalism*. Boulder, CO: Westview Press.
Zanetti, F. (2011) Labor market institutions and aggregate fluctuations in a searching and matching model. *European Economic Review* 55(5): 644–658.

Index

Note: The following abbreviations have been used – f = figure; n = note

abductive methodology 113, 114, 116n
abstinence 154
abstract theory 157, 265, 280
Accumulation of Capital (Robinson) 176
adaptive systems 242
Addison, J. 279
age of representation (classical episteme) 105
age of resemblance 105, 106
agency/structure model 140–1, 142, 144, 146, 155, 228–9
agent-based modelling 36
aggregate income 225
aggregated entities 143, 144
Akerlof, G.A. 95–6
American Economic Review, The see 'Uncertainty and the welfare economics of medical care' (*The American Economic Review*) (Arrow)
analytical geometry 113–14
Anderson, P.W. 245
Angrist, J. 268
animism 43–4, 45, 121
'anti-complexity' economics 249–50
antitrust legislation 16, 126, 127, 128, 130
Arnsperger, C. 5–6, 21, 24, 69n, 184, 245; Post-Keynesian modelling 250, 251, 252n
Arrow, K.J. 15, 82, 84, 99n; competitive market model 85–9; early reception to ideas 89–96; enduring influence of ideas 96–8

Aspromourgos, T. 4, 68n, 71–2n, 177
asymmetric information 97, 186, 191
atomism 61, 228, 251, 257, 266, 296; age of representation 105; cumulative causation 136, 137, 138; emergent phenomena and appearance of novelty 139, 141–4; mainstream economics 22, 35, 37, 38, 40, 146; mathematical modelling and 238, 241, 242f, 243f, 244f; moral hazard and 92; neoclassical tension 269, 270
Austrian School 32, 50, 72n, 191
automaticity 129–32
axiomatic economic theory 57–8, 215, 262, 263–5
Ayres, C. 161

Backhouse, R. 174–5
Baudrillard, J. 183
Becker, G. 69n, 116n, 184, 186, 279
behavioural economics 103, 147, 186, 255
Bellman equations 297, 299, 302, 307n
Bentham, J. 172, 211
Beveridge curve 288–9, 296
Bhaskar, R. 202–3
Blanchard, O. 251–2, 291
Blaug, M. 171
Boisguilbert, Pierre le Pesant, sieur de 44
Boland, V. 99n
Borjas, G. 292, 293
Boumans, M. 284

bounded rationality 23
Bourbaki School 108, 283, 284
Bradley, F.H. 146

Cahuc, P. 277, 281, 283
Cairnes, J.E. 43, 44, 46, 48, 52, 73*n*; vulgar economics 153, 154, 155
calculus 113–14, 211, 261; infinitesimal 57, 151–2, 153, 210, 283
'Cambridge Journal of Economics' 10
Cambridge methodological tradition 111–14
Cambridge Revival of Political Economy, The (Martins) 17
Cambridge Social Ontology Group (CSOG) 8, 9, 25
Cantillon, R. 153
Capital (Marx) 176, 213, 218*n*
Capital in the Twenty-First Century (Piketty) 132–3*n*
capitalism 39, 76, 132–3*n*, 145, 157, 177; class relations 200, 203, 218*n*; mainstream economics 201, 205, 207; working class organisation 213
Caplin, A. 264
Caserta, M. 232, 234*n*, 250
causal-processual/-historical ontology 149, 223, 250, 264, 273; classical economics 51, 52–3, 57, 74*n*, 75*n*; emergent phenomena 37, 238–9; labour economics 274, 296–305; mathematical deductivism 122, 129; mathematical modelling and 240–1, 266–7; social reality and 55, 56, 59, 60, 62, 64; taxonomic science 39, 42, 43, 62, 66, 151; technological development 119, 120–1; *see also* cumulative causation; evolutionary science
cause and effect *see* causal-processual/-historical ontology; cumulative causation
certainty 86–7, 99*n*, 123, 129–32
Chamberlain, E. 127, 131
'changing face of mainstream economics' ('Review of Political Economy') (Colander *et al.*) 3
chaos theory 245

chaotic model of turbulent flow (Lorenz) 242, 243*f*, 244*f*
charity 87
Chicago, University of 127, 169
Chick, V. 106, 224, 232, 234*n*, 250
circular process of reproduction 160, 161
Clark, J.B. 56, 75*n*, 126, 151, 161, 170
Clark, J.M. 126, 175
classical geometry 113
'classical' growth model 176
classical political economy 30, 34, 41, 43, 56, 67*n*; aggregate quantities 158; certainty and 129; 'deductive school' 47; diversity versus continuity 3–8, 30–1, 61, 67*n*, 149–50, 163; 'empirical generalisations' 45–6, 47, 61, 73*n*; Marxian viewpoint 72–3*n*, 76*n*, 150, 153–5, 162–3; Newtonian roots 206–8; as respectable science 162; socio-economic reproduction 156–7, 158–62, 163; surplus approach 150, 160–1, 162, 163, 165–6; taxonomic science 47–9; *true* relationships 124–5, 130; underlying causes of value 153; utilitarianism 44–5; vulgar political economy and 153–5, 156, 160, 163, 206; *see also* mainstream economics; neoclassical economics
classical reductionist programme 57, 283
classification: economic theory 104–11
Clayton Antitrust Act (1914) (US) 126
Cliffe Leslie, T.E. 156
cliometrics 186
closed-systems 9, 12, 16, 19, 20, 23; atomism and 36, 37, 60; infinitesimal changes 152–3; mainstream economics 109, 201, 216; mathematical deductivism 26–7, 102, 107, 136, 149, 150–3; open systems approach and 103, 105, 106, 107, 108; orthodox economics 103; social reality and 25; *see also* event regularities; mathematical modelling; open-systems
Coase, R. 176
Cohen, A. 161

Colander, D. et al. 36–7, 18, 27n, 31, 70n, 77n; 'death' of neoclassical economics 194, 196n, 198n; heterodox economics 191; 'holy trinity' 169, 172–3, 174
Collins Dictionary of Sociology 176
commodities 123, 207, 249
competitive market model 85–9, 95, 125, 126, 127–8
complex systems 242, 245–6
Concise Oxford Dictionary 169, 170, 178
conditional closures 262, 266; open systems, *ceteris paribus* (OSCP) approach 225–6, 227–8, 229, 232–3, 234n, 235n
conditional logit estimation 265
consequentialist decision making 228, 235n
conservative philosophy 204
constrained optimisation 279–80
constructive empiricism 259
consumer demand *see* supply and demand
consumption 159–60, 162, 225
continuity 3, 163, 200, 202; cumulative causation 137, 138, 139; diversity and 3–8, 30–1, 61, 67n, 149–50, 249
Contribution to the Critique of Political Economy (Marx) 44
corporate power 127
Cournot, A. 151
CRE *see* Critical Realism in Economics
critical economics 155–8
Critical Realism in Economics (CRE) 19, 105, 106, 107, 116n, 183; academic economics 202–5; heterodox economics 103–4, 109, 165; mathematical modelling 113, 114, 115; neoclassical tension 256, 257, 260; social ontology 158, 180
CSOG *see* Cambridge Social Ontology Group
cumulative causation 11, 12, 17, 36, 42; social reality 54, 55, 83, 136–7, 142, 146; *see also* causal-processual/-historical ontology; evolutionary science

Dallery, T. 250
D'Auria, F. et al. 281, 282, 306n
Davis, J. 31, 228–9, 284
Davis, J.B. 106
Dean, A. 264
death of neoclassical economics, The (Journal of the History of Economic Thought) (Colander) 6
Debreu, G. 215, 284
deductivism *see* mathematical deductivism
Denis, C. *see* D'Auria, F. et al.
Dennett, D. 257
Descartes, René 113–14
Dictionary of Economics 174
differential calculus 151–2, 157–8, 164
distribution 85
diversity: continuity and 3–8, 30–1, 61, 67n, 149–50
Dobb, M. 67n, 164, 170
Dorfman, J. 171
Dos Santos, C.H. 250–1
Dow, S. 106, 173
dual labour market theory 281
Dubner, S. 268
Dupuit, J. 155
dynamic credit supply curve 230–2, 235n
dynamism 23

econometric analysis 23, 113, 130, 152, 180, 266–9
Econometrica 124
economic activity: reproduction of 158–62
economic imperialism 186, 187
economics *see* behavioural economics; classical economics; feminist economics; healthcare economics; institutional economics; labour economics; mainstream economics; neoclassical economics, orthodox economics
Economics (Samuelson) 4
Edgeworth, F.Y. 155, 172, 214
effective demand principle 227
efficiency 85, 186; wage approach 281

Ehrenberg, R. 292, 293
elasticity of demand 100n, 124
Elliott, R. 278
emergent phenomena 245; agency/structure model 140–1, 142, 144, 146; appearance of novelty 139, 141–4; definition 36–7, 70n, 71n; internal relatedness of social reality 145, 146; labour economics 274, 296–305
empiricism 9, 263, 264, 265
Engels, F. 157–8
equilibrium theory 6, 31, 62, 169, 186, 193; central principle of neoclassical economics 68n, 173, 215, 249; complex systems 243, 244, 245–6; healthcare economics 85; inconsistencies 151–3; labour economics 274, 277, 278, 280, 289, 290f; methodological equilibration 69n, 244, 250–1
Esteban-Pretel, J. 294, 295
event regularities 35, 36, 37, 46–7, 60, 70n; closed-systems 228, 229, 233; fundamental physics 262; labour economics 276, 303; moral hazard 92; social reality and 137, 146, 222, 261; *see also* closed-systems; mathematical modelling
evolutionary historical approach 6, 11, 16, 23, 66, 76–7n; certainty/uncertainty 129, 132, 136; classical political economy 163; heterodox economics and 147; mathematical modelling and 122–3, 135, 147; realism 201; social reality as causal-processual open system 83; taxonomic economics and 41, 42, 49, 50–1, 52–3, 72n; *see also* causal-processual/-historical ontology; cumulative causation; open-systems

'fair playing field' 126–7
Fallon, P. 293
Fayazmanesh, S. 68n, 71n
Federal Trade Commission Act (1914) 126
feminist economics 32, 38, 201
Ferandez-Blanco, J. 295

Fine, B. 5, 26, 63, 69n, 185
fixed point theorems 152
Fleetwood, S. 26
'folk ontology' 22, 23, 24; natural language 259, 260, 262, 269; *see also* ontology; social ontology
formalism *see* mathematical modelling
Foucault, M. 105
Foundations of Economic Analysis (Samuelson) 6, 263
'freakonomics' 268
Frege, G. 215
French, S. 258, 259
'freshwater economists' 67n
Friedman, M. 85, 127, 169, 176, 212; labour economics 293, 307n
Frisch, R. 124, 235n
Fujomoto, J. 294, 295
Fullbrook, E. 77n
'fundamental' physics 257–8, 259, 262

Galí, J. 291
gambling addiction *see* pathological gambling (PG)
game theory 215
General Theory of Employment, Interest and Money (Keynes) 128–9, 176, 206, 232
German Historical School 156
Gifts of Athena, The (Mokyr) 132n
Glimcher, P. 264
Gödel, K. 215
Gorman, W.M. 248
Gossen, H.H. 155
Göttingen School 215
government intervention 93, 96
gravitational theory 207
Great Depression (1873) 213
Great Depression (US) 16, 128–9
greed 169, 172–3
grounds of finality 41–2, 66
group theory 262–3, 270–1n
Gulf War 183

habituation 159–60, 162, 300–1, 306
Hahn, F.H. 68n, 113, 184, 294
Hall, R. 286, 291
Harcourt, G.C. 99n, 114, 161, 176, 223–4
Harris, D. 230

Harris-Todaro model 281
Hart, N. 171
Havik, K. *see* D'Auria, F. *et al.*
healthcare economics 84, 85–9, 90, 91, 92, 99*n*; moral hazard 95–6
Heckman, J.J. 116*n*
Hegel, F. 157
Heraclitus of Ephesus 138, 139, 140, 141
heterodox economics 1, 7, 12, 21, 84, 195; change in mainstream economics 70*n*; classification as neoclassical 102, 103, 221–5, 232–3, 234*n*, 255; contrast with mainstream economics 37–40, 203; critical realism 104; definition of 191–4; inconsistency 192; interdisciplinarity 181, 165–6; mathematical deductivism 63, 64, 113; mathematical modelling 108, 109, 222, 233, 250–1, 240–1; methodology and social ontology 125; non-taxonomic categorisation of 107; open-systems approach and 103, 107, 116; orthodox economics and 164; reasoning relationally in agency/structure terms 147; reclassification of 97–8; self-identifying 37, 164; *see also* evolutionary economics; open-systems
Hicks, J.R. 6, 67*n*, 129, 164, 170, 177; equilibrium theory 193; labour economics 278–9
Hilbert, D. 57, 122, 215, 283, 284
historical cause-effect sequences 139
history of economic thought approach 4–5, 15–16, 17, 18, 20, 27*n*; academic economists 68–9*n*; use of 'neoclassical' as term 170–2, 182
Hobbesian approach 20, 202, 205, 208–12, 217
Hodgson, G. 69*n*, 184, 234–5*n*, 276
Hollis, M. 7–8
Holt, R. *see* Colander, D. *et al.*
'horses for courses' approach 114
Hotchkiss, J. 279, 280
human capital theory 186
human nature 209
Hume, D. 105, 116*n*

Humphreys, P. 256, 269
Hunt, K. 171
Hutchison, T. 172
'hydraulic Keynesianism' 129, 130, 235*n*
hypothetical state of nature 209

ideology 27
idle curiosity 120
'Immanent critique' 10
immutable laws of human nature 209
inconsistency 111
increasing returns 86
individualism *see* methodological individualism
'inductive' approach 156
Industry and Trade (Marshall) 125, 151
INET *see* Institute for New Economic Thinking
information asymmetries 23
Institute for New Economic Thinking (INET) 71*n*
institutional economics 16, 32, 38–9, 162
instrumentalism *see* methodological instrumentalism
insurance schemes: government intervention 93, 96; healthcare economics 87–8, 89, 90, 91–4, 98, 99*n*
interdisciplinarity 181
internal relatedness: social reality 139, 144–6, 157
IS-LM approach 129
isolationism 36, 37, 38, 40, 157, 257, 296

Jary, D. and J. 177
Jevons, W.S. 67*n*, 123, 154, 169, 171, 172; scientificity 209–10, 213, 214
job creation curve 288
Johnson, M. 259
Journal of Health Politics, Policy and Law 96
Journal of the History of Economic Thought 7
Journal of Risk and Insurance, The 95–6

Kalecki, M. 224
Kant, I. 157, 257, 270*n*
Katzner, D. 230

Kaufman, B. 279, 280
Keane, M. 267, 268
Keen, S. 67n
Keynes, J.M. 44, 109, 112–13, 114, 132, 197n; mathematical deductivism 176; Great Depression (US) 128–9; long-period equilibrium 251; supply and demand 206, 227, 232; use of words/numbers 165, 224
Keynes, J.N. 51–2, 53, 83, 150; classical political economy 153; mathematical modelling 105, 107, 108
Keynesian theory 21, 27n, 38, 51–3, 216
Kim, K. 218–19n
King, J. 279
Kirman, A. 247, 248
Klamer, A. 3
Kregel, J.A. 226
Krugman, P. 67n, 191
Kurz, H. 27n
Kwon, H-S. 279, 281

labour economics 306; command theory 208; defining 277–82; emergent, causal processual, historical and open systems 274, 296–305; mathematical modelling and 273, 274, 282–4, 301–3, 305; search theory and realisticness 273, 274, 281, 290–6; searching and matching approach to 284, 285f, 286, 287f, 288–9, 290f; supply and demand 23, 274, 277, 278, 279, 280–1; theory of value 207, 208, 212
labour market agents 275, 276, 299–301, 302–3, 304, 306n
Ladyman, J. 256–7, 258, 259, 260, 262
Laing, D. 280, 292–3, 298, 304–5
laissez-faire ideology 62
Lakoff, G. 259, 270n
Lautzenheiser, M. 171
Lawson, T. 10, 115, 120–1, 157, 158, 162; capitalism 218; definition of 'neoclassical' 175–6; heterodox economics 165
Leamer, E. 267, 268
Lees, D.S. 90–1, 92, 99n
Leibniz, G.W. 151, 152
Levitt, S. 268
libertarianism 90–1

'limitations of marginal utility, The' (Veblen) 75n
Lindeboom, M. see Mendes, R. et al.
linear regression 267–8, 270
linear systems 241
'locking up without ignoring' 226, 227–8, 229, 234–5n
logical positivism 114
Lotka-Volterra predator-prey model 241, 242f
'lowest common denominator' economics 270
Lucas, R.E. 234n

McCarthyism 189
McCloskey, D.N. 108, 173
McFadden, D. 265
McMorrow, K. see D'Auria, F. et al.
macroeconomics 128, 152, 186
Maddy, P. 270n,
mainstream economics 12, 19, 21, 26, 27, 193–4; Cambridge methodological tradition 111–14; capitalism 201, 205; change in 70n; classification and rhetoric 106, 108–11; closed-systems approach 109, 152; contrast with heterodox economics 37–40, 115–16; deterministic ontology 180, 189, 196n; distinction between neoclassical economics and 81, 84; divinely instituted 45, 53; evolving character 190; failings of discipline 32–3, 34, 165, 194–5, 212, 277; generalisation 261; historical relationship with neoclassical economics 84, 215; labour economics 280–2; lack of tension between method and ontology 147; nature and role of classifications of 104–8; philosophy and methodology of 8–10; as respectable science 9, 162; social sciences and 181, 196n; spectrum classification 106, 116n; 'statements of uniformity' 54; technical architecture (TA^1/TA^2) 185–8; transformation from neoclassical 81; see also atomism; classical political economy; mathematical deductivism; mathematical modelling; neoclassical economics; orthodox economics

Mäki, U. 294, 307*n*
'Making of an Economist, The' (Colander and Klamer) 3
Malthus, T.R. 112, 153, 155, 206
marginal productivity theory 161, 279
marginalism 5, 20, 40, 67–8*n*, 71–2*n*, 171; branch of classical economics 151; differential calculus 158, 164; historical context 202, 205, 212–13, 215; limitations of 55, 56, 75*n*; mechanical laws of human behaviour 209, 211; subjective elements 153, 154–5, 155–6
market demand *see* supply and demand
market incentives: healthcare economics 87, 98
'market for 'lemons': Quality uncertainty and the market mechanism, The' (The Quarterly Journal of Economics) (Akerlof) 95–6
market price 159
marketability 85, 90
Marshall, A. 6, 40, 74*n*, 83, 123, 171; 'biological perspective' 74*n*; Cambridge tradition 111; classic political economy 153, 155, 163; competition/monopoly 125, 127, 128, 130; economic principles 125, 127, 128–30, 131, 132; equilibrium theory 62, 151–3, 163; evolutionary approach 150, 151; internal relatedness 157; mathematical modelling 112, 151–2, 158; 'neo-vulgar' economics 163; orthodox economics 164; static/mechanistic nature of the new economics 214; taxonomic science 51–3, 54, 61, 67*n*, 68*n*, 71–2*n*, 73; trustfulness 95; vulgar economics 156
Martins, N. 17, 26, 111, 113
Marx, K. 44, 56, 176, 209–10, 218*n*; classic political economy 72–3*n*, 76*n*, 150, 153–5, 162–3, 206; critical realism 157, 203; differential calculus 157–8; internal relatedness 157; last classical economist 164
Marxian economics 5, 18, 32, 39, 50, 173–4
Mason, E.S. 127, 131

mathematical deductivism 18, 19, 26, 27, 32, 77*n*; anti-deductivism 248; closed/open systems approach 102–3, 107, 222, 225–32, 262, 263; deductive-nomological (D-N) models 200–1, 202, 204, 205, 211, 218*n*; as indicator of neoclassical theorising 115, 149, 164, 175, 180–1, 280; logic and 246; mainstream economics as form of 33, 35, 37, 162, 189, 192–3; perceived as essential for proper science 84, 165; preconceptions (of economics) 59–61, 66, 152; seen as necessary and sufficient 112; social reality and 122, 283; taxonomic science 55, 56, 57, 58, 62, 64
mathematical modelling 17, 18, 20, 32, 102, 116; alternative models and certainty 131–2; as (an/the) indicator of neoclassical theorising 115, 119–20, 172, 176, 187–8, 195; atomism 35, 36, 37, 39, 146–7; change to number of *possible realities* 122–3; closed-systems and 26–7, 107, 136, 150–3; generalization 260–2, 265; 'good servant but bad master' 223, 224, 225, 234*n*; labour markets 273, 274, 282–4; mainstream economics 201, 205, 216; 'mythmatics' 246–9; need to rule out 81, 115, 135, 137, 141; neutrality 198*n*, nonlinear dynamic systems and atomism 241, 242*f*, 243*f*, 244*f*; open systems, *ceteris paribus* (OSCP) approach 20–1, 152, 153, 222, 223, 225–32; prediction 85, 269–70; rise of discourse in economics 56–8, 70*n*, 123–5, 128–32, 185–6, 201, 260–5; science of general patterns 258, 259, 260; taxonomic science and 57, 59, 76–7*n*, 83, 132; *true* relationships 124, 125; unrealistic formulation 38, 39–40, 71*n*, 204; use of 21–2, 22–3, 24, 26, 146, 189–91; *see also* closed-systems; event regularities
Mátyás, A. 171
Mearman, A. 105, 115
medical profession *see* healthcare economics
Mendes, R. *et al.* 291
Menger, C. 67*n*, 154, 156, 169, 171

meta-axioms 31, 69n, 244–6, 252n, 262
meta-theory 31, 68, 273, 274, 282–4, 305
metaphysics *see* ontology
methodological barter 244, 252n
methodological equilibration 69n, 244, 250–1
methodological individualism 6, 68n, 69n, 198n, 269, 303–5; complex systems 244, 245, 247–8, 249, 251; labour economics 274, 277, 278, 280, 289, 299
methodological instrumentalism 25–6, 30–1, 69n, 85, 244, 251
microeconomics 152, 186
Mill, J.S. 43, 44, 46, 73n, 155, 156
Milonakis, D. 5, 26, 185
Mirlees, J. 97, 98
Mirowski, P. 123
Mitchell, W. 124
modelling *see* mathematical modelling
modern economics *see* neoclassical economics
Mokyr, J. 132n
monetarism 67n
monopoly 125, 126, 127, 128
Montes, L. 218–19n
moral hazard 15, 94, 97–8; healthcare economics 81–2, 84, 87–8, 89, 91–2, 100n
'More is different' (Anderson) 245
'more than the sum' idea: emergent entities 143, 145
Morgan, J. 115, 132n, 133n
Morgan, M. 124
Mortensen, D. 278, 281, 298
Moscati, I. 214

National Health Service (NHS) (UK) 90
natural language 258–60, 261, 269, 270n, 271n
'natural order' 43, 44, 45, 73n, 121, 133n; classical political economy 150, 155; science and 213–14
natural selection 49
nature of heterodox economics, The (*Cambridge Journal of Economics*) (Lawson) 10
Nell, E. 7–8, 172, 174
neo-Hellenism 169

'neo-Platonism' 178
neo-scholasticism 169
neoclassical economics 58, 84–5, 87, 94, 96, 99; arguments for abandonment of term 65–6, 81, 135, 137, 150, 166; basic divisions of 63–7, 103, 104–5, 239–40; conception of 49–51; as 'counter-classicism' 170; definition of 10, 13, 25, 82–3, 147, 174–6; developmental consistency of meaning 34, 67n; dominance of 1–2, 3, 4, 26, 94; dualistic thinking 173–4; essential features 68n, 84; evolving variability 185; existence of 181, 182–3, 184–5, 187–8, 190–1, 197n; focus on individual 172; as form of criticism 30, 67n, 164–5; future developments on use of term 177–8; historical context 212–16; 'holy trinity' of characteristics 172–3; inadequacy of 35–40, 64, 65, 89; interchangeable with mainstream/orthodoxy 196n; 'legitimate' alternatives 2, 3, 4; methodological inconsistency 149–50, 152, 158, 164, 182, 192, 200–1; multifaceted system 200; need for better definition of 115, 221–2, 255–6; term persistence of 129–32; seen as 'bad economics' 7, 32–3, 190–1; state of suspension/euthanasia 188, 190–1, 198n; synonymous with/ subset of mainstream economics 4, 10–12; term as figurative speech 168–78; wrinkling/complexity 187; *see also* classical political economy; closed-systems; event regularities; mainstream economics; mathematical modelling; taxonomic approach
neoclassical tension 108, 111, 146–7, 182, 256, 266; evolutionary historical approach and taxonomic science 151; folk ontology and 269–70; lack of tension between method and ontology 147; moral hazard 82–5, 87, 94, 96, 99; *see also* ontology
neuroeconomics 197n
Newhouse, J.P. 100n
Newton, Isaac 113, 114, 151, 152, 261; classical political economy 205, 206–8, 212, 215, 217

NHS *see* National Health Service (NHS) (UK)
non-atomistic mathematics 241, 242f, 243f
non-identity 137, 138
non-profit institutions 86, 88, 100n
non-redundant patternhood 258, 259
nonincreasing returns 85
nonlinear dynamic systems 22, 241, 242f, 243f, 244f, 252
nonmarketability 86, 88, 90
'normal position' 150, 158–9
normality 43, 47, 48–9, 52, 55
Nuñez, R. 270n

objectivity 2, 8
Olympic sports 184–5, 197n
ontology 53, 66, 103, 135, 192–3, 222–3; metaphysical preconceptions 41–5, 49; open-systems 232, 233, 239; philosophy of science 256–60; tension between method and 58, 64, 65, 66, 67, 82; *see also* 'folk ontology'; neoclassical tension; social ontology
open systems, *ceteris paribus* (OSCP) approach 20–1, 152, 153, 225–32, 234n, 235n
open-systems 9–10, 12, 18, 20–1, 23; closed-systems approach and 103, 105, 106, 107, 108, 216–17; labour economics 274, 276, 296–305; mathematical deductivism 102, 113; mathematics and 26–7, 112; social reality and 24, 25, 115, 136, 137, 149; *see also* closed-systems; evolutionary science
Opticks (Newton) 206
organization: emergent entities 143, 144
orthodox economics 165, 174, 196n, 203, 216, 255; closed-systems approach 102, 103, 104–5, 106, 108; 'counter-classical' approach 164; inconsistencies 111, 115; mathematical modelling 108, 109, 116
OSCP *see* open systems, *ceteris paribus* approach
Oxford Dictionary of American Art 170

pair-wise relationships: internally relatedness 145
Pareto efficiency 23, 274, 277, 278, 280, 286

Parmenides of Elea 138–9, 142
pathological gambling (PG) 266–7, 271n
patient-doctor relationship: healthcare economics 86, 88
Pauly, M. 91, 92–3, 94, 95–6, 97, 99n; moral hazard 98, 100n
Pesant, Pierre le *see* Boisguilbert, Pierre le Pesant, sieur de
Peterson, M. 96
Petridis, R. 280
Petty, W. 44, 153, 155, 163
philosophy of science 8, 9, 271n, 274; cumulative causation 137; mathematical modelling 274, 284, 295; natural order 200, 203; realism 256, 257, 259, 263
physicians: healthcare economics 86, 88, 92–3, 94, 100n
Physiocrats 43–4, 155, 159
Piketty, T. 132–3n, 197n
Pischke, J.-S. 268
Pissarides, C. 281, 296, 298–9, 306n, 307n; labour economics 286, 287f, 288, 289; realisticness 290–1
'Place of Science in Modern Society, The' (Veblen) 120–1
Planas, C. *see* D'Auria, F. *et al.*
pluralism 1, 25, 27, 37
political economy approach 5, 19, 20, 21–2, 25–6
political sciences 49, 56–7, 73n
Population Variety Reproduction Selection 25
positive feedback processes 137
positivist theory 9, 203, 204, 215, 284
Post-Keynesian theory 21, 24, 25–6, 32, 201; mathematical modelling 222, 226, 231, 250, 251
postmodernism 183
Pratten, S. 74n
preconceptions of economic science, The (Papers I-III, Quarterly Journal of Economics) (Veblen) 11, 65–6, 72n, 120, 121, 129; metaphysical preconceptions 41, 42, 43, 49
prediction 256
price systems: abolition of 90, 92, 99n; axiomatic economic theory 265;

commodities 123; discrimination 86, 87; indeterminateness 214; reproduction of economic activity 158–9; supply and demand 153–4; uncertainty and 94; zero reduction 92–3, 95, 99n
Principia (Newton) 206
Principles of Economics (Marshall) 74n, 95, 112, 125, 127, 128; differential calculus 151
Principles (Ricardo) 208
proceduralism 228
professionalisation: economic theory 213
profit 86, 87, 88
provisional closures *see* conditional closures
public choice theory 186

quantitative reasoning 141
quantum physics 215, 257, 262, 264
Quarterly Journal of Economics 11, 41, 43, 47, 73, 95–6
Quesnay, F. 153, 155, 160, 162
Quine, W.V.O. 215, 257, 263, 272n

Raciborski, R. *see* D'Auria, F. *et al.*
'Rainforest Realism' 22, 257, 259
Rational Economic Man: A Philosophical Critique of Neoclassical Economics (Hollis and Nell) 7–8
rational maximisation 274, 289, 299, 300–1, 302; defining labour economics 277, 278, 279, 280
rationality 23, 92, 110, 169, 172–3; atomism 61–2, 69n
realism 9, 11–13, 20, 155, 201, 203
reality *see* social reality
Reder, M. 169
reflexivity 17, 137–8, 139
regularity 43
relationality 38
relativity theory 215
Reorienting Economics (Lawson) 175–6
'reswitching' problem 113
'Review of Political Economy' 3
Ricardo, David 44, 111, 112, 128, 169, 206; classical political economy 153, 154, 155, 159, 163; labour theory of value 193, 208, 212–13; Newtonian approach 206, 207–8, 212
Rice, R.G. 90, 91, 92, 99n
risk 85, 87, 90
risk measurement 266–7
Robbins, L. 171
Robinson, J. 67n, 113, 127, 131, 161, 176
Roger, W. *see* D'Auria, F. *et al.*
Rogerson, R. *et al.* 301, 302–3, 306n, 307n; supply and demand 286, 291, 293, 296–7
Roll, E. 171
Ross, D. 256–7, 258, 259, 260, 262
Rosser Jr, B. *see* Colander, D. *et al.*
Rossi, A. *see* D'Auria, F. *et al.*
Rowthorn, B. 173–4
rule following 23, 24
Russell, B. 215
Rust, J. 267

sacrifice 154
Samuelson, P. 4, 6, 27n, 67n, 129, 169; axiomatic economic theory 263, 264, 271n
Say's Law 206
Schmoller, G. von 156
Schroeder, S. 172, 174
Schultz, H. 124, 130
Schumpeter, J. 67n, 171, 235n
science 2, 8, 9, 11, 23, 119; economics as respectable 162; idle curiosity and 119, 120–1, 132n; natural language 258–60, 261; positivism 284; realism and 256–8
scientific economists 5–6
scientific-realist methodology (Newton) 20
scientificity 209–11, 213, 214–15, 217
Screpanti, E. 171
searching and matching approach: labour markets 23
self-referentiality 143–4, 146, 186
Senior, W.N. 153, 154, 155, 156, 206
set theory 258, 259, 262
Setterfield, M. 225, 230, 232
Shafer, W. 248
Sherman Act (1890) 126
Shimer, R. *see* Rogerson, R. *et al.*
Siebert, W.S. 279

Smith, Adam 76n, 105, 153, 155, 169; economy as divine institution 43, 44, 45; 'invisible hand' 249, 280; Newtonian approach 206, 207–8, 212; price of production 159, 193; surplus approach 162
Smith, R. 292, 293
Smith, S. 279
social economics 32, 73n
social ontology 17–20, 25, 191, 193n; critiques of 8–9, 136–7; cumulative causation idea 137–9; emergence and appearance of novelty 141–4; internal relatedness of social reality 144–6; political economy and 26, 27; problems of neoclassical economics and 35–40, 83, 102; realism and 11–12, 13; social reality as processual/highly transient 139–41, 228–9, 275; 'underlabouring' function 10; *see also* 'folk ontology'; ontology
social reality 11–12, 17, 36, 37, 70n; agency/structure interaction 140–1, 142, 228–9; causal-processual nature 55, 56, 59, 60, 62, 64; cumulative causation 54, 55, 83, 136–7, 142; emergent phenomena 139, 141–4; event regularities 225; internal relatedness of 139, 144–6, 157; mathematics and 256, 257–8, 233; modelling and distance from 85, 222; open-systems and 24, 25, 115, 149, 152, 226–7; as processual/highly transient 139–41, 228–9, 275; stability in 140, 141
social science 16, 17, 49, 56–7, 97, 268; mainstream economics and 181, 196n
socio-economic phenomena 275–7, 299–300, 301–2, 304
socio-economic reproduction 156–7, 158–62, 163
Sonnenschein, H. 248
Sonnenschein-Mantel-Debreu (SMD) theorem 246–7
Soros, George 71n
Spiegel, H. 171
Sraffa, P. 113, 153, 161, 164

stability 21, 162
Standard Oil Trust 126
Stata 267, 268
state of nature theory 202
Steindl, J. 224
Stevens, M. 291, 298
Stigler, G. 164, 169, 177, 196n
Stiglitz, J. 97, 98, 191
structural modelling 21
subsistence level 159
substantive economic theory 205, 207, 210, 211; labour economics 273, 274, 277, 282, 305
substitution principle 279
superposition 241
supply and demand 23, 86, 123, 186; demand theory 245, 246–7, 248; labour economics 274, 277, 278, 279, 280–1, 286; value theory 153–4, 155, 157, 163
surplus approach: classical political economy 150, 160–1, 162, 163, 165–6
Sutton, J. 284, 306n

taxonomic science 11, 12, 23, 104, 119, 129; causal-processual/-historical ontology 39, 42–3, 62, 66, 151, 240; certainty/uncertainty and 127, 129, 132; as division of modern economics 63–4, 66, 147, 155; emphasis on 61, 137, 149; equilibrium theory 62; limited scope of 122; marginalism 151; mathematics and 57, 59, 132; open-/closed-systems approach 107; Veblen and 42–3, 47–51, 52, 54–6, 72n, 73–4n
technical architecture (TA^1/TA^2) 185–8, 191
technology: Veblenian dichotomy 161
Theory of the Leisure Class: An Economic Study of Institutions, The (Veblen) 184
Tilly, C. and C. 279
'Toward a theory of nonprofit institutions: An economic model of a hospital' (The American Economic Review) (Newhouse) 100n
transcendental method *see* critical economics

transformational model of social activity 25, 162
true relationships 124–5, 130
trustfulness: healthcare economics 86, 88, 94–5
trusts 125–8, 130–1
truth 138–9, 269

uncertainty 85–6, 87–8, 94, 108, 123, 222; mathematical modelling and 129, 132, 227–8, 235*n*
'Uncertainty and the welfare economics of medical care' (*The American Economic Review*) (Arrow) 82, 84, 99*n*; competitive market model 85–9; early reception to ideas 89–96; enduring influence of ideas 96–8
unemployment insurance 297, 302, 303
United States (US) 16
'unity of opposites' 138, 140
University of Chicago 127, 169
utilitarianism 45
utility and production functions 63, 156, 186, 197*n*, 214; mathematical logic 246–7, 265, 268–9

Value and Capital (Hicks) 6
value theory 273, supply and demand 153–4, 163, 207, 249
Van den Berg, G. *see* Mendes, R. et al.
van Fraassen, B. 259, 263
Van Treeck, T. 250
Varoufakis, Y. 5–6, 21, 24, 69*n*, 184, 245; Post-Keynesian modelling 250, 251, 252*n*
Veblen, T. 34, 129, 184, 255; classical political economy 41, 44–9, 71*n*, 105, 106, 120–1; conception of neoclassical economics 49–51, 72*n*, 83, 119, 149, 182; critique of social ontology 136–7; cumulative causation idea 137–9, 143; evolutionary approach 41, 43, 47, 73*n*, 150, 163; first neoclassical economist 164; level of consumption 159–60; on Marshall and Keynes 51–3; metaphysical preconceptions 41–4; neoclassical economics as 'school' 30, 65, 68*n*, 196*n*; neoclassical/evolutionary thinking 53–6, 64, 65, 66–7; 'normal people' and uncertainty 123, 131; originator of 'neoclassical' 4, 11, 12, 14, 16–17, 18; proprietary rights over 'neoclassical' term 168; science and technology 120–1; surplus approach 160–1, 162; taxonomic science 42–3, 47–51, 52, 54–6, 72*n*, 73–4*n*; vulgar economy 153, 155, 156
Veblenian dichotomy: technology 161, 162
Verry, D. 293
von Neumann, J. 176, 215, 224
Von Thünen, J.H. 151
vulgar political economy 5, 20, 44, 72–3*n*, 76*n*; classical political economy and 153–5, 156, 160, 163, 206

wage bargaining theory 281, 282, 287–8, 296
Walras, L. 154, 169, 170, 171, 306*n*; equilibrium theory 193; marginalism 6, 67*n*; scientificity 209–11, 213, 214–15
Waugh, F. 124
Wealth of Nations (Smith) 207
Weintraub, R. 68–9*n*, 111
'welfare economics of community rating, The' (*The Journal of Risk and Insurance*) (Pauly) 95–6
'Why is economics not an evolutionary science?' (*Quarterly Journal of Economics*) (Veblen) 41, 43, 47, 73*n*
Wright, R. *see* Rogerson, R. et al.

Zafirovski, M. 67–8*n*
Zamagni, S. 171
Zanetti, F. 291
zero price systems 92–3, 95, 99*n*
Zezza, G. 250–1
Zylberberg, A. 277, 281, 283